THE VOYAGES OF FISHERS HORNPIPE

Reuel B. Parker

For Tony —
with love,
Reuel

PARKER MARINE ENTERPRISES
P. O. BOX 1214
ROCKLAND, ME 04841

Published by Parker Marine Enterprises

ISBN number 0-9778393-0-3

Parker Marine Enterprises
PO Box 1214
Rockland, ME 04841

Printed by Friesens
Author photo by Scotty Folger. All other photos courtesy of the author, except as noted.

DEDICATION

In Memoriam:
Captain Lane Briggs
Navigator Becky Smith

AKNOWLEDGEMENTS

For Karren Tart, and the friends from my life before sailing, who helped me on my path. For Ray Farnow and the Village Boatyard, for George Loukes (who taught me rigging), and for the good folks of Half Moon Bay, California. For sailmakers Bob and Billy Henderson and Suzi Gray, who made the beautiful wings with which we flew. For Perry Fly, Michael Lannigan, Cyndee Horner, Paul Newman, Elliot Greenspan, Holly Hunter, Bob Tillotson, Teresa Rodriguez and all the many kind, wonderful fellow-travelers on *Fishers Hornpipe* who were my helpers, lovers, friends and crew from 1974 to 1984. For Captain Lane Briggs and the gang at Rebel Marine Service. For Beth Blessing for typing the newsletters into the computer. For Jeff Thomas for reading the early manuscript and making hundreds of good suggestions.

And for *Fishers Hornpipe* herself—*long may she live!*

A NOTE ABOUT THE PHOTOS

The photographs in this book are not in any way meant to be offensive or shocking. They simply and accurately represent *how we lived*, and for that matter, how we still live. Readers who have never lived on a cruising sailboat may find this unusual, but I assure you it is not. The old and the young, the fat and the skinny, the ugly and the beautiful, all look much better in a full-body tan! And they feel better too.

Most of the photos were taken with a circa 1960 Yashika 44 twin-lens-reflex 1.5” square-format camera (size 127 film). The later photos were taken with an Olympus OM-1 single-lens-reflex 35mm camera. Photos were prepared for publication using Adobe PhotoShop.

A NOTE ABOUT THE CHARTS

The charts were gleaned from various sources, which include many from the time period of these voyages. I deeply regret having traded all my Pacific (California, Mexico and Central America) charts for Caribbean and Atlantic charts with a sailboat passing west as we were headed east. I reworked the charts for publication in PhotoShop. I agonized over the choices of charts to include and exclude, and only hope that my final choices will help readers understand where we were in the world.

TABLE OF CONTENTS

INTRODUCTION vi

PROLOGUE vii

VOYAGE ONE—CALIFORNIA 1

CHAPTER ONE—DOWN FROM THE MOUNTAIN 3

CHAPTER TWO—BUILDING 9

CHAPTER THREE—HALF MOON BAY 17

CHAPTER FOUR—SAUSALITO 23

CHAPTER FIVE—HALF MOON BAY TO SAN DIEGO 31

VOYAGE ONE PHOTOS 37

VOYAGE TWO—CENTRAL AMERICA 53

CHAPTER SIX—NORTHERN MEXICO 55

CHAPTER SEVEN—SOUTHERN MEXICO 63

CHAPTER EIGHT—MEXICO TO COSTA RICA 67

CHAPTER NINE—COSTA RICA TO PANAMA 77

CHAPTER TEN—COLUMBIA TO KEY WEST 89

VOYAGE TWO PHOTOS 101

VOYAGE THREE—THE ATLANTIC 119

CHAPTER ELEVEN—KEY WEST 121

CHAPTER TWELVE—THE BAHAMAS 125

CHAPTER THIRTEEN—TO THE NORTH 131

CHAPTER FOURTEEN—TO THE SOUTH 141

VOYAGE THREE PHOTOS 149

VOYAGE FOUR—THE CARIBBEAN 159

CHAPTER FIFTEEN—TO THE ANTILLES 161

CHAPTER SIXTEEN—PUERTO RICO AND THE VIRGINS 169

CHAPTER SEVENTEEN—THE LESSER ANTILLES 177

VOYAGE FOUR PHOTOS 187

VOYAGE FIVE—ENDINGS 203

CHAPTER EIGHTEEN—ONE MORE ROUND 205

CHAPTER NINETEEN—THE LAST VOYAGE 215

VOYAGE FIVE PHOTOS 221

APPENDICES 237

APPENDIX ONE—NOTES 239

APPENDIX TWO—PAUL'S JOURNAL OF TRAVEL 243

APPENDIX THREE—ALBUM 247

INTRODUCTION

The first five chapters of this book were written in 1983 and '84, around the time I started to consider selling *Fishers Hornpipe*, and while my memory of events was less than ten years old. I have edited, filled in details and added stories as I have remembered them in the years that followed.

I started my lifelong practice of writing newsletters in Mexico. They form the backbone of this book, starting with Chapter Six. Although I have rearranged their structure, I include them pretty much in their entirety, as they were written during my travels. I have also added passages and information from both Logs (formal and personal), and I have added many comments from my traveling companions. Where the newsletters are out of sequence with events, I have reorganized them—and where information is lacking, I have written new passages to fill the gaps. Doing so may have caused a disparity of writing-styles in places, but I hope this is compensated for by the spontaneity and enthusiasm of the original newsletters.

Reuel B. Parker
August, 2001
South Thomaston, Maine

PROLOGUE

It is the last day of 1983. A cold, wet, rain-dreary day—unusual for South Florida. A fire crackles in the aft-cabin stove; the wind moans fitfully through the rigging. My spirits are way down—I'm in limbo. *Fishers Hornpipe* is for sale. The only way I can help you understand how that feels is to have you imagine selling your only daughter, your home, your freedom, your soul, your *very life*—all at once.

For over four years I have cruised—lived and traveled on the water. More than 30,000 miles sailing on three oceans, over fifty crew members come and gone, twenty countries visited, a passport completely filled—not one little square left unstamped. Those many salty miles that roiled beneath *Fishers Hornpipe's* keel—they're not at all like highway miles beneath your rubber tires. Rolling down the highway at 55 can't be compared to sailing on the living sea at anywhere between one and eight knots over a constantly changing surface, usually for days at a time, watch on watch, powered by an ever-changing wind. And there aren't any motels, coffee shops, grocery stores, garages, police, or hospitals out there. You take it all with you.

I got tired. The life-style is relentless. *Fishers Hornpipe* is a little tired, too. All those maintenance jobs pile up to create a monster: paint, oil, varnish, sew, repair, replace. At some point you have to stop constantly moving and be in one place for a while, to earn enough money to do all this work—and to earn enough money to go on traveling. In my case, the only way to get a real break is to stop altogether. As Ken Kesey used to say, "You're either on the bus or off the bus." There's more to it of course. You'll see as my story unfolds...from the beginning....

VOYAGE ONE: CALIFORNIA

Voyage One—The California coast from Half Moon Bay to Sausalito to San Diego.

CHAPTER ONE—DOWN FROM THE MOUNTAIN

The Earth does not belong to us. We belong to the Earth.

Chief Seattle

In the early 1970's I was living in a community called *Starhill Academy for Anything* in the Santa Cruz mountains of California—what the unknowing would probably call a "hippie commune." For most of my adult life I have lived close to nature, frequently in communal lifestyles. The 'communal lifestyle' part began with college dorms and army barracks. The 'close to nature' part came afterwards. Henceforth I lived in tents, old trucks, ruined cottages and cabins in the woods before living on boats.

You would have called me a hippie. I had very long hair and a long beard. I was skinny as a rail. I played music, worked as an itinerant carpenter, and ate healthy food. I used drugs. I made love to a lot of beautiful girls with furry armpits. I was a product of my time.

Like so many young men of my generation, the Vietnam War had permanently affected my attitudes toward 'western civilization.' My college education had been more-or-less permanently interrupted by Uncle Sam, who drafted me out of Columbia University in 1967.

At the start of Basic Training, after surviving the battery of tests during the induction process, I was told I would be in the artillery. I declared I was a non-violent person by nature and insisted upon a non-combatant 'MOS' (military occupational specialty). This didn't go over well, and I increasingly found myself in an untenable situation. I eventually declared myself to be a conscientious objector, which made matters worse.

As I was backed further and further into a moral corner, I finally became a deserter during the climax of the Vietnam War. I discovered that I was a radical, much to my own amazement, and soon I was wanted by the FBI. While I was 'underground,' my best friend was killed in Vietnam, having been there two weeks. Something irreparable snapped inside me. I became involved in trying to end the war. When I finally turned myself in, I was charged with 'subversion and espionage' against the US Government. After a long legal battle, never knowing from one day to the next whether I was going to spend many years in a military prison, I was discharged as an 'undesirable'—(*unrehabilitatable radical*)—'for the good of the service.' I spent much of the next two years lobbying Congressmen and Senators in Washington DC to end the war in Vietnam. I worked with Clergy and Laymen Concerned; I worked with the American Friends Service Committee (Quakers); I worked with Students for a Democratic Society. My young wife and I were tear-gassed in the March on Washington in 1969. We were there when the American flag came down the pole in front of the Department of (In)Justice and the Vietcong flag went up. It was a time of great passion, confusion and anger. We wanted to change the world—and the US Government—into something that cared.

* * *

In January of 1971 I rode a Trailways bus to San Francisco with all I owned on my back—carrying my guitar, mandolin and dobro. I was joining a folk-rock band with an Army buddy, called *Doc Savage*. The band didn't last long. Later that year I found myself at *Starhill*, among people who, like myself, didn't want to live in mainstream American society any more.

At Starhill, my tiny cabin was tucked down in a redwood grove in the forest, remote and beautiful and peaceful. I had no money, I was alienated from my family, I had few possessions (tools, books, musical instruments, a truck), and no obligations. My marriage was history, though a life-long friendship survived. A few girlfriends came and went. I worked as a carpenter in the flatlands or played music in bars when I needed money. I didn't need much. *Starhill* raised most of its food—big gardens, hogs, chickens and goats.

The community was not structured. It had no charter. We were bound together by one force: a deep, nearly fanatic love of Nature and the Land. Indeed, we worshipped Nature, though informally. We would gather at sunset on the grassy point of Star Hill, overlooking miles of forest and green hills rolling down to the Pacific, and gently sing the setting sun into the sea. At night we sat around our campfires, played music, and watched the stars and planets circle across the clear California sky. We lived as a tribe, the way human beings had lived for hundreds of thousands of years, before things went wrong, before 'the great forgetting.' We lived in harmony with ourselves, each-other, the world around us and with Nature. Our land was huge and beautiful: 1,800 acres of redwood and Douglas fir forest. Our neighbors included the Folger (coffee) Estate, Doctor Gerossi's SMIP Ranch (Sytex Made It Possible), Jimmy Chub's Funny Valley Farm (Celestial Seasonings Teas) and Neil Young's Broken Arrow Ranch.

There were 45 of us at most, and we were a diverse group. More than half were women and children. We lived organically, tending gardens, raising livestock, building simple (often primitive) structures, raising children, fighting erosion, restoring man-damaged land, and being involved in the greater community around us as each of us chose to. We lived nearly without money.

Unfortunately, our idyllic paradise was a little too close to 'the real world.' Taxes, lawsuits, things involving inconceivable amounts of money (twenty million dollars in back taxes) were destroying us. We knew our time was coming to an end. In California, property tax was based, in part, on the standing board-footage of redwood trees. These trees were dear to us to the degree that we would do anything short of violence to protect them. We eventually ran out of options, and we lost the battle, our land, and our trees.

I had not wanted to see beyond *Starhill.* My life was there—I was happy there. I was deeply suspicious of the civilized world and wanted to turn my back on it forever, to escape back into Eden. There is, of course, no way to do that—and by then I guess I knew better. My ordeals with the U.S. military and the Vietnam War had left unhealed scars, deep anger, and bitter awareness.

With the end of *Starhill* in sight, I sat down to take an inventory of my life. I took a big sheet of white pasteboard and began to write: What do I like? Dislike? What can I do? Not do? Want? Not want? Extend back in time; Extrapolate forward in time (follow the infinite possibilities of 'time lines'), and so on. I came to one clear answer, perhaps an extension of my 'escape syndrome,' but also a learn/grow/explore program—*The ARK!* Build or acquire a sizable sailboat and take off after that setting sun. Realize that childhood dream. Why a boat? Why not?

Ignorance sometimes enables the over-ambitious to tackle the impossible. Occasionally providence lets them succeed.

In 1973 I started looking for a boat. I worked more, becoming an 'outlaw contractor' (no license, no bond, no business card, no workman's comp, no phone, no union dues). I rapidly became known, respected and in demand through word-of-mouth. I was designing, building and remodeling houses, restaurants and bars for the elite and well-heeled folks of Woodside, Portola Valley, Palo Alto, San Mateo and Santa Cruz. But the kind of money I was putting together wasn't going to scratch the surface of acquiring a large sailboat.

My Colorado Grandmother died, and left me some stocks and bonds. They cashed in at a few thousand dollars, very few, by the time the Vampires took their share, and I thought I was rich until my ignorance about the cost of things was educated away.

I put a deposit on an old wooden ketch named *Shangri-La* of all things and flew to San Diego to see her. She was the only vessel I ever saw in my price range ($6,000), and I didn't even have that much, but I knew I could earn it.

I walked from the airport to the harbor, a nearly impossible thing through a tangled maze of super-freeways, fences, concrete walls and a total absence of sidewalks. Clearly it was one of those 'you can't get there from here' expeditions. The thought of paying for a cab on top of airfare was beyond consideration to one used to living on nearly nothing and aspiring to buy a boat.

There she was, rotting in her slip, rusty pipe-fittings for hardware, TV antenna at her mast head. She had been built in her owner's father's backyard in Arizona in 1938, his one and only such effort. *Shangri-La's* owner's mother had sewn her cotton sails, rotting in their bags since 1938. The ancient Chrysler Crown flathead gasoline engine, it's sparkplugs rusted solidly in place, the ceramics broken and the ignition wires wrapped around the bent studs, actually started and ran. The boat had been motored over to Catalina Island once every year or two for a week's vacation. She had never been anywhere else; perhaps she had never even sailed.

I crawled around inside her, peering and poking, with a friend who knew a lot more than I did and kept shaking his head in disbelief. I did know a little about boats, especially small boats. I had built and repaired several in my youth. And certainly I knew about wood. I knew that *Shangri-La* was hopeless for fulfilling my vision of sailing off into the sunset. She would either sail off into a broken heart and an empty pocketbook, or into a watery grave, but not with me aboard. Her hopeful owner lowered his price a thousand dollars to no avail.

I walked the docks and hit the brokerages and combed the bulletin boards and newspapers. At some point I added boat-brokers to my shit-list of Vampires—used-car salesman, insurance agents, real-estate brokers, middlemen, lawyers and politicians—opportunistic blood-suckers that get between you and what you want or need, and then have the audacity to charge you for it. I did learn that in San Diego, in 1973, you could by a smallish cruising sailboat, modestly equipped, for about $15,000. Looking back from today [1984], that's rather amazing. But at the time it spelled doom for my plan. I couldn't conceive of ever having that kind of money in my life. I flew home infinitely discouraged.

Then I met Patrick Cotten. Starhill wasn't far from the quaint fishing village of Half Moon Bay. It wasn't really close either—out several miles of bad dirt road, then over many miles of twisty narrow pavement down through the mountains.

But I made the trip often, to earn money playing music in the Miramar Beach Inn—a dive waterfront bar (reputedly one of Al Capone's clandestine prohibition-era whorehouses)—and to enjoy being by the sea. I used to eat in a wonderful little greasy-spoon seafood joint called The Crab Cottage in the village of Princeton by the Sea. Princeton was a few miles north of the town of Half Moon Bay on U.S. One—sort of a dip in the road that could be missed by a blink of the eye. There used to be a rusty sign that said 'Princeton, Pop. 71.'

Half Moon Bay itself is long and open to the sea, somewhat protected from it by a long rocky barrier reef with two breaks in it, one north and one south. At the north end of the Bay, the Army Corps of Engineers built a rock breakwall enclosing a small natural harbor from the beach to the foot of a high promontory called Pillar Point. That's Princeton, and it is a beautiful, moody, isolated place; or rather it was in 1973, before it was "discovered."

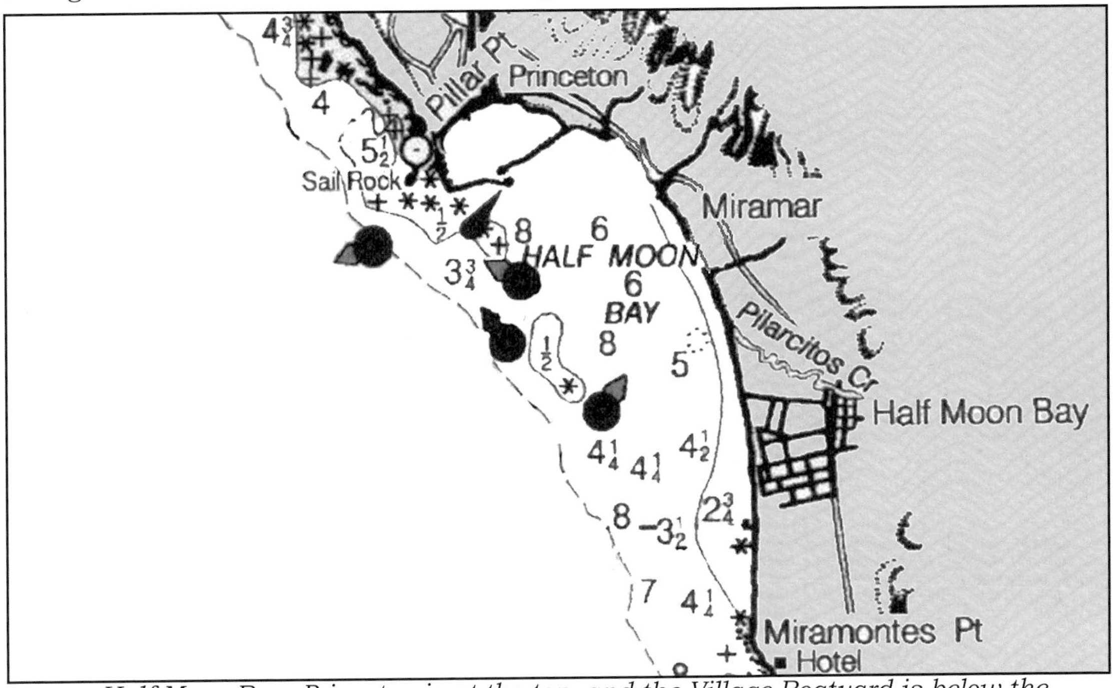

A mutual girlfriend had told me about Patrick, "this neat guy who designs and builds ferrocement boats," but I wasn't anxious to meet what I assumed was another California crackpot. Ferrocement boats? Not even a radical like me could buy that one. I knew and respected ferrocement—I'd used it in houses for years—slabs, foundations, grade-beams and walls—but not boats. I think my love and understanding of wood just didn't leave room for much else. I had no interest in steel or fiberglass, though I had worked aplenty with them also.

Patrick was a real salesman—a dream merchant. He was also hungry at the time. Just starting to build a large new boat for himself with a partner who hadn't worked out, he had passed a crossroads in his life that left him with nothing. He was starting over. We had a lot in common, but he was older and wiser, and infinitely more seaworthy (I hadn't been "to sea" yet). I don't know why he was in the Crab Cottage the morning I met him; he never went into restaurants, preferring to use his money more effectively. Perhaps it was an orchestrated trap. Or perhaps Nadine, our friend in common, was waitressing that day and had invited him in for pie and coffee, her treat. At any rate, I wandered in, met him, liked him, and found him very engaging to talk to. He clearly knew his stuff, and he believed (still does) in ferrocement hulls to the virtual exclusion of all others. Realizing there was much to be learned from Patrick, I became interested in his new boat as well as his designs. He was building in the local Village Boat Yard, not far from the Crab Cottage, and he took me to see his boat. The huge bulbous conglomeration of wood and steel and chicken-wire that loomed above the Monterey fishing boats in the yard didn't at first impress me favorably; my eye was used to other shapes. I remember thinking (please don't hate me, Pat!) that *Harmony*, as she came to be named, was the result of crossing a fat Dutch shoe with a California art-nouveau Spanish galleon. As I studied her, and Patrick explained the armature of the hull, I became more respectful of the incredible diversity of the building medium ferrocement.

Half Moon Bay. Princeton is at the top, and the Village Boatyard is below the "P" in Princeton. The Miramar Beach Inn is to the left of the "M" in Miramar.

What impressed me more was Patrick's design work. The man obviously understood *ARK*. His boats, at that time ranging in size from 36-feet to 72-feet, were full-bodied, flush-decked, deep, full-keeled, all-weather passage-making vessels. But they were also a life-style, a home environment I have never seen in the work of other designers. Patrick created dreams. And for their girth (they were beamy) and mass (they were heavy), they had sweet, easy lines: Picture in your mind a beautifully-proportioned fat woman. Inside these buoyant, pleasing shapes was room! Every cubic inch was accessible to be used, and there were *many* cubic inches. The boats had full-standing-headroom throughout, as much as you wanted. They had center cockpits that didn't make big holes in the deck, the only openings being hatches, skylights and companionways. Inside, the boats were full of light and air and open space. I have never seen designs like Patrick's: He was telling the world that you could go to sea without suffering, without deprivation—you could even put a small car in some of his larger boats! You could go to sea in safety, comfort and style, and you could take it all with you. Quite a dream.

In his portfolio was a design "with my name on it"—forty feet on deck, fourteen-foot beam, six-foot eight-inch draft, twenty-one-tons displacement. There were several being built in Southern California, and I knew I would have to go see them. It was 1974, and the Big Gas Squeeze was happening. I lashed a 55-gallon drum of outlaw gas to my old Ford flatbed and headed south. What I saw in San Diego left no doubt that what I wanted was a Cotten 40. I think the vessel that really convinced me was *Quest* (see photos). I must add that the folks who were building Patrick's designs were as delightful and helpful a bunch of eccentrics as I have ever had the pleasure to encounter.

An unusual feature of all the Cotten boats I have seen is that they are fair—no lumpy hulls allowed. And most are nautically finished: They look like traditional vessels by and large, not ugly caricatures and cartoons of boats as do so many other ferrocement, steel and fiberglass designs. Ferrocement boats were getting a bad name, and now have a worse name because most of them are poorly-designed and amateur-built. Pat's boats had nothing in common with these others—even his construction methods were very different.

For my part, I still wanted a wooden boat, and I was considering building Pat's design with traditional plank-on-frame construction. Pat was exasperated. Why would you sacrifice ten percent of your interior space to leak, be eaten by worms, rot, stink, make your clothes moldy, and quadruple maintenance? To say nothing of costing three times more money and time to build the hull? I did some serious thinking about all that and concluded there was much wisdom to it. But a ferrocement hull?

I started helping Patrick with his hull—for apprenticeship and working off the cost of my blueprints. I was shocked when he told me the plans would cost $350. Dreams are expensive, but what a dream! I paid half in cash and worked off the other half, which was really to my benefit. As I worked, my respect deepened. It was so simple, so pure a method.

Patrick had sailed a 26-foot converted Navy Whaleboat all the way to New Zealand back in 1966. He said it was like being locked in a tiny bathroom which was then violently heaved and thrown around for weeks on end while every few minutes someone would open the door, throw a bucket of cold salt water in your face and slam the door. When he got to New Zealand and saw all the ferrocement boats, he was skeptical too. While crawling around in the bilges of one that was several years old and well-used, he discovered a handful of dry sawdust. The owner told him it must have been there since the boat had been built, and something in Pat's head snapped. All that soggy cramped suffering! He learned, starting then, everything he could about ferrocement boats, including how to design them.

I did my own comparative research. Steel was out—I hate rust, and the gently curved sections of the hull, while lending themselves well to steel construction, would probably take a highly skilled and experienced steel craftsman of the kind found mostly in Europe. The materials in steel would be reasonable—perhaps four or five thousand dollars. In fiberglass construction, one faces the problem of making a mold; fiberglass best lends itself to mass production. "One-off" glass hulls tend to be very expensive and frequently unfair. A new method was around involving glass rods not unlike the steel rods used in ferrocement. This would cost $10,000 and six months of working with one of the most poisonous, insidious, obnoxious materials on earth, to which I am highly allergic. (How can anyone not be allergic to having myriad microscopic glass slivers constantly imbedded in your skin, lungs, and eyes, to say nothing of breathing polyester resin and other highly toxic fumes?) No way would I build in fiberglass. In my youth I had spent a summer working in a fiberglass factory on Long Island, and it was a true glimpse of Hell.

To build the hull in conventional wood would cost six or seven thousand dollars and take the better part of a year. Patrick's hull-shape would have lent itself to cold-molded wood—strip-planked and/or multi-diagonal construction using epoxy lamination, a method becoming more popular with the advent of the *West System*. That would cost around $10,000, take the better part of a year, and require weather-proof shelter—greatly increasing yard costs. The big question was: What could be gained by building in another material? I researched everything I could find about ferrocement, and I found only one real drawback: resale value. At the time, that seemed as relevant as worrying about the sky falling. Why would I ever sell my creation, my key to freedom, my life? At the time it was beyond consideration. Ferrocement construction, Cotten style, was fast, cheap, strong, tight and dry, and I went for it.

I rented the boatyard space next to Patrick's,

traded some labor for use of a dilapidated garage nearby, loaded my portable redwood cabin back onto my Ford flatbed and drove it down to the dead-end dirt road by the boatyard. Patrick's arrangement was similar—a plywood camper on the bed of an old Chevy pickup. For the better part of two years we lived there, the two trucks side by side, moving only rarely when the police or Board of Health might nose around (several times a year). Right beyond the trucks and *dreams-taking-shape* was Princeton Harbor—moody, beautiful and beckoning.

CHAPTER TWO—BUILDING

I have spread my dreams under your feet;
Tread softly, because you tread on my dreams.

W. B. Yeats

In May of 1974 I lofted my frames on the floor of the garage, using the traditional method with battens and tacks. Pat made fun of me for being too thorough—he uses butcher paper, a pattern wheel, and half the time. The sacrificial pine frames then went to the boatyard where I meticulously set them up and "trued" them, which took nearly a week. Then I had to work for a week or two for money. I shirt-sleeved the whole operation: Work on the boat until broke, line up a contracting job, go do it, buy materials, go back to working on the boat. At night I often went to my girlfriend Karren's apartment where my compact drafting studio was set up, and designed houses, additions and made remodel-job blueprints. Seven days a week and many nights I worked my ass off. I knew I had to keep this up for years, with no breaks. I was a fanatic and I loved it; I was possessed by *THE DREAM* and I couldn't stop until I got there and made it a reality. Patrick was right there beside me doing the same thing, and not much later Larry and Sue were on the other side of me, going at it just as hard.

I had only one awful setback. It came during those first weeks. I came home from working in the flatlands across the mountains one evening, my heart thumping in anticipation of seeing the skeletal ribs of my Dream and—she was gone! I came a little unglued—was the whole thing a fantasy? Had I slipped back a cog in time? Running terrified into the boatyard I saw my meticulous efforts in a broken pile on the ground! Who could have done this? I was ready to kill when Pat and Ray (the yard owner) came over and told me about this incredible gust of wind that struck from out of nowhere and disappeared into nowhere—not unusual for Princeton weather. Had some malevolent god descended with a little test for me, and in one divine playful puff leveled and broken my Dream? Buddhism teaches us to be thankful when God chooses us for a little humbling test—well, I was pissed. I cursed God and the Wind and Buddha, then set about untangling the mess and repairing and truing the frames. Another week of hard work and they were standing again. "More accurate than before," I said, "maybe that's why it happened."

And Patrick said, "Good—I've seen other men walk away and quit after an incident like that."

"Not me," I said. "The wind can blow 'em down again and I'll bloody well put 'em up again!" But secretly I thanked Buddha for letting me pass the test.

The Cotten method of building a ferrocement hull might be fast, but it was not without pain. The steel and wire mercilessly carved my hands into hamburger. In my sleep (and later, even when I closed my eyes) all I could see were the hexagonal patterns of chicken wire. After all the mesh was on, I had to tie something like 80,000 wire ties to compress and strengthen the armature. Fortunately, many of my wonderful and crazy friends came to help. Marijuana helped ease a lot of the tedium, and gave us a better eye for divots or deformities in the armature surface.

A useful fairing technique was to shine a flashlight (at night) along the hull at a flat, tangential angle—any dark shadows were caused by "hills," or high spots. These were then beaten flat with a large rubber mallet. [After the hull was plastered and cured, the flashlight technique was repeated: the shadows, or divots (low spots) were then circled with a magic marker, to be filled with epoxy fairing-compound.] A fair armature is essential for a fair hull, and many hulls, especially those using other methods, go irrevocably awry on this point.

On rare occasions, near the end of construction and the approach of plaster day, cocaine and speed kept us going all night. Drugs were plentiful and high-quality during that time. For those of you who are shocked and look down your noses, please remember that many things can be abused, including alcohol, religion, money, television and even gasoline. We Princeton boatbuilders all stayed away from self-defeating alcohol, with the occasional exception of good, cheap California wine.

As a measure of our dedication and fervor, I remember Larry—building his Dream beside mine—pushing himself so hard that he got a hernia. Furious that he would lose a few days work and have to pay for an operation to boot, he grudgingly went into the hospital. The next day after he came out, he went right back to work, shat his pants once, washed them out on the spot, pulled them on soaking wet, and continued working.

Patrick was poorest financially among us, though that's a moot point. For months at a time, he would live on those large institutional cans of ravioli and big boxes of Bisquick. Every penny went into the boat—it could be no other way. There were times when he simply didn't eat, but worked instead.

We scrounged for material; we bought in bulk; we recycled; we salvaged; we begged, borrowed and stole; and we built.

In September of 1974 we plastered the hull of *Fishers Hornpipe.* I hired a professional crew of six, and invited about 30 friends to the work party, most of whom had come to help staple or hog-ring or tie wire during the preceding months. The total cost of the hull was under $3,000, including rent, plasterers, food and even champagne on plaster day. Plaster day alone cost $1,000 of that total. I had been working nights a lot getting ready for the deadline, and I was exhausted. The plastering alone took 12 hours, with many hours of preparation before and cleanup after. The first step involved shooting the wet concrete—Chem-Comp Type V with sand, pozelans and chromium-trioxide added—with a Gunite-nozzle and pump. The professional crew followed Reggie, the gun man, with hand trowels, compacting and smoothing the concrete right to the wire armature. The second step involved shooting a second, light coat over that, which was again troweled, very carefully this time, as this coat protected the steel by about an eighth of an inch. This second coat also became the visual surface and had to be perfectly fair and smooth. The professional crew were really artists. Reggie's wife told me, while we were watching him work, that he was rubbing my hull with the same soft, skilled touch that he used when he rubbed her bare bottom! I saw my hull as a huge, beautiful fat woman, and Reggie and the gang were making love to her!

We then loaded concrete into 5-gallon buckets, and a dozen helpers climbed inside the hull and began plastering the inside by hand. This was hard, exhausting work, and it went on for hours. My friend Trippe fell from the sheer into the bilge at one point; she got right back up and continued plastering. It was critical that no air voids be left in the armature, and that the inner and outer layers of cement made solid, uniform contact, with no "cold-joints."

As the wet concrete began to set up, we *sponge-floated* it to give texture and "tooth" for coatings, and late that night we *dry-floated* the hull to knock off protruding grains of sand. Everyone involved said it was the fairest hull they had ever seen, and I was proud! Karren passed out sometime during the afternoon and didn't surface until the next day. She had been helping me during all her time off work, and she was exhausted. Looking back, I wonder if I would have made it without her. Early the next morning I had to crawl out of my own total exhaustion and set up the water-systems which would keep the hull wet-curing for 30 days. Then I started making deck beams.

When you tackle a project which is seemingly interminable, you can't think too much about all that is involved—it is self-defeating. You just keep the Dream in mind, the carrot before the donkey, and keep slogging away through the project at hand, hard as you can, planning just far enough ahead to prepare for the next step. Ignorance helps. I don't know how Patrick did it—he knew so well what he was into. He was, perhaps, careful not to tell us too much. I remember telling him, very early in the project, that I intended to build my whole boat in a year, at a cost of about $10,000. He laughed, but didn't say much more. Years later he painfully reminded me that I had even gone so far as to say I would wait for him to finish (his boat being much larger), so we could sail off into the sunset together.

My friend Ken had a Mobile Dimension Saw, an incredible machine that consists of a hotrod VW engine track-mounted on modular steel box-booms. He would take a bucked log of any diameter—up to twenty feet long—and lag bolt stacked 4x4 wood cleats on the butt ends. The boom rested on the cleats, off to one side, while the mill ran up and down the tracks, spinning one 24-inch vertical blade and two 12-inch horizontal blades. The operation is largely automatic, utilizing an ingenious arrangement of linkages and cables and gears and bellcranks. Two people could mill a thousand board feet of lumber a day, and the results were clean and accurate with very little waste.

With this monster machine we drove into Big Basin National Forest that summer and milled most of the lumber that would go into *Fishers Hornpipe*—and there was a lot of it. The tree we milled was ancient and huge, a first-growth Douglas fir (Psuedo Tsuga) which had died a natural death of old age—'cone' rot up through the roots into the heart. The leviathan had fallen across and begun to damn up the creek beside which it had grown. The Park Commission bucked it into twenty-foot logs and dragged them with a bulldozer onto an adjacent flat. The deal was that they got half the milled lumber for park projects (mostly large timber), and we got the other half.

For three days that VW's extractor exhaust pipes shattered the pristine silence of the forest, but in the end there was lots of clear, heart, vertical grain, natural air-cured old-growth Douglas fir milled and stacked in our trucks, and the chips mulched the nearby young firs. This lumber was virtually invaluable, and the heart and soul of that magnificent thousand-year-old Tree-Being are now the heart and soul of *Fishers Hornpipe.* Along with my own blood, sweat, tears and soul.

The deckbeams took time. I built a jig that could laminate two at a time, after Pat's one-at-a-time model. I scraped and planed and routed and sanded and varnished for what seemed an age. I laminated the sheer clamps inside the hull, using through-bolts, after it was cured and I had removed the pine frames. The finished deckbeams were bolted to the clamps, blocked between, and the double-layered Douglas fir plywood deck nailed and glued over, after pre-painting the underside of the first layer between the deckbeam glue surfaces. This decking method is the strongest, simplest, most rot-proof and beautiful one I know of. (Thank you, Mr. Cotten—I still use it.) My decks went on in early 1975. The plywood got covered with *Yellowjacket* (polypropylene-coated fiberglass open-mesh cloth) and Arabol (liquid latex rubber lagging compound), which years later got painted with epoxy and sand in non-skid patterns. This excellent covering was cheap, fast, attractive, waterproof and pleasant to live with.

Christmas came while I had my nose to the grindstone, and brought my brother-in-law and close childhood friend Jim Schaefer from Colorado for a visit. I was so unprepared for the holiday that I didn't even have any food in my camper. We were both broke, and couldn't afford a Christmas dinner in a restaurant (even if one was open). I had some old eggs—hence we had scrambled eggs for Christmas dinner. Sorry, Jim.

The bare ferrocement hull with wood decks looked for all the world like a giant musical instrument—and the acoustics were incredible. I had a moment of maritime doubt in which I thought of building a piano harp-frame right into the raised quarter deck, with a recessed seat in the main deck before the keyboard, and gigantic cables across a bridge overhead (bass strings). During moments of confusion about what to do next, I spent time playing drum rhythms with my hands or fists on various bulkheads, mesmerized by the sheer volume and tone quality.

1975 went slowly. Maybe I started to realize what I was up against. I had to work away on jobs a lot, to get money to buy materials. The interior started to get roughed in. I drew the interior layout twenty-two times, consulting often with Pat; and it changed a little more in the building, but I got it right. I used every one of those many cubic inches as well as I could. Patrick's plans rarely included interiors in those days; that was your end of the Dream. He gave you that incredible space—you figured out how to use it. However, he was always available to his ever-growing number of followers for help, work, consultation and design, and earned most of his money that way.

Diesel engine, tanks, machinery, hardware, fasteners, through-hull fittings, pipes, wiring, cabinetry, shafts, gears, chain, bearings, plumbing; on and on I slogged. Work, buy and scrounge parts, put them into the boat, work again. Day and night, seven days a week, week after month after year.

Patrick hit the water in February of '76. Larry and I were killing ourselves to launch together later that year in time to beat the rainy season, which usually turned the boatyard into a quagmire of mud and sand—impossible launch conditions.

At some point I moved out of my truck-cabin, faithful home for over four years, and into Fishers Hornpipe to live with plywood and sawdust and tools and formidable piles of parts. I sold my tiny redwood cabin to a woman who took it back into the forest as her home. I sold the faithful old truck to a man who used it to deliver redwood hot tubs. I went through an identity crisis—I had never lived in a boat. I had never been to sea. I had never even sailed a big sailboat. What the hell did I think I was doing? My poor mother and stepfather back in New York, who had more or less given up on me as bananas years before, were now convinced I was completely mad.

* * *

We always had a problem in the boatyard with sightseers—rubber-neckers, busybodies, curiosity seekers. These people would come into the yard, into our work-space, and bombard us with questions, feeling somehow that they were doing us a favor by interrupting us to talk. With few exceptions, the conversations went like this: "Sure looks like a lot of work." "Yup." "Been at 'er long?" "Yup." "Your boat?" "Yup." "Gonna sail to the South Pacific?" "Maybe." "What's it made of?" "Ferrocement." "You mean concrete?" "Yup." "You know concrete don't float, dontcha?" "Yup." "Well, how come you're building a boat out of it?" And here you had to decide whether to waste your time explaining that the air contained in ferrocement floats—hell, steel doesn't float either. Since that usually took too long ("Yeah, but concrete don't float!"), we often got creative with our answers, especially after going through the explanation a zillion times or so.

The first man to build a ferrocement boat in Princeton was a tall, red-haired commercial fisherman with perpetually bloodshot eyes named Jim. Jim patiently explained how things float dozens of times, until he got tired of it. Then he started telling them about the pingpong balls. "...concrete don't float?" "It's the ping pong balls." "The what?" "Ping-pong balls." "How's that?" "Well, I put ping-pong balls inside the hull." "Oh." "But they wear out, so I have to color-code them. I got red ones, blue ones, and yellow ones, and I replace one color of ping-pong balls each year, so that every three years they've all been replaced." "I see...well, been nice talkin' to ya." "Wait, come on inside and I'll show ya...." But by then the pest was nervously backing away, and Jim was free to go back to work.

My worst sightseer experience involved no

words at all. Karren and I had been working and found ourselves in the mood to make love. Inside *Fishers Hornpipe*, where my bunk was to eventually be located, was a stack of plywood with an old foam pad on top. We crawled up on there and commenced making love. A particularly bold busybody came up onto my scaffolding during this time, and was walking around my hull closely examining everything. Because ferrocement is very hard to cut, the wire armature was formed around holes where portlights would be located, and wooden plugs were set in place before plastering. After my hull was cured, I left these plugs in place to keep rain from blowing in, but they fit rather loosely and could be easily removed. Well, this uninvited inspector, out of curiosity, I assume, pushed one of the plugs into the hull and reached his hand into the dark interior. It happened to be the plug over the stack of plywood on which Karren and I were deeply engaged in exploring the Yang, or left-hand (physical) path to true enlightenment. In our ardor we didn't notice the plug, or the hand, but lifting to implement a homing thrust toward "oneness with the universe," the left cheek of my ass slapped neatly and firmly into the outstretched hand of curiosity. Needless to say, I screamed, somehow realizing the hand was not that of my love (knowing, peripherally at least, where her hands were), and completely lost what was just on the verge of becoming a splendid orgasm. The hand and arm retreated very rapidly, leaving a little flesh and blood on the ragged rim of the ferrocement aperture where the plug had been. I rolled onto the cabin sole, screaming bloody murder (I guess there were some words involved), grabbing my pants as I flew out the companionway shouting anatomically-unlikely suggestions to the owner of the incredibly rude hand, who had fairly flown down the scaffolding and ladder to the ground, and was booking it toward his car somewhere out on the street. Patrick, on *Harmony* next door, looked up to see me trying to stuff my still tumescent tool-of-enlightenment into my pants as I was running down the scaffolding howling with rage. Later, when I explained, he laughed until tears were streaming down his cheeks.

After that incident I put a big sign on my scaffold ladder, blocking the way up. The sign said something to the effect of "*Keep the fuck OUT!*" The boat yard, and shortly thereafter the community at large, had a many a chuckle when they saw my sign and found out what had happened.

* * *

I had a major "wake-up call" during this time. One beautifully gentle, sunny Forth of July morning, I took off out to sea (out to the reef buoys) in the boatyard's twelve-foot play-boat, *Queen*. Someone had dragged *Queen* up from her grave on the bottom of a lake to sit forlorn and rotting in a corner of the boatyard. I, wanting a taste of sailing and a closer relationship to the Bay than just watching it, patched her up and got her sailing so we would all have a boat to play with. And we all did—*Queen* was a delight even if she was clunky and her sails were shot and she didn't respond very well. So off I went on this fine morning, had a beautiful sail out to the reef and most of the way back, when moody old Half Moon Bay changed her mood. The wind picked up to over twenty knots in minutes, and blew straight out through the breakwater entrance, which was laid out exactly parallel to the prevailing northwest wind by the clever Army Corps of Engineers. That made the entrance a dead beat into the wind for poor old *Queen*, who absolutely wasn't up for it. Many a larger and more able vessel had come to grief in that entrance. I hiked out, sheeted in (*Queen* didn't have quick-release sheets), and started beating in. *Queen* shivered and shuddered and wouldn't do it. I thought, "Oh, shit, what have I done now?" I turned off the wind and ran down along the breakwall to wait and see if the wind would ease or shift. At worst, I could put *Queen* on the beach a mile away and go get the trailer, somehow drive down the beach and with some help, retrieve her (however embarrassing that might be).

I smelled Buddha in the wings again. Sure enough, along came that same gust of wind that had leveled my frames way back when, and *WHAM! Queen* took a knockdown and put me in the water. Now the water along the coast of California is cold—cold enough that a grown, healthy person can die of hypothermia in an hour. I swam *Queen's* mast around into the wind and stood on her centerboard while pulling on a shroud. She came up, wet sails flapping, and kept going right on over. With a very sinking feeling, I noted that her cockpit never came to the surface of the water—*Queen* was so heavy that she floated too low in the water to even be bailed out! I realized I was in for the duration. The icy chill of the water began to chill my soul. I started looking for other boats—none. I could see people on the breakwall fishing. I waved, hoping to convey some sense of my danger. One guy waved back. It was a very long walk down the half-mile of rocky breakwall to get help, then back, and it became painfully obvious that he wasn't going to do it. I was out of shouting distance and drifting further away fast. My swimming was rusty, and I was getting cold enough to feel where the cramps would come. "Stay with the boat," my training said. The beach was a mile to the southeast, the breakwall now more than a quarter of a mile north. I seemed to be drifting south—bad news. It dawned on me that I could die. I thought about the huge sharks that occasionally ate abalone divers in the area. I fought against panic, fought against the cold, began to shake. I thought about a lot of things like, *"If I live through this, I'll never go near the fucking water again!"* Some serious evaluation of myself was happening; I was getting really scared. I fought back and forth between ration and panic. Mostly, I was pissed at myself—I knew I'd really fucked up.

Finally, the Harbor Patrol boat came to the rescue, its blue light flashing. When they hauled me out of the water, I was blue, too, and my lips were purple. I had been in the water for about thirty-five minutes. They dragged *Queen* back into the harbor on her side, while I huddled and shivered in the cabin of the patrol boat, feeling very low and stupid and embarrassed.

It turned out that the Fire Department across the street in El Grenada had seen me through their binoculars and called the Princeton Harbormaster. They very- possibly saved my life, but I was too mortified to go and tell them thanks.

I got *Queen* back to the beach, took a hot shower in the fisherman's bathroom, and went to bed. I was really low for a few days. I did some serious thinking and decided I still wanted to fulfill my Dream. I had been tested again and failed this time. If I was going to go messing around on the ocean, I was going to have to tighten up my act. *Thank you, Buddha.*

We all worked on tightening up *Queen* too. She got built-in flotation, new sails and quick-release sheet cleats, but I never took her to sea again. I did, however, sail her around the harbor a lot, even in nasty weather. I took Karren for her first sail ever in *Queen*, on a windy day. When I came about the first time I neglected to tell Karren to switch sides (I honestly thought she knew to). As we heeled sharply on the new tack, Karren's lovely ass dipped deeply into the cold water while she hung on to the cockpit coaming for dear life, screaming bloody murder! Boy did I catch it for that one—she never did completely forgive me.

* * *

I put a lot of energy into fairing my hull. First, I sand-blasted to remove leached-out lime deposits from the surface. Then I epoxy-soaked the hull, coating "wet on wet" so each subsequent coat would chemically bond to the previous one. I made my own fairing compounds after much experimenting, settling on talc as the thixogen for the epoxy resin because it made such a smooth, workable compound, and sanded easily. I learned the troweling technique from Patrick, who used a thin stainless steel blade 18 inches long, and troweled alternating vertical and horizontal thin layers of epoxy fairing compound. I used a long, flexible batten and "mapped out" the high and low spots on the hull surface. The topsides were covered with odd-shaped patterns having plus or minus signs or "high" and "low," and eventually various other graffiti too. At one point the whole hull was covered with weird drawings, symbols and notes, like some archaeological boulder. I wanted the finished hull to look like one of those Steuben blown-glass sculptures. I wanted perfection.

I spray-painted the hull myself and she came out looking like a blue mirror. Folks who had seen a lot of boats said she was one of the fairest hulls of any material they had ever seen, and I was very proud of my work. Her topsides were deep sea blue, her bottom red, and her bootstripe white (which I later changed to yellow).

There were now two more Cotton boats being built in the area—to Pat's new 28' design—and one of these belonged to a beautiful young woman. Late one night, with a full moon in the sky, I heard someone talking loudly outside my boat. When I came out to investigate, I found this woman on the beach, drunk and blasted on cocaine, soliloquizing about how beautiful and fair my hull was.... One thing led to another, and I took her inside to make love to her—which she had informed me I was going to do. But first she laid out several more lines of pure Peruvian flake, which I happily snorted up. The problem with cocaine and sex is that while it makes women horny and wet, it makes men limp as a wet noodle. Wanting very much to fulfill my obligation here, I dove for her muff, only to be rebuked: "Eat eat eat! Doesn't anyone fuck anymore? I like a man to climb on me and fuck me!" The following day I visited her boat and tried again with a little more success....

Larry and I decided to launch both our boats in November, and we commenced racing against time. Rubrails, pedestal, rudder, bowsprit, cleats, ground tackle, machinery, chainplates; I worked like a madman with a hellhound on his trail. I was tired a lot—we all were—and we had long bull-sessions over coffee and breakfast in a tiny waterfront coffee-shop called Ketch Jo-Ann's. The fishermen and boatbuilders congregated there to bitch about how rough life was and give eachother moral support and advice. Jo-Ann and her family kept us fed and helped us all through rough times. Many an idea was created and destroyed around the big square corner table; nothing was sacred, either. The crowd was rough and honest—the fishermen in particular lived a hard life there. We learned a lot from each other. Our women often complained that we had the same conversation day after day after day. One morning Karren pounded the table with her fist, stood up, and said "I've had it—this is the *third morning in a row* you turkeys have had the same identical conversation about water tanks!" –

and stormed out.

Other language oddities must include Mickey, a local craftsman who periodically burned out on speech altogether. He would show up at JoAnn's with a sign that said something to the effect of: "I am having a WORD FAST today—PLEASE don't talk to me!" To this day I think Mickey was the wisest one of all.

There were two other restaurants that helped keep me alive through my times of boat-building-induced poverty: Tillie's Lil Frankfurt, especially. Tillie was a character of great depth as well as physical size—you would not want to cross her path in a dark alley. From the time I met her, I knew she could squash me like a bug. She had survived World War II in Germany married to a Nazi officer, and told me incredible stories after we became friends. She always wore flawlessly shiny black military shoes, and worked in her little restaurant alone from before dawn until midnight. I survived on her soup—and no ordinary soup was this! Tillie bought sides of beef, which she butchered herself. The best cuts went into her delicious traditional German specialties; the rest went into the soup, which was made fresh every day in a huge stainless pot. For 80-cents, she gave me a *BIG* bowl of this fortifying meal, full of fresh meat and potatoes and vegetables and spices, plus a piece of *REAL* dark bread—not that chemical-saturated foam-rubber crap that Americans pass off as the staff-of-life. If I finished my bowl too quickly, she refilled it! The other Germanic treat that supplemented this hearty meal was a bottle of—now get this—*Optimator Doppelspatten.* I confess I feel pretty much the same about American beer as I do about American bread (where *DID* we go wrong?). Spatten means shovel—*two* of 'em on the label. This rich, dark, powerful, delicious beer cannot be compared to anything else on Earth—except possibly Guinness Stout.

When I had a little extra money, I would partake of Tillie's equally outrageous deserts, too. And we talked—more and more as we became friends. I think that Tillie probably wasn't friendly with many people—I would sit at her counter, even help clean up the tables and floors after quitting time—and she would tell me stories. One of the best ones involved smuggling linen and silverware across the Alps into Switzerland! She called me her little 'sailor boy'—I don't think she ever knew my name.

The other restaurant was a Mexican joint in Half Moon Bay, run by an inscrutable old gentleman named Adolfo Santana. I don't know why he took me under his wing either, but he was very kind to me, and his food was delicious. Because it was considerably more expensive than Tillie's soup, and a longer drive, I didn't go there as often.

* * *

As our deadline approached, our money ran thin. Larry and I were faced with building a trailer that could launch both our boats (there was no way to get them to the yard's marine railway). This would never have happened without the three men who ran the boatyard. They came up with a pair of huge, ancient truck axles that still had wheels and tires, though the latter were marginal. They had a welder, and plenty of scrap metal around, but we needed a lot more. The biggest and most critical component needed was a large, steel I-beam to form the backbone of the trailer. We scrounged unsuccessfully until one day Larry said he had found one on the side of the road in San Francisco. We grabbed our friend Chuck, who was building a big ferrocement *HMS Sultana* replica down the street from us, and headed up twisty US One to the City. Larry pulled off the street into what was obviously a steel construction supply yard. Around behind a huge pile of scrap steel, lying beside the road was exactly 'our' steel I-beam. Grunting and groaning and looking over our shoulders a lot, we muscled the monster into Larry's dilapidated station wagon, all the while protesting, "Jesus, Larry!—You said it was on the side of the road, like a public street or something...." The I-beam went over the seats to the windshield and hung several feet off the tailgate. The wagon's rear springs compressed all the way and then some. The front end was a little light, but somehow we crawled back to Princeton with the I-beam and gave it to Ray in the yard, who knew better than to ask where we got it.

Times got more hectic: We were all (including Chuck down the street) killing ourselves to get our three boats ready to launch before the rainy season. It became work day-and-night and not much sleep. The boatyard crew had the trailer nearly assembled, but it still needed a towing/steering tongue, which would require a healthy length of large-diameter steel pipe. We had no spare money, barely enough to eat on, so buying one was out. Larry and I cruised the flatland scrap- and steel-yards, combed dumps and industrial garbage-piles near and far to no avail. The only such piece of pipe we could find was on a steel fishing boat construction-site right there in Princeton. We knew better than to touch anything in our own backyard, and the fisherman to whom said pipe belonged was known to have a foul sense of humor. Well, we went so far as to pinch it and hide it and make one last desperate search everywhere we could think of. After a long, futile late-night cruise, we returned home and retrieved that pipe and put it in the boatyard by the trailer, to be fashioned into the tongue. We planned to find another to replace it with. Then we made the awful mistake of forgetting it.

All three boats hit the water together in

November of 1976 on the high tides. We launched Larry's *Wind Chariot* first, Chuck's *Drifter's Gold* the next morning, and *Fishers Hornpipe* later that same morning. The better part of the community of Princeton was up all night two nights in a row. It was like some strange religious procession, slowly walking three huge Arks through the town. Someone had to stand on deck lifting power cables and telephone wires. The Fire Department cordoned off the streets, and dozens of the Bay's good folk walked with the boats—fishermen, divers, boatbuilders, cooks and waitresses, local police and fire department, harbor officials, and friends—everyone who had watched us doggedly struggle for years... for our day had arrived. Ketch JoAnn's made batches of coffee and sandwiches for free and sent them to us by bicycle!

It was only a quarter mile from the boatyard to the municipal launch ramp, but it took most of the night to move *Fishers Hornpipe* carefully out of the rough earth yard and through the streets of town, past the Crab Cottage, around several difficult corners and into the municipal harbor parking lot. The trailer was very simple and the old truck tires, nearly flat under the massive bulk of the *Hornpipe*, registered 100 pounds of pressure. Painfully slowly, we backed down the entrance road to the harbor launch ramp. Every little operation took planning and expertise. Without Ray Farnow and the boatyard crew, it wouldn't have happened.

After the epic ordeal of getting to the launching ramp, I still had to work the rest of the night bolting down the anchor windlass. I passed out, exhausted, sometime during that process.

The launch would have both excited and terrified me more than anything in my life if I hadn't been nearly catatonic with exhaustion. All my friends—San Francisco people, Princeton people and my Starhill people were there. Karren blasted the stem with a champagne bottle. It bounced off the first time, and when she hit it the second time, had the hull been fiberglass, she would have taken the stem right out! Karren bestowed the name *Fishers Hornpipe*, and instead of a christening, she laid a huge bouquet of wildflowers on the bow—our own Pagan Ceremony. At first, everything went smoothly, beautifully, like a dream—the biggest and most ambitious dream of my life. The boatyard lowered *Fishers Hornpipe* slowly and carefully into her true element from the ancient winches of their W.W. II Army-surplus Duck (amphibious vehicle) whose name was *Mother Ducker*—which in turn was chained to a friend's huge semi-tractor. On deck, I stared mesmerized over the side of the hull at rising salt water instead of the yellow and white daisies I had been accustomed to seeing for years. Upon checking through-hulls for leaks, I heard the nightmare sound of gushing water (sinking!) and found that the rubber hose connecting the packing gland to the propeller shaft-log hadn't seated and was leaking badly. In sheer terror (I was new to all of this) I worked feverishly to fashion a new clamp and add it on behind the existing one to stop the leak. Whew!

Everything worked! I had built strongly and thoroughly. Larry and I had just enough energy to motor around the harbor in our beautiful brand-new boats. We brought them alongside slowly and jumped across and drove each other's boats, so we could each admire our own under way. It was heady stuff. Looking over at the *Hornpipe*, my friend Roger said "Reuel, your boat is full of beautiful women." I looked over—and she was! Then we all collapsed; got safely anchored and crashed. All three of us on our three respective boats came down with the *post-launch virus* and were seriously sick and out of it for a couple of weeks. Just around the time we thought we were going to live, Ray corralled Larry and me and said something to the effect of: "Okay, you assholes, where the fuck did you get that last piece of pipe?"

Uh-oh—we looked at each other.

"Never mind—I *know* where you got it," he growled. "Now I've been accused of stealing it, and you're both going to *shit* a new piece of pipe! *Or else!*"

Well Ray isn't really big, but he can be incredibly ferocious and certainly we loved him and respected him and no way did we want him unhappy with us. So the Great Pipe Search commenced again. Now there was *absolutely* no money. I don't even know what we were eating—I think friends were feeding us. I got psychic. That night the three of us again headed for the flatlands, with just a little moonlight. We went to a scrap/surplus yard that had lots of junk lying around in a large unfenced area, and I walked straight to that piece of pipe. We brought it the next day to one very pissed-off fisherman (Ray virtually dragging us by the scruffs of our necks), along with a bottle of scotch that we'd borrowed the money to buy. A month later that junkyard got fenced in. We were all relieved we didn't need any more big pieces of steel!

CHAPTER THREE—HALF MOON BAY

I am incapable of a profound remark on the workings of destiny. It seems to get up early and go to bed very late, and it acts most generously toward the people who nudge it off the road whenever they meet it.

Beryl Markham, *West With the Night*

The pressure didn't diminish with launching the boats. To the contrary, the biggest and most demanding commitment of my life started the day *Ms. Hornpipe* hit the water. Sailboats are so vulnerable they are often compared to infant children. They are tethered to the sea bottom by a fragile strand in an unpredictable and ever-changing environment. My good friend Perry Fly says boats are always trying to commit suicide. Perhaps it would be more fair to say that everything is always trying to murder them. Even their supporting fluid, our dear Mother Ocean, is essentially battery acid. Sun and salt combine to literally burn their skins of paint and varnish off. The wind attempts to dislodge their tenuous connection to Terra Firma and batter them on the nearest hard object to leeward; if none is available they get deposited on the beach where the surf pounds them to fragments. In fact *the only place a seagoing vessel is anywhere near safe is at sea.* The biggest danger *there* is being run down in the night by a ship. The sea herself, even in the full fury of the storm, is unlikely to harm a well-found, well-handled sailing vessel. Placing a boat in the protective security of a marina costs vastly more than traveling in her; all this I suspected and eventually had confirmed by experience.

The fickle Half Moon Bay weather caused me many a sleepless night and troubled day. To go to work over the hill, I had to leave a phone number where I could be reached, and several times I had to race back to the harbor as fast as I could to deal with weather emergencies. If a gale came up, I would stay with my boat, often for days, even if I ran out of food and had to fast. I did this alone, and I learned about weather and solitude. The storms, to my amazement, often made me horny. Perhaps it was being totally surrounded by nature's uninhibited release—but I dearly craved female companionship during my stormy boat-sitting. The few times I had it, I often found my companion too frightened to share my response to the storm, with perhaps one exception....

There was a pretty, petite young woman who waitressed at the Crab Cottage who consented, during a rising gale, to come boat-sit with me. That night, during the height of the storm, we started to make love. I remember, during the process of kissing her all over, being delighted that she smelled and tasted like a delicate, smoked oyster. I kissed her female center for a long time, and after she achieved a really good orgasm, with the *Horny Fishpipe* pitching deeply and rhythmically at her anchors, and I was crawling on top of her, she stopped me, saying "I'm sorry, no—you can't—I save *THAT* for my boyfriend only." *Boyfriend?!?* I politely crawled off and lay there beside her, throbbing with desire for hours until sleep mercifully overtook me. She offered no alternative. I didn't invite her out again.

During one southerly storm that reached hurricane force, I helplessly watched twenty-six boats break their moorings or drag anchor and hit the beach to be smashed by each other and the surf. The huge seas damaged the stone breakwall so severely that it had to be rebuilt. Some of the boats were repaired, but many of them never floated again. This was not a rare occurrence; there were many gales in an average year, and one or two or more boats might be damaged or destroyed in perhaps every other gale.

One morning, when I was still living in my truck on the beach, I watched, half asleep (my bed had a big window over the cab of the truck), a very young man die out in that harbor. A commercial fisherman was bringing his boat from the public dock to his mooring (it was dangerously rough on the docks), and the young man was running out in an outboard-powered dory to bring him back. The dory's bow was riding much too high, and the wind caught it and flipped it over. The boy went in the water. Apparently he couldn't swim. After a brief hesitation, the fisherman dove in and somehow dragged him aboard his boat—a nearly impossible thing to do. It was a foolish accident in an average storm, but the victim died on the docks from the reaction of his lungs to violation by salt water: He died of pulmonary edema, which could have been prevented by an injection of Lasix. Two other men died in that harbor while I lived there, one by murder. [*Never* mess with a fisherman's wife.]

I kept pushing to fulfill my Dream as soon as I'd recovered from the initial shock of launching. This came to involve a lot more than I had anticipated; I found that I lacked other essential kinds of knowledge that might be vital to cruising besides ocean-sailing. Consequently, during those years in Half Moon Bay, I took some classes. I took a course in oceanography at a nearby community college with Karren. Chris Zones, the instructor, taught me much more than was in the course syllabus. He was a very inspired teacher, who had that remarkable ability to make his subject matter come alive. For part of another year, at night, I studied emergency medicine at another community college, stopping just before becoming an E.M.T. (emergency medical technician). This was especially hard for me, because I was terrified and mistrustful of doctors and hospitals to such a degree that even the smell of alcohol gave me the heebie-jeebies. I got over it. I worked several shifts in the Stanford University Hospital emergency room. I got the basics of how to sew people up, set broken bones and deal with all the basic medical emergencies (they even taught me to deliver babies!). The things I learned were part of changing and growing. I became so fascinated by surgery that I got permission through a friend who worked in a dialysis ward (also building a Cotten boat) to attend a five-hour kidney-transplant operation. The doctors performing the operation were fascinated by my unusual desire to watch such a thing, and generously went to extra pains to ensure that I saw and understood every detail of the operation. It was *truly* a mind-expanding experience.

I took a navigation class with a local sailor, Jack Hill, who had a small sailboat (an old Columbia 26) in the bay and voyaged, sometimes single-handed, to Hawaii every couple of years. He was most generous in opening his home twice a week to as many of us hopeful, future navigators as wanted to come and learn. He taught us to shoot and reduce noon-sights using a somewhat unusual method of plotting a series of sights on graph paper and reducing them using only the Nautical Almanac. He would have taught us much more but we were an unruly group and we all too often, Jack included, lapsed into storytelling and bull-sessions about everything under the sun. However, we learned a lot that way too.

During those years, I read everything I could about boats and the sea and sailing. I read several hundred books, magazines and technical publications, which were a very essential part of my education.

The ongoing construction of the boats slowed down somewhat after launching. Working on a boat at anchor is difficult at best; electricity had to come from generators, and materials had to be carried by dinghy (imagine transferring sheets of plywood). At times we could bring the boats into the commercial pier, but there were limitations to that imposed by the weather, the cost, crowded conditions and the regulations of the harbor.

We four boatbuilders all went to the pole yard in Stockton and searched through thousands of poles to find our masts. *Fishers Hornpipe's* mast came from a solid 56-foot Douglas fir pole that had been pressure treated. It cost $100 to buy and nearly that much again to get it home. We bought seven poles for our four boats to consolidate and share delivery costs.

I used my Alaskan chain saw mill to rough-shape the mast, nailing 2x6's along each side for the mill's rollers. I finished the shaping with my Skilsaw, plane, and belt-sander. The boatyard crew drove their crane down to the docks, and Larry and I stepped our masts together, followed by a somewhat raucous 'erection' party. I remember being stuffed into a bosun's chair and hauled, protesting loudly, up to the spreaders where I clung like a cat until they promised to let me down.

For years I had been having this recurring nightmare about being up a flagpole in an earthquake—being whipped violently back and forth like a fish on a fly rod. When it came time to go up to *Fishers Hornpipe's* masthead to measure for her standing rigging, I was scared to death. I waited for a calm, sunny day, and had my friend Ron haul me up. I told him to drag me to the top, regardless of what I said, did, barfed, pooped, whatever. He did. Once up there, fifty feet in the sky, with the unstayed mast swaying back and forth terrifyingly, I wrapped my arms and legs around the mast so tightly that they cramped up and I couldn't let go to come back down. As I dangled the end of the hundred-foot-tape down to Ron, my hands shook so badly that I could hardly read the measurements. Then my nightmare came true—a fishing boat came roaring alongside the dock, Jimmy 6-71 diesel screaming as nothing else can, setting up a monstrous wake that began to roll the *Hornpipe* violently side to side while the mast-head whipped me back and forth...like a fish on a fly rod. The experience cured me forever. I don't have acrophobia anymore—I can go up damn near anything. I often work as a professional rigger—and I don't have that nightmare any more.

On the site where I built my hull, I erected a quick and dirty shed using plywood, electrical conduit and plastic. It looked like a giant, plastic conestoga wagon, and lasted well except for replacing the plastic once or twice after the sun and gales had their way. In that humble shelter I made the components of my interior, laminated my hollow Douglas fir booms, cured lumber, made cabinets for construction jobs, and even slept a few times.

In our community there lived a generous and skilled man who helped all of us rig our vessels: George Loucks. George had worked on the Pacific Northwest fishing schooners in his distant youth (he ran away to sea at seventeen) and was by trade a ship's rigger. He was long-retired, but his love of boats and people drew him out constantly to help us with our rigging. Out of all of us boat builders, I became the most interested in learning his trade;

and he graciously undertook to teach me as much as we had time for, which turned out to be a hell of a lot. He taught me about life and people too, and about sail making, of which his knowledge was extensive. All of *Fishers Hornpipe's* standing rigging was hand-spliced, the strongest and best way to terminate cable ends, and also the least expensive in materials. George taught me the nearly dead art of marlinspike seamanship; not the decorative stuff that sailors made in their spare time, but the methods that hold rigs together. He taught me the old ways, the traditional ways, but he didn't look down his nose at modern materials and methods; he knew those too. He was the kind of man who always had an open, inquisitive mind and, even in his eighties, was always learning something new. The knowledge he shared was invaluable.

Rigging a vessel for going to sea is more expensive than building the hull, often by double. Doing it traditionally was the least-expensive, most-versatile, and probably the strongest and longest-lasting way. One reason it has all but died is the ever-evolving mania for racing, which virtually controls yacht design and construction. The other is marketing: the economic disease of constantly inventing elaborate, expensive hardware to replace simple, inexpensive, traditional components—solely (as far as I can tell) to separate fools from their money.

The above-deck components of a large ocean-cruising sailboat are shockingly expensive. I have to admit that some of my fellow boatbuilders who needed essential rigging components, like shackles, for example, would come out of a yachty store like West Marine (having bought a couple) with pockets heavy with the ones they didn't buy.... Despite the Great Pipe Incident mentioned previously, I couldn't bring myself to do this. Even so, there was no way I could ever afford to simply go out and buy what I needed. Even if I had had the money, many of the parts I needed weren't available; they had to be custom-made.

I searched for more than a year for the basic components and materials that I needed for my rigging. Scrap stainless-steel stock for chain plates, boom bails and masthead trucks, surplus 3/4-inch galvanized rigging screws (turnbuckles), 3/8-inch 7x7 wire rope (galvanized plow steel for shrouds and back-stays, and stainless steel for the head-stays), surplus or wholesale cleats, shackles and seizing wire. Many of the blocks I made myself, some I bought wholesale from an importer. I traded labor with friends for some of the finer, more visible stainless heliarc welding, but also did much of it myself on an old Miller buzz-box, reversing the polarity. George started the splicing, and as I learned how, I finished it. Many large components, like the anchor windlass, I built myself from mild steel and had them hot-dip-galvanized in a huge tank in South San Francisco. I made everything as simple, versatile, strong and easily maintainable as I possibly could.

Much of the mast hardware—gooseneck, wire-halyard winches, whisker-pole track and gear—came from an old mast that Larry and I salvaged. (It was another one of those daylight jobs....) The fifty-year-old bronze Merriman-Holbrook fittings needed restoration, but were superior to anything made since. And the price was right.

I drew and redrew my sail plan until I felt it was right (Patrick thought I was nuts to "second-guess" his work), then took a thousand dollars in cash to the Henderson Brothers Sail Loft in San Diego to start them on my sails. These identical twins eventually became my close friends (especially Bob), and kindly shared much of their vast knowledge with me. They taught me so much that it would take another book to relate. Sometimes we traded labor too—I restored their beautiful Whitehall pulling boat—but that was later. And like my other best teachers, they taught me a lot about life.

The sails and my diesel engine were the two things that I had to buy outright, for what to me was a lot of money (it took years of labor to pay for them). But they are the heart and soul of the vessel, and they have to be the finest possible.

My interior was only roughed in, and I found it difficult to make much progress with finish-carpentry at anchor. I did manage to make the bulwarks, and fasten them to the decks at the commercial docks, working for a few days at a time. But I needed a place to move *Fishers Hornpipe* to where the weather and the working conditions were more favorable, and the Sausalito waterfront seemed to be by far the most attractive. However, finding dock-space there turned out to be a time-consuming and challenging project.

It was a long, hard push between launching *Fishers Hornpipe* and going for our first trial sail, and when we finally did, it was with old second-hand sails and a lot of hastily-contrived temporary rigging. But that first sail was one of the ultimate thrills of my life. Once again, I was too excited and terrified to really relax and enjoy it, but at least I wasn't exhausted like I had been for both plaster day and launch day. The weather was beautiful and the sea was gently rolling with that long, easy Pacific swell. It was like a fairy tale—blue sky, warm sun and gentle wind. We sailed right out the breakwater and several miles out to sea, then turned around and came back and sailed around the harbor to show off for all our friends. Feeling the awesome power in the sails, one of the boatyard women sailing with us said "Holy shit! This ain't no toy boat!" Karren was so excited that she got drunk, and scared the hell out of me by falling overboard. Fortunately, she

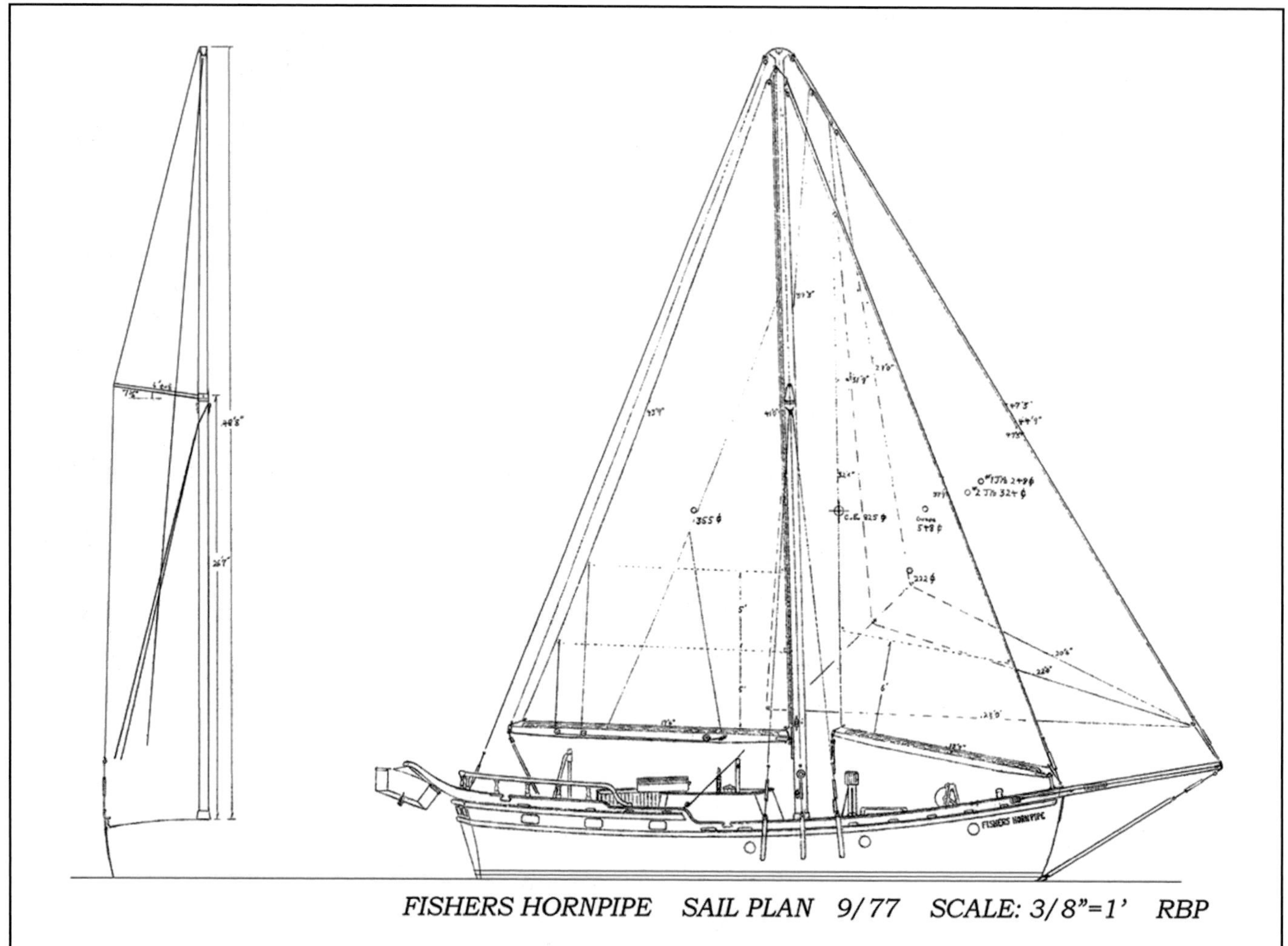

FISHERS HORNPIPE SAIL PLAN 9/77 SCALE: 3/8"=1' RBP

has very strong hands, and grabbed a lifeline on her way over, enabling me to get to her and pull her back aboard. Everyone felt proud and happy—the whole community had put something into *Fishers Hornpipe.* I tried to take everyone sailing, but I never got to them all. Each time we went out, there was some new part to the deck and rigging, a new piece of the evolving whole.

Our real 'maiden voyage' to a different port was made on December 24th of 1977. Larry and I, each with a handful of friends for crew, sailed from Half Moon Bay to Sausalito to celebrate Christmas in *Wind Chariot* and *Fishers Hornpipe.* It was during this trip that we first met UNCLE in the persona of the U.S. Coast Guard. Both boats were very unfinished, though quite seaworthy. But UNCLE is a stickler for details, judging a vessel on whether or not it conforms to the items they have on a list.

The day was brisk and overcast with a steady northeast wind blowing 10 to 15 knots. The sail was a joy until the Coast Guard cutter *Point Chico* hailed us at sea, in sight of the Golden Gate Bridge, and ordered us both to heave to and prepare to be boarded. That presented a problem for us, because we were just about to lose the favorable flood tide we wanted for entry to San Francisco Bay. When the current reverses, it can race up to four knots, which would delay our arrival in Richardson Bay (Sausalito) until after dark. None of us had sailed into these Bays before, and we greatly desired to enter in daylight. UNCLE didn't give a shit. The Coast Guard crew actually pulled the canvas covers off their deck-mounted 50-caliber machine guns. We obediently hove to and the coasties boarded our boats and thoroughly searched them, going so far as to pull up floorboards and tear up bunks. The 'routine safety inspection' bit is a crock of shit, obviously. The United States Coast Guard, ideally a noble and vital life-saving and coast-protecting organization, has had the responsibilities imposed on it of sniffing for drugs and inspecting marine toilets.

Larry and I both got tickets for very minor violations: Larry lacked one fire extinguisher, I lacked an 'approved' throwable life ring. (I had one that my crew and I approved of: a large truck inner tube with sail gaskets attached. People sail across the Gulf Stream from Cuba on these regularly—can you imagine sailing from Cuba on a Coast Guard approved one?) The *Hornpipe* was also missing her transom hailing port, because I was in the process of repainting the transom. (Her bow names were in place.) So UNCLE terminated our voyage and gave us an armed escort to Sausalito, very slowly

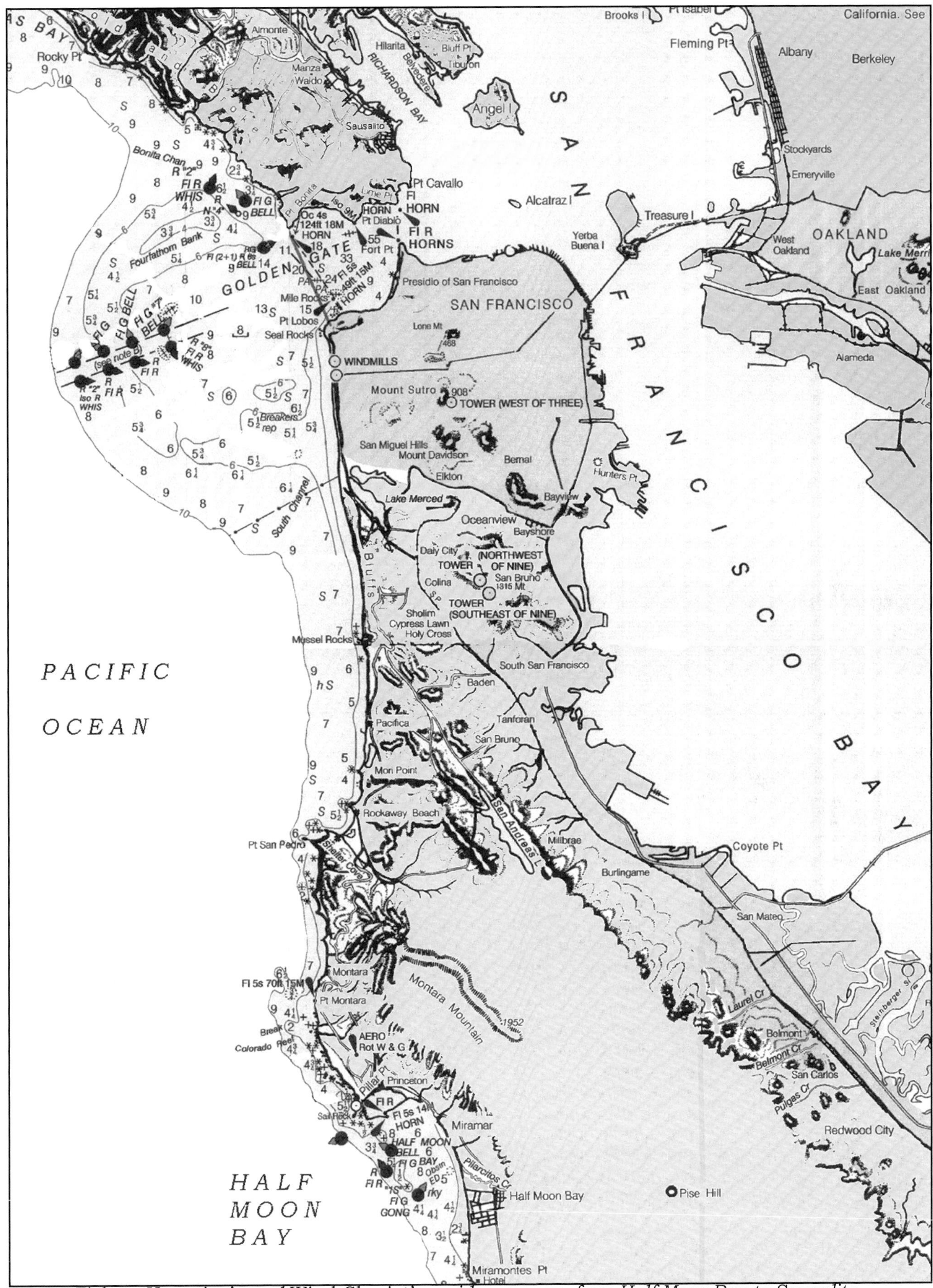

Fishers Hornpipe's *and* Wind Chariot's *maiden voyage, from Half Moon Bay to Sausalito (Richardson Bay) and back.*

slogging to weather against the tide in rain showers, which lasted several hours.

UNCLE again boarded us after we anchored, and forbade us to leave our vessels—we were, in fact, under house arrest. I still cannot imagine what the hell these people were thinking about. After all, this was Christmas Eve and we had turkeys and hams in our ovens, pies on our shelves and food cooking. Maybe they thought it was a Commie Plot to subvert Sausalito with drug-infested food. Of course there were no drugs on board either boat, not even a Christmas joint.

I want to stress the fact that we were all, captains and crews, polite to the boarding officers and crews. There were no antagonistic remarks, no rudeness or sarcasm. We were frightened and concerned. This experience felt very different from being pulled over by the California Highway Patrol—our homes were being violated.

Finally some officer got the bright idea to call the Half Moon Bay Harbor Master, who of course vouched that we were all okay, and UNCLE left us alone to slowly recover our shattered Christmas spirit. My anger didn't abate easily, and I wrote to my congressman, Leo Ryan, himself a Bay sailor, and he quite agreed that we had been treated obnoxiously and unfairly, and proceeded to write a complaint on my behalf to the HEAD CHIEF UNCLE in Washington D.C. The letter that came back shocked us all (I have lost it, or I would include it here), and put dear Mr. Ryan on the warpath. He was ready to tackle the Supreme Court with our silly case, except that first he got called to Guyana, where he was subsequently blown away by machine-gun fire during the Congressional investigation of the *Jim Jones Commune* mass-murder-suicide there. That was the end of the case for both of us.

The HEAD CHIEF UNCLE letter said, in effect: "We are the Fuck-ers and you-all are the Fuck-ees and when we say bend over and spread 'em, you *WILL* do just that. *Or else!*" More education. There sure is a hell of a lot to learn in the boating world. I was very naive, and I eventually learned that the U.S. Government is in no way unique in its attitudes. Most countries share them to some degree, and many are worse—though all sailors dread the U.S. Coast Guard and U.S. Customs and Immigration as much as any on Earth. No other country has such l-o-n-g a-r-m-s.

We did manage to recover and enjoy our Christmas feast in Sausalito. On Christmas Day, we found a fire extinguisher, an 'approved' life-ring, and I re-painted my hailing port back on the transom in the drizzling rain. We had a beautiful, uneventful return sail to Half Moon Bay on the twenty-sixth. (See Photos.)

My crew for this first voyage included two of the women in my life at that time: Linda and Nancy (see photo). I think I was seeing Nancy at the time of the sail—Linda had stopped being my girlfriend after complaining that she couldn't "compete with my other mistress." She was referring to *Ms Hornpipe*. I replied that the solution was a 'menage a' trois,' but she wasn't having that either.

Nancy brought her 10-year old son David with us on the sail. I liked him, and I think I could have been his friend—even his step-dad—but Nancy had this pre-existing relationship with a very violent, abusive man, and when he threatened to beat the shit out of both of us, she went back to him. I just don't get it—but some women seem to need that or respond to that. I wanted her, and I lost her.

One of my other Half Moon Bay girlfriends was Cheryl, who was a dental hygienist. She was pretty and petite, and loved her showers scalding hot and then freezing cold. One night we were out, and she kept 'draping' herself on me. Karren was there also, and remarked to a friend: "That's the end of *her*—Reuel hates being furniture." She was right....

I have perhaps been ambiguous about my relationship with Karren. I considered her to be my best friend, but really she was much more than that. She was always my lover, even when we were both seeing other people, even when they disapproved. (Looking back, I think that California in the seventies was very different than any other time and place.) Karren was really my second wife—my second long-term soul mate. My partner. Our relationship was turbulent, intermittent, difficult and passionate—but we loved each other very much. Years later it would occur to me that I failed her—that she somehow deserved more from me. That feeling has haunted me ever since.

Now that *Fishers Hornpipe* was truly ambulatory, it was time to move her to a place where I could efficiently finish her. I needed dock space and a shop. After no small amount of research and negotiation, in April of 1978 I packed up my life and migrated to Sausalito to live, work and finish my boat.

CHAPTER FOUR—SAUSALITO

"...the last free ride is waitin' on the water...."

Joe Tate, *The Last Free Ride*

Securing dock space in Sausalito was a delicate, psychological victory. The "straight" people's marinas were ludicrously expensive and crowded, and the vintage wooden yacht basin (Pelican Harbor) was completely out of this world. When I inquired about a slip there, I mentioned that my boat hull was ferrocement and was informed that I couldn't afford a slip, even if I could afford it. That left the houseboat community, with which I had already fallen passionately in love.

The only dock that could accommodate the *Hornpipe's* deep draft was the condemned and very dilapidated Napa Street Pier. The location was excellent, the rent cheap, the neighbors colorful, and space unavailable. The Pier was then managed by an interesting character known to everyone as Fat Albert. Fat Albert ran a new/used waterfront marine store at the head of the Pier called *Wave Traders*. This interesting establishment was a boon for all us poverty-stricken boatbuilders. You could dig through piles of Fat Albert's junk and find the most amazing equipment. If you couldn't find what you were looking for, you often could find something that could be made to work. But to get dock space on Napa Street Pier, you had to convince Fat Albert that you *really deserved to be there*, that he would indeed benefit (at least monetarily) by your presence, and that you would in *NO WAY* create any problems either for him or the eclectic loose community of degenerates, hippies, junkies, drug dealers and eccentrics who already miraculously coexisted there. Then you had to wait for months while he evicted some poor unfortunate soul who was too strung-out to make the cheap rent several months in a row. All this I somehow accomplished, largely with the help of my dear friend Perry Fly. The key to Albert's heart (besides money) involved persistence and a good sense of humor. Perry and I worked on him together and separately for *two years* before he finally gave in. Making him laugh seemed to be our most persuasive weapon. I think he ultimately gave me the slip for comic-relief value, and we got along great.

A couple of years before I got there, Stewart Brand had rented a leaky, derelict ice-house out on the Napa Street Pier, in which he partially created his wonderful *Whole Earth Catalogue*. I partitioned off and rented part of that old studio and set up my woodshop. There was no electricity out on the pier beyond the ice-house, so I ran a power line under the dock all the way out to my boat. This was a clandestine operation which no-one could know about (it was strictly *verboten*—Albert was rigid on this point), but my next-door-neighbor Bill (who was building a ferrocement *Spray* replica) caught on and I had to let him in on it. At night we sneakily ran hundreds of feet of romex 12-2 wire back under the rotten, filthy, rat- and pigeon-infested pier from the boats to my shop. We were both finishing up cruising sailboats and *had* to have electricity. We invented some elaborate story about the twelve-volt inverters we had purchased jointly and which supplied our juice. The deception succeeded for a year and a half, until Joe Tate figured it out. I'll tell you more about Joe shortly.

The dock space was tricky to get in and out of, as it was shorter than *Fishers Hornpipe's* overall length. My neighbor in front was an elderly Buddhist recluse whom everybody called Uncle Bill. I got to know him better after returning from sailing one day, and in the process of docking the *Hornpipe's* twenty-three ton, 54-foot ponderous bulk into a 50-foot space during a gusty northerly wind (my slip was on the north side of the dock), I accidentally removed the tenuous stovepipe from his ancient, leaky ex-rumrunner houseboat with my bowsprit. Of course he had a fire going and I don't know whether the racket or the back-drafting smoke drove him out. The logistics of getting in and out of that slip discouraged me from doing a lot of day-sailing.

The Napa Street Pier was a place where *anything* could happen. One afternoon while I was puttering about on deck, a naked girl swam up to my boat and called "Hey, would you please help me up?" I directed her to the bobstay under my bowsprit and reached down to help her aboard. I got her a towel to dry off, thinking she would cover up with it. She didn't. She sat on deck talking with me for ten or fifteen minutes. She was very beautiful—a real mermaid with full, round breasts and long dark hair—and perhaps 16 years old. It turned out she was the daughter of an acquaintance who lived next door to Napa Street on the wreck of an ancient ferry boat (of which there were several in Sausalito at that time). People walking past us on the Pier may have noticed that I was sitting and talking with a beautiful naked girl, but no one ever mentioned it. Perhaps she did it all the time. Perhaps they knew something I didn't. After a while she stood up, golden body glowing in the afternoon sun, said "bye," dove back into the water and swam away.

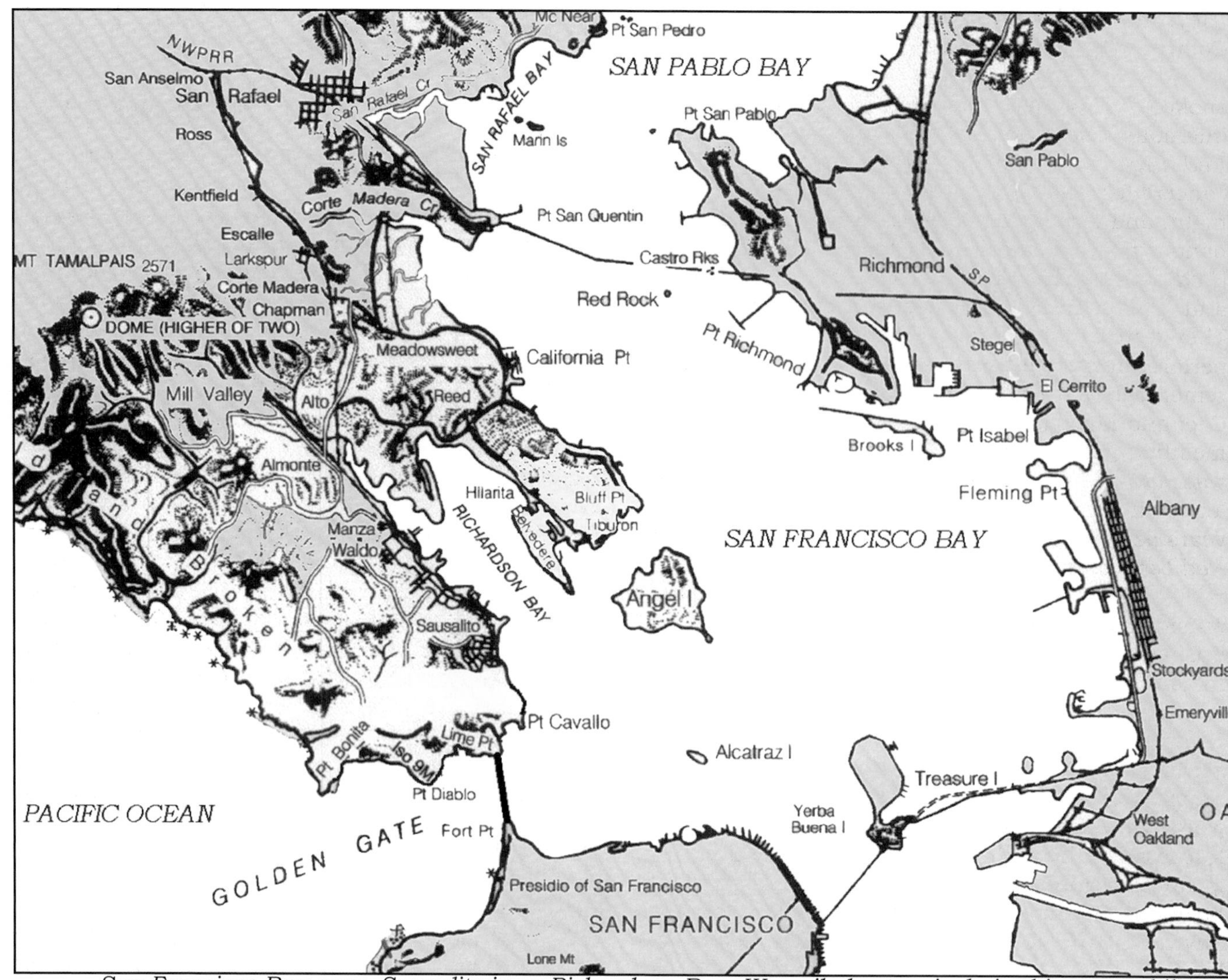

San Francisco Bay area. Sausalito is on Richardson Bay. We sailed extensively in this area while finishing Fishers Hornpipe *on the Napa Street Pier in Sausalito.*

My sex life improved in Sausalito. In Half Moon Bay it had been few and far between, and my lovers there quickly gave up trying to "compete with my other mistress," as Linda put it. Karren and I remained close friends after I moved to Sausalito, but we rarely saw each other anymore. We both knew the sailing life wasn't for her. In Sausalito there were crazy women: bright, radical, funky, hard-working, horny Earth-Mamas, and I made love to as many of them as I could. There was an incredible constant social scene in Sausalito—something was always happening—the houseboats were a real community. Life was very good.

I had an Italian girlfriend from Pier Three. She was a little crazy, and hot, and she liked my "left hook." But we argued a lot, and I remember one night we were playing pool during one such argument. There were a bunch of bikers waiting for the table. We were so involved in fighting that it took us forever to clear the table...those bikers were ready to kill us both when we finally fled for our lives.

Another girlfriend was Joni. She was blond, very pretty, and tiny, and I thought seriously about asking her to live with me and sail into the sunset... then her other suitor came to me, weeping, and begged me not to take her away!

My most embarrassing sexual experience involved a beautiful teenage girl who lived with her brother in an old bread truck near Pier Three. I asked her out to see the movie *The Wiz*, after which I took her home to the *Fishpipe* to make love to her. As I entered her, she cried out loudly. I thought she was coming (stupid me—I was hurting her), and I immediately came also! So much for romantic sex that night...thank goodness pre-mature ejaculation has never (usually) been my problem. Nevertheless, she never went out with me again.

I had another lover who liked to fuck really hard—I mean to bang together so hard that I was sore for days afterwards. She had a venus mound hard as a rock and sure loved to give it a beating. I remember saying something to Joe Tate about her, and that she sure loved to fuck. Joe replied,

"Hey, they *all* love to fuck!" And in the Houseboat Community, that certainly was true.

Joe Tate, sort of the organic mayor/ spokesman of the Houseboat Community, had an infamous underground rock-and-roll band called *Red Legs*. I remember the *Red Legs* opening a concert for *The Grateful Dead* at the Filmore one night, and earning the reputation of being the only band ever to be forcibly evicted from the stage. [*Red Legs* got their name from accosting strangers and painting red strips down their pant-legs.] They were a cut-up, wonderful, crazy band whose performances were completely unpredictable. I remember well the sweet, rich, powerful voices of Ceci and Maggie Catfish, the female vocalists. The members weren't always the same, but the band was always outrageous—those folks knew how to let it all hang out. I was fascinated, missing my years as a professional musician, and I soon joined *Red Legs* as their electric mandolin player.

The Houseboat Community had many musicians who were good (besides *Red Legs*), and during their bizarre and delightful parties I could usually find someone to play music with. I either rode my funky, rusty bicycle (*Air Force One*) or motored over in my patched up skiff (*Wendy*) with my mandolin whenever I got word that a party was happening. And often a sweet, misty-eyed houseboat woman would go home with the mandolin player. I sure miss those days. I know in my heart there is no place on Earth, never has been, never will be and isn't now (because it doesn't exist anymore) anything like the Sausalito Houseboat Community. Indeed, there is no place on Earth like California in the 1970's—I know this because I have spent the rest of my life looking for it.

Joe Tate, when he wasn't attempting to father another kid, getting stoned, making music or inventing some unlikely contraption that sometimes worked and usually involved some scheme to make money, owned and sailed an interesting vessel. The *Richmond* had been an ancient sea-going logging tug, converted to fishing boat, converted to Chinese junk-rigged schooner. She had a 1948 Harley-Davidson motorcycle seat for her helmsman's throne. The *Richmond* was big, 75 feet or so, narrow and fast and even seaworthy. At least Joe and a motley crew had at one time sailed her all the way to Costa Rica and Hawaii and back, managing to stay in trouble and catch tropical venereal diseases the whole way. Costa Rica's Puntarenas—funky as that place is—didn't fully appreciate *Red Legs* playing ear-shattering rock and roll (over the roar of the gas generator) from the deck of the *Richmond*, and eventually kept an armed guard on board until they could deport the whole outfit. A friend of mine who was on that trip as navigator told me that after they were well at sea, Joe went to each crewmember and took all their money—explaining it would be safer with him and that they wouldn't need it out there anyway.

Joe taught me some things I doubt I could have learned anywhere else on Earth. One jewel I have always remembered is "Beware the Deadly Underdose." Words to live by—and I have. Whatever it is that you want—make sure you get enough of it to thoroughly satisfy your desire—that way you won't want more right away. The most popular recreational drug around that time (drug-of-choice) was the "Speedball"—cocaine and crystal methamphetamine (speed) mixed together and intravenously injected. Rip your head right off. Good thing I hate needles!

There is an excellent underground movie about Joe Tate, the *Richmond* and the on-going battle between the Sausalito filthy-rich and filthy-poor called *The Last Free Ride*. If you ever hear of it playing anywhere (it was popular in Europe some years back where folks have a finer appreciation of these things), please go see it—I promise you won't regret it. Included in the film is the Sausalito funeral of their beloved poet and writer Alan Watts. There is a Joe Tate/*Red Legs* song that goes with it—"...the last free ride is waitin' on the water...." I remember the scene at the end with the newly-launched *Richmond*, with Joe at the helm dry-humping her steering wheel....

The on-going battle between the city-moneyed and the community-impoverished had profound implications for everyone in Sausalito. The City Fathers and Corporate Magnates wanted to eradicate the hippies and drug addicts, poets and prostitutes, saints and derelicts from the waterfront. They wanted this very badly. They wanted to develop the waterfront, and we were all in the way of progress. Money always wins, of course, but we made it as hard for them as possible. When they maneuvered a barge and pile driver in to build docks, a huge steel barge mysteriously broke loose from its moorings and sank on the spot. When the police tried to get it moved, the barge's ownership was traced to a countess in Europe. When they brought in the bulldozers, the poets and prostitutes laid their bodies down under the blades. It was a miracle no one got killed—it came close a few times. When salvage crews came to wreck the derelict houseboats and ferries, they found them occupied by women with babies in their arms.

Yes, there were prostitutes among the women (and men) of the Houseboat Community. One of them was my lover for a while, and she told me some stories I will never forget...but that's *her* book!

The people in the Houseboat Community were mostly very poor—really living in poverty. Maggie Catfish would regularly take her old station wagon on food-foraging trips. Everyone knew on which days the dumpsters behind the fancy supermarkets had the best pickins'—and a lot of people were ace dumpster divers (including me). The quantity of good food that came out of those dumpsters always amazed me. I remember one trip where Maggie found a lamb killed on the road. She got out to look at it, and it was still warm. She brought it back to that sunken barge I mentioned a couple of paragraphs back (the deck was dry at low tide), which had a kitchen built in it, and I cooked up a mutton stew that fed forty people.

* * *

During all of this, I kept hammering away at my boat and at being an outlaw contractor (mostly in Marin County, which everyone called *Moron* county) and did more and more work on other people's boats. My old friend/ex-brother-in-law Jim Schaefer had moved from Colorado to Marin County by then, and I occasionally did work for him too. I did fancy carpentry for wealthy people—ironic symbiosis.

Because I did high-quality detail carpentry, I found myself working on the beautiful wooden yachts at Pelican Harbor (the place that wouldn't let me in). I noticed a pretty, muscular young woman who worked there as a varnisher. At first she wouldn't even talk to me. I learned her name was Nancy Franklin, and I developed a wicked crush on her. Finally we found ourselves working on the same wealthy white man's yacht—she was varnishing my woodwork—and we slowly became friends. I invited her to sail with me to Half Moon Bay—*Fishers Hornpipe* needed a haulout—and she came. As I vividly recall, we were on deck working side by side on the main boom, and she just grabbed me and kissed me passionately. We staggered below, tearing eachother's clothes off on the way, and barely made it to my bunk before we were sexually devouring eachother. The rest of that week, we didn't get much work done, but the sex was incredible—some of the best in my life. But there was much more than that—I felt I had finally found my sailing partner—the woman I wanted to be with into the distant future. Was Nancy that elusive personified very female life goal?

Unfortunately for me, there was another man in Nancy's life (isn't there always?), and in the end he prevailed. I'm not sure why. The ferrocement thing looms large again...Nancy worshipped wooden boats. Near the end of our time together, Nancy came to be with me for a weekend. It was the weekend in which she was to have made her decision—him or me. I was on pins and needles. In bed, naked, she said "I have a present for you..." "What is it?" I asked, holding my breath. "Me!" My heart soared! She was mine! Then she dropped the other shoe: "I'm leaving next week with my other man to buy an old Alden sloop in Maine." I plunged a million miles...she was only mine for the weekend. I was so devastated I could not even make love to her.

Our friendship survived for years, nonetheless. She even flew back to California once and spent a passionate week with me. For a year after that, Nancy wrote wonderful letters to me about her adventures in *Dark Star*—but I never saw her again. I lost her forever.

* * *

Piece by piece, my basic interior was completed (some details weren't finished until years later). I capped my bulwarks with beautiful eastern white ash, made solid ash stern davits, built a center cockpit, finished electrical wiring and plumbing and water tanks, finished skylights and deck structure, and perfected the *Hornpipe's* rig. People still came to help me from time to time, and I visited friends in San Francisco, Bolinas (where Perry Fly lived) and Half Moon Bay. A wandering drop-out from The System—a talented watercolor artist named Michael Lannigan—had been helping me since we became friends back in Half Moon Bay, and he used to come to help me for days at a time, as did Perry Fly. Michael and Perry alternately were first mates on *Fishers Hornpipe* during those early sailing trips. We had great times, and perhaps a few rough ones too.

There was a Dream Journal published every few weeks in Sausalito that anyone could submit their dreams to: There were several little 'collection boxes' you could put your dreams in. One time I gave them a dream *Fishers Hornpipe* and I had in which both of us together had an astral-projection experience. We drifted together, man and boat, in our astral bodies, underneath the Napa Street Pier. I had a lot of those out-of-body dreams/experiences in Half Moon Bay and at Starhill, but living on the water had radically altered my sleeping habits and made my nights more conventional. After I started cruising, the nocturnal journeys ceased almost altogether, but the dreams have never ceased.

I worked as a shipwright on the large 1910 Baltic Ketch trader-cum-floating cocktail lounge *Lene Marie*, and increased my knowledge of and admiration for the surviving schooners and working craft of years gone by. I had always admired them, but now I was getting to know them intimately. Neil Young's Baltic Schooner conversion *W.N. Ragland* showed up one day and I became friends with her captain and crew. As I mentioned back in Chapter One, Starhill was close to Neil's *Broken Arrow Ranch*, and consequently many of us there had known Neil to some degree, myself included. The interior of the

Ragland (so named after Neil's grandfather) was a hippie dream—it looked as though it had been organically grown instead of hand crafted.

During this time Harold Sommers (a Red Stacks tugboat captain) and friends were busy restoring the beautiful German pilot schooner *Wanderbird*, and I would often go check on their progress. [Read Sterling Hayden's autobiography *Wanderer* to learn more about the history of this remarkable schooner.] Nancy Franklin and her (other) boyfriend helped out as volunteer labor. I remember they had to remove all the iron ballast, chip it and clean it, re-coat it with cement, and re-install it in *Wanderbird's* bilges. Evidently there was most of a disassembled 19th century German steam engine in there! I took a photo of *Wanderbird* from *Lene Marie's* crosstrees, which is included in the first group of photos.

Sterling Hayden visited Sausalito on occasion (he used to live there), and on one such visit there was a fund raising party for a new mains'l for *Wanderbird*. The party was held in *Lene Marie's* main saloon—the largest floating space available. A number of movies were shown, among them one contributed by Mr. Hayden. It consisted of some footage he had assembled to attempt to interest the movie industry in sailing films. One segment was an old news clip of the final race between Massachusetts' *Gertude L. Thibodoux* and Nova Scotia's *Bluenose*. It is some of the most exciting sailing footage I have ever seen—these huge (over 130') schooners were slugging it out in a full gale, and neither captain would shorten sail! The crew were all racing up and down the decks wearing waistcoats and bowler hats. The vessels were heeled dangerously over (they were 'light' for racing) with their lee rails and decks under water. The tops'ls were blown to ribbons, streaming and snapping tatters in the screaming wind. The sound track sounded like a howling steam freight train going full bore. After the fund-raiser ended, Perry Fly, Jeff (the captain of *Lene Marie*), and I watched the sequence again. Jeff broke out a bottle of Mount Gay Eclipse rum, and we drank the whole bottle while watching that movie over and over....

I learned to drink *aquavit* from Sterling Hayden, in the No Name Bar in downtown Sausalito. I had the great pleasure of getting shit-faced drunk in his company. He was living on a barge houseboat in France at that time, and had acquired the habit of saying "je suis d'accord" while pounding the table with his fist when he emphatically agreed with something someone said. He was a very talented and passionate man, a consummate sailor, and a fellow tortured soul. The world is a poorer place now in his absence.

* * *

I finally found myself wanting more and more to go cruising, and less and less to build what seemed to have become a lifetime project. I was feeling restless and tired and burned-out. This attitude shift got me working faster and more efficiently, and figuring what projects could be left for a future time without compromising the *Hornpipe's* safety, comfort and integrity. I worked on upholstery and running lights, and built my New England surf-dory *Gandy Dancer*. Perry Fly and I together built a pair of these dories, which I adapted from the turn-of-the-century Chamberlain model. John Gardner wrote about the type in his book *Building Classic Small Craft*, and published the lines of his adaptation. On a trip back east to visit my parents, I found a surviving Chamberlain dory in the archives of Mystic Seaport, and adapted my own smaller version of the design to be a yacht-tender and lifeboat. [Even after 25 years, I have never found a better all-around yacht tender. For *Gandy Dancer's* story, see my article in the Oct. 2003 issue of *Good Old Boat* Magazine.]

I bought an old German *Anker* zigzag sewing machine in the San Jose flea market for $35, and spent many days behind it. I now had most of my new sails from the Henderson Brothers (Bob Henderson had personally driven up and dropped them off while running errands in San Francisco), and I made my own sail covers. I bought all my fabrics and sewing supplies wholesale in bulk. I cut foam rubber mattresses with a razor-sharp fillet knife, and upholstered them myself.

I realized I was getting close to being able to take the first Big Jump, and I started looking for crew. All my faithful friends and lovers for one reason or another weren't going to be able to go; I realized somewhat sadly that I was moving into a whole new world and lifestyle, and that all 'my people' were not.

The search for crew was so difficult and unsuccessful that I started to feel very frustrated. Somehow I had thought that if I could bust my ass for years creating this *ARK*, I should have no trouble at all finding folks to help me sail her. I had even been naive enough to think we would have to rotate crew so that everyone would get to share in the experience. California Dreamin'....

Finally I met Cyndee Horner, who moved on board and started helping me get it together. After agonizing for years about where the first voyage would take me, I concluded that I wanted to head down the coast into Mexico and Central America, then through the Panama Canal and into the Caribbean. The other big option was to sail to Hawaii, thence either back to California or off to the South Pacific. I knew I didn't want to return to California, I worried that heading for the Pacific islands would not be economically feasible, and I was apprehensive about a maiden voyage of such long duration as sailing to Hawaii. Cyndee had kicked around Guatemala the year before, and wanted to return to the Caribbean by sailboat.

As we got to know eachother, Cyndee wanted us to become lovers. I resisted admirably—I didn't want to jeopardize my relationship with my new (and only) crewmember by risking a move that might complicate things. One morning, as I was sitting in the middle of the settee eating breakfast in the great aft cabin, Cyndee came in wearing a very light, pretty cotton dress—with nothing on underneath. She sauntered up to me, climbed onto the settee, and straddled me. I put my spoon back into my yogurt, fruit and granola. My brain was going "no...no...." And my body was going "yes... YES...." Cyndee looked me in the eyes and said "OK Parker—this is it!" So much for celibacy....

Perry Fly was to be first mate, but as departure approached we found we had too many differences of opinion, and eventually realized, to our mutual disappointment, that we weren't going to do the first trip together. He is a more conservative sailor than I am. An example would be the life raft argument: Perry insisted that either we get a life raft, or he wasn't coming. As far as I was concerned, these highly expensive rubber life-boats might work and might not. Their cost was so extravagant that I would have had to wait another year to earn enough money to by a good one the right size (I would have chosen an eight-man Givens Life Buoy). I knew in my heart that I would go stark raving mad if I had to wait that long. [Besides, I just don't believe in them, and to this day, after five cruising sailboats and over 100,000 miles, I still won't have one.] There's no way in Hell I'd let *Fishers Hornpipe* sink out from under me with everything I own. I put my energy instead into systems to protect her—I made a double-thickness foam-core "collision mat" which could be drawn over a hole in the hull from the outside, underwater-curing epoxy, an EPIRB emergency radio, an emergency tiller, and emergency portlight covers. If it ever came to going into the drink, we would go in the dory, which is the most seaworthy of all small craft. *Gandy Dancer* carried a sailing rig and two pairs of oars, and could carry six adults. I converted an old ice chest into a survival kit—equipped with water, food, fish-tackle, flares, first-aid kit, etc.

Cyndee and I found another woman, Debi Babarsky, and the three of us were to become the core of my crew for the first cruise. The same thing that had happened with Cyndee and me happened again, with Debi (except I think I started it). We had all tried to be lovers, but being friends and traveling companions worked out better and made more sense in the end. Also, to be honest, I did not feel that either of these two remarkable women was the 'soul-mate' I was looking for. Perhaps too much social/sexual experience had led me to be overly discerning in what I thought I wanted or needed in a life partner. While I never would have made a list of what I sought in a woman, I nevertheless could sense that a particular individual wasn't exactly what I was looking for. This defect in my character (what else could it be?) has caused me to search relentlessly my whole life for an elusive goal personified by a woman who probably doesn't exist. Although there were some marvelous close calls....

We went for practice sails on San Francisco Bay and environs as often as we could. And we took various friends with us. Even though I was no longer romantically involved with my crew, I still needed love and sex, and I still wanted a soul mate/ cruising partner. I was very attracted to a massage therapist named Monica—but she became involved with Perry Fly. I was to learn that finding a cruising partner is, for me, the hardest thing in the world. At the time of this writing I still haven't found her.

During one of our practice sails, we had an accident that resulted in an injury—the only serious one in all my years of sailing: My hand-made drum-type windlass was cranked by a long steel handle, which was not self-locking. Hence when you finished raising the anchor, it was necessary to lash the handle with a rope loop made for that purpose. If you neglected to secure the handle, and if there was any tension in the anchor rode (such as an anchor hanging from the bow roller), the handle could spin back around.

Cyndee had just weighed anchor, and let go of the handle without securing it. It spun back around and hit her in the head, just above her left eye. This caused a laceration that began to bleed profusely. We made her an ice pack, returned to the Pier, and I drove Cyndee to the hospital. The wound required several stitches, which were skillfully made by a young woman doctor.

The cut healed rapidly, and left no discernable scar (her eyebrow concealed it). But the incident upset me, because I saw how easy one of us could be injured. I ended up removing and discarding that windlass, and purchasing a used Simson-Lawrence windlass to replace it. Although not as powerful as the one I made, it had the advantages of being able to pull more than one anchor rode (mine could not), and the chain could be funneled below deck where its weight was lower (always an advantage).

After this incident, I always stressed that personal safety must be our first priority. A serious injury at sea, or in a remote place, must be avoided as earnestly as possible.

I had a hard time consolidating my life into *Fishers Hornpipe*. Everything that wasn't coming with us had to go. I had learned the lesson years ago that when I left someplace, I left it for good, leaving nothing behind that I ever expected to see again. (When I left New York in early '72 for the last time, I gave everything away: furniture, clothes, oriental carpets, a wife I dearly loved, several cats and twenty-two cars and trucks—many of which were restorable collector's items.) My music recording equipment I just had to leave with Perry—no one I knew had enough money to buy it. Several boxes of books (I hate to part with books) I gave away. I took some 750 books with me—onboard *Fishers Hornpipe* there were over 60 feet of bookshelves.

The medical chest was a real challenge, and a big expense. I read several books and magazine articles on the subject, and finally sat down with both a family doctor and a pharmacist to determine what was really important. I bought a military-surplus waterproof steel ammunition box, painted it with epoxy, and packed it full of medical supplies. These included antibiotics, various topical ointments, pain-killers (including injectable Xylocaine), Cavitex and clove-oil for dental emergencies, injectable Lasix for pulmonary edema, injectable synthetic adrenaline for severe allergic reactions, needles and suturing thread, splints for broken bones, plastic intubators, sphygmomanometer, blood-pressure cuff, thermometers, razors, scalpels, Ace-bandages, a neck-collar, many kinds and sizes of bandages, cotton, alcohol, witch-hazel, hydrogen-peroxide, and many other items I am forgetting.

In Sausalito we organized and re-organized the *Hornpipe* trying to locate everything where we felt it would be most accessible in emergencies, as well as convenient for every day use. In the scuttle box above the main companionway, I packed flares, a military-surplus gas mask, wool watch caps, and items needed on deck. The gas mask intrigued people: It was ostensibly for fire-fighting—to enable entering the boat in heavy smoke. But because the marine toilet was located just off the base of the companionway, it was occasionally used to enter the boat during very-smelly-poop conditions. Under the cockpit roof I bolted down an Airco arc-welder/ generator set and an industrial air-compressor. In the front of the cockpit I installed a large air horn—which startled crewmembers so severely that I had to warn them when I was going to sound it.

By early October we were ready to leave Sausalito and sail to Half Moon Bay for a final haul-out. There were many heart-felt good-byes and several good-bye parties, a couple of which were so good that I don't remember anything!

On October 4th of 1979, at 0710, *Fishers Hornpipe* cast off from the Napa Street Pier and sailed out under the Golden Gate Bridge for the last time. My crew included, besides Cyndee and Debi, several waterfront characters who would sail with us down to Half Moon Bay. These were Henry Tate (Joe's brother), Greg Baker (a local shipwright who sailed further down the coast with us), and Ted Barone, who built the famous caboose houseboat. [You can just barely see the miniature roll-top desk I built for Ted in *The Cottage Book*, p.73, by Richard Sexton.] Ted gave me his 22-magnum revolver as a parting gift—so I would always have protection wherever I traveled. I accepted it very reluctantly, thinking long and hard about whether I would ever be capable of using it for anything more than a signaling device. [I once used it to shoot out an annoying electric light.] This settled for once and for all the old question of "to carry firearms or not to...." Hence I also bought a fine old 12-gauge Remington pump shotgun from a friend at Starhill. You never know when you might really want a duck for supper (it came with a long full-choke barrel). I eventually bought a short, rifled barrel for it also, and several boxes of armor-piercing slugs. The shotgun also shoots flares.

In Half Moon Bay, we worked on finishing touches to make us seaworthy, like installing stern windows in the transom. Up until then there had simply been four rectangular holes back there and it seemed reasonable that something seaworthy should fill them, though in many years of sailing, I have never seen green water come anywhere near them.

There was a party for us at Starhill that I will never forget. Starhill no longer existed in the sense that it had years before; it was now owned by Jim Wickett, who had fought off the Vultures and Leeches for years, with great personal sacrifice, to save some of the land. He lost most of it, and lost many of the giant redwoods we had sought so earnestly to protect, but he saved the Point where we used to sing the sun to sleep, and some of the acreage around it that had been dearest to us. A few of the people had stayed on, and though everything was different, a special spirit had survived. My remaining friends threw the party. It was up in a beautiful, isolated meadow at Bill and Kathy's house. (Bill Butler and I had worked together as partners in the construction business years before—see photo.) All the food was fresh from the land. It was a warm, liquid night with a harvest moon. We cooked over hardwood coals outside. I felt very high that night, as high as I ever have in my life—grateful to be alive then and there with such good fortune and so many loving, special friends. It was almost too much for me, and I had to wander off to the edge of the redwoods to be alone for a little while. I started listening to the insects absently, until I began to hear patterns and waves of patterns in their music. I could hear one chorus end and another start and hear the creatures all shift and syncopate their music to the new wave, and I realized, for the first time in my life, *astounded*, that they weren't making random noises, that they were actually singing in huge harmonies, harmonies of sweeping waves, harmonies involving thousands of voices! Ripples of subtle shifts were repeated as heard and transmitted for as far in any direction as I could focus my hearing. I looked up at the sky and the clouds and the stars and moon, and I looked at the silhouettes of the magnificent trees around me, the motion of the branches in the gentle wind. I thought of my many friends who loved me, and I just broke down and cried and cried, and I couldn't stop, and I didn't care. I felt that rare oneness with the universe, that sense that maybe it all does mean something. I felt complete.

Jim Wickett had been studying law, and had just taken his bar exam. He had some free time, a rare condition in his life, and he asked if he could join us for the trip down to San Diego. I felt hesitant at first, but when I realized that he really wanted to come, I agreed. It was a good decision.

Back down the hill, in Princeton Harbor, we completed the final preparations for our departure.

CHAPTER FIVE—HALF MOON BAY TO SAN DIEGO

"Sailing is ninety percent boredom, and ten percent sheer terror."

Anonymous American Woman

On October 12, shortly after 0700, we sailed out of the Princeton breakwater bound for Monterey Bay. That was on a Friday, and you're not supposed to leave on a Friday, but I never cared much for superstition and perhaps I didn't know any better then anyway. The wind was southerly and we motor-sailed.

As we came into Monterey Bay, we were accompanied by black and white dolphins playing under the bowsprit—the first time for most of us—and we watched a beautiful sunset. We anchored in the commercial anchorage with the fishing boats and savored the first new harbor of our first real voyage.

Late the next morning, we left for our first overnight sail, the 150-mile trip to Morro Bay. When we started we had a nice ten-knot northwest wind, but it quickly became southwest and built up to 25 knots and brought the fog with it. The sea built up a short, steep chop (superimposed on the northwest swell), and most of us started to feel seasick. Greg, the only veteran sailor among us, soon lived up to his nickname, 'Barfing Baker.' That only made the rest of us feel worse. I put a reef in the main without taking up on the correct reef-clew outhaul and might have dismasted the *Hornpipe* if it weren't for the strength and flexibility of Douglas fir. When I got it all squared away, we were under-canvassed with the second reef in, instead of the first, and that made the motion even worse. Cyndee went below and cooked a huge pot of vegetarian chili in the pressure cooker, and we found that good hot food can drive away seasickness. I only wish it always worked that way...I think those beans were just too heavy to come up!

The wind eased by evening and remained light and southerly for the remainder of the trip. That first coastal navigating was a challenge for me, including my first overnight and fog experiences, and I felt really good when we picked up a mooring in Morro Bay after one day and six hours at sea. *Fishers Hornpipe* sailed right along at five or six knots in winds of ten and fifteen knots. At times she would exceed seven knots for hours at a time

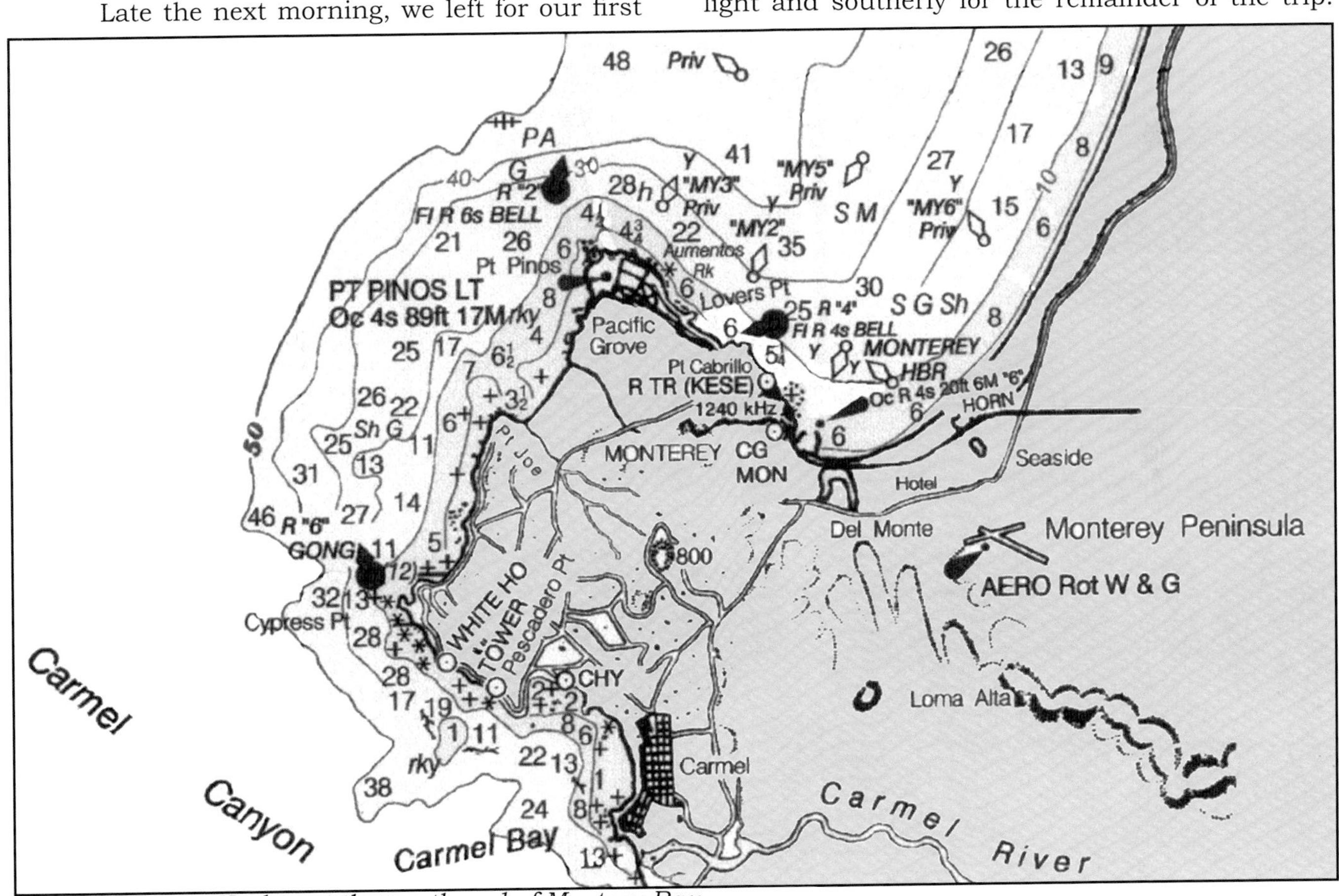

Montery Harbor at the south end of Montery Bay.

and I felt more and more confident that she was a pretty ideal sailboat.

Debi had to leave us from Morro Bay to return to Sausalito and work. She would join us later in San Diego for the trip south. After enjoying Morro Bay for a couple of days, we left for the Channel Islands late on the morning of the 17th. We were down to Greg, Jim, Cyndee and myself for crew. We had a broad reach the whole way to Santa Rosa Island with a good 15 to 20 knot breeze, and the huge pacific swells with lumpy seas superimposed on them gave us our first taste of how tiring it is to steer off the wind. In the middle of the night, Jim and I tried to tack all the way around in a 270-degree circle with a reefed mains'l because I was afraid to jibe, never having done it in that much wind and sea. [For you landlubbers: Tacking is turning into the wind; jibing is turning away from the wind, in both cases to get the wind on the opposite side of the boat and sails.] We were off infamously rough and windy Point Conception and needed to turn east into the Santa Barbara Channel. We finally had to jibe; we'd lost too much distance trying to tack, coming around in that big circle with only the reefed main, having to fall off to gain speed, and trying again. *Fishers Hornpipe* rarely misses a tack unless she is asked to do something unfair, like tack from a reach to a reach in the kind of large, nasty chop that dwells off Point Conception. Jibing was no problem at all, I was relieved to discover. I hoped all the many new lessons would be so easy. In the wee morning hours the wind died and we motored into Bechers Bay, Santa Rosa Island, exhausted.

We slept most of that day and left early on the next one for Santa Barbara, coasting along to explore the shoreline of Santa Cruz Island and anchoring briefly to take *Gandy Dancer* into beautiful Painted Cave. It was cold and foggy and drizzly so we didn't feel inclined to play as much as we would have liked. The Painted Cave was interesting, but a big swell, high tide and foolish lack of powerful flashlights (which always seem to plague my spelunking expeditions), kept us from seeing much of it. Cyndee was suspicious of oil clumps we kept spotting and we all pondered how much environmental damage was being done by oil

San Francisco to San Diego.

spills.

At 1830 [6:30 PM—I record all ship's time events on the 24-hour clock], with just a little daylight left, we came into Santa Barbara and tied up at the Harbor Master's dock. We stayed there two nights, which cost a very reasonable $12.80. Greg had to leave us there to return to work in Sausalito, and we said sad good-byes realizing we might never see him again.

We left on Sunday, the twenty-first, for Anacapa Island, and saw a pod of black Killer Whales (Orcas—really giant dolphins) cavorting off our starboard bow. The anchorage at Frenchy's Cove, Anacapa, was terrible and we rolled in the Pacific swell. By 0245 we couldn't take anymore and weighed anchor for Santa Catalina Island. We entered Avalon Bay that afternoon at 1630.

On the 24th we sailed for San Diego—our last stop in America. It was our first passage with twin jibs, held out by 24-foot-long aluminum poles. A snowy egret circled around and around us near San Diego, a huge black submarine surfaced near us—which scared the hell out of me—and to top things off, a beautiful barn owl with yellow wings circled us once and flew away—in broad daylight. I took this improbable visit as a good omen, though I knew not for what.

The next morning we had a great beat (tacking to windward) into San Diego Harbor, with Jimmy and Cyndee working hard and fast on the big center-mounted jib-sheet winch with its two-handed handle. [The *Hornpipe's* mains'l and stays'l were self-tending, but the jib had to be released and sheeted in on the opposite side with each

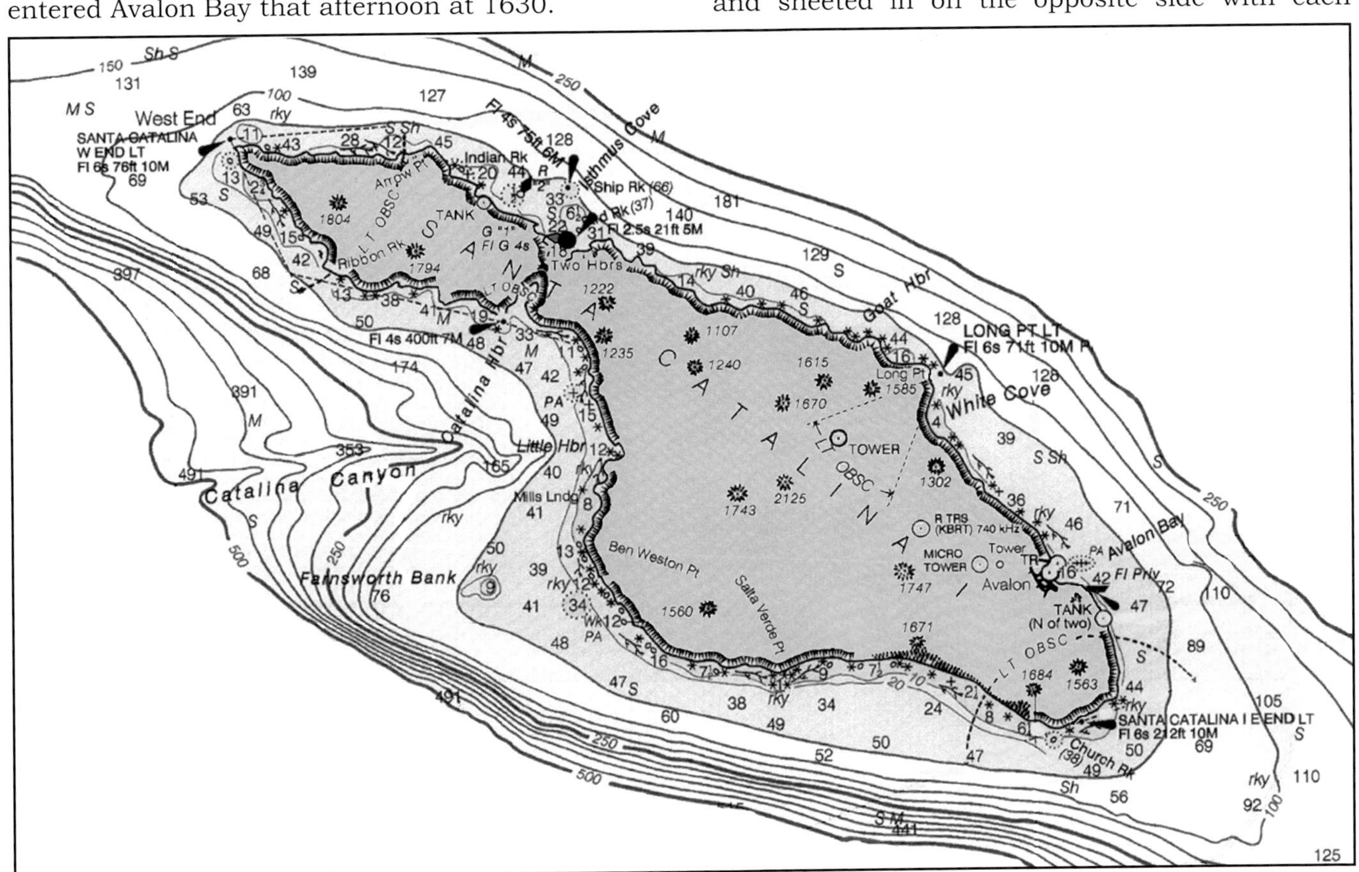

Santa Catalina Island. Avalon Bay is on the right.

We had a great time in Avalon. I took *Airforce One* (my rusty old bicycle) up into the Wriggly Estate's private land reserve, for which I had to obtain written permission, and spent a whole day riding around dirt roads and trails, exploring the intriguing vegetation and beautiful landscapes there. Jim went scuba diving near the edge of the harbor to a depth of 100 feet, and came up full of enthusiasm for the strange sights he saw in the kelp forest. For its close proximity to Los Angeles (26 miles), Santa Catalina Island is a hauntingly beautiful and relatively unspoiled place. There is even a small herd of Buffalo there.

tack.] We hooked a left into the Commercial Boat Basin and anchored among the colorful derelict boats and houseboats just off the Henderson Brother's sail loft. Steve and Marylin West sailed out in their dingy, and Bob Henderson rowed out in his Whitehall, all to give us a hearty welcome. The following day we moved over to 'cement boat alley,' where we stayed until finagling our way into a slip at the commercial dock. *Fishers Hornpipe* was documented with the federal government as a commercial vessel—cargo and mackerel fisheries. That qualified us as 'commercial'—stretching the point pretty far.

We spent four months in San Diego. I worked on the *Hornpipe's* sister ship, *Prelude*, for Steve and Marilyn West. Several years earlier Patrick Cotten and I had come down to loft and frame the *Prelude*, which eventually became a successful commercial fishing vessel. I also spent some long hard weeks up in San Pedro Boat Works (Los Angeles) working on *Lene Marie*, which had come down from Sausalito for a major haul-out and re-fit. Patrick was also in San Diego working on a new vessel to earn cruising money.

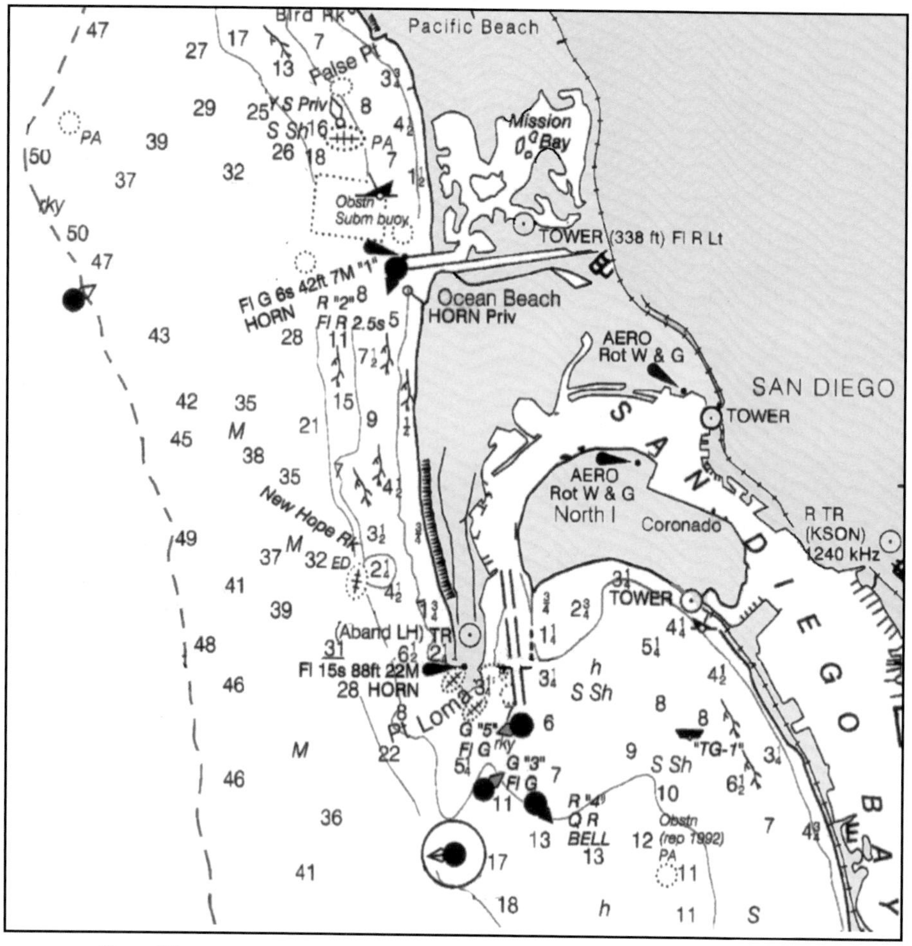

San Diego.

Cyndee had various jobs as waitress and receptionist at H&M Landing, a large commercial charter boat operation. Debi, who wasn't in San Diego as long, worked in a clothing store doing alterations, as well as in the Henderson's loft. As mentioned earlier, Debi had left us up the coast in Morro Bay when she had to return to work in Sausalito, and left again to spend the Christmas holidays with her family in Virginia. My Starhill friend Bob Tillotson joined us less than a week before we left, having been very busy finishing up his affairs in Northern California so he could come on an extended cruise.

We had the Henderson Brothers make us a big 650-square-foot genoa jib, of which Patrick disapproved—"Why are you in such a big hurry to go anywhere?" Bob took me aside and whispered, "You wait and see—now he'll want one too!" The Henderson Brothers insisted that we take a yankee storm jib with us—even though we didn't have enough money left to pay for it—and I can never thank them enough for the times that that sail drove *Fishers Hornpipe* safely and powerfully through storms at sea in the years that followed. As you will see.

During rainy days when we couldn't work outside, Perry Fly, who was visiting, and I would take guitars and mandolins and fiddles and concertinas up into the sail loft and weave fiddle tunes into the fabric of those beautiful sails. Bill Henderson stabbed himself in the thumb with his sail needle because he kept trying to figure out what *our* fingers were doing instead of *his*! I learned a lot too, because when Perry wasn't around, the Hendersons taught me how to do handwork on the sails, which was a great honor. George Loukes, back in Half Moon Bay, had started teaching me about sail making, and the Hendersons taught me a whole lot more. I made some long, straight Douglas fir layout-battens for the loft, and Bob taught me how to use them to lay out broad-seams, and to build shape into a sail by creating the curvatures of its perimeter. Bill taught me how to do handwork—sewing luff ropes, rat tails, attaching jib hanks—all skills I have used ever since.

I built a pair of huge oak entry doors for Bill Butler (my carpentry partner from Starhill), who had admired a pair I had previously made for a house in San Mateo I had remodeled for a friend. Bill wanted these doors for a house he would some day build for himself and his wife Kathy. [Many years later, I went to visit him, and there they were! I had completely forgotten about them.]

With help from Debi and Cyndee, I restored the Henderson Brothers' vintage Whitehall pulling boat (evidently she had been *Ticonderoga's* tender). The Whitehall project was part of our trading of energies.

I started seeing a tall, blond sail maker from the loft, Suzi, who gave me my first glimpse into punk culture. On our first date, she wore black gloves with the fingers cut off, and I knew I was getting into something very different from the hippie girls up north. I wasn't disappointed. She also taught me to love the music of David Bowie. Suzie and Bob took me to see Fleetwood Mac's new band (with the Buckingham/Nicks addition), and we also went to one of Bob Marley's last concerts before his untimely death.

Suzi came to spend the night with me on the *Hornpipe* on occasion. On one memorable night, three of us ended up in my cabin (the third being a visiting male friend). We made love to Suzi for hours, much to the delight (Cyndee) and disgust (Debi) of my crew. Looking back on that night from my old age, I must say it was one of the pinnacles of my youthful sex life. I had been in numerous sexual situations with multiple partners, but that one was especially memorable. Suzi was a beautiful, talented woman, and a fantastic lover—but I was not able to persuade her to come sailing with us.

On New Year's Day, 1980, we had a memorable raft-up of Pat Cotton's boats in San Diego Harbor—*Harmony*, *Kismet* (his newest creation), *Fishers Hornpipe*, and *Silverheels*—our friend Bosco's Atkins-designed *Eric* with a New England fisherman *pinky stern*. (Bosco called it a 'stinky pern,' as it included a palatial throne-with-a-view.) Soon after that, *Harmony* and *Silverheels* departed for adventures in the South Pacific.

The *W.N. Ragland* showed up at some point, and I will never forget some of the parties we had. There was a 'punk club' in San Diego—a meat-market where I learned about slam-dancing, sort of an impromptu martial arts dancing where the dancers basically beat the hell out of eachother. Suzi and some of the *Ragland* crew took me there, but I couldn't get into it. I'm not heavy enough, mean enough or crazy enough. Most memorable was my 34th birthday, for which we assembled the crews of the *Ragland*, *Prelude*, *Hornpipe*, and the Henderson's sail loft—over twenty people. Because of my big mouth, we got into drinking tequila—by the shot—before, during and after dinner. Earlier that day someone had asked me what my favorite pie was—to which I answered lemon meringue (it isn't anymore). Larry or someone from the *Ragland* had bought one and stashed it on the dock all evening—where it got really soggy in the cold San Diego winter drizzle. I don't remember too much of what happened after dinner, but I have this persistent image of a tip tray being passed around under the table with fat lines of coke and a tightly-rolled one hundred dollar bill.... I think someone had to carry me most of the way down the dock to my boat. But next morning, when I awoke to one of the most brutal hangovers of my life, my face was covered with large quantities of some sweet, sticky substance, and a gooey pie tin was folded and stuffed in my back pocket!

* * *

We spent weeks buying and storing food and supplies in the *Hornpipe's* many commodious cubic inches. Cyndee and I had researched and planned this project for months. We spent hundreds of dollars, much of it in health-food co-ops, buying bulk beans, rice, pasta, grains and canned goods. We bought 5-gallon containers of olive oil, honey and molasses. We repackaged everything meticulously, and some of that food lasted for five years.

In one huge closet/locker on the port side, we carried earth-working tools including picks, shovels, axes, wrecking bars, jacks, rakes, a hoe, and many packets of different kinds of seeds. After all, you never know when and where you might have to start life over from scratch. Being a product of my time, I lived with a big dose of pre-Armageddon consciousness—*ARK* syndrome.

Although *Fishers Hornpipe* did not have a separate (bulkheaded off) cargo hold, as do many of my subsequent cruisers, she did have a large shop/hold area just forward of amidships. There were large workbenches with tool bins and drawers port and starboard, plus the closet/locker mentioned above. I carried circular saws, drill motors, scroll saws, a table saw, planer, jointer, Alaskan chain saw mill, bench-mounted drill press and bench grinder, sewing machine, generator, arc-welder, air compressor, pneumatic tools and paint sprayers, all manner of hand tools, and many boxes of fasteners of all sizes and types, including kegs of nails. You can see why this was a heavy 40-foot boat.

* * *

On Feb 14th, the second night of a wicked southwesterly gale, *Fishers Hornpipe* was driven back in her slip into the concrete commercial dock, breaking her starboard stern davit. This setback depressed us, as we were anxious to leave San Diego for the rest of the world. I was able to repair it with epoxy and Dutchmen (wood inlays), and by late February we were ready to go.

There is an old adage that voyages with horrible beginnings have good middles and great endings. Well, we had a horrible beginning. We barely escaped San Diego on Tuesday evening, Feb 26th, 1980. Our departure was a nightmare—after hustling for months, we still hadn't finished all our projects or fulfilled all our commitments (never have, ever), and we were thoroughly irritable and burned-out when we said our final good-byes. We cast off our stern lines and warped forward to cast off our breast lines (made off to pilings port and starboard), to find one of them hopelessly jammed under the lines of a fishing boat that had come in after we had last gone out. By the time we got them free, having to cut the one out, our stern had swung into *Prelude*. After no small amount of yelling and cursing and running around waving arms in the air, we got away.

We circled around *W.N. Ragland* to say goodbye, and headed for the fuel dock to take on fuel, water, propane and ice. On our way there we ran aground, getting the *Hornpipe's* keel hopelessly stuck in the San Diego mud (black mayonnaise) until high tide lifted it out.

We didn't clear Point Loma until 1800 hours, all sail set for Mexico, at which point the wind utterly died and we had to motor.

The crew consisted of Cyndee, Debi, my dear friend Bob Tillotson from Starhill, and a teenage surfer named Michelle, who was our first paying passenger (I forget what we charged her, but we really needed the bucks—legally, of course, this was a 'donation-to-the-cause.') Storms had destroyed the road down Baja Sur to Cabo San Lucas, and Michelle was returning to her surf camp there with boards and provisions the only way possible—by boat. She was a warm, positive character and we all greatly enjoyed her company and help.

I was both ecstatic and terrified to be leaving America, for what, as far as I was concerned, might be forever. I had a boat full of beloved people, food, tools, books, and music. I had three hundred and fifty dollars, and I was headed south, to start the greatest adventure of my life.

VOYAGE ONE PHOTOS

Photo 1

The Corral

Photo 2

Starhill--The path from my cabin

Photo 3

Starhill--The saw mill

Photo 4

Reuel and Bill Butler, 1975

Photos 5 & 6

The Cotten 40 *Quest* in San Diego

Photo 7

Frames set up
Stringers going on
Scaffold in place

Photo 8

First layers of chicken wire and diagonal rods going on

Photo 9

Ready for plaster
Bill Edenson (left)
Reuel (right)

Photo 10

Shooting wet mud
Reggie on the gun

Photo 11

Reggie troweling

Photo 12

Skim coat and sponge troweling

Photo 13

Plastering finished
Beorne and Reuel

Photo 14

Reuel, Karren & Roger
(Beorne's ass)

Photo 15

Marine architect Partick Cotten

Photo 16

Deck beams going in

Photo 17

Jim Schaefer & Reuel, 1975
Plywood decks going on

Photo 18

The “banana” stage--epoxy primer
Roger & Leith

Photo 19

Ready to launch
From L to R: Ray Farnow in vest, Bob, Mike, Larry, HarborMaster, Bob Tillotson (leaning on tire)

Photo 20

Starting down the ramp

Photo 21

Splashing
Jack Hill on dock (Nav. teacher)

Photo 22 (above) She floats!

Photo 23 (below) Happiness (Joan Parker photo)

Photo 24

Spars and rigging finished

Photo 25

Reuel at the spreaders
(Joan Parker photo)

Photo 26

Early sail--Perry Fly and Reuel
Bulwarks under construction

Photo 27

Wind Chariot on her maiden voyage

Photo 28

Fishers Hornpipe on her maiden voyage--returning to Half Moon Bay at dusk

Photo 29 Linda & Nancy

Photo 30 Michael Lannigan

Photo 31

Sausalito--Napa St. Pier
Fishers Hornpipe on the left

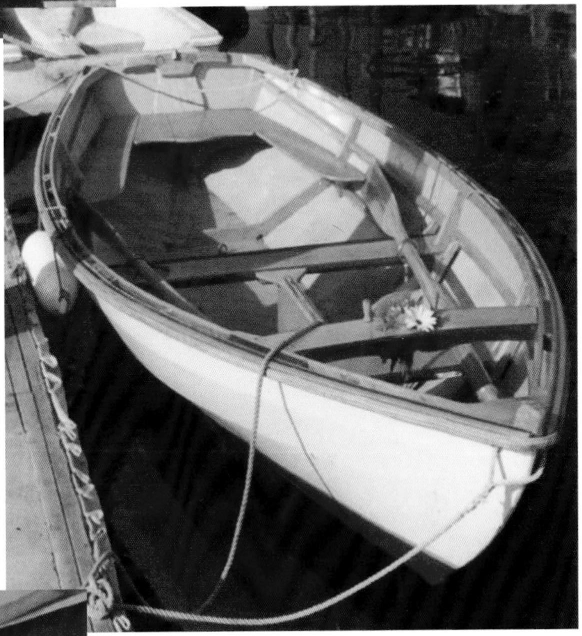

Photo 32

Gandy Dancer, my dory/tender

Photo 33

Reuel & Monica
San Francisco Bay

Photo 34 *Fishers Hornpipe* sailing on San Pablo Bay

Photo 35

Fishers Hornpipe sailing on San Francisco Bay--almost ready to go cruising

Photo 36 *Wanderbird* and *Freda* in Sausalito

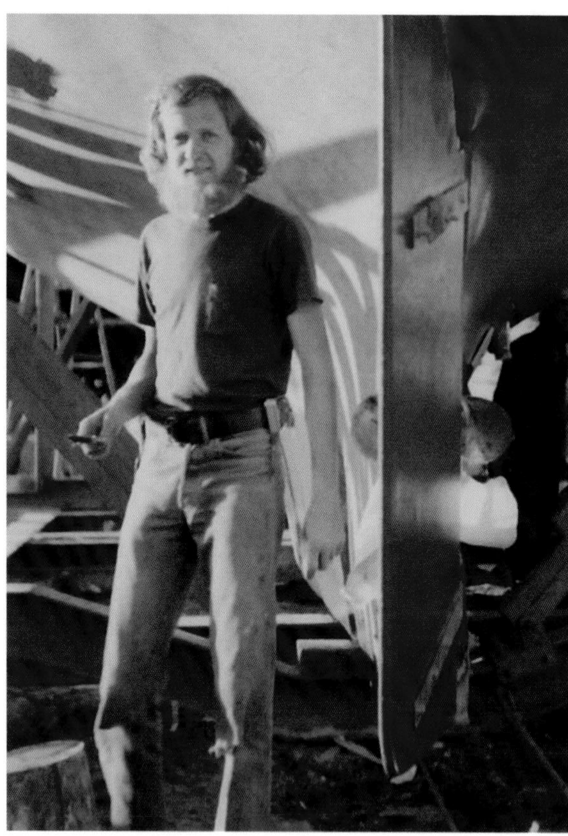

Photo 37

Reuel painting the bottom
Half Moon Bay, Oct '79

Photo 38

Bob Tillotson

Photo 39

Jim Wickett

Photo 40 (above) Cyndee & Debi

Photo 41 (below) Reuel in Moro Bay

Photo 42 Jim & Cyndee, Santa Catalina Island

Photo 43 The Raft--San Diego, New Year's Day 1980 left to right: *Silver Heels, Harmony, Kismet, Fishers Hornpipe*

VOYAGE TWO: CENTRAL AMERICA

Voyage Two—San Diego, California, Central America, through the Panama Canal, Western Caribbean, to Key West, Florida.

CHAPTER SIX—NORTHERN MEXICO

Other things being roughly equal, that man lives most keenly who lives in closest harmony with nature. To be wholly alive a man must know storms, he must feel the ocean as his home or the air as his habitation. He must smell the things of earth, hear the sounds of living things and taste the rich abundance of the soil and sea.

James Michener, *Return to Paradise*, 1950

As stated in the Introduction, I started writing newsletters in Mexico, to inform my friends and family of my whereabouts and adventures. In the following pages, I have integrated the original eight newsletters written during my voyages into this book, placing the text in italics. Although I have not altered the newsletters greatly (other than to correct them), I have frequently reorganized them sequentially in time, placing parts of them where they better maintain the flow of my story.

The newsletters were written on an ancient Smith-Corona *Sky-Writer* given to me as a going-away-present by my ex-brother-in-law Jim Schaefer. It was the best typewriter I ever had, and I sorely miss it. I had to make numerous repairs to get it working—and to keep it working—but it was well worth the trouble.

I also kept two logbooks—one for "official information" and one for "personal accounts," to which my crewmembers and I all contributed. I have added passages and information from both logs to round out my stories. In subsequent chapters I have also included much material from my teenage first mate Paul Newman (not the actor), who wrote a high school thesis based on his travels with me. Later editorial comments are in brackets.

* * *

After leaving San Diego and motoring across the invisible border into Mexico, our spirits lifted with the intoxicating excitement of what we were doing, and a gentle breeze came up around 0400 to carry us on our way without the motor. By mid-afternoon the next day the log says: *truckin'—threat of squalls—wind!* After that the wind died again, and we waited for more, which took an hour and a half. Finally the wind came and stayed—we were on our way!

Cyndee, Personal Log, Feb 27:

Off the coast of Mexico, bound for South America, a world away from here... is a ship that sails the sea... FISHERS HORNPIPE *sailing like she never has before! The new genny* [genoa jib] *makes such a difference. The new mule aids in stabilizing when the wind dies and the genoa comes down.* [A "mule" is a triangular sail—like a jib, but cut very flat. It is hanked onto a back-stay, hoisted and sheeted forward very tightly. It can be used at anchor to hold a vessel into the wind, or carried when running dead downwind to dampen rolling. Our storm jib doubled as a mule.] *Thank you a-thousand-fold Bobby and Billy Henderson! It's wonderful to be out at sea again. We've logged about 75 miles even after being hove-to many hours early this a.m. Seasickness is making its rounds...we're all a bit rusty on maneuvers and like the seasickness, it will pass. These beautiful days ahead promise sea legs, sea sense, and mucho smiles.*

Debi, Personal Log, Feb 28:

It's like one has to synchronize one's head to one's body to the motion of the boat and to the entire pulsating mechanisms and spirit that make Fishers *a working force on the sea. My body tried to rebel as did everyone's but Cyndee's. She's a blessing, cooking for us all. Approaching our third night, I feel a little less like it's a bad carnival ride I want off. We're rolling with twin jibs, heading back southeast instead of going to Guadalupe Island. The thought of mainland sounds appealing. We've done very little motoring. Yeah! It's great having five people on the boat. The sea seems to enhance one's appreciation of the human race. Onward!*

Sailing down the mountainous coast of Baja was a real joy for us. The weather was gentle, balmy, tropical and utterly thrilling for a first-time experience. The seas and wind were gentle, and the *Hornpipe* just rolled along at a comfortable speed averaging five knots. The log shows numerous sail changes made to meet the conditions of changing wind, but we didn't stop until we reached Isla Cedros on March 1st, well down the Baja coast.

I don't remember much about Isla Cedros, but the anchorages (we tried several) were very 'rolly,' as the Pacific swell wrapped around the island and set the boats dancing. This phenomenon is endemic to many Pacific anchorages—particularly

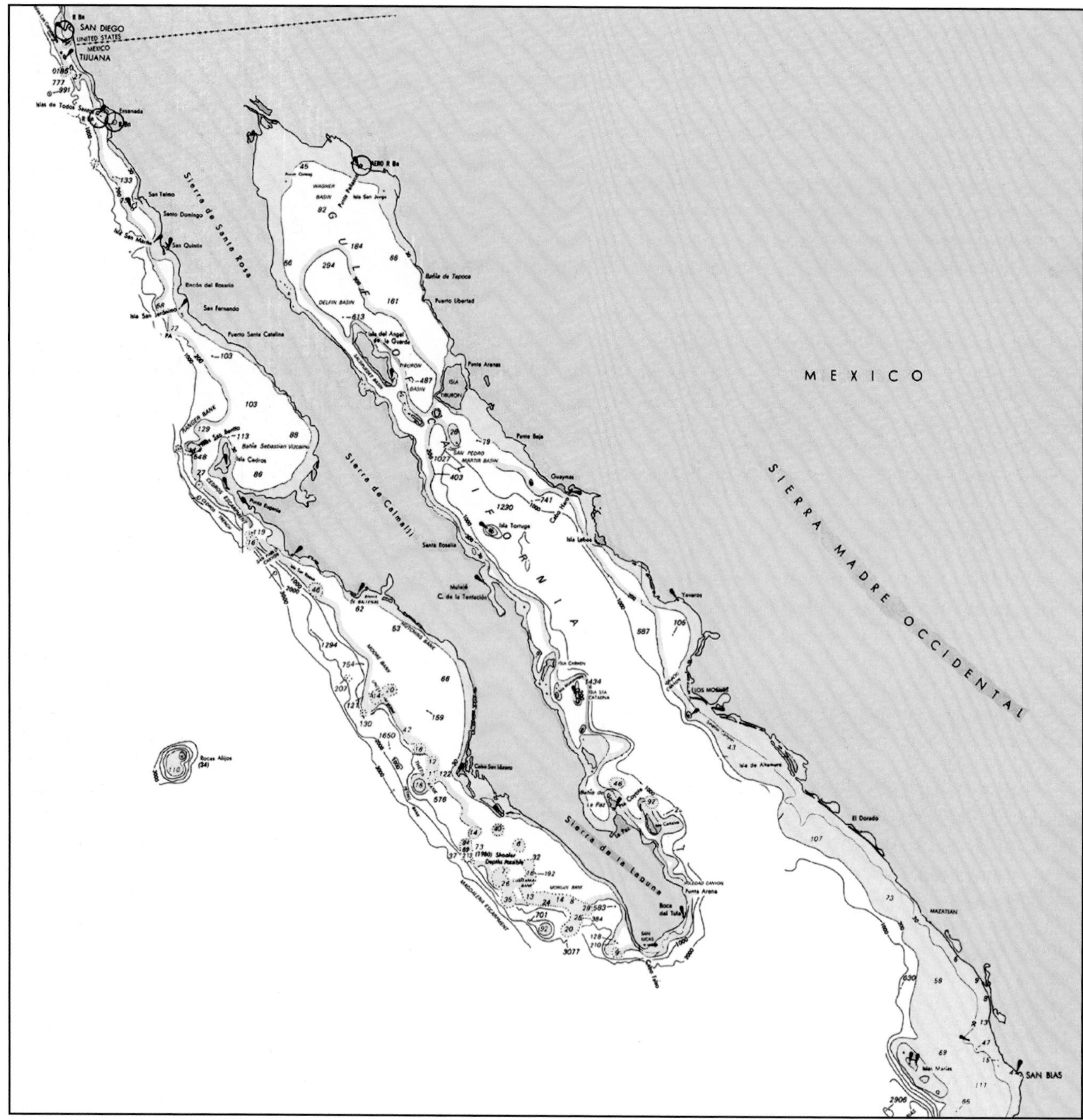

Baja Sur, Mexico. San Diego to San Blas.

those in the lee of offshore islands that are not surrounded by extensive reefs. In Isla Cedros we traded with some local fishermen for two huge, delicious lobster. We did some hiking there—I followed a canyon and creek for miles up into the mountains.

Newsletter, Mar 23, 1980:

Between San Diego and Cabo San Lucas, we stopped only at Isla Cedros and Bahia Santa Maria, breaking the trip roughly into thirds. It was a good shakedown with no problems or gear failures. Fishers Hornpipe *is more than two tons overloaded, much of it distributed out fore-and-aft as well as amidships, and her motion is heavy although still comfortable. Friends from other boats who come aboard are amazed at the amount of stuff we can leave lying around. Our speed is also affected, as is the increased difficulty steering downwind in lumpy seas. All in all, however, we have it fat-city: the boat is dry, very comfortable, powerful, and controllable. We can carry more sail longer, and have less difficulty getting it down than most vessels in either our size or weight range.* Fishers Hornpipe *is well-ventilated and well-lit, and has numerous places to escape to in which to be alone—so essential in cruising.*

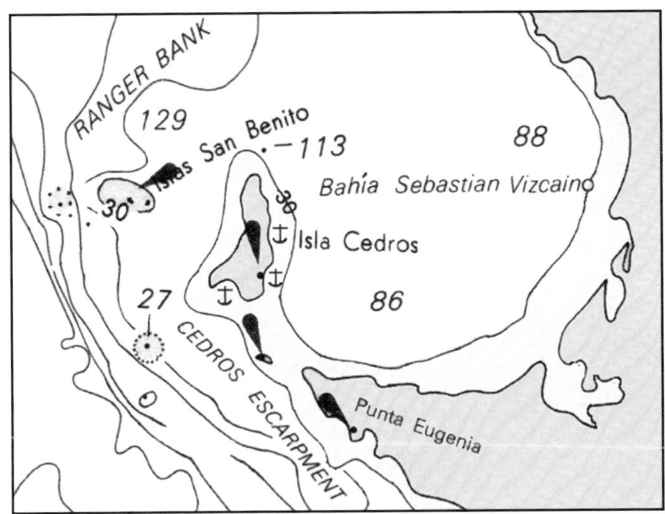

Isla Cedros, Mexico. Wherever we anchored, we rolled in the surge.

We stopped on the evening of March 6th in Bahia Santa Maria. The large anchorage was deserted, except for us. We went hiking and exploring in the surrounding arid hills, and I very nearly jumped on a large black snake while I was running down the rocks—we both about jumped out of our skins (the snake *and* me)!

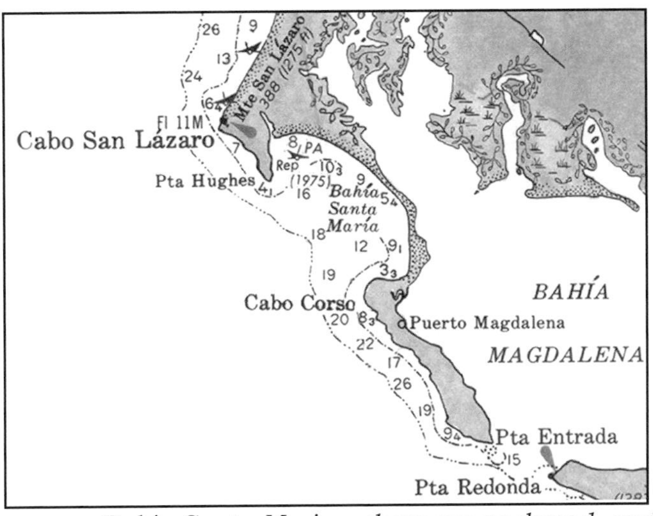

Bahia Santa Maria, where we anchored, and Bahia Magdelena, to which we walked.

Down on the beach, Debi was in her underwear, alone, washing her clothes when three young Mexican fishermen appeared out of nowhere (we had thought the whole place was deserted). They were very polite, and very interested, and they gave her a fish—our first jack, I think, though the Mexicans called it a *torrito.* We cooked it for dinner and found it all but inedible. Bahia Santa Maria was a desolate, lonely, beautiful place.

As we proceeded south, the weather became increasingly hot, balmy, wet and tropical. The winds were variable and gentle, and mostly from behind us. We rolled happily south, full of anticipation. We ran our first water tank dry and used up our first propane tank out of the States.

We anchored in Bahia San Lucas in the wee hours of March 10th. We stayed for four days, and had a very good time. The biggest attraction for me was Cabo San Lucas itself, a most incredible playground of sea, sunlight and huge rocks—carvings-by-nature—that looked like the art placed in university plazas by famous sculptors—hundreds of them. Michelle left to join her surf camp just up the coast. By this time we were all very fond of her and knew we would miss her company.

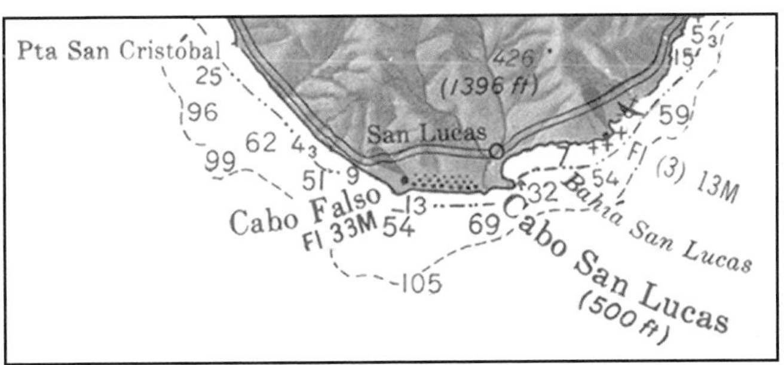

Cabo San Lucas

The town was small and tourist-oriented. We hung out in one roadside restaurant (Taqueria) that had good one-dollar breakfasts, real coffee, and other cruising people as well as Mexican clientele. The paperwork in San Lucas wasn't bad (my first experience), although I had to walk many miles down hot dusty roads.

At dusk, returning from one such excursion, a 'low-rider' car came slowly along side me. The driver, his face hidden from view, said "Que quiere?" My reply was "el mundo!" I was learning Spanish... he was peddling drugs.

Cyndee hitched a ride up to La Paz and over to Todos Santos, where Michele's beach surf-camp was located. She says it was surfer's heaven—as perfect a lifestyle as any on Earth. Just a bunch of friends living in tents and old Volkswagon buses on the beach, surfing all day, cooking outdoors, smoking dope and making love all night under the Mexican stars.

We filled our water tanks from a well by backing *Fishers Hornpipe* up to the beach, anchoring fore and aft, and rowing in to pull out an incredibly long ganglia of garden hoses. The water contained a fair amount of debris and dead bugs, so we added chlorine. [The formula I use is one cap of Clorox bleach per 50 gallons of water.]

San Lucas was our first real foreign port, and we found it funky, friendly and charming. We learned about the *single-hander's club*...those unfortunate single guys cruising alone. "Single-handed" really refers to a single person operating a boat—as in a "single deck-hand"—but it acquired a new meaning among the cruisers on the Mexican coast: single-handed sex. Rumor had it that the "club" would rendezvous on VHF radio when single women were spotted: "Breaker, breaker—bambinis on the beach—let's hit 'em from both sides and launch a rubber-duck assault from the harbor…." Another new phenomenon was the cruisers' version of the old soap *As the World Turns*, called *As the Anchor Drags….*

In many profound ways, a whole new life began for me. I was actually doing it—cruising, traveling, exploring a new country, embarked on a new life! Learning (painfully and slowly) a new language, new customs, eating new food, seeing new land unlike any I had seen. My life was unfolding before me, shared with friends, in new vistas and dimensions, and this was just the beginning! I was thrilled, excited, terrified, all at once. We were also seeing intriguing new dimensions of nature—whales, dolphins, killer whales, birds, deserts, lush tropical paradises—rich new smells, sounds and sights.

We were also meeting people on other cruising boats, some of whom we would meet again and again in other countries and on other oceans. Some of these cruisers became life-long friends, and some we would lose touch with too soon. Among the long-term new friends were Michael Starbuck on *Starbuck* and David Edwards on *Azulao*.

* * *

At 1030 on March 14th we departed San Lucas to work our way east along the bottom of Baja Sur, intending to enter and explore the Sea of Cortez. We anchored at dusk the first night just east of Punta Gorda—although we never knew for certain if that's where we were. The anchorage was dangerous—it was full of rocks. With Cyndee on the bowsprit watching for danger (look out!—port, port!), me casting the lead line (we had no depth sounder) and Bob at the helm, we somehow got in and anchored. Just then, we managed to back over our fishing lines, which in the excitement, we had forgotten to pull in. I spent half an hour diving down in near darkness, hacking away at the mess without success. We spent a very restless night there, not knowing if we would be swept onto an unseen rock by a change in wind, tide or current. I slept on deck and awoke every fifteen or twenty minutes to look around. [This I had trained myself to do; indeed I spend many restless nights, especially at sea in unsettled weather, and any change in wind, wave or sound wakes me up.] The next morning Debi and I both spent an hour diving, cutting, and untangling the prop.

The next day we sailed to Los Frailles. The anchorage there was beautiful; behind it was a huge, rocky mountain that projected out into the Sea of Cortez, like an entry gate. The following morning we started beating our way north, trying to enter the Sea of Cortez. At first the winds were light and fickle, and we had to motor-sail to avoid being swept back into the Pacific by the strong current running against us. Darkness fell before we could get through Canal Cerralvo, between Isla Cerralvo and Punta Pescadores.

We hove to on the offshore-tack for the night, not wanting to attempt the passage without visual aids, and suspecting that the light on Isla Cerralvo was not functioning (we never saw it). The wind steadily increased throughout the night, a miserable one, until daybreak, when we resumed trying to beat through the channel. With the wind over twenty knots, a strong current against us, and close, steep, "square" waves hitting us with considerable force (the Sea of Cortez has a reputation for this), we finally gave up and ran for Mazatlan on the mainland coast. We simply could not get through Cerralvo Channel, gateway to the East Coast of Baja Sur, which we really wanted to see. Cyndee had been reading my well-worn copy of John Steinbeck's *Log of the Sea of Cortez* and was especially disappointed. Sorry Cyndee.

At first we had a good sail running off on a broad reach in 25-knots of northerly wind, but as night fell, the wind fell too. By the next morning it died altogether and I regretfully started to motor, much to Bob's displeasure. I think he would rather sit in the ocean for days, rolling and slating about, waiting for wind, than to have to motor. That next night the wind came back—10-knots out of the north-west, and we headed for the distant glow, or "loom," of Mazatlan. At 0230 on the 19th we anchored in our first mainland Mexican port.

[Years later, I came to know that we probably used the motor less than any other boat I have ever met—that had one. We would lie at sea in the rolling swell, sometimes for days, waiting for wind, rather than destroy our peace and quiet—or offend our sense of smell—with diesel fumes and racket. The other consideration was the cost of fuel…. Now, in my old age, I am a little ashamed to admit that when the wind dies—or even falls too light—I fire the diesel up and go.]

David Edwards sailed to Mazatlan on *Azulao* around the same time we did, and had a very different experience. He had a young crewmember—a teenage boy—who was new to sailing. This boy was a clean-living fellow—he did not, for example, eat candy. During the night of the long crossing, the wind began to blow harder and harder. While the boy was on watch, he felt fatigued and decided to break his rule and eat a candy bar to keep his energy up. Just as he bit into it, a huge freak wave hit *Azulao* and capsized her! She was knocked down so far that her mast and sails went under

The southern tip of Baha California. Michelle's surf camp was in Todos Santos, just above Punta Lobos on the west side. We anchored at Punta Gorda and above Los Frailes, on the east side, on our way to the Sea of Cortez, which we were unable to enter at Isla Cerralvo.

water. Much later, in Mazatlan, having recovered and arriving safely in port, David found the candy wrapper plastered to the underside of the coachroof where the sea had deposited it—the boat had gone so far over that she took many gallons of seawater inside, which in turn picked up anything in its way and washed it head-high in the cabin. It was a close call for *Azulao*. That lad never ate candy on that trip again!

Newsletter, Mar 23, 1980:

Windy night in Mazatlan Harbor. Just returned from a most exhilarating sail in Gandy Dancer, *our dory/tender. Cyndee, Debi, Bob and myself left late this morning to explore a beach we heard was not polluted by gringos. No wonder—apparently the place is virtually inaccessible except by boat.*

We sailed out between the breakwaters to sea, after an abortive attempt to reach the place by landing on the breakwater and walking across. The trip was about 3 1/2 miles, between steep rocky islands through sizable swell, and landed us through

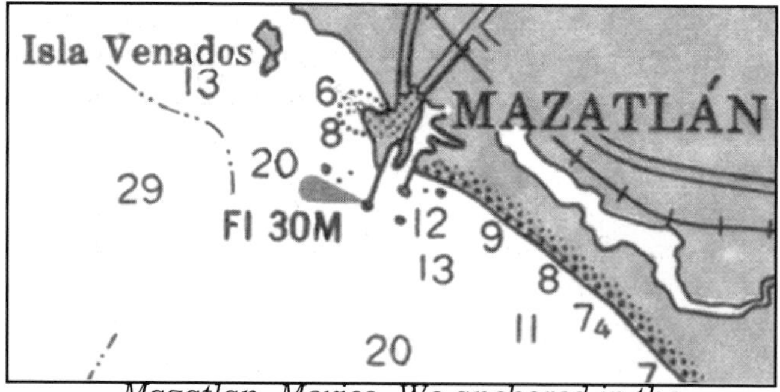

Mazatlan, Mexico. We anchored in the protected harbor and sailed Gandy Dancer *outside to the beach.*

light surf on the north end of miles of beautiful white sand beach backed by palms and rocks.

On the beach, a large pavilion (several pavilions linked together) covered many tables and chairs and concessions. Beneath their palm-thatched roofs were many people, two dance-floors with bands, fresh fish cooking on open fires, fresh coconuts, tamalitos, beer, juices, etc. The fish were being brought in by fishermen as they were needed—fish were leaping all along the surf line, even among the swimmers. Frigate birds were circling around snatching the smaller ones up (fish, that is).

Evidently this beach scene occurs every weekend, but this one is probably special as this is President's Day—the beginning of two weeks of holiday celebrations. Also, school is out. Even so, less than a fourth of the beach had people on it (just an occasional couple rolling around on the sand).

Farm tractors were towing surrey-type trailers full of people to and from ferryboats, which came from somewhere in Mazatlan. Perhaps Bob and Cyndee will tell us, as they are going to return to the harbor by that mode of public transportation. Yes, we temporarily lost half our crew in this magic place—romance of sunshine, wisps of cloud, good chemistry, sparkling water and off they went in search of an adventure. The beach was a picture-post-card of paradise in the tropics—it was magical!

Today, I met Joel, a Mexican surfer. Joel and I talked for an hour or more, a remarkable feat for one who can't speak Spanish and the other who can't speak English. We drew a lot of pictures in the sand, literally. I think I am a language-dummy. Joel wanted to know how many millions of dollars I had! I was unable to communicate that I didn't even have any hundreds of dollars. Or maybe he just didn't believe me....

A few days ago, while attempting to order yogurt in a roadside yogurt and juice stand for my trashed-out Montezuma's Revenge stomach, the waitress was trying to explain to me what flavors she had. After about the third time around, I confessed: "Yo no comprendo Espanol"; Cyndee looked at me incredulously and said, "Reuel, she's telling you in English!" "Yo no comprendo Inglis," I confessed further.

Joel had perseverance. We actually covered a lot of ground....

Debi and I left for the return-trip alone and sailed into the sunset, literally. And into increasing wind and seas. Today Mother Pacific was good to us, as was Gandy Dancer, *and we made it back to* Fishers Hornpipe *only moderately soaked and shivering. It took an hour beating into five-foot seas in gusty, variable winds with big wind-chop in a twelve-foot dory with a twenty-five-year-old blown-out cotton sail! A robust, exciting end to a perfect day, really. Only a dory could perform like that. I felt confirmation that I had chosen a good design for my tender.*

Newsletter, Mar 28, 1980:

Arrived in San Blas yesterday afternoon. San Blas is a small coastal village about one hundred twenty miles south of Mazatlan. For us, it is the first true tropical paradise. Lush green, thick forest, miles of sandy beaches.

The sail down started slowly, in baffling light wind (more than ten sail changes and adjustments during the second morning out, after being nearly becalmed most of the night), and ended up in a sleigh-ride with the genoa jib poled out on one side, the newer yankee poled out on the other side, and full mains'l up behind, the wind being off the starboard quarter. One-thousand-four-hundred-fifty square-feet of Dacron running downhill like a freight train, requiring much attention at the helm, making around eight-knots over the bottom with a helpful current. Fishers Hornpipe *is not a fast boat, especially now with more than a two-ton overload. That was as fast as we can go.*

We shared a feast dinner last night with friends David and Beth from Fianna *on board* Fishers Hornpipe. *Fresh fish (a peculiar dark meat almost reminiscent of good liver), fruit salad, vegetable soup, cauliflower with cheese sauce, and homemade muffins (pineapple-zucchini). Yummy!*

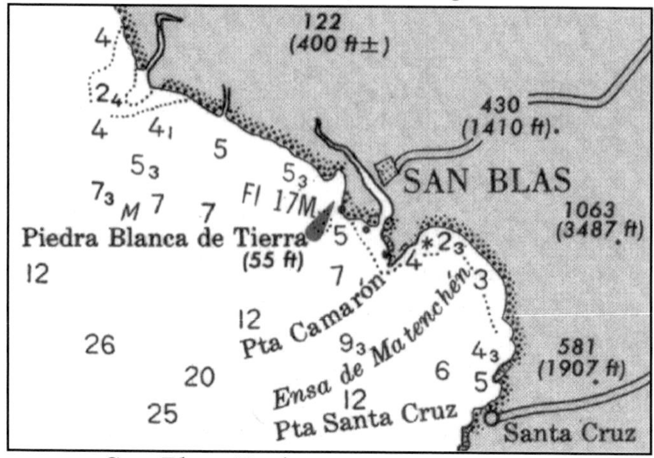

San Blas, Mexico.

Newsletter, Mar 29, 1980:

We hitched a ride into San Blas yesterday and found the town unremarkable. The bus ride back out was more interesting, as the bus was very near death and required much nursing by the driver. The town has several ruins, which we hope to poke around in today, as we have decided not to leave until tomorrow. There are many small outdoor restaurants along the beaches, but we seem to have neither the stomachs nor the pocketbooks to try them.

Bob left us at Mazatlan, deciding to travel by land for a while (the Hornpipe's *diesel grossed him out) and meet us in Costa Rica. It was impressive that a hermit for the last seven years could live happily in a boat with three other intense people for a whole month, although I wish it had lasted longer. Now we are short-handed and must look for crew in Puerto Vallarta (our next stop) and if that fails, in Acapulco.*

Even with work-bucks and money from Michele (our surfer/passenger), I am now nearly broke. The boat trip gobbles up money much faster than I can acquire it. In San Diego I earned and spent the better part of $5,000—I now have less than two hundred dollars. Poof! The boat is well-equipped in some areas, and totally lacking in others (electronics); our survival depends on our extensive tools, hardware, raw materials, and inventive initiative. We will have to find work and opportunity as we travel, relying on ourselves and hopefully avoiding yelling for help from friends and relatives, or having to bail out altogether. It is going to be tight.

There are many things to say about what I have learned so far. Some of the trip has been hard—and I haven't felt at ease much. There have been numerous difficulties: The responsibilities can be overwhelming, the work is often exhausting, there is strain among crewmembers as well as love and cooperation, there are money problems for all of us, there is the discomfort of being a foreigner in a foreign land—the language barrier, the laws and paperwork, the constant vigil of navigating—and the gnawing awareness of the sea slowly and systematically eating Fishers Hornpipe.

There are no breaks from these things. Hurricane season is coming on fast, both on this coast and in the Caribbean. There are many miles to go yet; the hardest and most dangerous are yet to come. We are in serious need of more crew with real experience, and enough time and money to travel on. I need to find work, or somehow acquire money. Same old story.

Been smelling homemade crackers baking for hours in my sleep. Debi makes a lot of crackers—we can keep them down. I just crawled back out from another attack of whatever-the-fuck-it-is. None of us has had a straight stomach for very long. At first mal-de-mer did its number on all but Cyndee's cast-iron gut. Then, ever since Cabo San Lucas, one or more of us has had whatever-the-fuck-it-is. Sore stomachs, cramps, barfing, drizzle-shits, headaches, lethargy, vaginal disorders, weakness, unrequited hornies (not just me!), ravenous appetite, no appetite, etc. Ain't cruisin' fun?

I almost forgot to mention perhaps the worst malady of all: The Farts. This has been, regrettably, almost solely my malady. I no longer need to rely on feet for motivation. I merely turn in the direction in which I desire to go and let loose a couple of blasts. In my wake lie unfortunate deceased small animals and plants. The crew regularly don gas-masks, or ban me from various parts of the boat. I slink off to hide in shame, having to tie myself down for fear of floating away in the night. Bob's similar affliction of years gone by is now dwarfed by mine. Although he does still wake us up, sometimes himself included, with his musical blasts: "Thphhhhpt." "Hark! I hear a nightingale!" "Huh? Oh, uhn, wha??"

We are rolling back and forth in the Pacific swell. Rolling, rolling, rolling, rolling. Everything goes "click clack" or "bimp bump." In the middle of the night I lie awake trying to figure out what the hell it is this time. The rolling pin in a drawer. The boathook on the foredeck. A stray flashlight. Right now it's a box of fuses behind the tape deck. It's hopeless! Every "bimp bump" is masking yet another "click clack." The bane of most Pacific anchorages, that insidious swell sneaks into almost any harbor and sets all the boats to rolling, rolling, rolling....

Here in San Blas we are among "no-see-ums" for the first time. These are the tiniest of black bugs, which, seen under a microscope, become a huge pair of teeth with wings attached. They go right through the screens. And they eat for steak-sauce the Army-surplus bug-repellent that burns skin, dissolves paint, lacquer, and varnish off the aft cabin table. They are biting me right now.

There is a delicious cool breeze weaving through the boat. We sleep naked under one sheet or sometimes a thin blanket or bedspread. As we go further south, it's going to get much hotter.

Tomorrow we leave for Puerto Vallarta. There, we will look for crew, replenish stores and fuel, and repair the whisker-pole car rings, which broke due to poor design—my only such screw-up so far. They consisted of bronze swivel rings to which we clipped the pole-ends, in such a way that if the poles got cocked they could twist the rings off—which they did.

The only other thing that broke is the handle to the head. It is also bronze, and has been around since WW II. It fatigued and broke off at the shaft. Picture this visual—of Debi spooning her turds into a jar to dispose of them. She neglected to add enough water to make the jar sink, and it floated merrily off over the horizon. Some kid in Japan will receive a message in a bottle. A Mexican in Mazatlan brazed the handle back together for twenty pesos.

From Puerto Vallarta we will coast-hop to Acapulco. That will probably be our last Mexican port. There we will make the final preparations, there we must have crew together, to go offshore and sail to Costa Rica. This offshore course will take us around the Golfo de Tehuantapec, across which blow the dreaded "Tehuantapecers" (pronounced—I kid you not—"Tuh-wanta-peckers") which can reach hurricane force, and which are in season. The two approaches to crossing this body of water are: A) To travel with one foot on the sandy beach, always ready to anchor close on shore, and B) To get way the hell far and gone to sea where you feel them anyway, but with less intensity (and no sand). The drawback to Plan A is that a tehuantapecer can literally sand-blast the paint right off your boat! Because of that, and lack of time, I have elected to do the latter...although I may change my mind.

Once well along the coast of Central America, skipping Guatemala, El Salvador and Nicaragua (all politically unstable at the moment?) we may sail out to Cocos Island, and thence to Costa Rica.

[Isla del Cocos is a remote, verdant, mountainous naturalist's paradise several hundred miles off the Central American coast. Surrounding reefs include one of the world's largest breeding grounds for sharks, and are known for their spectacular diving (better bring your "bang-stick!"). Most regrettably, we did not sail there.]

But I'm getting ahead of myself....

CHAPTER SEVEN—SOUTHERN MEXICO

"... and I dug you diggin' me in Mexico..."
Donovan Leitch

We departed San Blas on the morning of March 30th. That evening we anchored off a beautiful beach just east of Punta de Mita. On the 31st we sailed to Baia de Banderas (where we first saw Mangrove trees growing in the surf) to anchor in the busy harbor of Puerto Vallarta. We didn't like it there.

Reuel, Personal Log, Apr 1:

Puerto Vallarta: Miles of hi-rise hotels, stacked all over the hills and crawling down to the beaches. Paved roads, tourists, restaurants, taxis—diseases of a city totally prostituted to the tourist trade. Cruise ships coming in and out daily, huge ferries to Cabo San Lucas, yachts packed into a cramped harbor, sport-fishing boats, para-sail tow-boats, tour-boats...gross. Puerto Vallarta is a city operating beyond its capacity. Hence the age-old problem of an intimate relationship developing between human feces and drinking water. Or for that matter, water for washing vegetables, cooking, cleaning—all water. Enter the Amoeba. The result is an incredibly debilitating sickness that can severely alter human life for years, if it doesn't terminate it (rarely, fortunately?). According to the Merck medical manual, the infection-carrier rate in the tropics can be over 50%. Cruise ships were leaving Puerto Vallarta last month with half their passengers flat in their bunks.

Everything in Puerto Vallarta is geared to separate the gringo from his dollar. Expenses were as high as in fancy Marin County restaurants. Piña Colladas at the hotel Playa de Oro were about three-and-a-half-dollars each.

Cyndee, Personal Log, Apr 2:

Puerto Vallarta—another dirty harbor. It seems where the gringo scene is utmost, there is pollution and sickness. Un-consciousness breeds dis-ease. This morning there are two cruise ships... one pulled right up to the dock...the other anchored out, requiring a shuffling of the tourists back and forth to shore by those 'gunboats.' Reuel calls the Pacific Princess and such "Love Boats"...fitting. Vallarta is also home of many hotels, but so different from Mazatlan. Gringo Gulch is full of the older, more wealthy tourists than Mazatlan.... It's pretty much day-sailing down the coast to Acapulco—this coast is studded with bays and holes—all tucked up into rich green foliage. Ah! The tropics. The sun, she grows hot, the waters warm. It's a crime to be cooped up in a harbor such as this.

We stayed there three days, largely because I was sick as a dog with Amoebic Dysentery. It comes and it goes. I finally started a cycle of Tetracycline to try to knock out some of the Amoebas, and to prevent secondary infection, as well as to cover the possibility of the infection being bacterial. I didn't know what to do.

Being that we were short-handed anyway, Cyndee and Debi were hesitant to go to sea until I was somewhat better. I just wanted out of Puerto Vallarta. So as soon as it seemed possible, we took off for Yelapa, on advice from numerous sources. Yelapa is tucked between jungle-covered mountains on the south coast of Baia de Banderas; a cove so small that we had a deuce of a time finding it.
The departure from Puerto Vallarta was a bitch: our stern hook snagged something and we had to dump all 300 feet of stern line with a buoy, raise the bow hook, and go back to raise the stern hook with the windlass. I *hate* anchoring fore-and-aft. The decks were covered with mud and wet line, and I was totally exhausted from what was more of a big hassle than any big problem—had I not been so sick.

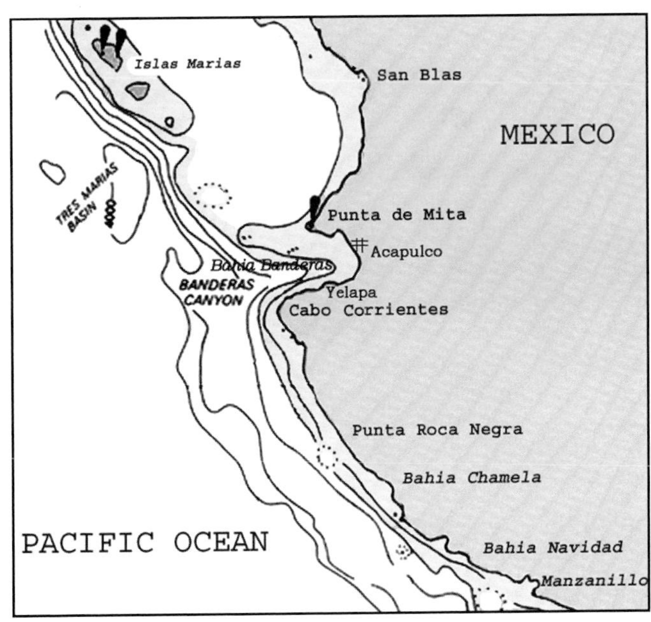

San Blas to Manzanillo, Mexico.

The sail across Baia de Banderas was slow and frustrating—all to windward against a strong current, trying to find a nearly invisible cove for which we had no chart, with dusk coming on. When we found it, I couldn't believe that anyone in their right mind would anchor there. The cove is nearly bottomless, small, surrounded by rocks, and open to the northwest swell—which was breaking somewhat violently against the beach and rocks. So we anchored (there were other vessels there) fore-and-aft once again, with a stern hook damn near on the beach, crowded between another boat and some ominous looking rocks, and commenced to pitch and roll in the swell like a bucking bronco in the ring.

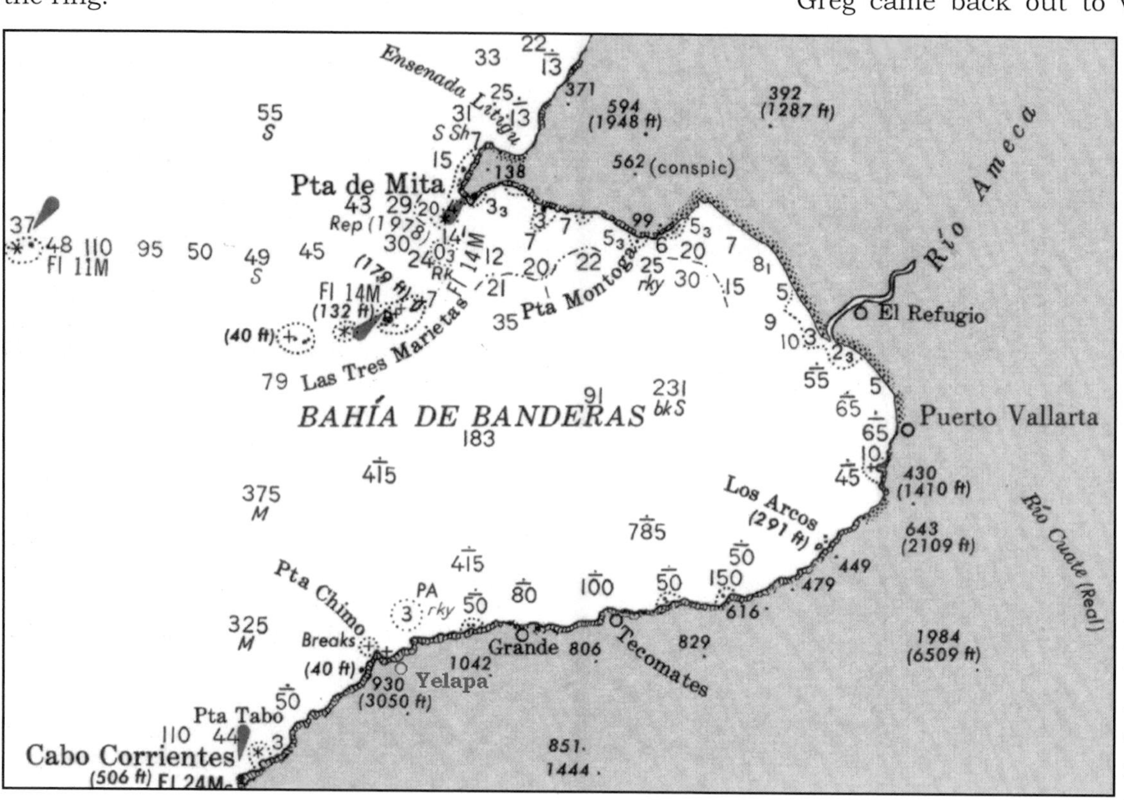

Bahia Banderas, Puerto Vallarta and Yelapa.

After a very uncomfortable night during which I programmed myself to wake up and look out a porthole (for position reference) every twenty minutes, the violent motion finally worked a shackle-pin loose between the stern line and chain (it should have been seized), allowing *Fishers Hornpipe* to swing 180 degrees on her rode. Miraculously, she avoided hitting anything or tripping her bow anchor.

As we were all scrambling like hell in the sunrise light to remedy this situation, someone hollered to us from the rocks. It turned out to be Greg from the *W.N. Ragland*, with which we had hoped to rendezvous in the Sea of Cortez. Greg, newest crewmember of the *Ragland*, was on vacation in Yelapa waiting to hear from the vessel, which was in the La Paz area, as to whether he would be needed for the next leg of their travels. *W.N. Ragland* is Neil Young's converted Baltic cargo schooner (in case you forgot), and her comings and goings were encumbered by that man's complex and often turbulent life. Greg had some time on his hands.

He swam out to greet us, and helped us get turned around and re-anchored. This was no simple task—ultimately I had to dive for the loose end of the chain, swim it up to the surface and hand it to Cyndee in the dory, where she reconnected it to the nylon rode with a new shackle (we never found the pin to the other one). Two stern-anchor bummers in a row.

Greg came back out to visit us later—we had much news to exchange—and he invited us to come see the village and the palapa were he was staying. This we did, and there met his friends and roommates, John and Mary.

Here I learned about a new architectural type: A palapa is a free-form open-air tropical Indian house; generally with a high, ventilated thatched roof, a stone, tile, concrete or dirt floor, often stone or adobe partial walls, woven mats for wind-breaks and sun-shades, and no doors or windows. One or more sides of the structure are totally open except for low partial walls. This particular palapa we visited had various levels, including two sleeping lofts, a kitchen, dining area, large living room, a study on a different level, a beautiful steep rocky yard, and a bathroom and shower under a separate roof. All spaces were open to eachother and to the outdoors. The water came from a near-by creek, and there were virtually no mosquitoes (there were, however, scorpions). What an ultimate way to live. (See photo.)

Describing Yelapa makes me want to abuse superlatives—which I do all too often. I hesitate to use that dangerous descriptive *paradise*—but it was. It was...an Indian village woven into the side of a hill...dirt and cobblestone paths—all steep and winding—full of colorfully-dressed people, burros, small horses, livestock, children...small markets (tiendas) in the front rooms or porches of haciendas and palapas...steep creeks and springs with cascading waterfalls...fishing boats moored in the tiny bay...lush green jungle pouring out onto a pure white sand beach...a tiny hotel...a community of Indians, Europeans, artists, musicians, movie stars and film-makers...a well-kept secret? Well, not anymore.

The population consisted of roughly 700 Mexican Natives (indigenous aboriginals) and 60 people of other nationalities, mostly American (some Canadians, French, Dutch, German). Many of the foreigners were immigrants. The land is essentially a community, deeded by the Mexican government as Indian Land, or native land. *Individuals from outside the tribe must be formally accepted by the community before they can even be granted rental property.* Consequently, gringos cannot own land, but can lease it in some circumstances. This is different from other land arrangements in Mexico, where foreigners can purchase and own land—if I understand all this.

Yelapa felt more like a real *community* than anything I had experienced since the communes of California (like Starhill) or the Sausalito houseboat community. It broke my heart that Bob didn't stay with us long enough to experience Yelapa; it is the place he had been looking for and dreaming about all his life. He would walk into Yelapa and never come out. [Decades later Bob would wander into the interior of Thailand, marry a local woman, start an organic farm and never come out.]

From the beach in the tiny harbor, a stream winds back up into the hills—a thundering river during the rainy season. John and Greg led us on an all-day hike for miles up trails that switched back and forth across the stream, among small farms, herds of cattle, through jungle with trees reminiscent of coastal California (madrones and live oaks?) mixed among palms and ferns. Parrots just ahead of us signaled our intrusion into paradise, strange nuts and berries and nests of termites and hornets hung from branches, and we had to brush off tiny ticks on occasion. At last we came to groups of waterfalls under which we sat naked; refreshing therapeutic water rushing down over our heads and shoulders and backs. We spent the day like that, leaving *Fishers Horpipe* to surge nervously at her moorings waiting for us. Greg told us how he had brought a California tourist girl up here the week before, and how she took off her bikini, wrapped her long, tan arms around his neck and murmured "I want the *total* experience...."

That night we ate a fresh fish dinner in the palapa, and Greg and John volunteered to spend the night on *Fishers Hornpipe*, inviting us to have an evening ashore in paradise—a first night's sleep on shore in a *long* time. These two men were both professional mariners, and we had grown to like, respect and trust them in the course of but one day. We accepted.

The next day they both set sail with us. I guess it is easy to leave paradise knowing you will return in a few weeks. And the romance of the rolling Pacific was calling them (to say nothing of the romance of Cyndee and Debi). I had not been romantically involved with either of my fair crew-members since California—we were close, intimate friends. I cannot stress how vital this is to health and happiness aboard a cruising sailboat! There are times when sex can complicate things, as well as times when it can simplify them.

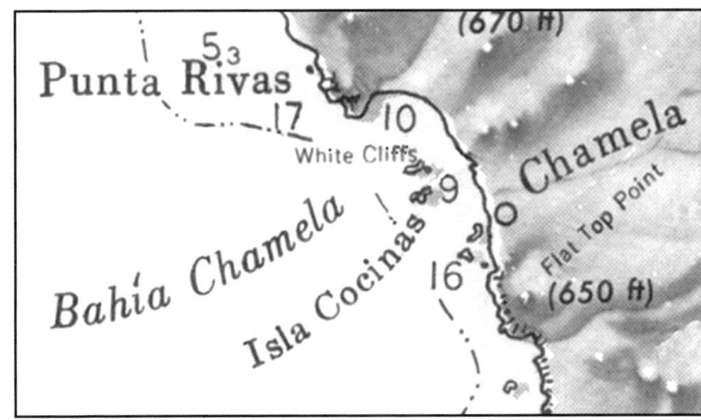

Bahia Chamela, Mexico.

So for the time being, our crew was five, with some real professional help on board. Greg and John were both licensed charter sailboat skippers, with experience. This took an unbelievable burden and strain off me, for the first time since the trip started. There was a possibility of Greg or John continuing to travel with us, and I extended the invitation.

We sailed on the 5th to Isla Passavera in Bahia Chamela, where we dove to scrape off some of the ominous jungle growing on the hull (*Fishers Hornpipe* needed a haulout). I am ashamed to say I don't remember much else about this place. It is unclear from the log whether we even stayed the night—a very unusual omission—but on the 7th and 8th we sailed to Manzanillo.

Newsletter, Apr 8, 1980

We sailed into Manzanillo Harbor a little before noon and anchored in the commercial part of the bay off the freight loading yards. On the short row ashore we stopped at a trimaran to ask the usual information: location of customs and immigration, port captain, post office, central market place, etc. The woman we spoke with looked remotely familiar, and sure enough, she asked if I was Reuel—turns out she worked at Boatbuilders Supply in Redwood City and knew me during the embryonic stages of Fishers Hornpipe. *Small world out here. We are travelling in a society of wanderers—we have made many new friends and are constantly running into old ones. We are not alone.*

Paperwork was easy here, things being more centralized than ever before, and the officials being courteous and helpful. After entering and clearing the harbor in one action, we went downtown to shop and run errands. At last—a city with no gringos! This is an industrial city that does not rely on tourists for its support. It is nearly 1,000 miles by road from El Paso, Texas, and over 100 miles from Guadalahara, the nearest big city. I can't remember the proximity of any airport. Hence the people we dealt with were friendly, conversational (when possible), and eager to help us—a contrast to Mazatlan and Puerto Vallarta, and even to small villages like San Lucas and San Blas, where we often felt like ripe avocados about to be plucked (or fucked). In Manzanillo we found smiles and friendly faces.

The climate is now truly tropical—hot and humid. The breezes on the water make it bearable. We stay naked most of the time. We jump in the water a lot. We are at 19 degrees latitude and heading south! Jackson Browne is singing on the hi-fi. [The *Hornpipe* really has a hi-fi—I built it into her using hi-tech 12-volt components.] *The sun is setting and we are going ashore for dinner. I'm thinking of all you folks who will read this.*

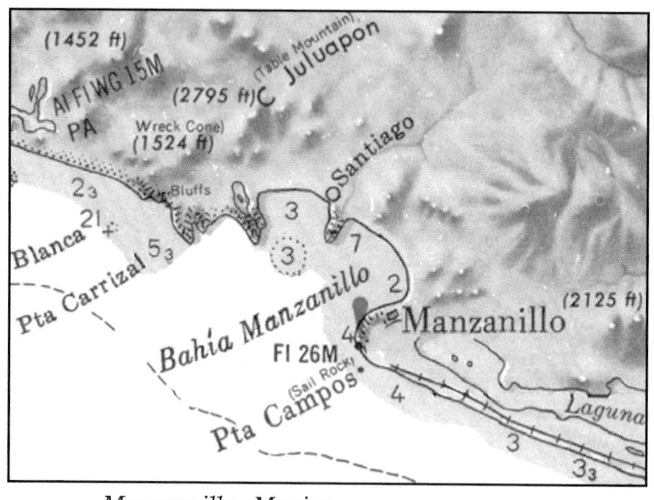

Manzanillo, Mexico.

Newsletter, Apr 10, 1980:

This afternoon we took on fuel and water. We took on food stores yesterday and this morning. Going to get fuel was quite an experience. We made a deal with a clerk in the Pemex office for somebody's friend or relative to fill a 55-gallon drum with diesel fuel and truck it ten miles to a deserted, broken-down municipal pier up in an inner harbor—really back in the boondocks. Evidently this is the only way a yacht can take on a large quantity of fuel. The alternative is going to the local Pemex station with five gallon jugs, lugging them a mile back to the beach, and rowing them out to the boat. Promptly at the predetermined time, we showed up at the boondocks and tenuously maneuvered up to this pier. Somebody's pal or nephew didn't show up. So we found a garden hose nearby with water of questionable origin (all water from Mexican garden hoses is of questionable origin) and proceeded to take showers. Still no show. We washed our clothes by a stream. Then I went for a bicycle ride. No show. Meanwhile, some Mexican fishermen came and we got to talking to them. Upon explaining our predicament, they volunteered to go get us some fuel, but they wouldn't be back until later in the evening. We agree—off they go. Another hour passes, and of course somebody's buddy or brother shows up. We tell him what happened and that he's several hours late. He wants a hundred pesos for his trouble. He is a big, imposing, impatient type. He says that he knows the fishermen, and he agrees to catch up with them and tell them that he is, after all, supplying the fuel. Fine, we'll take it. But to our shock, off he goes. He doesn't even have the fuel yet; he still has to go and get it, which he didn't let on! Another hour passes. We give a tour of our boat to some upper-class Mexican families who walk onto the pier, an interesting exchange.

All this time we have also been talking to this strange Mexican hobo, Miguel, who wears funky dark glasses and has pockets full of cigarette butts and dead fish (this is true!). Because he spoke better English than we spoke Spanish, he sort of acted as a go-between and translator during all these transactions, bending them slightly with his own interpretations and opinions. I think he had more than a few loose screws.

Finally, the big guy, the original somebody (who showed up after the fishermen) comes back with the fuel, which I hastily drain into the Hornpipe's *tank. The hobo, Miguel, would like to have a cup of coffee and get to see the boat for his efforts. Fine, but let's make it quick as it's getting dark and I want to get the hell out of there! He drinks his coffee s-l-o-w-l-y. He won't get off the boat. We cast off the mooring lines and I politely take his hands and drag him onto the dock. Whew. We just got away before the fishermen came back. The big guy never told them. But I understand that they will have no trouble selling the fuel to the next yacht to come along....*

* * *

During siesta time, we have been hanging out in Bar Social *in downtown Manzanillo. For the price of a beer they bring out plate after plate of food: ceviche, tacos, guacamole, refritos, ceviche (fish-lime salad), tortilla chips, etc. A trio of chamber-musicians wanders from table to table playing Spanish classical music. A distinguished-looking gentleman at the bar noticed me watching them, and asked me for a request, which he "bought" for me. I asked for La Cumparasita and they played it—the best I ever heard.*

This evening we will sail across the harbor to the fairy world Las Hadas Hotel*—touristas again—to anchor for the night. Then we sail south with the first sign of good wind.*

CHAPTER EIGHT—MEXICO TO COSTA RICA

All luxury is the same, but misery for each person is miserable in its own way.

Leo Tolstoy

We intended to sail over to Las Hadas for the night, but it ended up being two nights. Las Hadas was truly bizarre—like Disneyland in the middle of Mexico. Curving concrete spires, sculpted hi-rise hotels, walled-in winding paths, palapa-style bars at every turn, a suspension bridge over the pool, colored tiles and whitewash. The hotel's name was imprinted on *everything* including the sand in the ash buckets! There were armed guards at the gates.

I took a long bus ride into town to print copies of the last newsletters, which turned into an all-day adventure, and when I returned, the guards wouldn't let me in. Well, eventually they did, after much explaining and several phone calls.

The next night we had a party with friends from other boats, again on *Fishers Hornpipe*, and early on the morning of April 11th, we sneaked into the posh hotel marina before dawn, filled our water tanks and headed out for the open sea.

We left just in time: The next day (we learned later) a friend on *Panacea* (anchored off Las Hadas) was hailed from the water by someone swimming out to his boat with fish in his pockets and a kilogram of tortillas tucked in his shirt, looking for us. He talked about following *Fishers Hornpipe* to Acapulco to join us, and he wouldn't get off the boat!

The sail from Manzanillo to Zihuateneo (as beautiful as the name) was pleasant and uneventful. A starry night and dolphins at dawn. We caught a bonita on the 12th, and came into the anchorage early the next afternoon. Zihuateneo is a beach tourist town, in a beautiful quiet harbor—clean, well laid out, full of both Mexican and American tourists. It even had a 'health-food' restaurant and several good *hamberguesa* joints. We stayed there for three days, and had another really good pot luck dinner on *Fishers Hornpipe*. Hell, when you've got the only big aft-cabin around, you end up with parties in it. Zihuateneo was a special meeting place for cruising sailors. Here we found Shane and Debby on their beautiful little *Monk*. We found *Swirl*, several of the California trimarans, and David and Beth on *Fianna*, who had decided to head for Hawaii. They asked Greg to come with them, as he was due to rejoin *W.N. Ragland* there soon. Other coastal companions who arrived were *Eagle*, *Cora Lee*, *Brisa*, *C-Dream*, and *Panacea*.

I was still sick with 'whateverthefuckitis.' At times I almost felt all right, and tried foolishly to act like it. At other times I was weak and sick and weird. Profoundly affected. The Merck Manual and Physician's Desk Reference were scaring the shit out of me, and rightfully so: Amoebic Dysentery, if the culprit, is no joke. Our friend Shane made me aware that I could buy *Flagyl*, the World Health Organization's recommended cure, across the counter at a local drugstore. I got sicker. I bought some. Having Greg and John on board was a lifesaver at that point, as I really needed help. The cure was brutal—as bad as the disease—*Flagyl* turned my aching guts totally inside out!

Of the five of us on board, Debi and John and Cyndee and Greg had become couples. Their relationships were intriguing, had depth and charm, and came about slowly and thoughtfully—considering the limited amount of time available. I might mention here that I didn't always get along with John, a bright, complex, intense man going through changes. However, I did enjoy his company in small doses. I think he would have continued with us to Costa Rica, but neither Cyndee nor I were up for it.

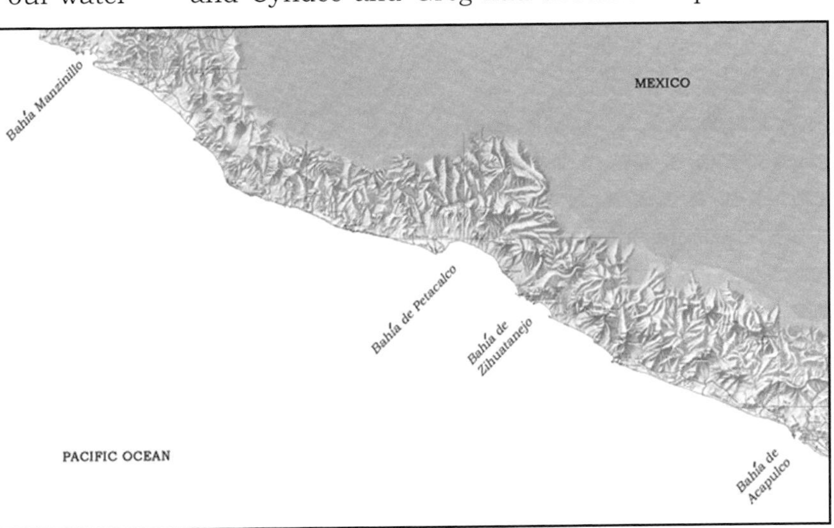

Manzanillo to Acapulco, Mexico.

Reuel, Personal Log, Mar 20:

Departed Zihuateneo 4/16 and arrived

Acapulco 4/17. Huge city, ugly and beautiful—Rico y Pobre. Here many changes have come down. Greg is sailing for Hawaii on Fianna, *and Cyndee has an invitation to do the same. John goes back to Yelapa, and Debi has left to go back to the States. Cyndee and I more or less asked her to leave—for Cyndee it was coming down to being one or the other. I am much closer to Cyndee, as well as aware of her superior sailing skills and intimate knowledge of* Fishers Hornpipe. *Debi has simply not learned a gut feeling for the art of sailing, although she definitely appreciates it—a paradox.*

The personality conflict between these two remarkable and dramatically different women has been evident from the beginning. Cyndee has at various times expressed an impending inability to continue traveling with Debi, and this time I took it seriously. Day before yesterday, I brought all this out in the open in an intimate conversation with Debi, after which she made the decision to leave Fishers Hornpipe. *I guess I had unconsciously worked up to this a few days earlier by saying that I would like to "clear" the boat in Acapulco, and have some time and space to myself. Now that it is here, of course, it's frightening.*

All four left for Mexico City this morning. Greg and Cyndee will return in a few days—John and Debi will not.

Well—I ache and ache. I feel horrible right to the depths of my soul. This is a strained and unhappy time for me. The prospect of being stranded alone in Acapulco with the hurricane season nearly upon me, with no money and no crew, and still feeling weak and sick is the darkest nightmare I can imagine, short of losing everything I have worked so long for. Indeed, they could amount to the same thing.

I am trying like hell to shake this disease I have had for nearly a month now. Yesterday I completed a cycle of Flagyl, which may have made me as sick as whatever I had (amoebic dysentery?). If I were religious, I would pray for recovery—but I believe it can only come from within me and from the arbitrary(?) moves of the giant hand of Fate. And with some pharmaceutical help....

Cyndee lifted my spirits yesterday by saying she wouldn't abandon me and Fishers Hornpipe *here. I needed that solidarity now more than any other single thing. Thanks Cyndee! I know she wants to be with Greg, and wants the learning/ growing experience of a trans-Pacific crossing with Greg and Beth and David. I am touched that she would sacrifice that, even knowing that if she had decided to go, it would also involve sacrificing this trip down the Central American coast. I hope it is fulfilling for her.*

While I was sitting here typing, Debi returned from the bus station briefly to get her traveler's checks, which she forgot were hidden under her bunk. Our eyes met briefly—a heavy flash—sad and strange. I felt miserable.

We were all honest—always—and that has made our interrelationships work. But it seems so desperately sad that things had to end here and now—even though Cyndee and I both wanted them to. Today it seems the price for everything is sky high.

* * *

That was the low point. Within a few days I began to get well: the effects of the Flagyl wore off, I gradually was able to eat and digest again, and my strength, both physical and emotional, began to return. I think the turning point was leaving the marina docks and crossing the street to a Mexican Dairy Queen, where I ravished a big dish of ice cream called *Las Tres Marias.* I made a couple of phone calls to the US and asked for financial help, which came quickly thanks to the combined efforts of my folks in New York and Jim Schaefer in California. Also, there came a badly needed short wave radio, hand delivered by a very helpful woman who flew from Oakland to join another boat in Acapulco.

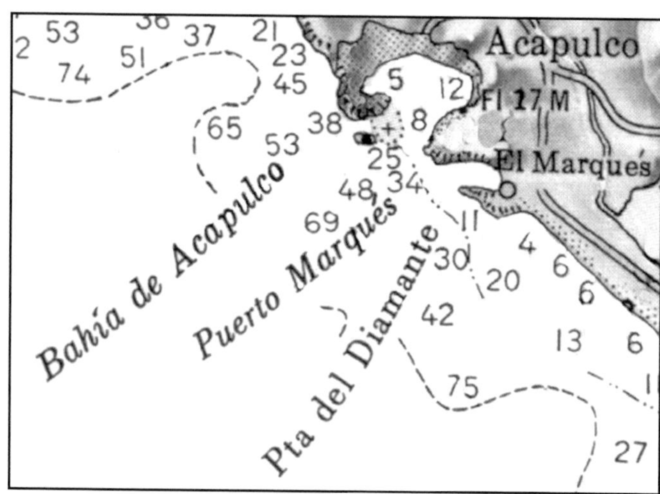

Acapulco.

A young man named Gene Wedge caught up to me at that point, and I asked him to come back to talk some more—and to stay on board—after a few days had passed. We had met Gene briefly back in magical Yelapa, and he followed us down the coast to see if he could sail with us. On the day Gene arrived, I very much needed some time and space to myself, and could not make a decision about a new crewmember without Cyndee meeting him first.

Cyndee came back, Gene came back, we three hit it off, and we decided to set sail for Costa Rica as soon as possible. We said farewell to Greg and *Fianna*, and Cyndee was pretty distraught for a few days. We worked hard putting in stores, diving

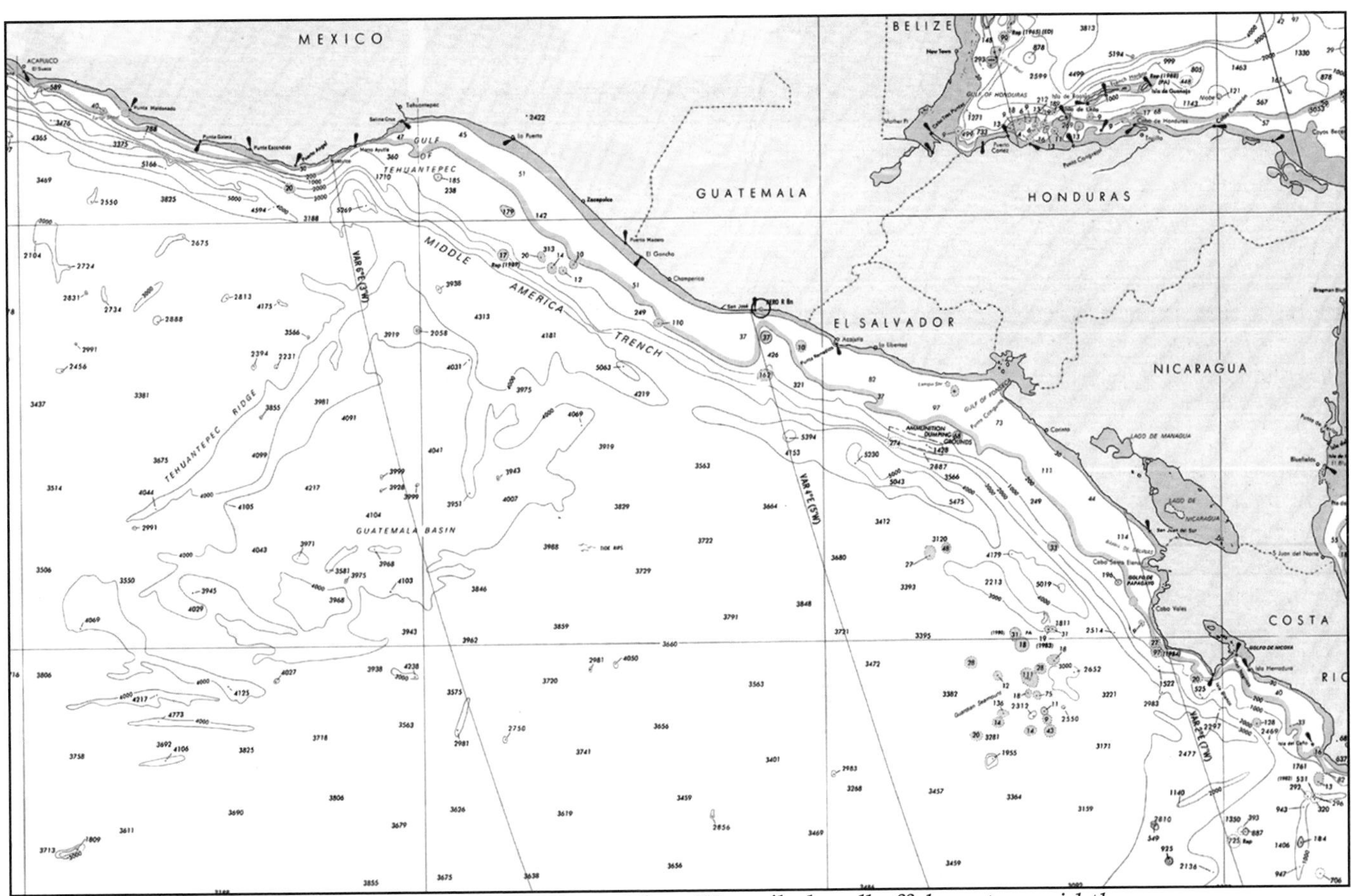

Acapulco, Mexico, to Punta Arenas, Costa Rica. We sailed well offshore to avoid the tehuantapecers, *but were caught by violent* chubascos *as we approached Costa Rica. The voyage was 1,100 miles and took twelve days.*

and scraping *Ms Hornpipe's* large bottom (Gene's initiation project), finding parts, supplies, gear, and taking on fuel and water (propane was a bitch in Acapulco). We cleared the harbor and the nation of Mexico (wherein lies a story in itself), and said goodbye to many friends, some of whom we would never see again. We set sail for Costa Rica on the afternoon of 4/29.

Gene, Personal Log, May 5:

A sleepy sun is begrudgingly taking over the sky from the gibbous moon. Its main excuse for not making a more spectacular entrance seems to be that it can't find the horizon. It must be jealous as it realizes it's not going to get much of a part in the day's celestial show. Little did I know of the show that was in store for us. About fifteen minutes after I wrote that passage, we were hit almost instantly by an impetuous little squall that shot bullets of rain with a 45-knot wind. For a few minutes, we had some real sailing, and then it left us in the dead air again with the five-foot jagged seas that it had kicked up.

The experience of the sea has been breathtaking. The animal life astounds me daily. From the Porpoises that saluted our departure to the lazy green turtle bobbing on the waves. Then there was the whale that spouted in my ear in the middle of a night watch and just about blew me out of the cockpit. The porpoises showing off their trails of phosphorescence under the bowsprit in the moonlight. The schools of bonita jumping frantically away to escape the vicious jaws of Fishers Hornpipe. *(We did catch one of the silvery little guys, and he did us quite well with a generous dousing of teriyaki.) The ever changing weather and sea, the lines of the boat and her full sails, and the peacefulness of the moonlit nights and sunrise watches all fill me with awe and wonder at the miracle of existence and of my being here to behold it all.*

There were only the three of us on this passage: Cyndee, Gene and me. Gene was a great addition to the crew. We stood watches 3 hours on/6 hours off; but we didn't stick to it rigidly. Everything flowed. Gene had never sailed offshore in his life, and had only gone sailing half a dozen times or so on other people's boats on day-outings. We taught him en-route. Being a bright and sensitive young man, recently escaped from completing his masters in metallurgic engineering, he learned quickly and was an excellent travelling companion.

Our course was as follows: We left Acapulco

gradually leaving land, until by the time we were off Golfo de Tehuantepec, we were around 175 miles offshore. Our course then veered slightly landward, for Costa Rica, which kept us around 125 miles off the coasts of Guatemala, Nicaragua, and El Salvador. The voyage took a little over twelve days (I had figured twelve to eighteen), and covered approximately 1100 miles, a daily average of 92 miles, for an average speed of a little under 4 knots. We saw nothing around us but beautiful deep blue sea for nine of those days. We had a comfortable and safe trip with none of the fancy gear or electronics considered essential by the blue blazer/captain's cap yachting types. The rough times were exhausting, but the good, cooperative companionship and hard work brought us through them with no great hardship—one simply must cope with what the sea doles out.

We saw many playful schools of dolphins, who always came over to cavort with us. I sat down under the bowsprit on the bobstay and whistled to them and tried to rub them with my feet. Their sense of space and timing are uncanny, and they never let me quite touch them. While we were off the coast of Nicaragua, we found some good wind (15 to 18 knots), but it blew on our nose. While beating into it, the seas were short and steep, causing the *Hornpipe* to pound—something she never did before. She pounded so hard that the forward skylight slammed shut—a first—and she actually slapped her bowsprit on the water a few times. Things began to loosen up here and there throughout the boat—BOOM...BOOM—and I felt glad my *ARK* was strongly built. A large school of dolphins had been swimming with us for an hour or so, and they began to slap their chins on the water, making fun of *Fishers Hornpipe*. Very funny, guys. We also saw several whales and giant sea turtles.

The weather was hot, and we three were naked for most of the trip. I remember Cyndee asking me to come look at something...and there was Gene, snoring away on his back on the aft cabin settee...with a big hard-on pointing straight up. Cyndee was fascinated—"Is he having a sexual dream?" "No," I told her, "that's a normal thing that happens to all men in their sleep... it's called a piss-hard-on, on the theory that your bladder is full, and that you can't piss with a hard on." "Which is of course bullshit," I continued. "Carl Sagan in his book *The Dragons of Eden* explains that it's much more complicated than that—perhaps some kind of primitive genetic-preservation instinct—just as men often get an erection and may even ejaculate in the moment of death." This only fascinated Cyndee more, and next thing I knew, there she was sliding up and down on Gene's genetic-preservation...and I can't blame her. He was a very sweet, very attractive guy.

Our cheap ($85) and cheaper ($25) plastic sextants both worked satisfactorily. We all shot noon-sights and graphed them the way Jack Hill back in Montara taught me, and the results seemed very accurate. Thanks Jack! Betcha never thought I'd remember. At night, the stars were brilliant, and we started seeing the Southern Cross, which is beautiful. I became addicted to Constant Comment tea, especially before late-night and early-morning watches. We saw many freighters, some of which came frightfully close: They are by far our biggest danger on the sea.

We had both favorable and unfavorable currents, a lack of good steady wind (typical, especially that time of year), some excellent sails, a lot of motoring (around 400 miles of motoring out of 1100 miles total), and some engine trouble. We had excellent food (as usual), good navigating and dead reckoning (I really learned on the way), and no Tehuantapecers! The dreaded infamous Gulf of Tehuanepec was like a giant lake, and we had to motor across it (far out at sea). We were lucky.

On the morning of May 9th I awoke to the green coastline of Costa Rica, after ten days at sea. Winds were baffling—light and variable and nonexistent. Our passage had been a good one, fairly fast (thanks in part to the Japanese taxi cab engine in the bilges), and mostly very comfortable. As we approached the coastline, we calculated that we were caught in the grip of a landward two-knot current. Because our sailing speed was only two-and-a-half knots, we found ourselves being swept toward a rocky, dangerous-looking shore. We tacked offshore, losing distance toward our destination, and as evening fell, ominous dark clouds began gathering all around. The wind fell lighter still, and we started the engine and motor-sailed. The diesel, for the first time in four years of faithful service, suddenly quit. The cause was simple enough: air in the injectors. I bled the system and all was fine—for a while. With increasingly shorter periods of running, the engine continued to stall due to the same malady. I was unable to solve the problem; hence we sailed very slowly for Punta Arenas. It became clear that the Mexican fuel we took on in Manzanillo or Acapulco was of poor quality: dark and dirty, it burned with a foul exhaust, and was prone to "sudsing." It also seemed that our fuel didn't last as long as it should have, and as we ran low the motion of the boat sloshing the fuel around in the tank may have allowed air, water or dirt into the fuel-pickup line. [There is always a small amount of water present under diesel fuel, condensed from the air in the tank—because water is heavier than fuel, it goes to the bottom. The other likely culprit was a type of algae that grows in diesel fuel and plugs filters. At that time I had never even heard of it.]

As our motoring capability became

increasingly limited, we headed well offshore to avoid danger. A good thing too—within an hour the storms commenced. Violent squalls, blinding rain, thunder and terrifying lightning flashed all around us (a nervous experience on a sailboat, the highest grounded point for miles around). Winds would come screaming at us from one direction, stop dead calm, blow moderately from another direction, shift in a split second to a violent squall, stop dead again, leaving us pitching and rolling in steep confused seas, then come screaming again from behind us. *At one point I swear the wind blew like hell straight down on us from above!* [It would be years before I learned what a *micro-burst* is.] We were carrying maximum light-air windward working sails: genoa jib, stays'l, and full main. We raced around in zig-zags and circles for the entire night, with no let-up or rest until dawn. I kept all sails on until I felt we were well offshore, navigating strictly by the seat of my pants, with no visibility and not having time or inclination to record all those course changes in the log. We were blown out to sea (perhaps thirty miles) and completely lost our position.

When I felt we were safely away from land, the wind had increased to between 30 and 35 knots, and I donned safety harness and lanyard and cat-walked out into the horizontal maelstrom of water to wrestle down 650 square-feet of violently-whipping Dacron genoa. This can be done only by good technique, not sheer muscle (human muscle is comparatively irrelevant). Cyndee put our bow into the wind while I tripped the brake on the 50-year-old Merriman-Holbrook wire-halyard-winch, and hauled on the downhaul. Down she came neatly inside the lifelines, but wet and whipping. Under conditions like this, everything happens in painfully slow motion. The sailor has to use one hand to hang on, one hand to work with, and both feet and all muscles to maintain some semblance of balance.

At 0730 on 5/10 we once again sighted land, far off in the haze, as the storms gradually abated. We slowly began working our way back toward shore, sailing in very light air and sloppy hangover seas. I spent the day, after a few fitful hours of sleep, down in the bilges with the diesel, trying to get it running dependably enough to safely navigate the powerful currents and light air we expected to find (and did) in Golfo de Nicoya. At some point during all of this, a copper tube I had installed to facilitate oil changes fatigued, broke and commenced dumping the contents of the crankcase into the bilges. I pumped what fuel I could out of the tank into a five-gallon jerry can, examining every inch of fuel line and every fitting. I fabricated a new oil-drain-tube with a rubber hose damper/sealer on it, cleaned the mess out of the bilges and stored it in a bucket to be disposed of ashore, rerouted the fuel line using the jerry can as temporary fuel tank, and refilled the crankcase with oil. Then I bled the injectors and got the monster running, to have it do the same thing: quit. Sweet mysteries of life! Of course, that isn't what I said at the time (even *I* can't print that!). While in Costa Rica, it simply got added to the long list of projects, with a number-one priority; but I didn't know what to try next.

The *chabasco* storms, as they are called locally, tore both our worn-out American flag and new Costa Rican flag to shreds. Cyndee spent several hours sewing them back together, and they looked like little patchwork quilts.

Reuel, Personal Log, May 9:

We are the only boat out of approximately twenty we talked to, or even know of, to make the trip offshore. All the others planned to hug the coast and make some stops, so we will be the first ones to arrive in Costa Rica.

*Off El Salvador we were hit by several early morning squalls, one of which blew between 40 and 45 knots, causing us to sail through it under single-reefed main and stays'l alone, the only time we had to reef the main on the passage. The local storms—*chabascos*—which hit us off Costa Rica, didn't blow harder than 30 to 35 knots, but were much more dangerous.*

Fishers Hornpipe *rides like a '56 Buick Roadmaster, trucking comfortably over the ocean. Our long passage from Acapulco has been a very pleasant one, and I found the most rare thing—Peace of Mind—which I had not really enjoyed since Sausalito, and rarely there, because I was so possessed by the goal of getting this whole trip together. There have been both incredibly peaceful, beautiful times and very upsetting, trying experiences—which is the way of the sea. The transitions-transmutations between them are unique.*

Fishers Hornpipe *is ready for some long-deferred maintenance. There is painting and oiling; replacing of worn out, chafed line, cable and gear; a new windlass handle to be made (I accidentally threw the last one overboard in Acapulco); new whisker-pole hardware to be designed and made; an extensive bottom job needs to be done soon—including sandblasting and epoxy resealing of the hull below the waterline; and many parts and systems of* Fishers Hornpipe *need to be finished, modified, or replaced. As my old friend Perry Fly back in Bolinas used to say: "Boats are always trying to commit suicide." Actually, everything is just always eating at them (and consequently, I might add, at their masters).*

I am ready for a change of pace—the chance to be somewhere for a while, even a whole country, is appealing. Time to think, write, design (which I am *very turned on to), play music, make love, work, and yes, hang out in coffee shops and restaurants. Get to know the people around me. There are likely to be upwards of 40 cruising boats hanging out in different corners of the country, especially Golfo de Nicoya. They will be here for the summer, waiting out the storm season, deciding where to go next. We are too late in the season to make the Caribbean crossing I had intended to make, so here we are too. An option for me could even include a trip back to the States to collect needed parts, materials, people (crew) and money. This kind of life is very expensive—although that is of course relative. We haven't assessed all our costs yet, but it seems certain that we have exceeded our monthly individual expense goal of $150. So we must find work soon.*

[Looking back on this from twenty-five years later, I am amazed to find that I lived and traveled on *Fishers Hornpipe*—including all maintenance expenses—for well under $3,000 per year. The arrangement I had with my crew was that we evenly shared travel expenses—food, fuel, port fees, etc.—and that I paid all maintenance costs for the boat. We all shared the maintenance work. At that time a US Federal program provided medical coverage for all crew (and captain, if he/she did the same work as the crew) in US military hospitals anywhere in the world. This included dental work, eyeglasses, and prescription medicine. The program was terminated during the Reagan era.]

I am anxious to be in the trade winds of the Caribbean. But first, there is much to do and see in this part of the world, and it is likely that I will be in Costa Rica long enough to get really involved with a place for the first time on this cruise. I intend to explore the country, both by land and by sea, and I am excited about this. There are still supposedly DC-3's flying up to San Jose, Costa Rica's capital, (one of my all-time favorite airplanes), and a narrow-gauge mountain railroad (an even greater favorite)! San Jose is at a cool 3,700 feet up in a broad plateau surrounded by Costa Rica's green, heavily wooded mountains.

Newsletter, May 11, 1980:

Love at first sight! This gulf may be as beautiful as any place in the Universe. Steep slopes, wooded with deciduous hardwoods and tropical jungle, hundreds of hidden coves and small beaches, as well as mile-long white paradise ones, and no hotels! White blossoms, clear turquoise water full of tropical multi-colored fish, playful dolphins and huge sea turtles. All size and shape islands, constantly changing skies, sculpted rocks, winding canyons, waterfalls—WOW!

When I started typing this afternoon we were entering the Gulf; now, at night, we are anchored in the roadstead of Punta Arenas—yes, off the goddamn disco, as usual (all through Mexico, the only available place to anchor seemed to be off the disco). Fishers Hornpipe *is rolling and pitching just a little too much to ignore. We are the victim of a wicked tidal current, small, short steep seas, and the 10-12 knot breeze that drove us here—onshore, of course. The seventy-five-pound CQR plow is down (our working anchor), and well set. The lead-line revealed a long, constant-sloping mud/sand shelf with a depth of five fathoms where we are anchored, approaching high tide.*

I cooked a spaghetti dinner, and we had chocolate-coconut cookies for desert, which I baked this afternoon while we sailed in. Busy little captain, eh? Sailing has a profound effect on hunger.

It is very hot and humid here. I am sweating on the typewriter!

On 5/15 we took on stores and fuel (which cost nearly $100) and left Punta Arenas for Isla Jesusitas, across Golfo de Nicoya.

Newsletter, May 17, 1980:

The beat across Golfo de Nicoya was possibly the most disjointed and dangerous sail Fishers Hornpipe *was ever subjected to. Cyndee and I were hot, drowsy, and a little too laid back. Friends had arrived on* Free Spirit, *and they took us out to lunch, where we had a couple of beers. Cyndee stayed a little longer than me with her new flame, Steve, skipper of* Free Spirit. *So our energies were dissipated, but the eight-mile trip to Jesusitas seemed like it would be a very easy day-sail.*

As soon as we rounded the point we started to wake up fast. It was blowing a good 25 knots, and the wind chop across the shallow bar was brutal. We ran around securing flying objects, and in so doing I came across the open portlights in the shop, through which were sloshing many gallons of water—all over my tools and supplies. Next I noticed that the daggerboard wedge was not in its slot in Gandy Dancer, *but I couldn't fix it until we got into deeper water where we could heave to. During all this hassle and distraction we narrowly missed a moored ferry boat, and then passed close to what looked like a ship's mooring buoy. As we went by it, Cyndee looked down to see the hulk of a* wrecked ship *just beneath the surface on the starboard side. We then hove to while I dropped from the stern davits into* Gandy Dancer *to bail her out and tie in her wedge.* [We trail *Gandy Dancer* astern only on day-sails or short trips on safe waters—theoretically. At all other times we raise her into the stern davits where she is five feet above the water.] *That taken care of, I fell to the task of hooking the fuel line back to the tank, bleeding the injectors, and eliminating the temporary Jerry jug fuel tank, which I should have been doing instead of going out to lunch!*

Just before leaving our Punta Arenas anchorage for the fuel dock on 5/15, I had discovered that the new oil-drain-tube, which I had installed at sea, had fatigued and cracked and once again drained the crankcase into the bilges. This time I eliminated that system altogether, plugged the oil pan, and refilled the crankcase. I can only assume that increased engine vibration caused the copper tubing to fatigue and break—twice in a row.

The sail across the Gulf was a dead beat the whole way, and it got dark before we arrived. We felt our way by the seat of our pants through the islands and the shoals, and with the help of lightning flashes and good luck, found our anchorage off Isla Jesusitas. Free Spirit *had arrived hours ahead of us (they motored across at 9 knots) and their masthead light, some 85 feet high, helped guide us in.*

We joined Free Spirit *for a salad, a couple of bottles of wine, and some music, which Jeff and I made—the first in a long time. Of the things I really miss, playing music is second only to the companionship of a woman partner. These two things can never be contrived; they have to happen of their own volition.*

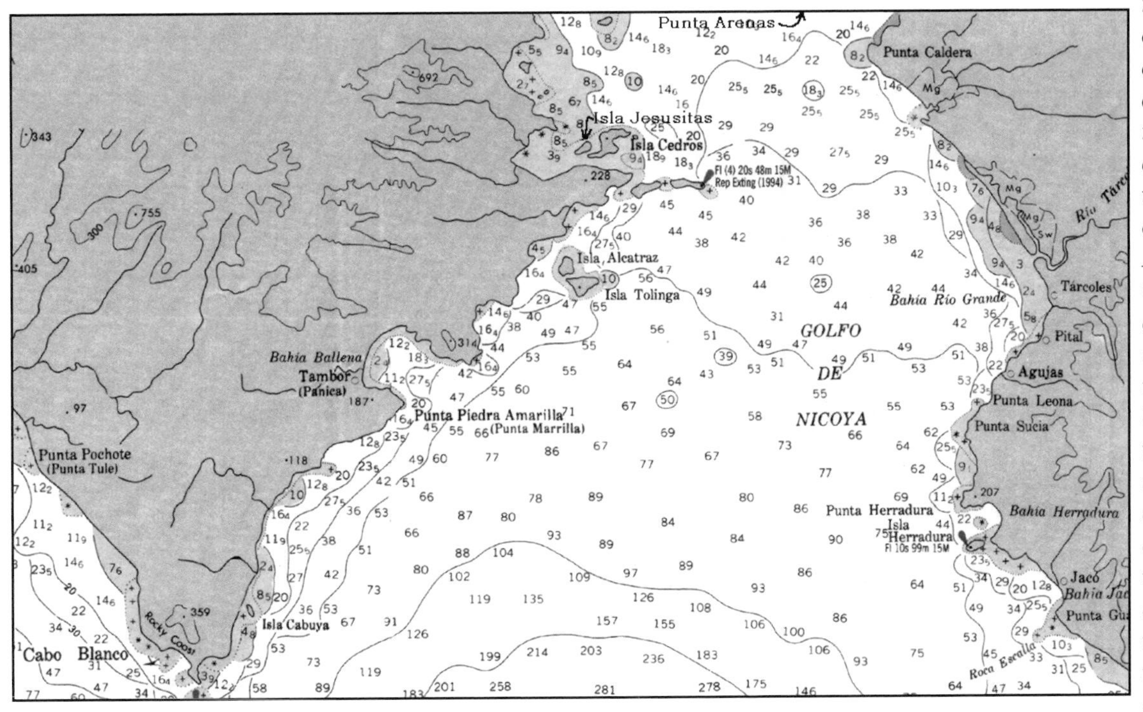

Golfo de Nicoya, Costa Rica.

This morning, early, a local powerboat from the Jesusitas Resort came by and Carlos, the manager, asked if we would help to unload a generator plant in exchange for desayunos (breakfast). This turned out to be an interesting expedition: The generator weighed about 500 pounds, and we had nothing to move it with save manpower (six of us) and a piece of pipe. This took several hours of grunting and sweating, after which we were covered with grease. While working in the brush, I encountered red ants for the first time—also called fire ants or piss ants. As I was wearing flip-flops, they swarmed onto my bare feet and bit the living shit out of me. This cracked up Carlos. I quickly rowed out to the Hornpipe *and came back wearing boots!*

Breakfast was scrambled eggs, pancakes, good strong coffee, tomato juice with chile in it, and good conversation. Carlos, the man who recruited us, is the new manager of the island's tiny resort hotel. [Later, when we came to know each other pretty well, he told me he had needed to keep "a low profile" for a while....] *Isla Jesusitas is 1000 yards by 500 yards, with cabins and a motel-like building. The resort and restaurant are open year round, but the rainy season, now starting, is their off season.*

We are anchored between Isla Jesusitas and Isla Cedro, both of which are a five-minute skiff ride to the peninsula, where there is another fine anchorage, an excellent beach for careening (beaching) vessels to do bottom work, and the Hacienda de Nicoyana. *The Hacienda is a little restaurant which serves hamberguesas only, and has a lending-trading library full of English-language books! All about the rafters of the roof over the large communal table are the carved names of yachts and their crews who have visited over the years. Here we met Kurt Gahn, who keeps a log of visiting vessels—today we will sign his log-book. Other than these two resorts, the occasional house or shack, there is a tiny village a few miles back in the jungle, and that is the extent of civilization here. And this is the most civilized part of Golfo de Nicoya beyond the port of Punta Arenas.*

Today is a Saturday, and we are plagued by powerboats coming over from Punta Arenas. For some unknown reason, they seem to favor the dangerous passage between these two islands (where we are anchored), and are all but destroying the peaceful solitude of this place. I hope I live to see the day when fossil fuel becomes so dear that the crude, insensitive people who race around polluting the air, water, and peace of Earth with fast, noisy,

Isla Cedros, Isla Jesusitas, and the Hacienda de Nicoyana.

dangerous gas-guzzling monsters are driven from the water forever. The vast majority of the power-boaters we have encountered have had no sense of privacy or safety, and race their speed boats within scant feet of Fishers Hornpipe, *sending out horrendous wakes which beat* Gandy Dancer *against the hull of her mother ship. Put out more fenders!*

Last night we had a talk about what we're going to do next. The consensus seems to be in favor of continuing to move, taking time to enjoy each place we come to as we see fit. Gene is interested in continuing with us if we keep moving, putting off for a while his destination of Peru. Cyndee wants to keep moving. I need more information about how to deal with the impending hurricane season, but I would prefer to keep moving also. Costa Rica seems like a good place to hole up, but prospects for work here are slim, other than nickel and dime projects on other boats, few of which have much money. We will stay here a little while at least, until our friends catch up with us, and until we have had time to explore the country. Next week we will take turns leaving the boat and exploring the Costa Rican interior.

I definitely still need crew, and the chances of finding them here are pretty darn slim. I know I am being redundant, but I really do want a female partner in this venture, one who is experienced and dedicated to this life-style, and I wonder if I am going to have to sail to the ends of the Earth to find her.

Fishers Hornpipe *needs that haul-out more than ever, and I am still investigating the possibilities of doing it in Punta Arenas. If not, Panama has grids on which to careen vessels to do bottom work between the tides.*

Upon arriving here we found a letter from our crewmate Bob, explaining that he had bailed out and gone back to the U.S. This was a big disappointment, as we were looking forward very much to seeing him and hopefully reuniting as travelers. We hope he is high and we miss him very much.

* * *

During the long hot months in Costa Rica, we did manage to explore some of the country. Cyndee and I took turns taking trips into the interior with friends from other boats (someone had to always remain on board the *Hornpipe*). I remember taking a bus up to San Jose, where I rented a jeep with two friends. We traveled north through Costa Rica's rich interior farm country, up the volcano Irazu, 11,260 feet above sea level. The fertile hills on the lower slopes of the volcano reminded me of Vermont—I saw huge heads of lettuce growing. As we traveled higher, it kept getting colder, until we could scarcely believe we were in the tropics. After hiking up to the top, we looked way down what seemed to be thousands of feet into the huge crater, which appeared to have its own clouds—pretty spooky.

Back in San Jose, I enjoyed the museums, architecture and restaurants of the city. San Jose felt very sophisticated and European after Mexico. I developed a real taste for the national dish, *gallo pinto*, and for cabbage salads with lime juice and salt for dressing. For those of you who speak Spanish, gallo pinto will mean 'painted rooster.' In reality it is just the same old rice and beans—but spicy and good!

At *Isla Jesusita* and *Hacienda de Nicoyana*, a whole summer community formed among cruisers waiting out hurricane season. While anchored there, I found new friends, slowed down in the heat and torpor of the season, and took a long rest from my hectic pace.

I stayed in Golfo de Nicoya from May 11 through September 14—over four months. I hung out with Michael on *Starbuck*, Steve and Tarey Lea on *Zephros*, David on *Azulao*, all of whom became life-long friends. Other friends included the crews of *Tangerine*, *Windborne*, *Satisfaction*, *Rhonguild*, *Unlikely VII*, and *Kathi II*.

We spent our time reading, partying, playing music, cooking and eating (and getting fat!), swimming, day-sailing, hiking and making love when possible. (The "Single-Handers Club" at least had the whorehouses of Punta Arenas when all other endeavors failed.) I tried to stay clear of the whores—I remembered the horrible stories from the crew of the *Richmond* back in Sausalito about the tropical venereal diseases they contracted here. But the whorehouses were unavoidable—every bar was a whorehouse. I remember hanging out with Michael Starbuck one afternoon for happy-hour, when two young *Ticos* (Costa Ricans) got in a knockdown drag-out fight over a very beautiful young lady-of-the-night. They rolled around the floor trying to kill eachother until they rolled over to

Michael, who without interrupting our conversation, simple stuck his foot out to keep the contestants from rolling under our feet in their ardor.

On another occasion we were in Carlos' car (manager of the resort at Jesusitas), parked in front of a bar, when several whores came out to proposition us. One of them got a hold of my beard and wouldn't let go—or take no for an answer! I yelled to Carlos to get us away from there, but he was laughing so hard he couldn't get the car in gear!

One or two cruising sailors found lovers among the nice girls of Punta Arenas—but this was very rare, and very frowned upon. Costa Rica is a very Catholic country, with as extreme a double standard as I have ever seen. Once a girl has sex out of wedlock—particularly if she gets pregnant—she is branded as *puta* for life, abandoned by her family in most cases, and cast out into the streets to be a whore. To me, this is a sign of a very sick culture, controlled by a very sick religion. Hispanic countries are places of extreme contrasts.

After many weeks without sex, I finally couldn't stand it anymore, and I propositioned a pretty young prostitute while anchored in the river at Punta Arenas. In broken Spanish, I asked her to come to my boat with me for dinner and sex. Offering to cook for her confused her, and did nothing to offset her fee, which was $10 US. I wanted her to spend the night, but she declined, as she had a small child to get home to.

After dinner, which was awkward (we could not converse), we retired to the *Hornpipe's* fo'c'sle—for fear of crab lice I didn't want her in my cabin. I undressed, and she undressed herself. She had a lovely, petit body, beautiful olive skin, small, firm breasts, pretty hair and eyes—and she was perhaps the worst fuck of my life. I wanted her on top (*arriba, por favor*), but she adamantly refused. So I got on top, and she used that ancient whore's trick of locking her legs on mine so that I could only penetrate her half-way. It was awful. She was clearly afraid of me (Jesus, I'm not *that* big!), and no amount of gentleness on my part could alleviate her fear. I felt horrible—disgusted with her, disgusted with myself. But she was warm, and tight, and blessedly wet, and I made myself come. We got dressed in silence and I rowed her ashore. I felt very dirty and ugly, and I vowed never to do that again.

* * *

Across the Gulf, near the *Hacienda de Nicoyana*, we met and made friends with numerous American expatriates living simply and comfortably in the jungle and on the beach. The US dollar went so far in Costa Rica at this time that a person with a small pension could retire and live quite comfortably. The houses consisted mostly of a roof and screens—it never gets cold.

We took hikes up trails into the hills behind the Hacienda—and followed streams up to crystal-clear pools where we stripped and went swimming in the cool mountain water (see photos). It was heavenly.

One memorable experience happened during a hot morning, when a small cruising sailboat ghosted alongside and hailed me. An attractive young woman was single-handing, and I rafted her alongside. Things happen rapidly in the tropical heat—we sat and talked for a while, took our cloths off, went for a swim, came back on board and made very sweet love. She was the daughter of an Australian sea-captain, and was cruising around Central America on her own. I cannot find a mention of her in my logs or notes—and I am ashamed that I cannot even remember her name. But I remember her kindness and her love—however fleeting. A week or two later, we were both anchored in the estuary behind Punta Arenas, when I went to visit her. While I was aboard her small sloop, I became stricken with a fever, and collapsed. She put me to bed—there was no romance in it this time—and nursed me back to health. Shortly after that she sailed away, out of my life forever.

Cyndee and I took *Gandy Dancer* for long sails among the islands in Golfo de Nicoya. I remember that Cyndee went off sailing on her birthday, and by late afternoon still hadn't returned. I started to worry about her—though she is an excellent sailor, and the wind was good, she was overdue. Finally, as darkness fell, she came back with *Gandy* under tow behind a fishing boat. It turned out that she had sailed full-bore onto a hidden rock (the water there was always murky) and hit the steel daggerboard so hard that she tore the trunk right out of the boat... and sank! Being very smart and resourceful, she stood on the rock, got the board out of the trunk, tore open a kapok float cushion (probably with her teeth), and used the stuffing to caulk the slot in the bottom of the boat! To do this, she had to remove mast, rig, oars and all gear from the boat, turn the 12-foot dory upside down, caulk the slot, turn the boat back over and bail her out. She set the heavy steel daggerboard on the rock near her feet (underwater), retrieved it and put in back in the boat. Since the trip home was upwind, she couldn't make much headway without the board, and consequently was lucky to catch a tow from the passing fishing boat. Cyndee was an amazing person: a great companion, an excellent cook, one hell of a good sailor, a fantastic lover, and a very dear friend. I did not know it, but I was about to lose her.

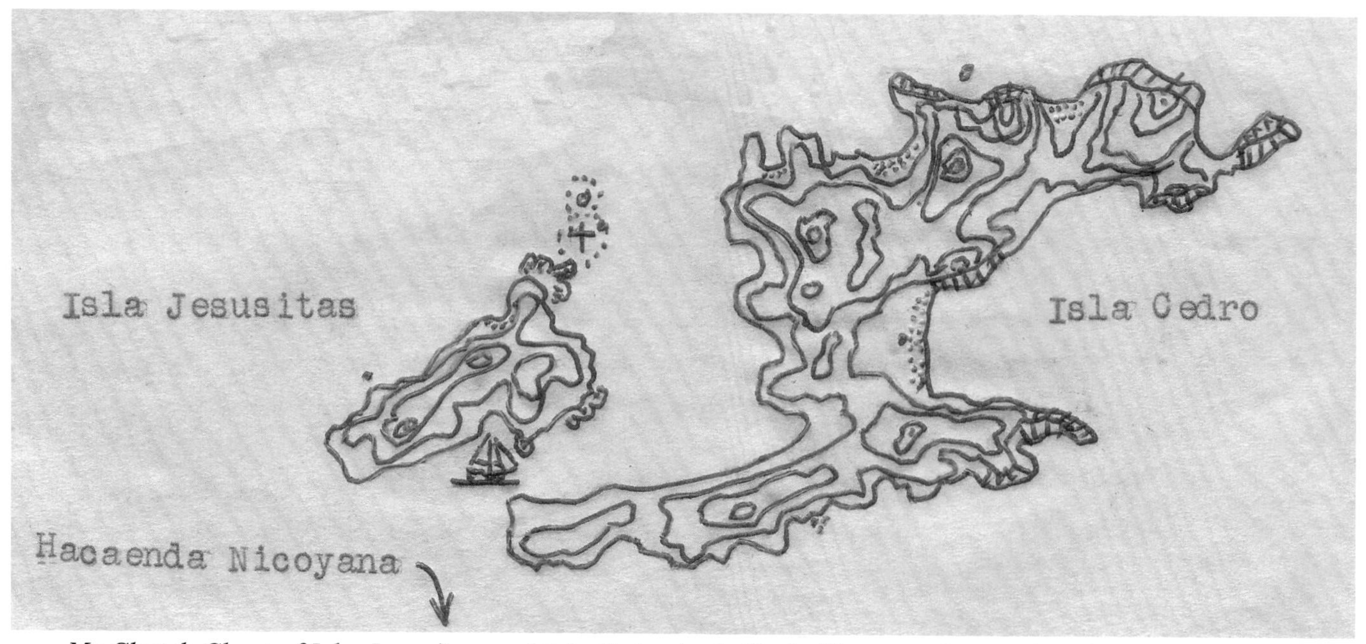

My Sketch Chart of Isla Jesusitas and Isla Cedro in Golfo de Nicoaya, Costa Rica--from a Newsletter

CHAPTER NINE—COSTA RICA TO PANAMA

Pur e lascia a gratare.

Dante, *Purgatorio*

I worked the last couple of months I was in Costa Rica for Carlos. He had an old wooden sailboat named *Nimbus*—someone's broken dream that got left behind. She was in rough shape, but was still beautiful and restorable. I worked on her—on and off—for months. I learned a lot about Costa Rica, met many people, had some adventures, and improved my lousy Spanish. Carlos also arranged for me to do some charter sails for the hotel, and even haul some cargo, and I made a little money those ways. We had a symbiotic relationship, we learned from eachother, and we did some serious partying together.

There were the two girls on vacation from the University of Miami, for instance.... They spent a few days at Carlos' resort on Jesusitas. As fate would have it, I got the shy one and Carlos got the nympho—Carlos always managed to get the best of any deal.

Around this time, all the cruising sailors were getting ready to head for Panama, and our new friend Rob agreed to give a lecture about Panama. Rob lived on an old sailboat (the *Roach Coach*) near Cristobal, on the Caribbean side of the Panama Canal, and had extensive knowledge of the area. The lecture was held in the dining room of the resort, and 15 or 20 cruisers came to it. As Rob was lecturing, Carlos took that horny U of M student upstairs to his room and proceeded to fuck her brains out. She screamed and yelled and gasped through the entire hour-long lecture! All of us downstairs tried our level best to concentrate on the fine points of navigating the Panama Canal and avoiding being mugged in Cristobal...but we feared making eye contact, lest we lapse into hysteria (or cheering).

I took the other girl out to see my boat, hoping for a similar stroke of fuck...er, luck—but she wasn't having it. We climbed up the ratlines to the *Hornpipe's* broad spreaders, thirty feet above the water, and shared a glass of wine as the tropical sun went down.

Carlos introduced me to some of the local Indians, and we visited a couple of the tiny villages on the peninsula. I came to know one man, in particular, who worked for Carlos on occasion. He had a dark, beautiful young daughter, with whom I was infatuated. This went nowhere, as she spoke not a word of English...but one day she was walking down the pier behind the resort, and opened her shirt for a long moment. She didn't see me until too late, and so I got flashed by the most perfect little milk-chocolate breasts I think I have ever seen. I feared she would be embarrassed (she did blush), but she only smiled at me as we passed each other.

There were a number of Americans who spoke fluent Spanish, married *Ticas* or Indians, and settled in the jungle to garden and raise beautiful children. I could see the sense to this, but I wasn't ready to swallow the anchor—I had a world yet to see.

In the end, Carlos and I parted on less than great terms, but I had enough money to get out of that place, and to get some badly needed work done on the *Hornpipe*.

In addition to her many qualities enumerated previously, Cyndee was an expert varnisher too. She spent weeks that summer preening the *Hornpipe's* long-neglected woodwork. In July, Cyndee met and fell in love with Marcus Rizzardini, the handsome captain of *Unlikely VII*. On July 25th, she told me of her decision to accept Marcus' invitation to sail around the world with him, as paid crew—the proverbial "better offer." I felt panic-stricken—but I knew it was the right thing for her. [We have stayed in touch for many years, and I know they had a wonderful trip, got married, bought a farm in Oregon and raised a family.] I have a photograph (at the end of this Voyage) showing Cyndee with all her possessions in *Gandy Dancer*, about to carry them to her new home aboard *Unlikely VII*. [Years later, in Key West, I would meet Reese Paley, the owner of *Unlikely VII*, and read his wonderful books on cruising.]

In September, *Fishers Hornpipe* finally got her long-awaited haulout, at the Cooperativa Boatyard in Punta Arenas.

Reuel, Personal Log:

Sitting on the marine railway at Cooperativa Boatyard *on the edge of "lovely" downtown Puntarenas. Two nights up on this rickety old car with a cracked diagonal girder on the starboard side. Many hassles—usual haulout-time bummers. Mosquitoes bite all night long here—voracious mother fucking scourge-of-the-earth bastards. Even smoke coils don't hold them off. Carlos lied to the lovely 22-year-old woman, Haiti, who runs the yard, about us not needing yard labor—hence she is very pissed off at me.* [This was a typical thing for Carlos to do.] *I am anxious to go. Hope to leave at noon this Friday.*

Crew came together, typically, at the last minute. I met Tage With (pronounced Tayah Vitt), a twenty-nine-year-old Danish man who was finishing a job for Plumrose meat-packing company in Costa Rica and wanted to try some cruising. I had also received a letter from a 17-year-old man, Paul Newman, in Rockland County, New York, and after a small amount of correspondence he joined me. Paul had been romantically involved with Valerie—youngest daughter of the Feuers (close, old friends from New York) and he had been following my trip through my letters to them. Paul flew into San Jose, found his way down to the coast, and tracked me down in a waterfront bar eating a *hamburguesa* and drinking beer—all without speaking a word of Spanish.

Paul took to sailing instinctively, and soon became first mate, if there was such a thing on *Fishers Hornpipe*, and hence my right hand. He was a "larger-than-life" young man, and he felt stifled in his too-restricted life in suburbia and high school. He needed adventure—and adventure needed him! Looking back on my own high school years, I think it is criminal to take vibrant, hormone-intoxicated young human animals and lock them up inside stagnant prison cells masquerading as schools—let 'em all out! Let 'em live! They will learn more in the School of Life. (Leave the classroom doors open—they'll go back in when they're ready.)

On the morning of Sept 14th, we finally weighed anchor and sailed out of Golfo de Nicoya. We island-hopped our way down the coast to Golfo Dulce, Costa Rica, where we kicked around for a week or so cruising the Gulf. We stopped at several small farms, called *fincas*, and hiked up a remote jungle river to a magnificent waterfall (more about this shortly).

From Punta Arenas to Golfito (and Golfo Dulce) we had Tage's 19-year-old Costa Rican girlfriend, Rosie, with us too. She was able to take two weeks off from school to make the trip—altogether an unusual experience for a young *Tica*. Because I was the "chaperone," I had to go and meet her parents—a very uncomfortable experience (which perhaps influenced a dream I had later).

I knew Tage was having sex with Rosie—and I knew what that meant in a Catholic, Hispanic country. Although she neither spoke nor understood a word of English, she fell in love with my ancient Roy Orbison tape, and made me play it over and over. Rosie virtually swooned over *Running Scared*. She was head-over-heels in love with Tage, who was obviously her first lover. I felt bad for her, because Tage had told me that she was just a "plaything" to him. He knew he would never see her again, and this trip was simply his idea of a goodbye present. She had hoped for a ring....

The island we hopped on our way to Golfito was Isla del Caño—a remote, deserted paradise—off which we anchored for two days. At dawn on 9/15, we were beating to weather in ever-increasing

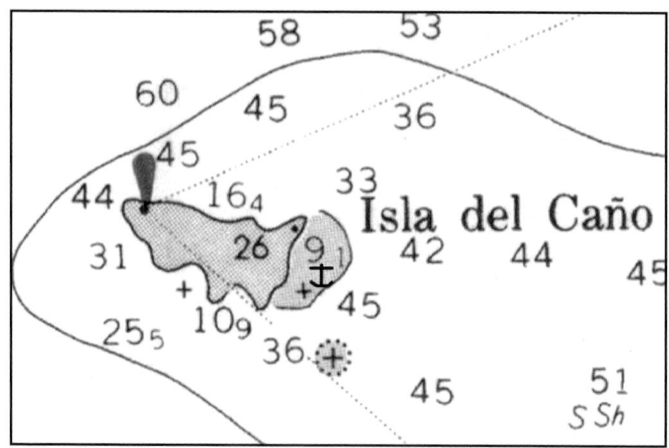

Isla del Caño.

winds. At 0730, the formal log states that a school of dolphins escorted us away from the reef off Isla del Caño, by repeatedly swimming in front of us and sharply turning to one side. I know this will sound incredulous to many readers who are unfamiliar with dolphins; and I also know that the blue-water sailors reading this will perhaps smile and remember similar experiences. Without the dolphins we would very likely have sailed right onto the reef.

Reuel, Personal Log, 9/16:

Second day anchored off Isla del Caño. Had to motor almost entire way. Hove-to late at night for a few hours waiting for dawn (sighted the island in the dark—afraid to come closer). Had a dream that Caño was a large New Jerseyish waterfront island with a large navy base and mothball fleet—rows of old decaying ships. Met a pretty young woman and fell in tingling lust—went to tell her mother she was coming with us—very upset she was. This girl petit but sturdy, very small breasts with large delicious nipples—exuding tomboy sensuality. Last thing I remember is her mother in the next room upset over the prospect of losing her daughter, and this girl and me teasing eachother mercilessly and me saying "let's go make love," and her saying "yes...." Then I woke up, of course. Vivid dream—I even remember the funky yellow-painted walls and blue window trim.

A breeze came up and I woke up Paul and we got up the genny and the breeze became wind and kept on increasing. Fishers Hornpipe *laid over and took off over the Pacific swell. Single reefed, then double reefed the mains'l, left genny up. Put rail under and kept it there. Wind about 30k with gusts maybe as high as 40k. Never saw wind here before! Delicious—but of course it was a southerly—dead on the nose. Tacked over to Caño and anchored inside the reef* [thanks to the dolphins!]—*but as we did, a short steep sea got all mixed up with the westerly swell and we got the shit pounded out of us. Paul and Tage enjoyed the sail much—Rosie hid in the foc's'le and wouldn't come aft where the ride was comfortable. Shook loose all the shit that wasn't tied down—above and below deck—but didn't break anything. NE end of Caño fraught with rocks & shoals—fair swell at times and not at others.*

Finally relaxing from tension of getting everything together and heading out with green crew—and barometer falling on first day out had me on pins and needles—although I didn't say much about it, I was worried about a "tropical disturbance." Not likely this far south, but.... Going skin diving today—then head for Golfito.

1600 hrs. Great day skin-diving & hiking & doing laundry in a crystal-clear stream, drying our clothes on the shrubs, native-style. Rowing out with clean dry laundry through the surf, a big one broke over us and put some salt back in everything. Got another bucket of shrimp (a gift this time) from a passing shrimp boat. Discovered a rock not ten feet below the surface where we are anchored in 40 feet of water! Can see the Nylon rodes all the way down to where the chain connects.

Multi-colored fish in the rocky submarine canyons. Couldn't find any lobster, but they're here—saw one carcass. Paul & I hiked a quarter mile or so up our laundry streambed through the jungle—beautiful, green and wet. Mosquitoes.

Will leave this evening and head south. First, a soup of vegetables & shrimp, a salad, and fried shrimp!

We arrived in Golfito on the afternoon of Sept 17th. We had a nice sail in, until the wind died, and we anchored with some difficulty in very deep water near *Zephros*, with whom we had planned to rendezvous.

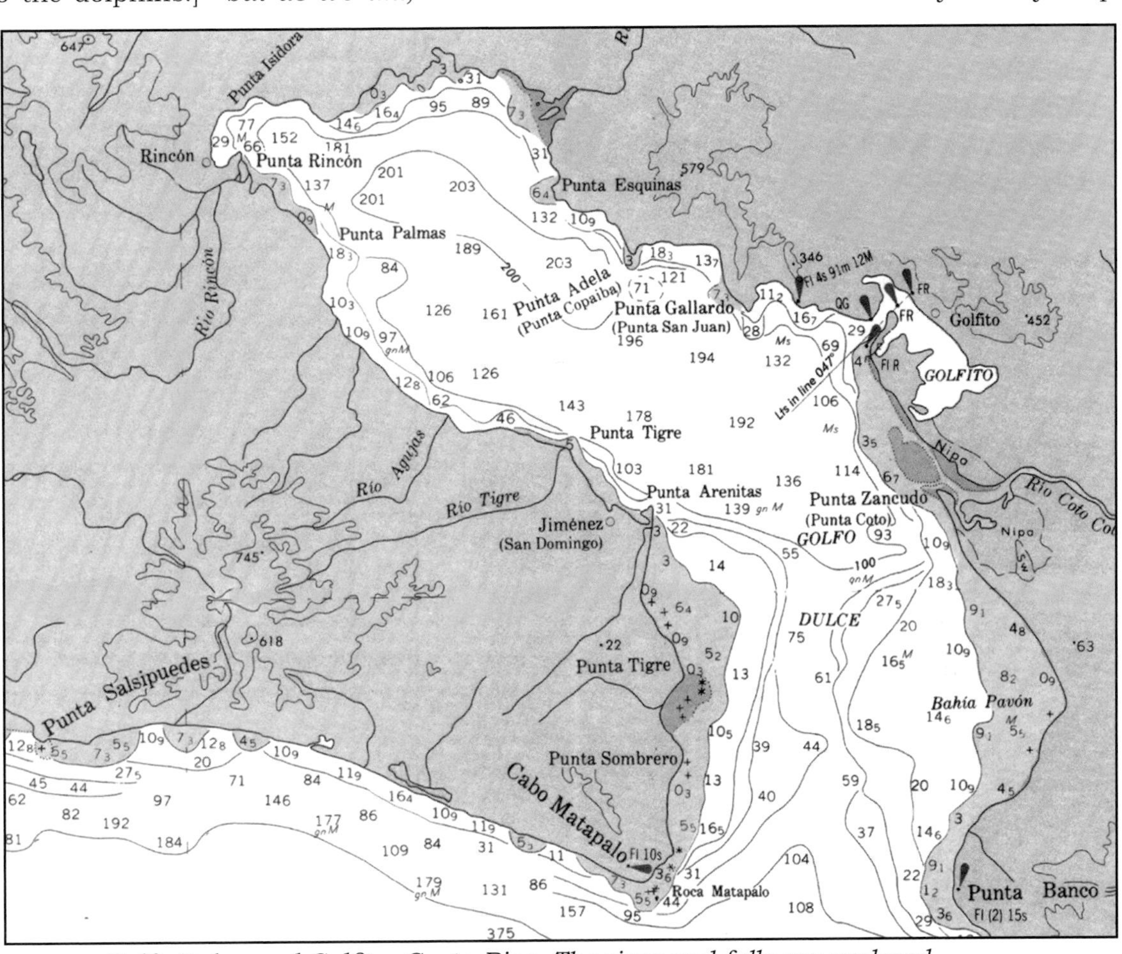

Golfo Dulce and Golfito, Costa Rica. The river and falls we explored are just above Punta Esquinas.

The village at Golfito was small and charming, and Tarey Lea (from *Zephros*) showed me around. The harbor was a banana-shipping port, and both Tarey Lea and Steve had lived and worked there to earn money to return to Key West. Steve built *Zephros* of ferrocement, and got a job near Golfito as a foreman building ferrocement barges. Tarey Lea painted beautiful signs for several of the local businesses. Steve and Tarey Lea were to become some of my closest friends, and we often sailed in company or met each other in different ports.

On the 19th we sailed to nearby Golfo Dulce, where we spent a couple of days exploring the pristine jungle. We met several Americans who bought land in Golfo Dulce, and retired there, creating small subsistence farms. We anchored off Lit and Lil's place—a perfect example—with a stern line tied to a palm tree (see photos). When we left, they loaded us with many fruits and vegetables.

Another friend we had met in Costa Rica, Joe, bought a *finca* (farm) the previous year for almost nothing—and we anchored nearby on the 20th and hiked way back into the jungle, where we followed a stream to a beautiful waterfall. We hiked up the rocks alongside the falls, and soon realized that we were in a place so quiet and remote that perhaps no white people had ever been there before—a true wilderness. One might literally hike up that waterfall for days—even weeks—before finding any sign of human habitation. The nearest road, or village, or jungle camp, might be many miles up beyond the coastal mountains somewhere in the distant interior. (See photo.)

Paul's *Journal of Travel*:

After walking two miles along jungle paths, we heard the roar of falling water. It surprised me, for the stream wasn't fast-running, but the waterfall was tremendous. The first drop was of sixty feet. From the base we could see two smaller falls above, each dropping maybe ten feet. Rounding the bend, the falls continued upward out of sight. I immediately took to the ascent.

The jungle around the falls was steep and dense, making it hard to find a way on the side. I also found that the stones that the water continually beat down upon were secure, while the ones off to the side were dangerous as hand- or foot-holds. This meant that I had to climb up through the water with my camera. All for the sake of being nuts.

Upon reaching the top of the first drop, I discovered the waterfall climbed on around each bend as far as the eye could see. I waved goodbye to the people below and yelled an inaudible "see you later" and didn't reappear for some two hours.

I spent a good part of that day on that mountain, going deeper into jungle where the only inhabitants are fifteen-foot boas, jaguars and such. [This was true.] *The terrain became less and less inclined, and the stream became wide and shallow. The sound of swiftly rushing water was replaced by the sounds of the jungle as I made my way up the now quietly-flowing stream. The sun fell soft, being filtered by the many canopies of growth. All was tranquil.*

There I found a feeling of enchantment. I felt an emotion that can only be found through direct experience. It was as if I had reached some other world in thought. I sat there for a long time, on a rock in the stream, thinking nothing in particular, very comfortably observing the world around me. This feeling would come again, but never in the same way. Very few people had sat where I was sitting. Maybe none. Joe or Mo hadn't climbed the falls. Why should I think any native might? People are usually too wrapped up in survival to appreciate the beauty around them. No, very few had been here. I was soaked to the bone. My only joint was un-smokable but also un-needed. My mind was altered by a sense of magic. I felt that nothing could enhance it... but it could end. The skies were clouding over. The soft light turned dark, and reality returned with the afternoon rain.

On 9/25 we anchored with *Zephros* and *Starbuck* off Captain Tom's place—an American expatriate who had sailed into Golfito many years ago, married a *Tica* and went totally native—and signed his famous guest book. There must have been a dozen naked little children running around—all his.

The sail the rest of the way down the coast to Panama was a little rough at times. There seemed to either be no wind, or lots of wind on the nose, until the early morning hours of 9/26, when we headed for the north end of Isla Coiba with a sweet following breeze that saw us flying wing-and-wing all day. We anchored at 1440 in the bay east of Punta Baltasar, carefully picking our way among the many rocks there. We left on the morning of 9/28, and got hit right away by a series of white squalls, interspersed with calms. Just past midnight we were abeam of Punta Naranjas, with no wind, but by shortly after dawn we were running off again with a good westerly breeze. The wind began to back after noon, and the barometer fell, but by late afternoon we were motoring again—frustrating. At 0335 on 9/30 we hove to in heavy rain to wait for the dawn. The Log states *wind moaning in rigging and deck pipes has taken the voice of a ghost whose message I cannot understand—brutal thundershowers and squalls—zero visibility.* By the light of dawn, when I scanned the distant horizon, the land that I could see was in the wrong place. I drew a sketch of what I could see (a practice I used frequently), and took magnetic bearings with my hand-compass. Then I compared my sketch and bearings to the chart, to see where the hell we could be. The Log states *hopefully headed to Ensa Playa Grande* in the Las Perlas group, and as fate was kind, we anchored there that afternoon.

[I contemplated removing all the weather data from the above paragraph, but decided to leave it to illustrate how stressful and difficult coastal navigation can be.]

The islands we visited along the Panamanian coast were beautiful and mostly deserted. We washed our laundry and bathed in fresh-water streams and waterfalls, and occasionally traded with shrimp boats for buckets of fresh shrimp. The coastal fishermen and shrimpers craved 22-caliber bullets and Playboy Magazines, both of which seemed like the wrong things to give them.

They also accepted T-shirts and old blue-jeans. We caught one delicious 8-pound dorado on a hand line, but by and large had poor luck fishing.

The Las Perlas Islands, in the Gulf of Panama, were the most beautiful I had ever seen, and the black people who lived there were warm and friendly. Miles of white beaches, coconut- and banana-covered islands, and of course, *Panama Red.* A native was along side in his cayuga before our anchor had set at Ensenada Honda, Isla Pedro Gonzales, offering any quantity of the stuff for twenty-five bucks a *pound.* When we just stared at him, dumbfounded, he said "OK, for you, twenty." Not yet knowing how loose things were, we refused to buy any—It just wasn't worth the risk. But the smiling native grabbed a big handful of the sweet herb and dumped it on deck, saying "You try it, you like it." Paul's eyes bulged out of his head. Throughout Panama, people were always giving us small quantities of the stuff—enough to enjoy and get rid of before entering civilization. We saw other cruising sailboats which had arrived in Islas Las Perlas months or years earlier, with long beards of marine growth hanging from their hulls. They anchored, discovered Eden, got very stoned and never left! You could live there on coconuts, bananas, fish and Panama Red for the rest of your life—on the most beautiful beaches on Earth.

Paul's *Journal of Travel*:

Anchored at the far side of the [bay] *was another yacht. We went and found the owner, a Frenchman named Michael, aboard with his wife and family. Michael had built his yacht, a forty-foot cutter, in France, and had sailed to Antigua where he met his mate, Roger. Roger was the only person who spoke English, and had to translate our conversation.*

We sat on deck and had tea and coconuts, smoking the local crop. We spent much of the day talking. It seemed they had nearly run out of money and almost had no stores left. They were living at the moment on any fish they could shoot and whatever else is free, such as coconuts and bananas. Michael's wife had a bandage wrapped around her head, and Roger explained that she had taken a bad fall. Reuel, who is trained in paramedics, looked at the wound. It seemed quite bad, so he advised her to see a doctor as soon as possible. 'Til then, Reuel had pills on the boat to help her with the pain. We invited them all to come to dinner....

That night we feasted. We dined on lobster dipped in butter and vegetarian spaghetti. Michael's children were especially delighted by Reuel's peanut butter cookies. These two boys, being only 6 and 8, were very mature kids. They didn't seem to complain or whine, and didn't ask to be taken home when they got tired. They slept 'til 3 o'clock on deck. I guess growing up on a boat, [kids] *mature faster in many ways.... We had a really good evening, and by the end of the night, we were all rather wasted. Roger had stopped translating earlier, but when it got so he no longer understood what Michael was saying, we knew that we were all rather far gone.*

One boat [we met a few days later] *was especially beautiful, and had a warm, comfortable feeling about her. On this boat lived a young couple—Pierre and Nala. They had been traveling for years, and they pick up what little money they need to live on. Pierre is a talented craftsman. When I met him he was working on a sculpture done in black coral. This he was to sell for one hundred dollars. The money would last them for one month, the time it would take them to sail to the South Pacific, their next destination. We spent a lot of time with these people and grew to enjoy them very much. We had many pleasant evenings out on their boat.*

These people made me think of how well I live and how great it is that I know that if I ever really need money, I can have it sent from home. The money I spent for myself in one month would have lasted Michael and his whole family for that much time. The last of their money would go for stores to reach the South Pacific. It must be a lot for Michael to support the family while traveling. I hope everything turns out for the better, and that they've reached the South Seas without too much hardship.

The other places we visited in Islas Las Perlas were Isla Bayoneta, for its perfect deserted beach, and Isla Contadora, which had a good anchorage. At one island (I wish I could remember which), we swam and dove with dozens of large rays—many with wing-spans of five or six feet—who were so unconcerned about us that we could reach out and touch them! The water was crystal clear, and it was like floating among living, flying clouds.

On October 4th we sailed from Islas Las Perlas to enter Balboa, on the Pacific side of the Panama Canal. As we came in, wind and seas were steadily increasing to such a degree that the designated anchorages were untenable. Violent seas raised by the strong seasonal SW winds were actually breaking in the anchorage off the Balboa Yacht Club, where they broke moorings and battered boats. We tried to anchor off the Yacht Club when we came in, but were told by Canal officials to move out to the mandatory Flamenco Island anchorage (an open roadstead) because the Club was closed on the weekend.

On October 4th we sailed from Islas Las Perlas to enter Balboa, on the Pacific side of the Panama Canal. As we came in, wind and seas were steadily increasing to such a degree that the designated anchorages were untenable. Violent

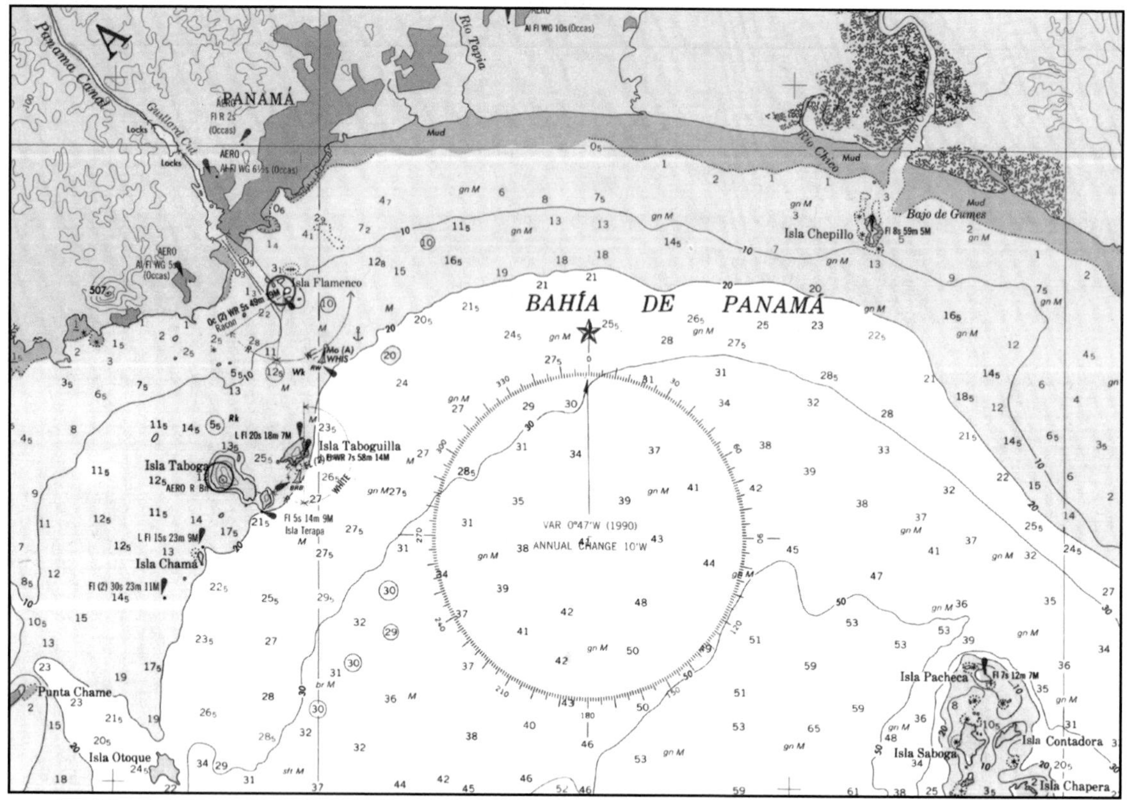

Bahia de Panama. Las Perlas Islands (lower right) to Canal Entrance (upper left)

seas raised by the strong seasonal SW winds were actually breaking in the anchorage off the Balboa Yacht Club, where they broke moorings and battered boats. We tried to anchor off the Yacht Club when we came in, but were told by Canal officials to move out to the mandatory Flamenco Island anchorage (an open roadstead) because the Club was closed on the weekend.

We got more than the usual bureaucratic runaround, had to anchor *eight times*, and sustained quite a lot of minor damage. Back in the Flamenco Island anchorage, in breaking seas, we parted our 5/8" nylon anchor snubber (the lizard), ran backwards over *Gandy Dancer's* painter, broke her transom, and beat up *Fishers Hornpipe's* paint work while trying to get off the lee shore. Paul dove into the breaking seas with a knife in his teeth to free our propeller, saving us from becoming a shipwreck—we were in ten-foot breaking seas and 25- to 30-knot winds, scant feet from going on the rocks. For feats such as this (and there were many), Tarey Lea gave Paul the nickname *Wonder Boy*. I even broke my best mixing bowl (it jumped right off the counter).

Finally, after arguing vehemently with Canal officials on the VHF radio, they allowed us to return to anchor near the Yacht Club. We anchored where we were instructed to, only to have the *Hornpipe's* keel pound on a hard sand bar at low tide, which damaged her rudder bearings and steering arm (I was able to repair this the next day). Canal officials normally insist on boarding yachts in the roadstead off Flamenco Island, which was impossible under those conditions. We waited for more than two days for a boarding officer. During the past year my opinion of bureaucracy and officialdom has declined, if those of you who know me can imagine such a thing.

Our transit through the Canal on 10/9 was an awesome experience. Friends from *Indian Princess* transited the canal with us as line-handlers (four are required by Canal Regulations), so we had to reciprocate the next day as line-handlers on their transit. We went through the huge lock systems side-tied to an ocean-going tugboat—standard procedure. We motor-sailed (all possible speed was essential) across Gatun Lake, and our pilot (Advisor McFarlin) looked the other way while we hauled buckets of fresh water on deck, stripped and bathed. On the Caribbean side of the canal, we anchored *Fishers Hornpipe* in the flats off Cristobal and took the train back across to Balboa to grab a few hours of sleep in that miserable hell-hole (it was still blowing) before the transit on *Indian Princess*. I left Paul behind to hold down the fort.

Paul's *Journal of Travel*:

Few people realize what, in fact, the Panama Canal really is. It is an engineer's marvel, stamped with concrete and steel into the earth. Connecting two massive bodies of water, the whole thing will probably last as long as the surface of the earth. Ships of all kinds use these waterways, and at any given time you can find dozens of these monstrous vessels going through the locks or steaming across the man-made Gatun Lake. There are two sets of locks on each end, each with three levels. The Lake's 163 square miles was created by the making of the canal. What was a valley is now a lake. What were mountaintops before, now sit as islands. 211 million cubic yards of earth was moved to build the locks and the dam on the Atlantic side alone. The Panama Canal Company takes in thousands of dollars for each ship, depending on tonnage and length. For this reason, small yachts are considered an annoyance....

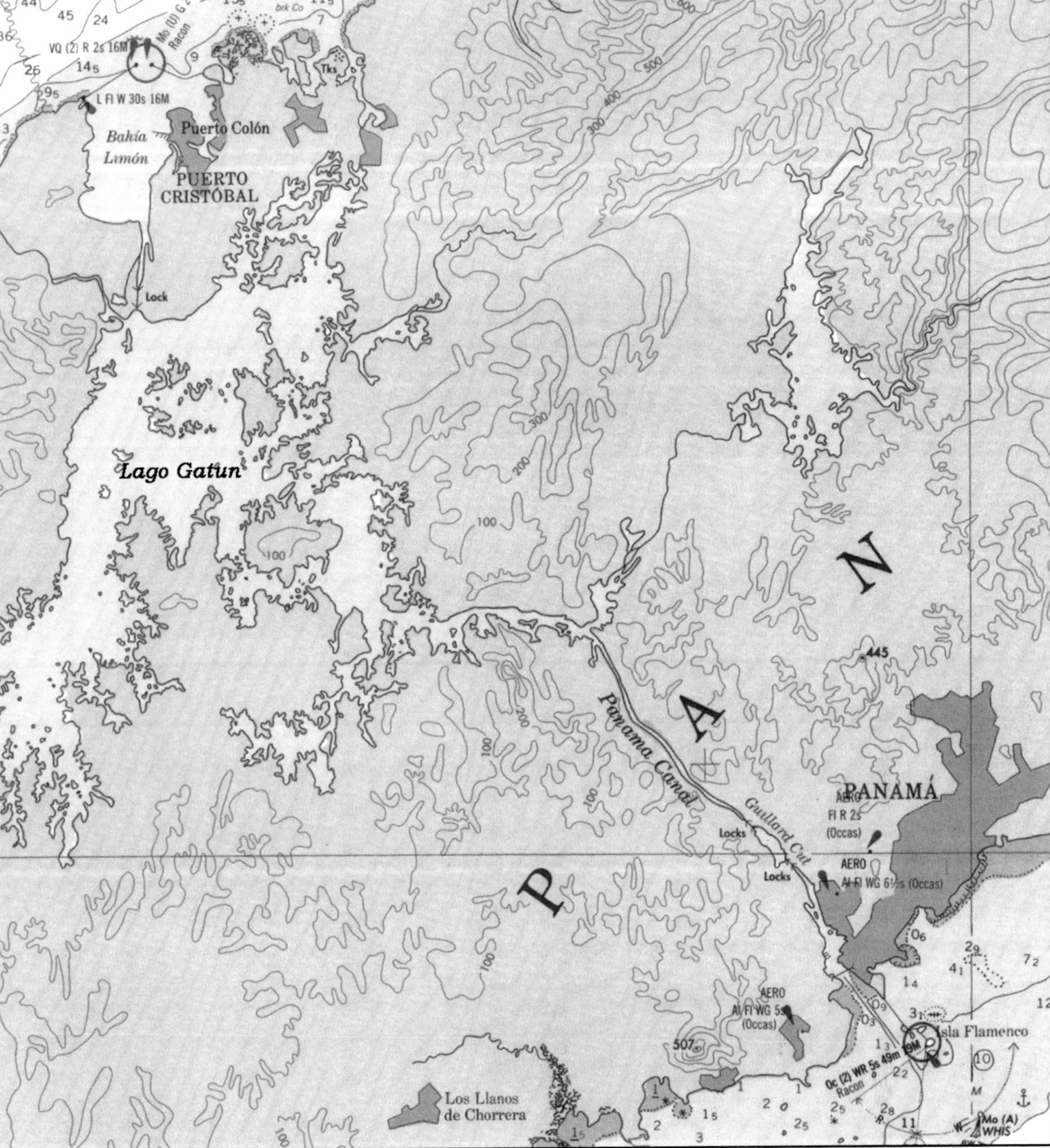

The Panama Canal.

We found many old friends in Cristobal, but I was disappointed to not find even one letter from my stateside friends or family. (I did get one letter in Balboa from Jim Schaefer.) Time and space do take their toll. I hoped they were all living such full and happy lives that they simply didn't have time to write! We found some new friends also—the Personal Log mentions Nadine and Eva, who came to dinner one night. In Cristobal we also took on a fourth crew: Anne Bertrand, a 29-year-old French woman who had been bumming around the Caribbean and South America for the last couple of years.

We had met our first French cruising boats in Islas Las Perlas, and met many more in the Caribbean. Most were on their way to the South Pacific. I must say that of all the new people on cruising boats I met on my first voyage, I have enjoyed the French ones the most. French sailors are sensitive, creative, funny and refined—though usually very poor, as Paul's *Journal* indicated above. They avoid bureaucratic paperwork and fees with great skill. Their boats are simple, seaworthy and beautiful, full of love and art and the best music and cats and garlic and hash pipes and rich old fabrics. We have shared many fine meals and parties. And I love the way French sailors dress: During the day, away from civilization, they don't—same as us American hippy sailors. When social etiquette deems it necessary—as in a first introduction—the men might don shorts. And at night, for dinner, the women wrap themselves artfully and charmingly in a single piece of colorful fabric—much more erotic than nudity—as guests see innocent yet teasing glimpses of the wonderful body parts that "straight" society deems be hidden from view.

On Dec 14th we took a slip at the Panama Yacht Club for four days to get the boat together, make repairs and load supplies. Colon is a fascinating but blood-chilling town. We wandered around it in as much as we dared, including one night with Rob—our friend and part-time resident who gave the distracted lecture back in Carlos' resort. Rob took us out to a very good Chinese restaurant. He carried a riot gas cartridge in his right hand at all times on the street. Lest anyone get the wrong impression of Panama: the problems are in the cities. In the country we were treated as guests, and often invited into homes and given food and drink and gifts.

As an interesting footnote I should add that while in Panama City one time, three men knocked Tage into the street, and with razor blades deftly removed and took his pants and money belt, which contained three hundred dollars and all his papers. He wandered into a back yard, covering his genitals with his hands (they took even his underwear), where he encountered a kind woman taking in her laundry, who gave him an old pair of pants.

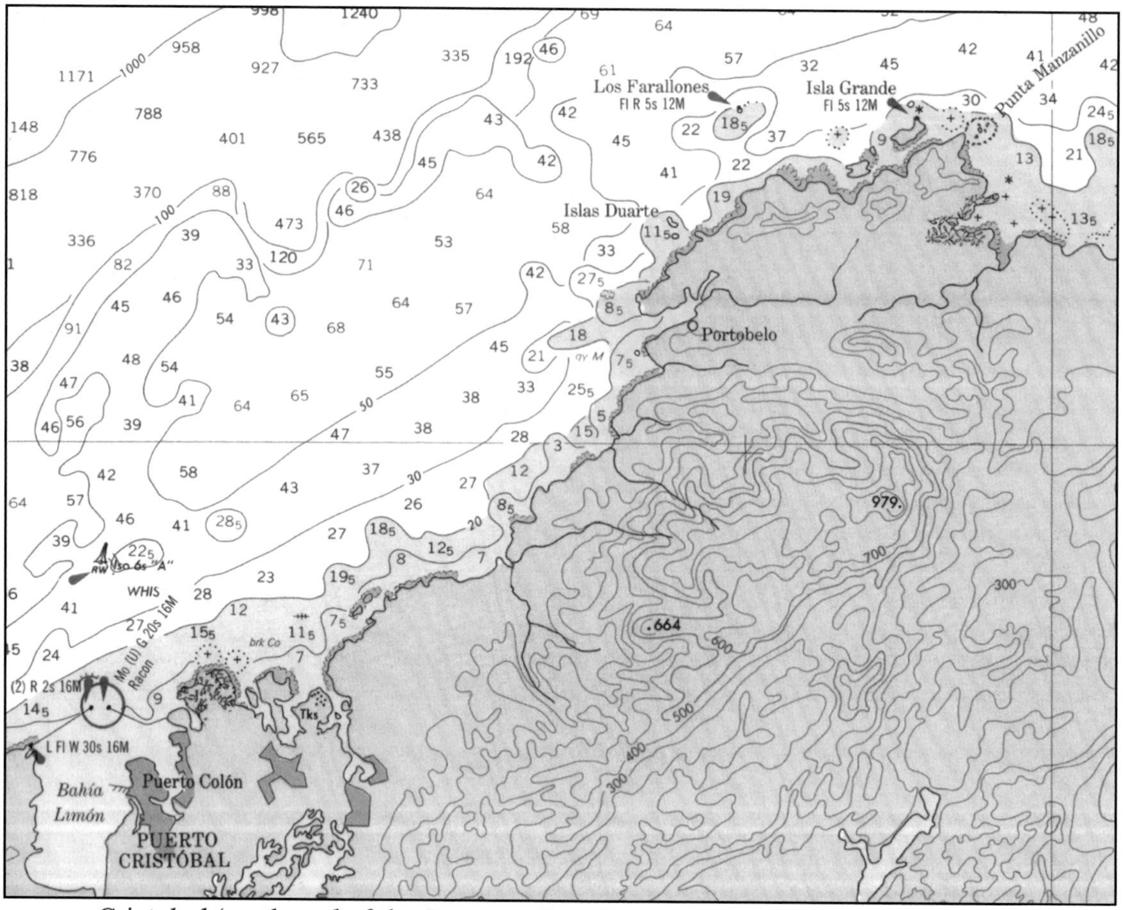

Cristobal (north end of the Panama Canal), to Portobelo and Isla Grande.

Another interesting footnote is that I was asked, on several occasions, to pack the *Hornpipe's* large hull full of drugs, run straight up to the US, and meet a vessel off the coast. *One trip* would make me a wealthy man. Very tempting.... I declined, of course—*Fishers Hornpipe* was my only home, and there was no way I would risk her, or my own freedom (or that of any willing crewmembers) for mere physical wealth.

While in Colon I met a professional smuggler who worked (at times) for the rock star David Crosby. He told me this wonderful story about breakfast one morning in Crosby's house: David emerged from his bedroom with a beautiful young woman. He announced to the table (I guess it must have been quite a scene, with many people there), "Hey, you all *have* to hear this woman sing..." And she did. It was Joni Mitchell, before anyone knew who she was.

* * *

Our provisioning and repairs completed, we left for Portobelo on Oct 19th. In addition to our crew of four, we brought with us two nautical hitchhikers: a 34-year-old Frenchman, Jean-Paul, and his 30-year-old Venezuelan woman-partner, Silda (see photo). This gave us an international crew of six. Silda and Jean-Paul were delightful people, but not accustomed to the regimens and demands of life on the water, which made things a little awkward at times. Their unique personalities, however, made up for any lack elsewhere.

Paul, *Journal of Travel*:

We met Jean-Paul and Silda through [the French] *boats. Jean-Paul is a Frenchman who, while in California a few years ago, bought a milk truck and has been traveling in it ever since. He met Silda, a Venezuelan, in Mexico City. He had to sell the milk truck because the only way to get a car or truck to South America is by freighter. There is no road, and the freighter costs too much.*

They were sort of a ying and yang. [Jean-Paul] *is the kind of person who didn't like to forsee the future and was not very organized.* [Silda] *totally had everything together.* [She] *helped out tremendously on the boat, while Jean-Paul, though trying to help, always left some kind of a mess behind. I grew very fond of these two very fast. It was hard to say goodbye when it was time to go our separate ways in this enormous world.*

When we met her, Anne [Bertrand] *was staying on one of the French boats waiting to go through the Canal. The people on these boats are all very down-to-earth travelers. They did all the work on their own boats. They lived very simply and had none of the modern conveniences on most yachts.*

Anne was always cold. She never really opened up. I never met anyone who traveled the way she does and still be so closed. She refused to see anything except what pleased her. I think of this as not seeing the full reality, but sometimes, when the ugliness surrounds me, I wish I could see the way Anne sees.

It struck me as strange at first—the rate at which friends are made when you travel. I don't mean just acquaintances, but real friends. People who, years later if you appeared, say in Paris, at their front stoop, they would make you at home. Real friends are hard to come by and I don't mean everyone you meet and even live with for a while is a very close friend. At home it takes much longer to really know somebody. I think that maybe securities at home are tighter so people are more apt to be cautious with strangers. Not as open. Life cruising is very demanding so it seems important to get to know somebody. I don't mean even to like them, just to open up to know them. When you sail with somebody, there usually is a spirit of working together, and playing. In the open sea there are many life and death situations, and it can be crucial to know what can be done with people as a team. Also, people who choose a life of travel usually are rather out-going. It makes life much easier when people can open up to eachother.

Newsletter, Oct 22, 1980:

Last night was the last of The Festival of the Black Christ *in Portobelo. We stayed for much of it, although I couldn't make it through another night of dancing 'til dawn. We were in the church when the magnificent life-size black Jesus and His cross were lifted up by many bearers and slowly paraded, a few steps forward, a few steps back, through the town, and we were there when He returned. We were packed in like sardines, sometimes being held upright by the sheer press of hot, sweaty human bodies. We were among large throngs of worshippers, some of whom had walked the Los Cruxis Trail for days, many in purple robes and with shaved heads. Our white faces shone oddly among the thousands of black ones, reflecting the light from candles and magnificent fireworks.*

We were told the Black Christ statue was shipwrecked here on its way from Europe to the Vicar of Peru centuries ago. There was a terrible plague at that time, and a handful of survivors waded out into the sea to salvage the wreck. They found the magnificent sculpture and dragged it ashore, and thereby ended the plague on the people. The sad eyes of the Black Christ showed, to me, the centuries of degradation and suffering of black people everywhere. His journey, the thousands of black people who traveled to Portobelo for this occasion, symbolized to me the birth of the age of the black man, of all third world people, at long painful last on the threshold of their inheritance of the Earth. Among these people—their sweat and smiles and handshakes and music and honest ways and the strength of their blood, I knew that Earth cannot help but be safer in their hands than it has been at the ineffective false-mercy and unflagging greed of the white man.

Portobelo represented the epitome of greed and cruelty of the Spanish Empire. It was here that stolen gold and silver were brought to be loaded aboard the Spanish treasure fleets bound for Spain—it was here where death and disease and murder ran rampant. Thousands of natives and slaves died on the Los Cruxis trail carrying Spanish plunder. Sir Francis Drake died here of dysentery in 1596. Henry Morgan raided Portobello in 1699, as did many other pirate and buccaneer fleets. The quantities of precious metals that passed through this port are legendary—every scoundrel on Earth had to have a crack at it.

One of the women I had met in Panama came to see the festival, and to stay with me on the *Hornpipe* for a couple of days. She was English, and had left her abusive husband in the Canal Zone. He had sailed on into the Pacific without her, leaving her with little more than the clothes on her back. I don't remember what her plans were, exactly, but they didn't include anymore cruising—at least for a while. She struck me as a very gentle soul, and I hope wherever she is in the world, that she is doing well.

The morning after the festival, I had to go ashore to search for half of my crew. I found them passed out in hammocks in the villager's huts! The kind and generous people of Portobelo had slept on the ground so that their unexpected guests would be as comfortable as possible. It took us a while to get it together to leave.

Moss grows on the undersides of the huge rusty Spanish cannons in the crumbling ruins of the fortress of Portobelo. Flowers and grass and huge land crabs and cow-shit have taken over the garrisons which fought the ancient battles. The walls reek with history (see photos). But it came time to leave.

On November 22nd we rode the Northeast tradewind out of the beautiful bay which Columbus first visited in 1501.

* * *

Our next stop was at an island group

centered around Isla Grande; we anchored behind Isla Juan Joaquin. Friends on several other boats joined us there, and we had a good party on the night of 23rd. Several of us dropped acid (I think it was the last of my Owlsly *Windowpane*)—which I had brought with me from California—and I remember Paul and several friends from other boats talking, lying on their backs. One of them was gazing up, and said "Wow, the stars are really incredible tonight," to which Paul replied "Oh man, I hate to tell you this, but you're looking at the underside of the awning...."

Newsletter, Oct 23, 1980:

Listening to Miles Davis' Bitches Brew *to candles and lamplight on deck. Just had another feast with friends from* Tangerine *and* Windbourne. *Today's divers came back with a dozen small lobsters, a few huge crabs and three pink fish, which I cooked with tomatoes and spices and onions and garlic and yucca, etc. into a chioppino. Klem brought two bottles of rum which made alternately Pina Coladas (fresh young coconut milk, pineapple juice, lime juice, cream and sugar and rum) and lime-rum punch. Also many pipes of Panama Red, and two spice cakes with orange icing (from Dennis). The sea water is as warm as the air—very comfortable tonight—making it easy to wash our naked bodies after dinner. Diving off the deck into dark crystal....*

On the 25th we sailed to Bahia Nombre de Dios, where we anchored between the river and the town. We went for a long walk through town—which was quiet and very neat—into the country, where we came to some farms. Local people there saw us, invited us into their courtyard and served us cold drinks. As always, the hospitality of the country people is the best.

My French crewmember Anne called October 26th "the day of catastrophes." We weighed anchor at 0630, and sailed out to beat into the trade winds toward the San Blas Islands. Foolishly, we forgot to check the boat before our departure, and someone had left the ports open in the foc's'le. Someone had their bed thoroughly soaked with sea water. Even the books on their shelves got wet. Here I should explain that once anything in a boat is inundated with salt water, it never dries out. The salt crystals continue to absorb moisture from the air, making a damp soggy mess that eventually leads to mold, fungus and rot. Salty, damp bedding is miserable to sleep in, and causes body sores that take forever to heal. Mattresses that get salt water on them must eventually be thrown away. Bedding and clothing must be thoroughly washed in fresh water, then carefully dried in the sun on a hot day with low-humidity. Hence I made a rule on board that crewmembers rinse off with a cup or two of fresh water and towel themselves dry before coming below decks, and leave salt-soaked clothing on deck or in the shower stall (immediately below the main companionway). I installed coat-hooks in the shower, and that is where we hung our foul-weather gear. At the foot of the main companionway I installed a teak grating, to allow dripping water to drain into the bilge.

We also foolishly made the mistake of towing *Gandy Dancer* instead of hauling her up under the stern-davits—sheer laziness or dumb optimism. The wind soon increased to over twenty knots, and the head seas gradually built to twelve feet. When I came on watch, I looked behind me to check on *Gandy*—and she was gone! We turned around and started a search—a good (wo)man-overboard drill—and found *Gandy* a couple of miles back, swamped with water, her painter parted. She was drifting toward some rocks, and we *just* got to her in time to tow her clear. It was a bitch bailing her out in those rough seas, and it was impossible to get her into the davits. We attached two lines to her and continued beating along the coast, motorsailing slowly to hold a course close to the wind, and (hopefully) safer for *Gandy*. Soon thereafter the wind died, and we had to motor. Shortly after that, a violent squall hit us, making us scramble to take down the genoa jib (which we had just put up), raise the yankee jib, and reef the mains'l. Several more squalls hit us—with calms between them—gusting to over 40-knots at times.

During this day, we saw our first two Columbian Copra Schooners—trading vessels that ply the coast and islands between Panama and Columbia. These vessels were long, low, with bald-headed rigs, often crudely-built, brightly painted and very romantic looking. One hailed us, but we stayed clear of her, having been told that they are often pirates. Indeed, we later learned that there had been a gunfight between a Columbian schooner and a Panamanian Costa Guardia (usually a very big outboard-powered cayuga, or dug-out canoe), in which several men had been killed.

At 1530 on 10/26, we came to anchor in the Chichime Cays. The Log entry says *Whew!*

Newsletter, November 3, 1980:

Islas San Blas: A yellow circle of sunlight drifts silently and very slowly across a bulkhead as Fishers Hornpipe *swings at her anchor. The circle lingers a moment on an old photograph—a girl with golden hair tumbling to her breasts. Her face, the colors, come alive, she smiles at me. The circle of sunlight reverses and drifts back from where it came.*

The San Blas Islands at last! Coral atolls, low

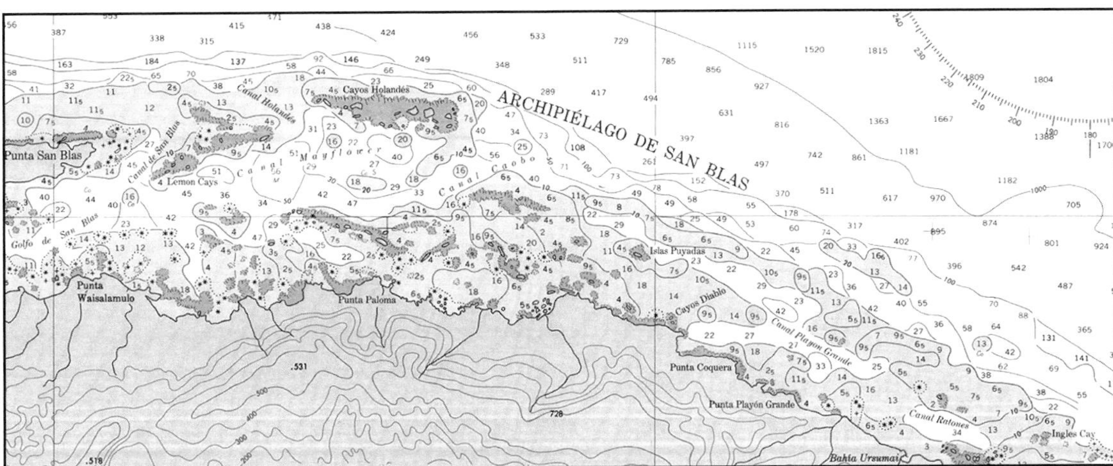

The San Blas Islands, home of the Kuna Indians. Porvenir is just off Punta San Blas. The Carti Islands are off Punta Waisalamulo. The Moron Cays, Pider Tupu, Ciedras, the Holandes Cays, Nargana and Tikantiki are to the east.

sandy islands, coconut palms, Kuna Indians. As isolated and naturally beautiful as this place is, and as integral as the Kuna race and society are, there is still a keen sense of commercialism among these people whose unit of exchange is no longer the coconut but the US dollar. Their molas, hand-sewn reverse-applique cloth panels, have found their way around the world; and their cash crop, coconuts and shredded dried coconut (copra), are exported all over the Caribbean, Central and South America. The Kunas still live in thatched huts with dirt floors, but one sees cassette players, electronic calculators, and French diving gear on the bamboo shelves.

On Oct 27th, we sailed over to the Carti Islands, where we were besieged by Kunas selling molas. We went ashore and met Jimmy—who took us to a tienda for a cold beer—and a private mola-buying visit. Molas are about 12x16-inches, and the Kuna people sew them onto their clothing (see photos). The applique subjects might be anything—birds, fish, flowers—I even saw one of a Grateful Dead icon. They cost anywhere from $5 to $25 at that time, and could often be sold to collectors and art galleries in Manhattan for $200. I only bought a few, as I had very little money. Some of the Kuna people were so aggressive about selling molas that they tied their cayugas alongside, boarded us and sat in the cockpit! This behavior violated my sense of privacy, and at one point I stayed below and refused to come out. This was a mistake, as my uninvited "guests" stole my rigging knife from the cockpit—evidently a rare incident. The only thing I learned in the Kuna tongue was "iggy maany""how much."

While we were ashore, we found some Kunas playing music and singing, and we made friends and hung out for a while. Jean-Paul and Silda were invited to stay ashore in a vacant house while awaiting a copra schooner to take them to Columbia, where they intended to spend the winter. The next morning they were back on board the *Hornpipe*, having been told by a village chief that foreigners were not allowed to stay on shore overnight.

On that same morning, 10/28, we were visited by the Panamanian Costa Guardia, who told us to go to Porvenir to have our papers checked. At 1130 we left to sail to Porvenier, and were met by another Costa Guardia en-route. This was a 30-foot cayuga (dugout canoe) with a big outboard motor and several armed soldiers. They boarded us, searched the boat, and placed an armed guard on board to make sure we went to Porvenir. The soldier—a mean little olive-colored man with little pig eyes—was very belligerent and kept waving his machine gun at me, shouting "Directo! Directo!" I was shitting bricks trying to explain that sailboats don't go "directo" anyplace directly upwind, which of course was where Porvenir was—especially when they are nearly out of diesel fuel! Silda finally calmed him down by enlisting his help making coconut drinking cups. What would diplomacy be in Hispanic countries without feminine wiles?

In Porvenir, the shit hit the fan big-time. It seems that allowing crewmembers ashore overnight was nearly punishable by death! And then Anne—typically French—had no Panamanian visa! How she got into the Canal Zone without one is beyond comprehension, so she invented—on the spot—this incredible story about being abandoned on a desert island by a jilted lover—captain of the boat she sailed across the Atlantic on. Improvising rapidly, she told how we had seen her as we sailed by, and gallantly came to her rescue! Voila—no visa! And you know what? *They bought it!!!* But not without hours of arguing and shouting in Spanish, Kuna, French, Danish and English! At one point the officials threatened to confiscate *Fishers Hornpipe* and throw all of us in a Panamanian prison to rot for the rest of our lives.

Just as we thought we had everything resolved and were hastily heading for the door, the Commandante said "Wait! You still have to pay your fines!" And the whole thing started over again—because we didn't have enough money!

In the end, they settled for kicking us out of the country. As we were (all six of us) packed into *Gandy Dancer*, rowing home across a shallow reef, we ran aground. Paul, always the first to react, jumped out of the dory to push—and landed right on the mother of all sea urchins! Screaming and howling in pain, we pulled him back into the boat, and somehow poled our way across the reef. Back on the *Hornpipe*, I tried to remove the spines from his feet, but they kept breaking off. All you can do is piss on the poor victim's feet—which neutralizes some of the toxins—and wait a week or two for the human body to dissolve and absorb the spines. The only consolation is having a pretty girl squatting over your foot, delivering "golden showers!"

After three days of incredible hassling, we finally escaped Porvenir for the Moron (pronounced Moh-rhon) Cays, only to find that the *Hornpipe's* Ship Documentation was missing. Fuck it—we left without it. [I found it later, mixed up with some other papers.]

The Moron Cays were deserted and very beautiful. We went diving on the most incredible reefs any of us had yet seen. I remember picking up a big sea fan that was dead—only to uncover a three-foot-long electric-blue moray eel that very nearly ate my hand for lunch.... I never did that again!

At dawn on the 31st a violent squall hit us, with winds above 40-knots. The plow anchor was down in coral marl—and I learned then and there that *you must always dive on your anchor and make sure it is set.* We dragged anchor to within ten-feet of the rocks...when the wind died.

On November 1st we sailed to Pider Tupu, where there was a hotel (it was closed), and we sailed on to Ciedras, where we bought some supplies. Later that same afternoon we sailed to Holandes Cays, where we anchored for the night, thence to the near-by Green Island group, where we were viciously attacked by hungry no-see-ums. Next morning we sailed to Nargana—also close by. The weather was *very* hot, especially when the wind ceased.

We sailed to Tikantiki on the 4th, still in the San Blas Islands, and rafted up to a Columbian copra schooner at the public landing, where we took on water and stores. Water was piped in from a steep mountainside on the mainland out to the island of Tikaniki through a miles-long bizarre network of pipes and hoses, supported by enormous scaffolds made of logs lashed together with vines. I added chlorine again.

The village was very pretty, and we learned that the Kuna Indians "alternate" in their living habitat. Some spend time in the lush hillsides on the mainland, farming and herding—then they trade places with other Indians and live in the islands, fishing and harvesting coconuts (and selling molas). All food and resources are exchanged freely between the mainland and the islands.

Paul, *Journal of Travel*:

The last few days spent in the San Blas were at the small island of Tikantiki. Here Anne had spent a number of weeks before arriving in Colon. She had lived with the family of one of the chieftains of the village [theoretically and legally impossible, as we had learned the hard way] *and was known throughout the island. As we stepped on to the land, all the children surrounded her, calling her name. She took us to the home of the chief, where we were greeted warmly. We spent more than three days there, and had more than one interesting dinner with our new Kuna friends. There I spent a lot of time being guided by some local kids through the village. I finally felt accepted enough on Tikantiki to bring my camera on shore and take pictures, something I had not done in previous villages.* (See photos.)

The Kunas are very proud and independent, and rigidly preserve their culture by not allowing outside influences among them. Marrying outside the tribe is forbidden, and is grounds for permanent banishment. Their hundreds of islands (Islas San Blas, also known as the Mulatto Archipelago) are spread throughout both Panama and Columbia, but the Kuna Tribes are an *intendencia*—an independent indigenous people—who only grudgingly accommodate officials from those two countries. Panama has its government seat at Porvenir, at the west end of the island group, and Columbia has its government post at the east end. The Kunas survived the Spanish depredations by playing invading pirates against them, guiding parties of raiders across the Isthmus of Panama, and by retreating deep into the jungle when necessary, where only they could survive. They have never been conquered. Their history is long and colorful.

We left Jean Paul and Silda in Tikantiki, where they caught a ride on the Columbian copra schooner we rafted up with. We were sad to part from them—we certainly had some great adventures together. Paul wrote in his *Journal*: *It was so sad to see them leave, but I feel that someday our paths will cross once more. I hope they carry their love to the ends of the earth.*

At 1015 on November 6th we weighed anchor and set our course north-west for Isla San Andres—300 miles away in the blue Caribbean Sea. Adios, Panama!

CHAPTER TEN—COLUMBIA TO KEY WEST

The sea, the isolating sea, confines one to one's own resources.

Richard Maury

Newsletter, Nov 11, 1980:

At anchor, St. Andrews Harbor, Isla San Andres, Columbia: The Caribbean. We arrived at San Andres two days ago after a robust and fast sail from the San Blas Islands in Panama. Fishers Hornpipe *is in her element: lots of wind and somewhat rough seas. Our twenty-four hour runs were 115 miles; an average speed of 5 knots, with some runs over 6 knots. Genoa flying most of the time in winds ten to twenty-five knots, on reaches most of the time. I'm thankful that Bob and Billy Henderson made the sails tough. Now they are just starting to show their 5,000 miles of hard use.*

Turquoise water, funky hotels, island mafia, unseen drug traffic, good restaurants, duty-free stores, corrupt officials, sewage stink in the city streets, sexy Columbian women, coconut palm-lined beaches, tourists, old churches, and down-island—the real people. San Andres. 300 miles north of the Panama Canal.

Paul and I rented a small motorcycle today on which we toured the island in the rain, running up dirt roads to farms and exploring the coast. Unfortunately we hit a pothole hidden in a puddle and dumped it—burning my leg pretty badly against the exhaust manifold. Tonight we have a party on Fishers Hornpipe *for some of our new friends here—I am cooking a huge Quiche and making sesame cookies.*

From here we go to Providencia, also a Columbian island, 50 miles North. Then through the Miskito Channel to Roatan and Honduras; then to Guatemala and Beliz and Cozumel and the Yucatan Pennisula, and finally to Key West. I decided against Swan Island as it would add many miles to the trip, and more expenses.

Nov 14—evening, compass heading 25 degrees, speed 5 knots, Tage on the helm, sky clear, wind Southeast 15 knots, barometer 31.00 steady. Beautiful sailing—beam reach, Fishers Hornpipe *trucking smooth and efficient and powerful. Dolphins weaving back and forth under the bowsprit clicking and squeaking their musical language. Half moon rising in clear black sky, spilling silver all over the sea. Main and genoa jib pulling powerfully.*

We weighed anchor from Haynes City just off San Andres at 1715 to start this night sail to Isla Providencia. Early the next morning winds fell a little lighter, but we continued to sail well. 0536: A black squall swept out of the night, bringing rain. Genny down/wait for dawn. 0640: Looking for Providencia. 0650: Land Ho! Hiding behind the clouds, high mountains in the clouds. We motored in as the wind died, winding along a beautiful green rocky coast with a lookout on the bowsprit. A man on the beach waved us further off—too shallow! Noon: Anchored in Catalina Harbor. Very beautiful island.

Zephros *was at anchor in the harbor, and we were very excited to be reunited after not seeing each other since Golfito, Costa Rica. Needless to say, a fine party ensued.*

Paul, *Journal of Travel*:

It was a twelve-hour passage to Providencia. This we made under the light of the moon. It was a little rough, but a fast, nice sail. We came in sight of Providencia in the mid-morning. The mist of white shoals parted to expose the jagged green peaks of this island. Providencia is a small island made up of the peaks of a subterranean mountain range. It is nearly six miles long and one and one-half miles wide, but the peaks go as high as 750 feet. We were immediately struck by its awesome beauty.... There seemed to be only one road encircling the island, and as we came close to the village, we could see that, although there were trucks and cars, the horse was still a common form of travel.

Reuel, Newsletter:

Providencia is a real treasure. It is one of the most mellow, friendly, beautiful and non-commercial places on Earth. The people are almost literally "one big happy family," all 4,000 of them, black and white all together, their blood mingled for hundreds of years from African, English, Spanish, and Pirate sources. Their language is a dialect of obscure and isolated English, Old English, completely unintelligible to me. They were kind to translate into musical contemporary English and Spanish for us. There is no prejudice and no crime here! The island's rocky green slopes are rich with livestock and farms. And growing in the cow patties, Psilocybin mushrooms!

Paul, *Journal of Travel*:

In the morning I rose early and went ashore to explore the hills, excited by the existence of cows. Not that I'm particularly into cows, or their droppings, but [I'm] *into what can be found growing in this*

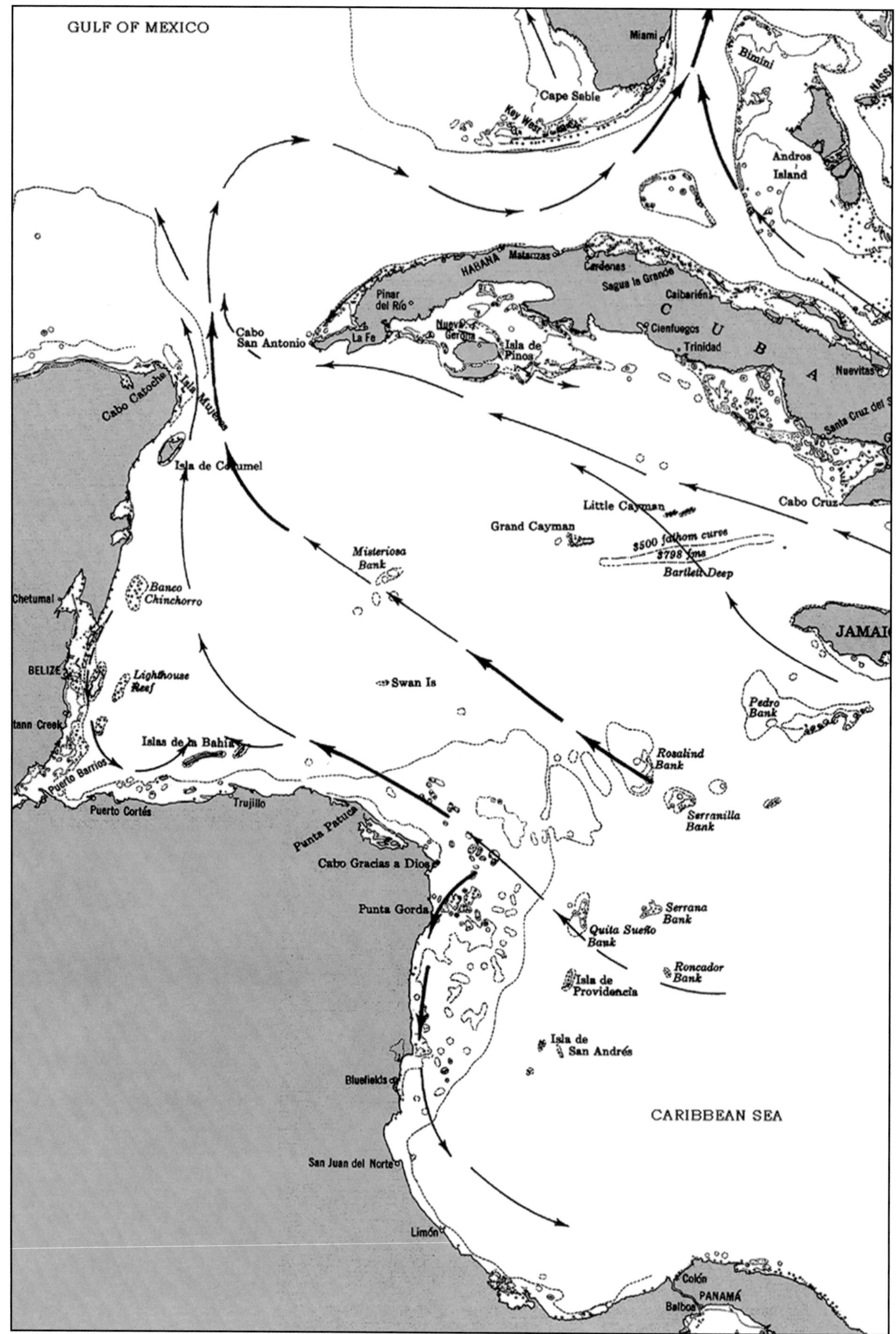

Panama Canal to Key West. Arrows denote currents.

Isla Providencia, Columbia. The island is surrounded by extensive reefs, which continue for several miles to the NNE. The anchorage is in Catalina Harbor.

rich manure. With only a few quarts of water for breakfast, and my camera in hand, I set out in search of mushrooms. I had been told they grew there in abundance, and Steve and Tarey [from *Zephros*] *had found a few the day before.*

For six hours I climbed from peak to peak, and only succeeded in finding three cow pies which yielded these magic mushrooms. Since I had only liquid in my body, these three took effect almost immediately. I came back out of the hills covered with mud and sweat, thoroughly abused by thorns and ants. Two cactus thorns, which are still in my wrist, I received after being chased by an angry heifer. None of these things seemed to bother me much, not even the sting of the salt as I relaxed on the beach. That night, while explaining my escapades to a local friend, he told me it would have been easier to walk down the road a quarter mile, turn left at a fence, walk into the pasture a hundred feet, and there would be all the mushrooms I could eat.

Reuel, Newsletter:

Here we met Asiento, a black fisherman; Simon, a white shopkeeper; and Bill, a teenager who became my self-appointed companion on a long walk about the island. They helped us in every way we could need. Asiento brought us fresh fish and fruit and took us diving—showed us a cave that could only be entered through a frighteningly long and dark underwater tunnel. Simon changed money, cashed traveler's checks, opened his store at odd hours and entertained us with his unique sense of humor.

The night before we left, the islanders invited us to a rum-dum, a party on close-neighboring Catalina Island, at the home of Providencia's high school physics teacher. A huge pot was filled with layers of yucca, (a potato-like root), platanos (plantain—a large banana-like fruit), fish, and much shredded coconut. This was cooked for hours over a wood fire, using no spices—not even salt. Beer and rum and marijuana were plentiful.

Paul, *Journal of Travel*:

Saturday night, we and practically the whole island, went to a small hall to dance to the reggae beat. Finally, after two months in Central America, I found music that I liked to dance to. Good people to dance with, too. I can't seem to enjoy the disco scene at the resorts. The night passed quickly as we drank, danced, and even tried to hold a few conversations over the volume of the music.

* * *

It was very clear that these islanders, for all their geographical and cultural isolation, were not unaware of the world around them. They were remarkably sensitive, refined people, with taste, generosity, discretion and open minds. They lived very simply, in harmony with eachother and the Earth, and they caused me to think that their way of life was very superior to life in more "civilized" cultures. They had no crime, no prejudices, no mental illness, no suicide, and apparently no unhappiness! The only overt symptom of genetic isolation seems to be their somewhat common tendency to stutter. The island seemed to have simply transcended the fact that it now, politically, was a Columbian possession. People's homes were full of books, and the best reggae played on cassettes in battery-powered boom boxes. The spirit was so warm and sharing and easy, I shall never forget it. We really regretted leaving, and we all promised to return. [While we were there, the islanders were installing electricity, planting power poles entirely by hand. I wonder what this magic place is like now, a quarter-century later....]

Asiento told us an interesting tale involving the short boat-ride to the party: He lives on Catalina Island, and keeps a dory, in which he fishes for a living. Several years earlier, he was at a party on Providencia, and got very drunk on rum. His friends—also drunk—took him to his dory, sat him on the thwart, put the oars in his hands and shoved him off. Asiento took a few strokes and fell into the bottom of the boat—passed out. When he woke up the next morning, at sea, his oars were gone, the sun was hot, and he had a brutal hangover. There was not a drop of water in the boat, and he was severely dehydrated. The trade winds blew him west, and the north equatorial current swept him north across the Caribbean Sea—almost 200 miles to Honduras. Asiento caught a few fish—very few—and ate them raw and drank their blood. At that time, Honduras and Columbia were not on friendly terms, as Isla Providencia was claimed by both countries. When Asiento's dory made the beach, he was arrested as a spy and promptly hauled off to jail. Of course he had no papers or ID. He was starving, terribly burned (black people get sunburn too), severely dehydrated and near death. The prison food made him violently ill, and a doctor was called. The doctor said "this man must have healthy food—lots of fresh vegetables." So Asiento was handcuffed and carried to the nearest Chinese restaurant—which he swears saved his life! After several weeks, the misunderstanding was cleared up, and both Asiento and his beloved dory were deported home to Providencia. He only drinks moderately now, and all the islanders are very careful about the 10-minute passage between Providencia and Catalina.

11/18, 0730, Log: *Weigh anchor for Swan Island (Isla del Cisne)*. We abandoned our plan to cruise Honduras, Guatemala and Belize—due to lack of funds. The new plan was to sail to Swan Island, from there to a couple of Mexican islands, thence around the west end of Cuba and to Key West—the most direct route.

Asiento ran out ahead of us in his outboard-powered dory (he also had oars and a sail) to show us out the channel and point the way through the reefs. Still, the passage was shallow and difficult, and took over an hour with the bowsprit-lookout weaving us around coral heads. Previously, at San Andres, we had hit several coral heads with *Fishers Hornpipe's* railroad track-ballasted ferrocement keel, broke the heads off and sailed through! This was a very bad thing, environmentally, when you consider how long a coral head takes to grow. Diving under the hull later, I could not even find scratches—there was no damage. Still my heart is always in my mouth when crossing coral reefs.

The wind came and went several times, including one strong squall. During the evening and night the wind came on strong and steady—the Northeast Trade—and I had to put a reef in the main. We had the Yankee jib and stays'l up, and at 0226 we had to hand the stays'l as the wind was up close to 30 knots. Our course was Northerly, so we lashed the helm and didn't have to steer. The seas were rough and confused, though rarely larger than ten or twelve feet.

By dawn there were more squalls to contend with, though in between them the wind dropped back to twenty knots. At 0845 my Log description of the sky was *shitty*, and we got socked by a 45-knot squall—gale force—which blew the tops off the rough seas. An hour later I was heartened to see a little patch of blue sky to windward.

I got a noon sight that day through partly cloudy skies and altered course ten degrees. I was laying a curving course to sail clear of the extremely dangerous reefs at sea off Cabo Gracias a Dios, Honduras, and I was very nervous until we sighted a shipwreck on our western horizon, which exactly confirmed our dead reckoning position and my noon sight.

The currents in those seas at that time of year were not totally predictable, and the reefs and banks presented a lee shore. That afternoon the wind was strong and oscillating in strength and direction, and I had to tie the reef back in the main that I'd shaken out after the early morning squalls. The next night passed with little difference except that the sky was clear and full of stars, a whole hemisphere of them in a black sky above and around us with a whole hemisphere of black sea beneath us. Looking under *Notes* in the Log, I see what prompted me to reef the mains'l: *1745—Hit very hard on starboard bow by freak wave—green water on deck to cockpit.*

At dawn I figured we should raise Swan Island (Isla del Cisne), the second most remote place in the Caribbean (after Isla del Aves). Because it is so low, we were within twenty miles of it before we saw a flat line on the horizon, which became beautiful low white cliffs fringed with green as we approached; a very gratifying landfall (see photos).

We anchored in the uncomfortable rolly harbor right next to *Zephros*! When the Honduran military officials saw us anchor, they swam out to *Fishers Hornpipe*, in uniform, holding their pistols in the air over their heads. Getting them on board and enduring the formalities of inspection was bizarre. Rumor had it that the officials here had been a real hassle for visitors, to such a degree that the Italian gentleman leasing and hoping to develop the island for tourism got mad and told them to lay-off. So we had it a little easier. This Italian gentleman (his name eludes me) opened his tiny *No Problem Bar*, built largely out of the shipwreck of a sailboat which Steve and Tarey Lea recognized as the old *Storm Signal* of Key West, which had belonged to friends of theirs. That night we were guests of this friendly and generous man and his family at a big spaghetti dinner attended by virtually everyone on the island, perhaps twenty people. He never let us give him a dime, even for drinks at the bar—"no money—no problem!"—and I was glad to give his wife a jar of preserves, which they were out of and wouldn't be able to get for weeks. There are no stores on the island—just the military barracks, a dirt airstrip, the defunct weather station and the Italians.

Swan Island was an isolated US weather station until Honduras claimed it and we gave it to them. Now the weather station is defunct, there being no Hondurans who know how to operate it. The day before we got there, the new Commandant on the island took our Italian host's Sunfish (a tiny sailboat) against his advice and without his permission, and set out to circumnavigate the island under the weather conditions I described above. After he capsized several times by himself, he ordered a soldier to go with him. They vanished at sea and were never seen again! Here Mo (whom we met in Costa Rica), who was sailing north on *Zephros*, took a ride home to Key West by private plane with a pilot we met there. She told me when I saw her months later how they blew a tire landing in Mexico, which scared the shit out of her, but the pilot's skill got the plane in without a scratch. Mo had a bad tooth and was grateful to cut short her time of suffering with it.

Swan Island was very desolate, and more than a little strange. We were glad to get our papers back, and left in company with *Zephros* the next day (11/21) at noon.

Working our way along the reef that reaches out from the Northwest corner of Swan Island, we were impressed by how large and rough the seas were. At times *Zephros* would be violently thrown almost completely out of the water and at other times she would drive into a huge sea and be buried in green water and spray (I imagine we looked the same). She was going to try to hold a course very close to windward, to round Punta San Antonio, Cuba and fetch Key West. We were heading for Cozumel, Mexico, where Anne would leave us. The wind was close to 30 knots, seas 12 to 15 feet, close together and rough.

Near midnight we tied a second reef in the main—the seas had grown even larger and rougher, and the wind was up above 30 knots. *Fishers Hornpipe* had been logging a constant 6.5 knots. Her point-of-sail was a close reach (I fell off a little to ease the motion) but she had been making the same speed close-hauled. She can take a hell of a lot more than I can, and I'm very grateful she can. *Fishers Hornpipe* was in her element—happy and showing us what she is all about, driving powerful and fast and safe, punching and shouldering into those violent seas like her ancestors before her in an age when boats *had* to be able to do that, because the lives and livelihoods of the strong men in them totally depended on it. I held on for dear life in awe watching her. I give her what sail she wants—she wants a lot, and she gives a lot. At midnight it was just too much for me in the ink black night with rain showers adding to things. So we handed the Yankee, no easy task out on the bowsprit in those conditions, lashed it tightly to the life lines, and put up the stays'l, which slowed us down to 4.6 knots, still very good speed, and made the motion gentler.

That day another freak wave hit us—so big and irregular that it broke against the cockpit coaming. *Fishers Hornpipe* has a center cockpit consisting of a two-foot-high coaming; her midships freeboard is over three feet. By now we were seeing an occasional sea with a height of twenty feet. The following entry from Log notes: *Salt water finding its insidious way into everything—every electrical wire, throughbolt, portlight glazing, deck pipes, cockpit, skylight, etc. Books wet, bedding wet, clothes wet, chainplate leaking in my stateroom, musical instrument cases wet, etc.*

At some point during this passage, the violent seas loosened up the tightly furled genoa jib. Before Paul and I could get the sail off and stowed below deck, more seas hit it and filled parts of it while we were working. Things were really touch and go—we were nearly pulled off the bow and into the sea several times. Anyone going overboard in those conditions would be almost impossible to rescue. We discovered later that the sail had been pulled by the weight of water across the catted fisherman anchor with such force that one sail panel was torn to shreds, and several other panels were badly damaged. This later cost hundreds of dollars to repair—the work was beyond the scope of my little German zigzag sewing machine.

Several times Paul or I went forward to re-lash sails, whisker-poles, anchors and the foredeck storage drum. Tage was useless for these tasks, but could hold a safe downwind course while we worked (we had to run with the wind and seas to work safely on the foredeck). The debilitating exhaustion experienced after one of these episodes—or of reefing the mains'l in these sea conditions—absolutely cannot be appreciated by someone who has not experienced it. A simple ten-minute task under normal conditions might take over an hour. I would finish the critical part of a task and collapse, gasping for breath, for five or ten minutes before being able to finish it, whereupon I would crawl someplace where I couldn't be thrown out, soaking wet, and pass out for an hour.

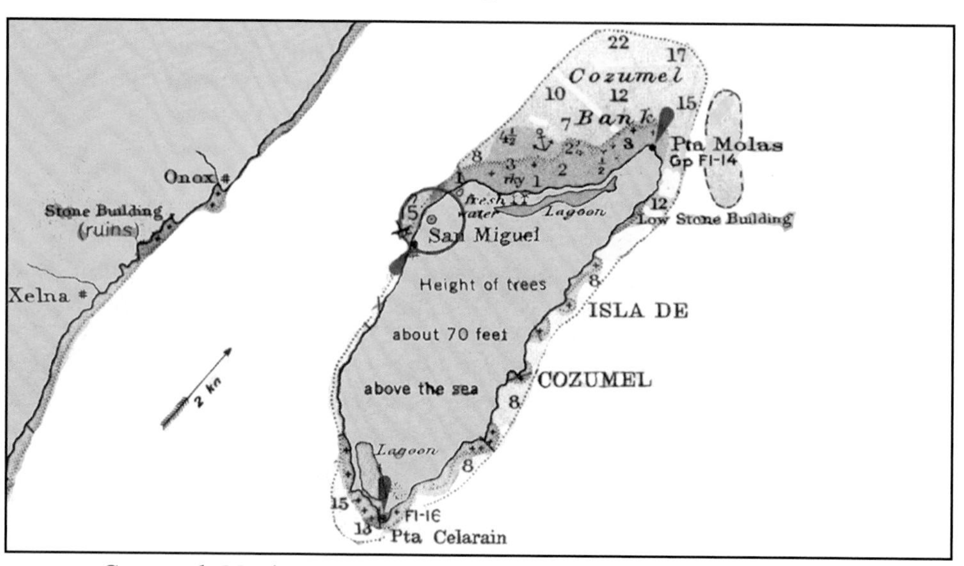

Cozumel, Mexico.

During this passage I remember declaring that I was forever cured from seasickness, and I even went below and cooked a spaghetti dinner to prove it. If only I had known what was yet to come!

The next day, 11/22, things eased a little, but not much. Wind was 30 knots. It was too rough for me to get an accurate noon sight: the figures made no sense. As the day progressed, things eased a little more, and I shook the second reef out of the mains'l in late afternoon. By night the wind had fallen very light and easterly, with an easterly 12' swell running, and a clear sky with a beautiful full moon. I was frustrated that night because I didn't know exactly where we were, and I was worried about running into the coast of Mexico. Around 0330 I sighted what I figured *must* be Pt. Celerain light on the southern tip of Cozumel, but I was uncomfortable for hours longer until I was sure. By the light of dawn everything made sense, and we sailed slowly and gently up the west coast of Cozumel. At 0830 we moored Mediterranean-style (stern to the pier) in the tiny *Club Nautico* in company with *Azulao*, *Trip Earth* and *Nikka*. Glad to be in a safe, snug harbor among friends we hadn't seen in months.

Unfortunately, the good feelings and relief were quickly spoiled by the Mexican officials in Cozumel—the greediest I had yet encountered. We spent three days there, and the fees were levied as follows: First to show up was customs; He inspected our papers briefly, along with those of another boat, and demanded $20 (USD) "for the taxi." When I complained, he said he would take ten. The government-operated marina—which didn't have even a *cold*-water shower—hit us for $23 (USD) for three days—for no water, no electricity, and filthy toilets. Migracion became a hassle that involved two trips to the airport (the taxi cost $3 (USD) each way—glad I had a bicycle!), and two trips to a huge office at the far end of town. Typically, I had to wait, or come back, for some paper-shuffler to scribble on some fucking paper. Migracion cost $13.33 (USD) for visa stamping and $11.11 (yup) for boat visa. The Port Captain, which involved four visits back and forth getting various papers stamped, charged me $8.88 (still US greenbacks) for "office fees." Three days cost $67!

Cozumel was a total tourist trap, and I regret going there. If I had had the money, I could have taken the ferry to the Yucatan mainland to see the Mayan ruins—but the damned *officiales* broke me. And wasted most of my time. We did, however, find time to dive on the airplane wreck off the west coast.

On Nov 26th at 0700 we weighed anchor

for Isla Mujeres, the next island up the coast. We stopped to speak with Steve and Tarey Lea on *Zephros*, anchored offshore and playing cat-and-mouse games with the officials, to borrow a chart. *Zephros* had been driven against her will into Mexican waters by the same winds and seas I have described—she was unable to maintain her desired course around Punta San Antonio, Cuba.

Anne left us in Cozumel to spend the winter in Guatemala, and Tage left to go Christmas shopping inland in Merida (he re-joined us in Isla Mujeres). Hence Paul and I made the trip alone—our first such. It was a beautiful, robust sail, with big seas and lots of wind. With our fast boat speed and a powerful north-setting current, we nearly sailed right past Isla Mujeres, and had to back-track to fetch the harbor. The surrounding reef was extensive and shallow, the current strong and dangerous, and the sea-buoys were very small and hard to find. We spent an anxious hour weaving among coral heads before we found the channel.

We anchored at 1500 in a crowded anchorage, and had to drop the hook three times before we felt safely anchored. The officials here were easy and friendly, but paperwork had been simplified by the fact that we had already cleared into the country in Cozumel. Other yachts in Mujeres warned us not to clear out of Mexico upon leaving, as we would be hit with more fees, and clearance papers from Mexico would not be required by a US vessel entering home waters. Isla Mujeres was nice—a little touristy—but low key. While we were there, Paul made fast friends with a street-performing monkey, and I think both their hearts were broken when we had to leave.

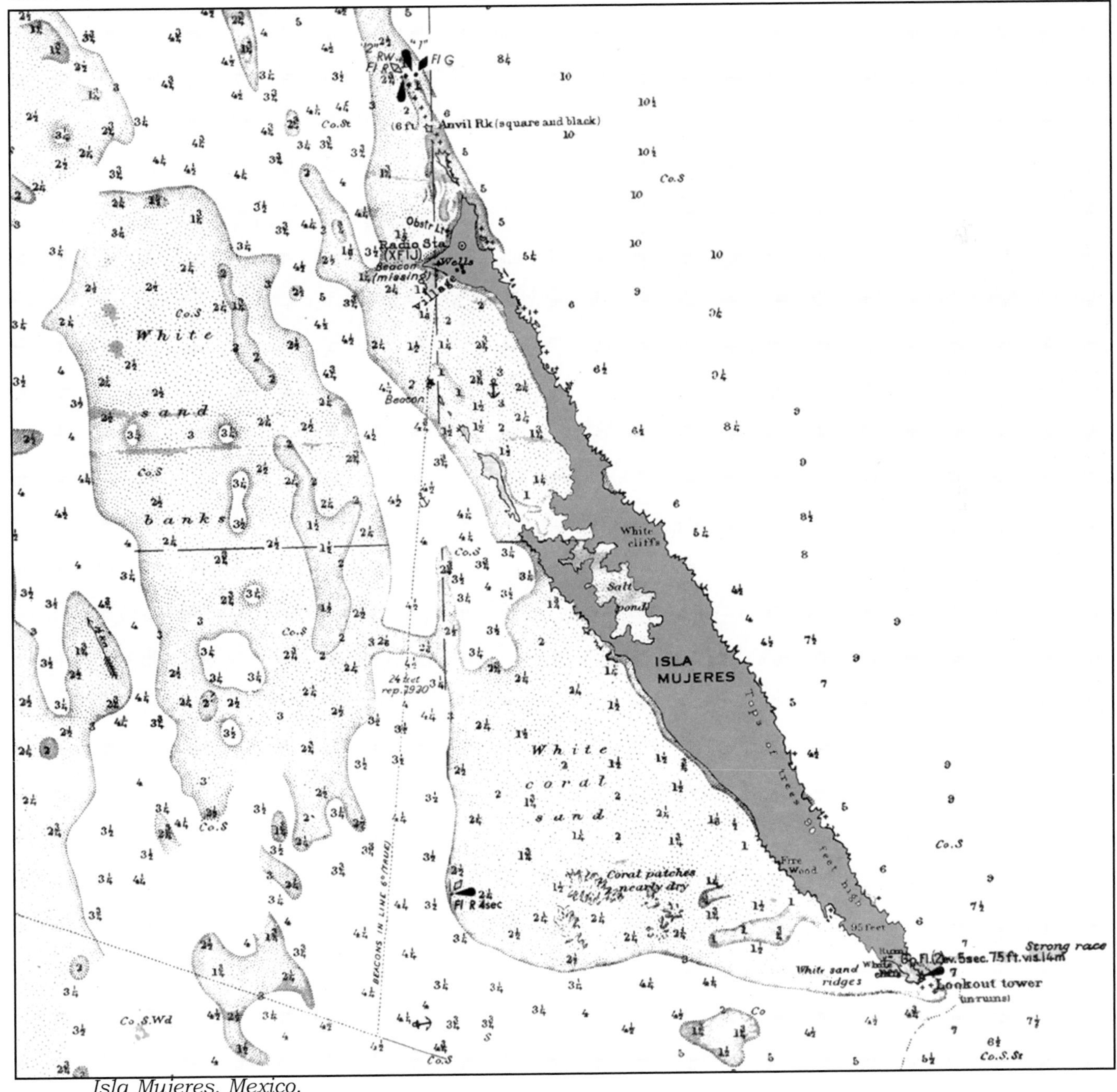

Isla Mujeres, Mexico.

Paul, *Journal of Travel:*

Isla Mujeres turned out to be very nice, mostly due to the absence of the resort hotels that [are overabundant on] *the landscapes of so many once-beautiful islands. In Isla Mujeres, the average "hotel"* [youth hostel] *was no more than a place to hang your hammock for 75-cents a night. This attracted more of the kind of people that interest me: the travelers of the world, instead of the American on vacation.*

Though the weather turned foul, I spent most of the week at Isla Mujeres on the beach. I had become very involved in finding shells that would work for jewelry. This beach had many different types that had potential.... Since the weather wasn't very [pleasant], *the people who only come to the beach for the sun stayed away. This left the people who came to this place of beauty just because of the environment. An ocean beach can be a very beautiful place during a storm. On a windy, blue-gray afternoon, while walking among the sand and the rocks, you will find the people who enjoy these different aspects of the beauty of nature.*

It was on one of these stormy days, while sitting on the beach searching for shells, that a young woman sat down next to me. She asked me to come and see the small fish that swam in the tide pools. We sat on the rocks and watched the world around us. We talked a little, but our best communication came from the eyes. I spent only the better part of an hour alone on the beach with her, but I felt as close as if we had known eachother a very long time. I left the following day for Key West, but when we said goodbye it seemed as if we would meet once again.

After a few days, Tage re-joined us laden with Christmas presents for his friends and family in Denmark, and we weighed anchor (noon on 11/30) for the remote Dry Tortugas at the west extremity of the US Florida Keys. While we were in Isla Mujeres, a violent two-day norther blew, and we felt concerned for *Zephros*, who had left Cozumel just after we had, and was probably half-way across the Yucatan Channel when it hit. The Yucatan Channel is famous for being rough during northers, as the northerly-flowing currents (which become the Gulf Stream above Cuba) oppose the strong north winds, setting up steep, short seas of impressive size and violence—more "square waves." Cal and Janet on *Indian Princess*—with whom we had transited the Panama Canal—were caught in the same norther further south. Janet had a very bad time of it as Cal was passing an extremely painful and debilitating kidney stone (he was rolling around on the cabin sole screaming in agony), leaving her alone to handle a vessel the size of ours.

We never once got accurate weather information from any persons or any radio stations anywhere in Central America. Some of the airports received teletype weather broadcasts, but couldn't de-code them! So we relied on asking fishermen and carefully watching changing conditions—but mostly we took what we got and made the best of it. When the fishermen at Isla Mujeres told me the sea would be "*muy tranquillo*," we took off on the heels of the shrimpers, weighing anchor at 1220 on 11/30. As soon as we got outside, the wind veered right back into the north. I was feeling very up-tight about the crossing, knowing it was 400 miles to windward, beating into large seas and strong NE trade winds, with the constant threat of a norther. We were sneaking between hurricane season—the last of which had just blown itself out—and the winter northers, the first of which had just struck.

We began beating close-hauled on the port tack, changing to the starboard tack when the wind clocked easterly; then to port tack when it backed to northerly, and so-on. We used the motor for a few hours during one rare spell when the wind fell light, as I didn't want to sit around waiting to get caught out. We had very little fuel, as I wanted the boat to be as light as possible for the passage—and because we were broke! I doubted we would be at a loss for wind.

By noon the next day the wind was a steady NE at 20 knots, and we stayed close-hauled on the starboard tack. That night I cooked a kingfish we caught with rice and salad for dinner, which we ate while watching a beautiful sunset. That night we enjoyed an exquisite starry night sail, during which we rounded Pt. San Antonio on the west tip of Cuba. By noon the next day, 48 hours into our passage, the sky was heavy overcast with rain, the wind very light, and we motor-sailed again for a few hours.

Motor-sailing has the distinct advantage of allowing a vessel to point much higher than under sail alone, yet make more speed than under power alone, thus advancing her on her desired course. This had become even more important than usual, as a norther would make Cuba a dangerous lee shore for us.

By evening the wind was ENE and blowing 30 knots, the seas very rough, and we were close-hauled on the starboard tack. Near midnight we tacked, and I tossed my cookies...thought I was cured—damn! The seas were violent, close together, irregular, and full of nasty freak waves. The night that followed was pitch-black and frightful. I thought of Debi saying that sailing in rough seas was like being on a really bad carnival ride—only you can't get off. Green water was constantly breaking across the decks, bursting through the cockpit scuppers across our bare feet and ankles. Spray was bursting

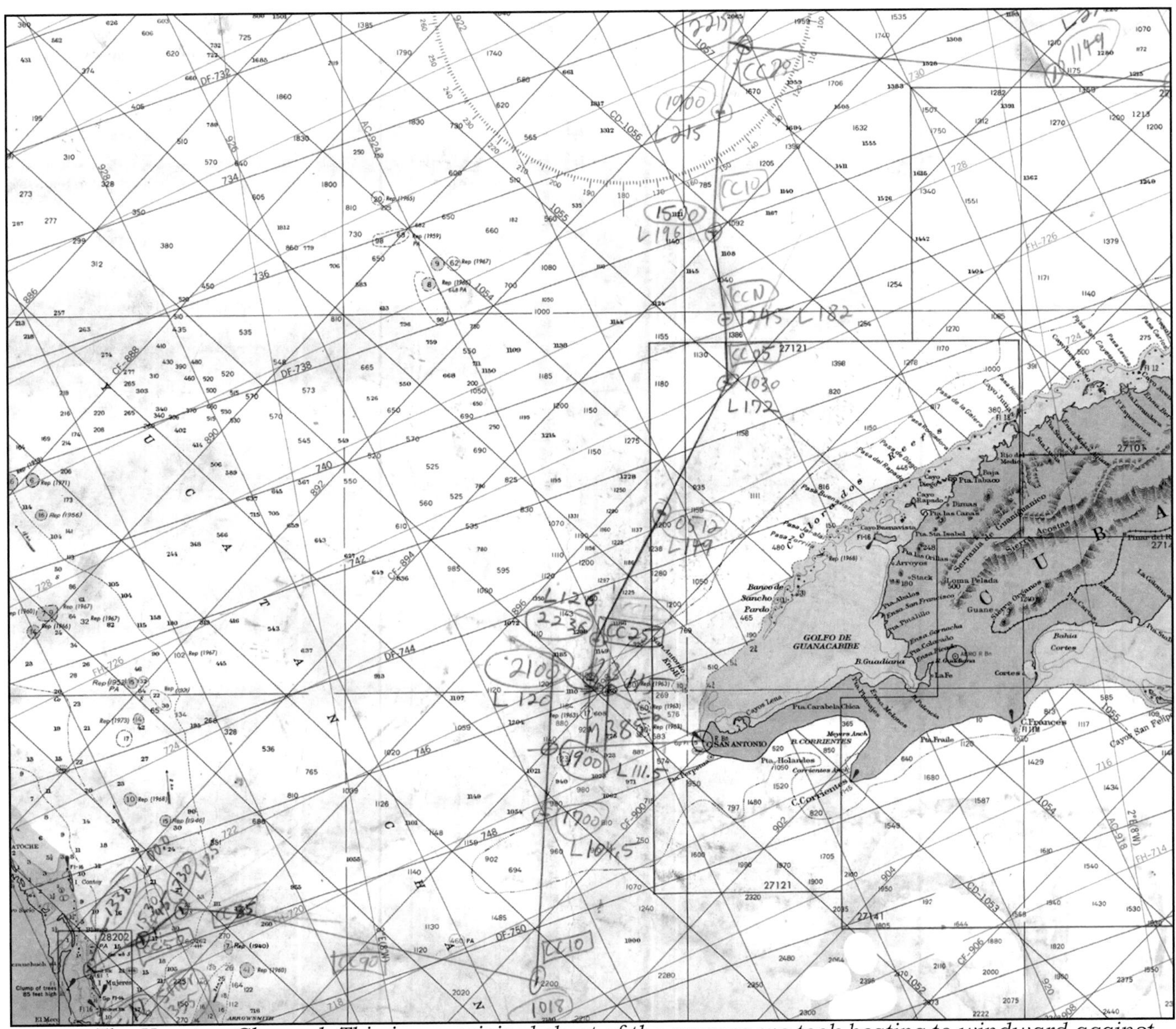

The Yucatan Channel. This is my original chart of the courses we took beating to windward against a violent Norther. Isla Mujeres is in the lower left corner; Key West is far away to the upper right.

over everything all the time—soon everything on deck, and much below, was soaked with cold salt water. It was unnecessary to leave the cockpit to piss or barf—and too dangerous to anyway. I pissed and barfed in the cockpit scuppers and the sea immediately washed it away. I could no longer go below to navigate, and I didn't even care anymore.

By noon the following day the wind was NE and close to gale force, around 40 knots. Paul and I slowly and painfully took down the yankee jib, and used every remaining sail gasket to lash it firmly to the lifeline, as high off the deck as possible, where water still hit it with incredible violence. The air was so full of solid spray it was hard to tell where the sea ended and the sky began. At times we were in green water up to our waists, hanging on for all we were worth. Without the jib, we sailed very slowly to windward, at around two knots, under double-reefed main and stays'l. We were being slammed and buried under huge green seas that came one on top of the other, the tops blowing right off many of them as they curled and broke. Some were a good twenty feet high, and often had bizarre shapes—square towers of water bursting straight up into the air before exploding into spray and being blown away—the result of current opposing wind. Maelstrom. *The Gulf Stream.*

During this time, whole obscure segments of my life swept through my mind. I remembered things I had never remembered before. We all slept a good deal, and ate almost nothing. During the whole passage, we did very little steering—because we were close-hauled, we simply lashed the helm, and *Fishers Hornpipe* blessedly steered herself. I did force myself to eat a little, during the less-violent spells, for fear of becoming dangerously weak. Tage, who fortunately doesn't suffer from seasickness, even cooked a meal one night, of rice and "donkey dick"—canned corned beef (Paul and I were teaching Tage American slang). That was the only meal he ever prepared during three months on board.

Both Tage and Paul had never sailed before joining me, and so were still learning, despite having now covered a lot of sea-miles under many different conditions. Tage loved sailing—especially when we drove the *Hornpipe* hard and fast—but he never really tuned in to the mechanics, nomenclature and procedures involved. Thus he was limited as a crewmember (and he didn't cook). Paul's energy, sensitivity, awareness and intelligence were highly developed at age seventeen, and he learned extremely rapidly. He had become my "right hand"—my first mate—very quickly. He was indispensable during rough times, and proved himself again and again. He was also fearless, but not reckless—valuable qualities in a mariner. I depended on Paul totally, though I was still teaching him how to deal with sailing procedures under different conditions. Hell—I was still teaching myself! Managing a sailboat in rough weather can involve a lot of technique—what might normally be a simple mistake, reversal of procedure or miscalculation can result in grave damage, severe injury or even death. It takes time and experience to make a good sailor, in addition to the above-mentioned qualities. I was lucky to have good crew—and we three made a damn good team.

During that next long night, the wind remained half a gale, and I felt like I had been in it forever and would be in it forever. At dawn I wanted to get the storm jib up because we were going so slowly. I had been thinking about this, building my strength for it, waiting for daylight. At dawn Tage ran us off down-wind while Paul and I struggled to get the yankee off the forestay and below deck, and hank on the storm jib. *Fishers Hornpipe* has twin outer (and inner) forestays, and I was pissed at myself for not hanking it on before leaving Mexico. I had intended to—it's so easy to be lazy when there is no storm, and then later you pay for it big time. This operation took over an hour and left me helplessly exhausted. *I was dehydrated and hadn't eaten anything that had stayed down for two and a half days.* But there was still much to do. Before setting the jib, we had shaken a reef out of the main, to gain more control while we dumped the stays'l. [I didn't want to carry both stays'l and storm jib; because the storm jib—really a small yankee—was larger than the stays'l, and more powerful to windward.] Now we had too much weather helm, and had to put the reef back in. This was another exhausting job under the circumstances. We continued on an easterly course on the port tack until after noon so I could get a noon sight. This was very difficult to manage over the stern on the other tack. The clouds didn't let me get a sight, and the wind and seas began to increase again.

We hadn't had a fix since the hand-held compass bearing on Pt. San Antonio two and a half days earlier. From my dead reckoning, I figured we should be south of the Dry Tortugas, so we came onto the starboard tack at 1245 and headed north. I hadn't added any vector for current into my course, as the Pilot Charts and Sailing Directions warned that the normally powerful east-setting current could be nullified or even reversed by northerly storms. If we were being set east, which indeed we soon found out we were, it wouldn't hurt us—only bring us closer to Key West. The wind was NNE at 35 knots, the seas close to 15 feet, and *Fishers Hornpipe* was driving, beating into it at an incredible 6.5 knots.

I thought of the Henderson Brothers often, and how they had insisted I take that nearly bullet-proof little storm jib with me, even though I didn't have any money to pay for it. And I thought about the other sails they made—so damn strong and good—billowing and straining as they drove us forward, meeting all that violence and energy—the random power and majesty of Nature—with fabric and thread and metal and knowledge and experience and love. Why is there so little of this kind of conscientious workmanship left in the world?

I thought also about all the criticism I had listened to about heavy-displacement, full-keel boats—about their being dogs, and unable to claw their way off a lee shore. I tried to imagine what these critics' little fin-keeled, high-aspect-ratio tupperware toys would be like out here, and I was very thankful for *Fishers Hornpipe*. I was deeply impressed by her. No-one had steered her for days—except while we ran off to make sail changes. Here she was sailing herself into all this sea and wind, close-hauled, going 6.5 knots by the taff-rail log (speedometer). And we felt safe!

Shortly after noon on 12/4 we saw two tankers on the horizon, and Tage got on the VHF radio to ask them their positions. For the first and only time in 14 months of hailing commercial vessels, the *Pisces* answered our radio call and gave us a position. Which placed us 45 miles south of Key West—60 miles due east of our D.R. position—a result of the Gulf Stream current which was there after all. They also told us the weather would remain the same—*shitty*.

By dusk we raised the lights of Key West, and carefully began to work our way in, working hard with the chart and a hand-bearing compass to identify navigation aids from the hundreds of lights we saw before us. We located the main ship channel, and as we came in, I tried to raise Customs and the Coast Guard on the radio. We anchored at 2100 off Wisteria (locally called Christmas Tree) Island, and

I finally got an answer from the Coast Guard. They told me it was alright for us *all* to go ashore and call a toll-free phone number for Miami Customs, who would most likely give us a "telephone clearance." Though I had no experience with this, people on another boat in Mexico (who had re-entered the U.S. at Key West) had told me it was likely. I was amazed that things could be so loose: we could have brought in—and unloaded—tons of pot! Little wonder Key West was reputed to be the drug capitol of America. *And there wasn't so much as a seed on board!*

Two days before, I had dug my little care package of personal drugs out of its hiding place in the bilge, and was throwing everything overboard, when Paul, who was watching, freaked out and made me stop. Even in that rough weather, he did his best to dispose of the last remaining *Panama Red* and *Peruvian Marching Powder* (pure crystal flake cocaine) without it being solely sacrificed to Neptune. I absolutely wouldn't let him have the last of the Windowpane acid I had brought all the way from California—or the beautiful crystallized mescaline—over it went. I had discovered that cruising under sail greatly reduced my appetite for recreational drugs. Reality was intense enough.

After getting safely anchored, we all rowed ashore, dying to get some food and booze, see women and walk on a surface that wasn't heaving around all the time. *I dutifully went to the nearest pay phone and called the toll-free number. I got a recorded message, which said the number was temporarily out of order!* I was very surprised, and tried to call twice more—and got the same message. I couldn't believe it—but there it was. [I later confirmed that I had indeed been calling the correct number.] We ate pizza and drank beer on Duval Street—salty, smelly sailors, home from the sea—and went back to the *Hornpipe* and slept like never before.

The next day I found the U.S. Customs office by accident in the old post office. I went in and told the officer there that we had arrived the night before and hadn't been able to clear in. He asked me where my crew were. I told him they were running errands, as the Coast Guard had told us it was alright to go ashore. *He had a major shit fit—red in the face, yelling at me—and ordered me to immediately round up my crew and move my boat to the customs dock.* This I did—paranoid as hell—about to run out of fuel, and so upset that I forgot to remove *Gandy Dancer's* daggerboard (we had sailed her to and from the distant anchorage), causing her to capsize and nearly sink (you cannot tow a small boat with it's board down). Paul, always the first one in the water in such an emergency, jumped in and made a line fast to *Gandy's* heavy steel daggerboard so Tage and I could haul it on deck. With difficulty, in a swift, dangerous current, we rafted *Gandy* along side the *Hornpipe*, and used lines tied to her gunwales to lift her hull above the water so Paul could bail her out. This involved lifting a five-gallon bucket half-full of water over his head, while swimming alongside. Somehow we managed to get it together, narrowly missing a channel buoy, and motoring up to the customs dock by the appointed time.

Once there, we again endured the plethora of paperwork, and lost all our still-fresh Mexican produce and delicious San Blas coconuts to the Agricultural Inspector. She also made me throw my beloved potted plants overboard—and wash out the pots! Fortunately she missed Harvey—my philodendron—who lived in the head and had been with me since Sausalito. The Customs Officer levied a $1,500 fine against me, the minimum (he told me) for allowing my crew to come ashore. I said "Why don't you just throw me in jail for vagrancy too—I've got less than ten dollars to my name!" He then grudgingly explained to me that my only option for reducing the fine was to write to the Customs Prosecutor in Miami, and explain that I had "extenuating circumstances." He hinted that if I was really good at browning my nose, I might be able to get a greatly reduced fine. [This I did, and my fine was eventually reduced to $100—still unfair, but I paid it.]

Meanwhile, another boat came in—*Azulao*—captained by my friend David Edwards—and the officials told him to just call the toll-free number—it was too close to quitting time, and they wanted to go home. By this time the toll-free number was back in service, and Miami Customs gave David a telephone clearance. No customs inspection, no produce thrown overboard, no immigration papers—nothing. And the same thing happened for the other boats that came in after hours. So I got crucified because a fucking government phone number was temporarily out of order. The US Government—like all governments—teaches us to lie. Would you tell the officials you had fresh produce and potted plants you loved if you knew what would happen? Wouldn't you even deliberately delay your arrival, so as to get a telephone clearance after hours? So does everyone else. So do I, now.

Lest I give a totally wrong impression here—by the end of our inspection, the Customs Officer was smiling and answering questions politely—another not-so-bad guy who just has a job to do—and does it by the book. [Which is what Nazi officers said during the Nuremberg War Trials after WW II.]

I would love to see all the government officials in the world—the pencil-pushers, paper-shufflers, little dictators and petty-minded bureaucrats—simply vanish from their posts. I firmly believe the world would get along just fine without them, and would even be a vastly better place. People could go back to doing real work—tilling the soil with their hands, pulling the fish from the sea, teaching the children how to live honestly, making the things we need with their hands. I don't know exactly where we went wrong (I'm working on it)—but we sure went wrong. I don't mean to imply that there are pat answers to the world's incredible problems. If there are, I sure haven't found them, and I think about it every day. But I am *sick unto death* of the pale, flabby, narrow-minded fascist automatons who suck our blood and energy and time and money to satisfy someone else's perverted sense of the order of things.

One additional item on this agenda: It is my sincere advice to all cruising sailors, and, indeed, to all world travelers, to exhibit their utmost understanding, patience, and polite behavior when dealing with any and all government officials. First off—it cannot hurt (unless you overdo it so drastically as to arouse suspicion). Secondly, *most* people (not all) respond to being treated fairly by treating you fairly in return. Offer the customs/immigration officer a comfortable place to sit, something to drink, and he or she will most likely be as helpful as possible. Finally—despite what I said in the last paragraph—even bureaucrats are human beings, and however they came to be who they are, they are still just trying to do their job. Even when US Coast Guard or Customs officials are tearing your home apart looking for drugs, it is essential that you do not blow your cool! Keep in mind that these people are armed, nervous, and doing their job. With all my leftover anger at governments from the time of Vietnam, it took me a while to learn this.

We stayed at the Customs Dock overnight—being dangerously low on fuel—and moved the next day to the Truman Annex transient docks. On the following Monday, I talked my way into a slip at the Truman Annex Marina. This was not easy, as they claimed to have no space available—and it was expensive: $175 per month. I didn't know how long they would let me stay—but since I was trying to rent shop space in the Annex (I needed to work!), I felt I had a chance.

Zephros put into Cuba to escape the norther we slammed through, and was held there for two weeks until the Cuban Coast Guard felt it was safe for her to proceed. During that time her crew was confined to the boat—though Steve and Tarey Lea later told me that the Cuban officials were polite and even friendly. They were so late to arrive in Key West that Tarey's mother and I filed an overdue report with the Coast Guard. Everyone else made it back to the US without major disasters—although they all had rough trips. Ours was the fastest passage by almost two days! So much for heavy, fat, slow deep-draft ferrocement tubs.

Newsletter, Dec 22, 1980:

Truman Annex Marina, Key West—Christmas songs on the radio. Cold crisp air all the way from Canada. The body and the mind feel more alive. I've been here a little over two weeks and it feels like home. My first job is restoring a little nine foot, 50-year-old Scottish lapstrake tender, and I love the old familiar sting of sweet oak sawdust flying from my carbide saw-blade into my face and nose. And the cramps from sitting too long at the drafting board designing her sprit-rig sail, spars, kick-up rudder and daggerboard. And fast early morning bicycle rides to Pepe's *for a scallion and cream cheese omelet and 3 cups of coffee (locals only—you can find it by the "closed" sign on the door).*

Pepe's *gave me a peculiar feeling of deja-vu. There was a miniature Count Rumford fireplace at one end of the small dining room, over which hung a painting of a black dog—behind which was a reclining nude woman eating an apple. One morning a vaguely-familiar man came in and sat at the next table, doing paperwork. I took an unlikely chance, and said "Allan?" The man looked up and said "Where do I know that voice from?" It turned out to be Allan Miller, from Martha's Vineyard, with whom I had worked briefly when I lived there years earlier. Allan designed and built the famous Black Dog restaurant, at one end of which was a full-size Count Rumford fireplace—over which used to hang a painting of a black dog.... Small world again!*

North America! On the Key West streets: beautiful women, outrageous women, gays and queens and dikes, bikers, drug casualties, drunks, freaks, shrimpers, tourists, Cubans, purse-snatchers, scam-artists, red-neck locals (called conchs*—pronounced* konks*)—Americans!*

This is the end of Fishers Hornpipe's *first extended cruise—from Sausalito, California, through Central America and the Panama Canal, through the western Caribbean, and terminating in Key West, Florida. The cruise began on 10/04/79, and ended on 12/04/80. We sailed over six thousand miles. I learned a lot, and have a lot still to learn.*

I like Key West, and I intend to stay and work here for several months as planned. There is much work to do on the Hornpipe*—to maintain, re-finish, refine and perfect her—before heading down into the West Indies and eastern Caribbean next year. Money must somehow be generated more efficiently—perhaps I will do some Caribbean chartering, or even begin to sell my designs. Who can ever know what the future will bring?*

VOYAGE TWO PHOTOS

Photo 1 Flying twin jibs off the Mexican coast. Note the bronze rings (pole ends) which broke

Photo 2 Cabo San Lucas, Baja Sur, Mexico

Photo 3 (above) Fishers Hornpipe in Yelapa, Mexico

Photo 4 (below) A Yelapa farm

Photo 5 John's Palapa

Photo 6 Greg, Cyndee & Debi in Alcapulco

Photo 7 John

Photo 8 (above) Isla Cedro, Costa Rica, from the Hacienda. Photo 9 (below) The Hacienda

Photo 10 (above) Fran & Reuel Photo 11 (below) L to R: John, Fran, Joe, Mo, John's wife, Dennis

Photo 12 (above) The meadow on Volcan Irazu, Costa Rica. Photo 13 (below) The crater, Irazu

Photo 14

Cyndee and all her belongings in *Gandy Dancer*--leaving to join *Unlikely VII*

Photo 15

Fishers Hornpipe
hauled out in Punta Arenas

Photo 16

Zephros sailing in Golfo de Nicoya
Steve and Tarey Lea

Photo 17 Jungle Paul on Isla del Caño, Costa Rica

Photo 18 Rosie on Isla del Caño

Photo 19

Lit & Lil's place, Golfo Dulce

Photo 20

Fishers Hornpipe off Lit & Lil's place

Photo 21

The waterfall above Joe's
finca, Golfo Dulce--
Paul climbing to heaven

Photo 22 *Fishers Hornpipe* anchored in Golfo Dulce, Costa Rica

Photo 23

Islas las Perlas, Panama

Photo 24 Tage, Janet & Cal on *Fishers Hornpipe*, transiting the Panama Canal

Photo 25 Lago Gatun, Panama Canal. Tage With

Photo 26 Jean Paul & Silda (Paulphoto)

Photos 27, 28 & 29

The Fortress at Portobelo, Panama

Photo 30 Paul in Portobelo

Photo 31 Anne in Portobelo

Photos 32 & 33

The Fortress at Portobelo

Photos 34 & 35 Columbian Copra Schooners

Photos 36, 37 & 38 Islas San Blas, Kuna Indian woman & children (Paulphotos)

Photos 39, 40 & 41 Isla Providencia, Columbia. *Fishers Hornpipe*, center of # 41

Photo 43 Providencia--
Where the 'shrooms grow

Photo 42 Bill, Providencia, Columbia

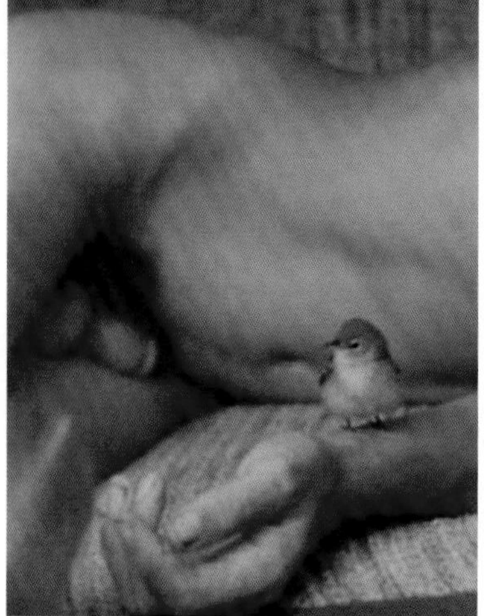

Photo 44 Pecker & peeper

Photo 45 Tage, Isla del Cisne landfall, Honduras

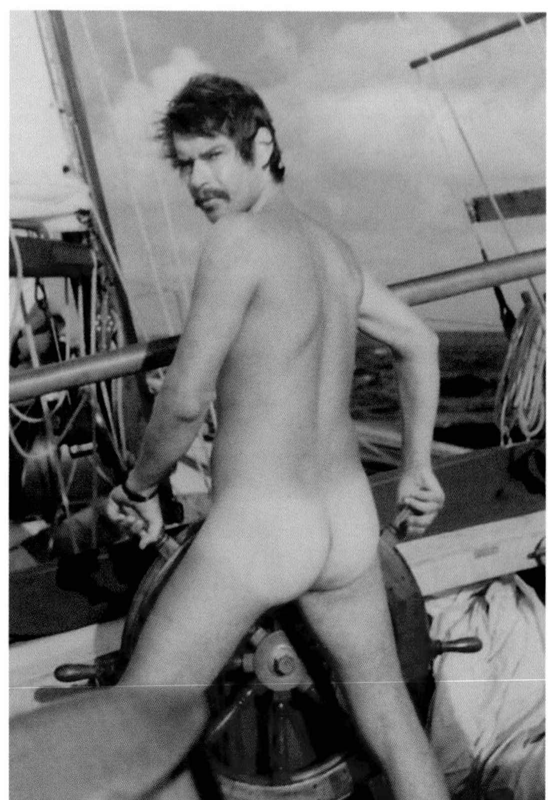

Photo 46 Anne, Isla del Cisne landfall

VOYAGE THREE: THE ATLANTIC

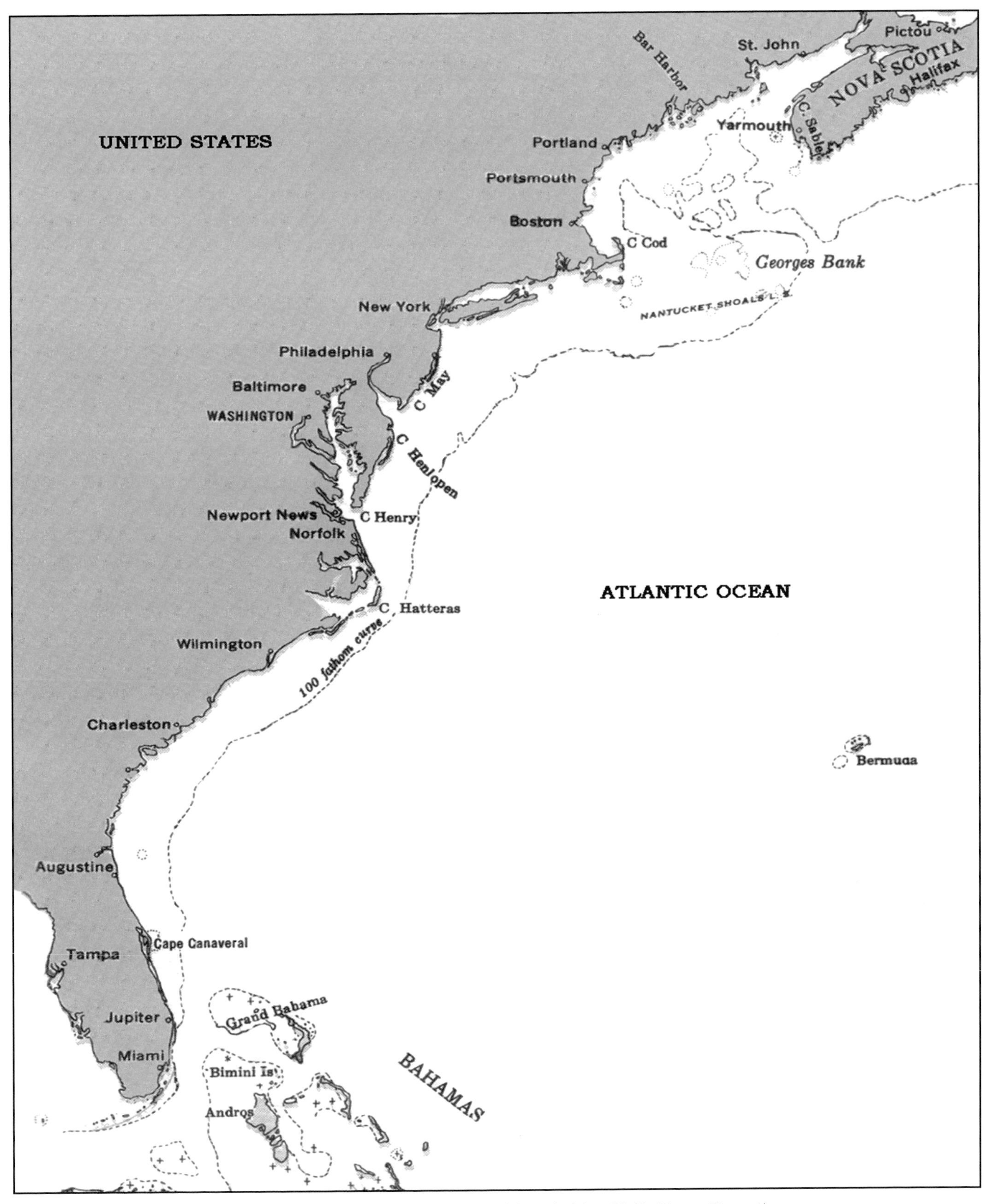

Voyage Three—The Bahamas to Maine and back (the U.S. East Coast).

CHAPTER ELEVEN—KEY WEST

"...up town, cross town, everywhere in town in Cayo Hueso..."

The Survivors, *In Cayo Hueso*

My four months in Key West were good ones. I worked a lot, but discovered that the expenses and wonderful distractions of the island took most of my money. My love life was incredible—even better than it had been back in Sausalito. Love—and sex—were really happening in Key West. It reminded me of Haight-Ashbury in the early seventies, but was very different. The atmosphere of tropical sunshine, flowering trees, minimal clothing, reggae music, island living—mixed with lots of dark rum—made a powerful aphrodisiac.

At night I would ride *Air Force One* (which was getting ever more rusty) down the narrow tree-lined streets of Old Town, stoned out of my mind on the sweet scent of night-blooming jasmine, warm tropical air, and the mellow sounds of music....

The best band—especially for dancing—that I have ever encountered in my life was *The Survivors*. They played in the small outdoor bars all over Key West—a blend of Reggae, Salsa, Soka and home-grown original songs that made me (and everyone who heard them) uncontrollably melt out onto the dance floor. Your hips would start moving on their own, your feet shuffling, your eyes would glaze over and you would be transported into heaven!

There were lots of cruisers in Key West—boats constantly coming from and going to the US East Coast, Canada, the Bahamas, Central America, Cuba, the Caribbean and even the South Pacific via the Panama Canal. The more humble voyagers were sailing the US East Coast, which I was soon to discover held some rich, varied and beautiful cruising grounds.

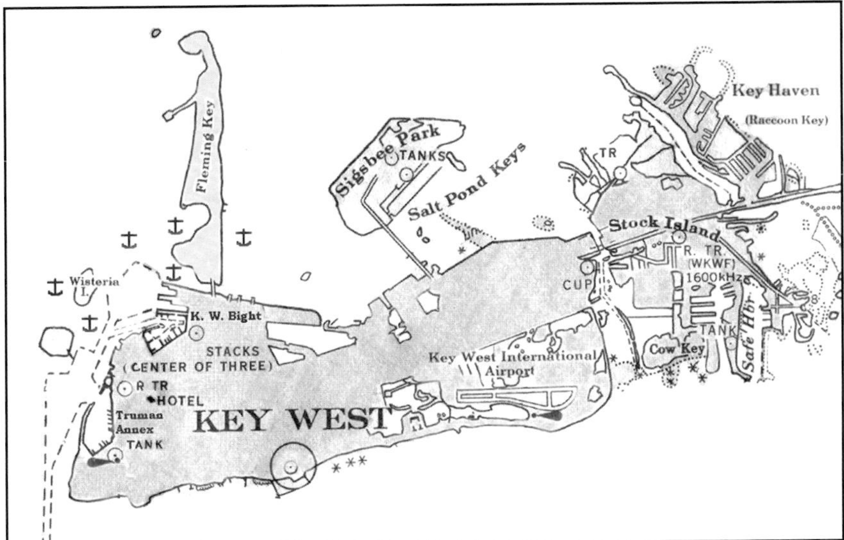

Key West in the late 1970's.

And there were lots of cruising women. I met Kathleen on Pier Five—her sloop was tied up across from the *Hornpipe*. We started hanging out together, and briefly became lovers. She was from Barbados—very beautiful, and very bright. She had co-owned a restaurant in Old Town, sold out, and wanted to go cruising. I wanted her to come cruising with me...but it was not to be. One night she spelled it out for me: "Reuel, I want *romance* in my life! I need to be *courted*!" "What could be more romantic than my lifestyle?" I countered. "Oh hell" she said. "You just don't get it, do you?" [Now, after all these years, I get it. And I wish I had then....]

I also met Kathy (and her teenage son and daughter), who had started cruising with a male partner. It was his dream—she went along for the ride because she loved him—not because she had any interest in cruising. After their first rough experience at sea, he packed his bags and fled! And Kathy fell in love with cruising, and kept the boat! I remember she had an old red convertible that we drove to Miami one weekend. This was before all the new bridges were built between the Keys—Route One ran across the old Flagler Railroad bridges—just barely wide enough for two cars to pass. When we got to Miami, we rented a motel room for the night, and one thing led to another.... Perhaps Kathy could have been my sailing partner—but I certainly wasn't ready to be a stepfather to her children. I was too immature—and I was having too much fun.

Steve and Tarey Lea, from *Zephros*, were around. They anchored behind Wisteria (Christmas Tree) Island, where many cruising boats were moored. Steve was gone a lot, and Tarey Lea and I hung out together much of the time. We shared meals, went dancing, and became really close friends. I was immediately taken with Tarey Lea when we met back in Costa Rica—she was a fireball of positive energy, tempered by a deep intuitive wisdom about the ways of the world. She was a talented artist and a consummate sailor. Like me, Steve became sea sick in heavy weather, and Tarey often had to manage *Zephros* at sea for days at a time—she was tough and pragmatic. She was also beautiful and sexy, and I would have given my left nut to have her with me. One night I told her that, and she said: "Reuel, be careful what you offer your left nut for—you never know if that's what you'll get (and have to give!)."

I used to wear baggy denim overalls a lot. With no underwear (ever). One day I was leaning over locking *Air Force One*—Key West was, and is, the bicycle-theft capital of the world—to a signpost in front of La Bodega, a great bakery/coffee joint, when a small hand darted surreptitiously through the opening at the side of my overalls—and grabbed my whole set of genitals! I yelled and nearly jumped out of my skin—to find it was Tarey Lea (and not some enterprising gay man, as I instinctively feared). She laughed so hard that she got the hiccups, and soon I was laughing with her.

A terrible thing (from my perspective) happened to Tarey. She and Steve had purchased a property in Golfo Dulce, Coasta Rica, near Joe's place (the water fall) we had visited the previous year. But she and Steve were having relationship problems, and Tarey went off to Mardis Gras with another man. Shortly after that, Steve was in Golfo Dulce, and Tarey flew to join him there. In the ferry (an outboard-powered dug-out canoe), a revelation hit Tarey like a ton of bricks—she was pregnant! Not by Steve. There was a very tearful reunion, with promises for change, and sincere commitments. But Tarey had to go back to the US to deal with her new situation. The child in her womb was not hers alone—and she felt responsible to its father.... When she told him, he insisted that they marry and become a family. This was not what Tarey wanted, but she eventually caved in under tremendous pressure...and guilt. The man involved was a Christian Fundamentalist, a born-again Jesus freak—and he would not take no for an answer. He was absolutely livid with rage that Tarey could have even *considered* an abortion and reconciliation with Steve.

Thus Tarey's life became a living hell, and Steve's heart was broken. He sold *Zephros*, sold his land in Costa Rica, and moved back to Hawaii where he was from. Tarey got married and had a baby boy named Gabriel. Her new husband was an absolute tyrant. He forbid her to have any contact with her friends from her previous life, including me (she had to send and receive letters through her mother). He kept her a virtual prisoner. He was worthless as a father—he would not even watch Gabriel long enough for Tarey to take a shower. But years later, when Tarey tried to leave him, he proceeded legally to obtain sole custody of Gabriel. In the end, Tarey told me she stayed with him just so that he would not be the sole influence in Gabriel's life. Eventually Tarey became pregnant again, and then one day the letters just stopped. I never heard from her again.

* * *

One visiting vessel was a small sloop which had sailed down from Cape Cod, bringing Marcia Peaslee as crew. Because I love Mexican food, I started hosting "pot luck" Mexican dinner parties on Pier Five. We placed a full sheet of plywood on two saw horses, covered it with a tarp, and as people from other boats (and from Old Town) showed up, we laid out a real feast. The rum and tequila flowed freely at these parties, and I remember (barely) passing out in *Gandy Dancer* (she was hauled up on the dock for maintenance) after one such feast. Marcia found me and somehow got me onto the *Hornpipe* and down into my bunk—and crawled in with me. I doubt I was much good for anything else but sleep that night, but there were many other nights...and I fell in love with Marcia Peaslee.

Although Marcia and I became very close during our brief time together, I was unable to persuade her to come live and travel with me. I was heartbroken when she left to sail home to Cape Cod. I felt that perhaps I had truly found the cruising partner I had so long been looking for...alas, it didn't happen, though I tried for years thereafter to make it so. [I'm still trying!]

* * *

We did manage a few short sailing adventures during our time in Key West. My old California friend Perry Fly came to visit me in January, and with some other new friends (a couple—John and Cindy) we made a trip out to the Dry Tortugas. We left on 1/8 and returned on 1/12. I remember trading some cigarettes (Cindy was trying to quit) with a shrimper. We gave him less than half-a-pack—with a joint we slipped in for good measure—for a full bucket of shrimp. I told him "That's a lousy trade," and he looked at me for a moment before saying "It's a *great* fucking trade!" I guess he was trying to quit too. Never underestimate the power of a nicotine fit.

We passed Mel Fisher's ghost ship on the way west. Mel was a major Key West player, and became America's most famous treasure salver. His most famous discovery would be, some years later, the wreck of the Spanish Galleon *Nuestra de Atocha*. During a salvage operation in the Keys, Mel's son and daughter-in-law (if I remember correctly) were drowned in a diving accident. Mel evacuated the ship used in the operation and abandoned her to rust away on location.

Coming into Fort Jefferson in the Dry Tortugas, it was blowing a norther, at night, with heavy rain—altogether nasty conditions. We found the piling that marks the entrance channel—just barely got around the right side of it, and went roaring full-speed up the narrow channel to the Garden Cay anchorage. I was shitting bricks negotiating the turns in the channel, and had no idea how we were going to stop at the end (it's a cul-de-sac). I might add that we were using a flashlight to find and identify the channel day markers—there were no lights. At the end there was *just* room to round up, drop the hook, and claw the sails down. Perhaps Perry remembered why he didn't come sailing with me way back when...but he was too polite to say anything.

We spent a couple of days exploring the Civil War era Fort, which was architecturally fascinating to me (see photos), and hauntingly beautiful. There was no one living there but a young couple employed as Park Rangers. Coming back to Key West was less exciting than coming into the Tortugas—mostly we motorsailed against the wind—which was a screaming *norther.* I saw J-24 sailboats for the first time racing around just off Key West—and I was very impressed with their performance in all that wind.

Paul went home at Christmas to be with friends and family in New York, and when he came back he introduced me to his close friend Eliot Greenspan. Eliot had been working in Miami in some huge mall, taking photographs of babies for money. He was tired of academia, having spent a year at Tufts, and was curious about the cruising life. He struck me as extremely bright, funny and pleasant to be around. He played music and was studying Tai Chi. He was literary, and wrote wonderful poetry.

I met Susan in the Truman Annex, where she was assistant Harbor Master (or should I say mistress?). She also was interested in the cruising life, and was splitting up with her boyfriend, who lived with his parents aboard their English cruising sailboat. She was the only one of my eight *Cayo Hueso* lovers who was willing to leave and come with me, hence I kidnapped her (she didn't resist).

The other addition to our group was a stowaway. Part of the problem of being tied up to a dock is that you get some uninvited guests. We got a rat. But we didn't find out right away.

We left Key West on April Fool's Day, 1981, with Paul, Eliot and Susan as crew. After island-hopping and running aground throughout the Florida Keys (*much* too shallow for the *Hornpipe*), we worked in Miami briefly, hanging out with Russell and James Frehling.

Russell had just bought a new cat ketch, and wanted some modifications made. We actually rented a slip in the marina (Monty Trainer's) where

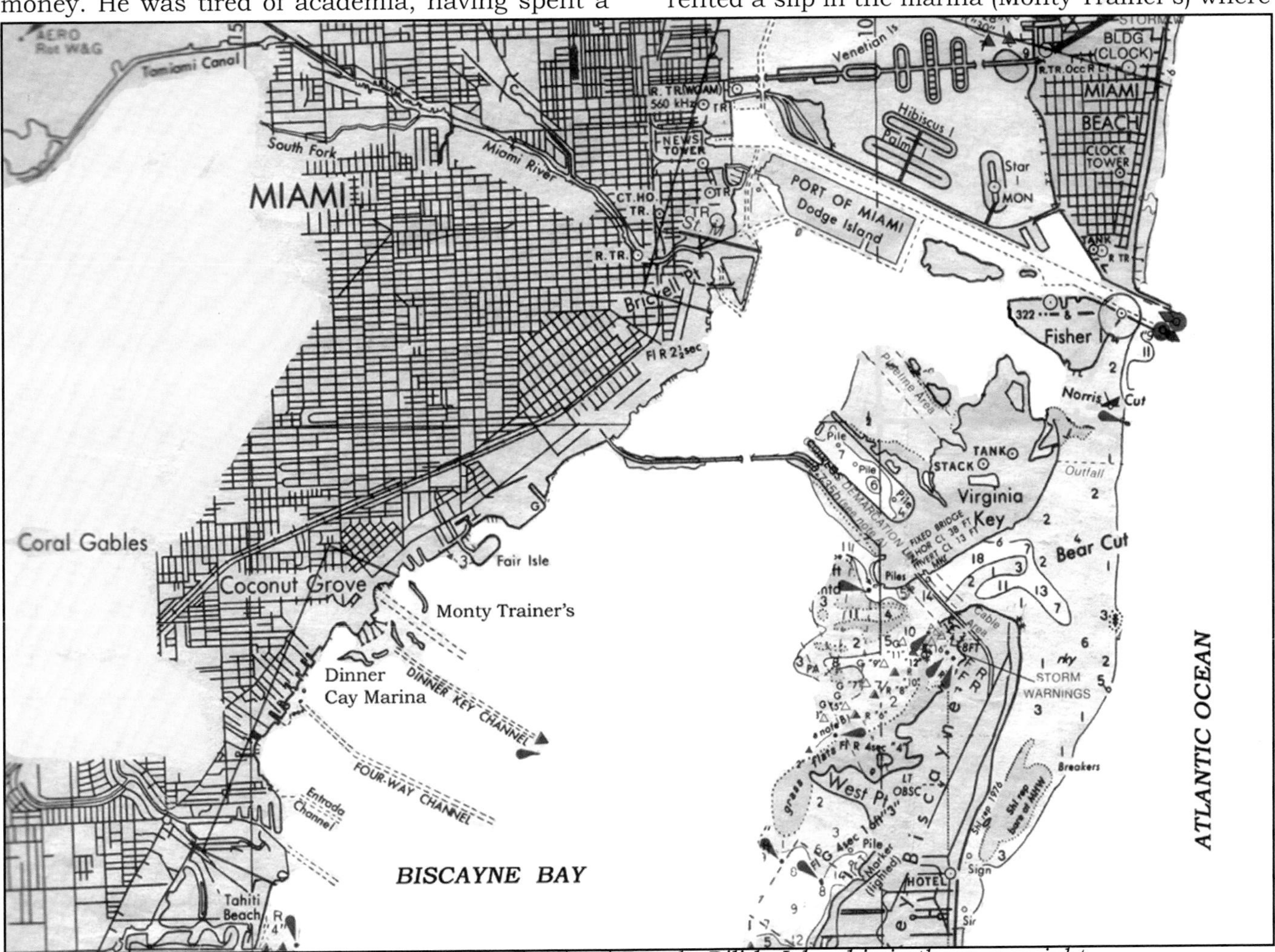

Biscayne Bay, Coconut Grove, Miami, Miami Beach. Dilido Island is in the upper right—the left of the three "lozenge"-shaped islands by Venetian Island.

Russell kept his boat in Coconut Grove. There we enjoyed a pleasant mixture of working and partying. Eliot had a close friend—Anne Knox—who worked at Monty's, and she kept us well supplied with cold beer. She also became a life-long friend, who would become one of my strong connections to Miami.

I had known Russell back in Bolinas, California—he was a close friend of Perry Fly's. Russell was a deep, complex renaissance man, who was an electronic musician, among other things. He worked with dolphin language electronically—recording and cataloging the sounds and reproducing them with synthesizers. After achieving some remarkable success, he took his equipment to Japan, in an effort to prevent the slaughter of dolphins so prevalent there. To prove his equipment and techniques to Japanese fishermen, he electronically called a large school of dolphins into a harbor. *The Japanese fishermen slaughtered them.* Russell took his equipment home and destroyed it.

There were four Frehling brothers. They inherited the Anheuser-Busch distributorship for South Florida. Some of them actively managed this operation, and some found other, more eclectic pursuits, like Russell. Brother James had a beautiful home on a canal on Dilido Island, Miami—one of the more impressive pieces of real estate I have ever visited in my life. We were his guests there before departing for the Bahamas.

Just as we left the dock behind James' house on April 18th, Bob Tillotson called. Instructions were shouted back and forth over the water, and we picked Bob up at the fuel dock in Miami Beach—and headed for the Islands.

CHAPTER TWELVE—THE BAHAMAS

"...your papa ain't your papa, but your papa don't know..."

Shame and Scandal in de Family

We had a slow, pleasant trip to Great Exuma in time for *The Family Island Regatta* (a week of native sloop races). It was traveling south along the Exuma Islands chain that I most profoundly realized the limitations of deep draft for cruising. We seemed to run aground a lot—not that this was anything new—but we also couldn't go to many of the places we wanted to see, nor navigate many of the island passages which were attractive to us.

If you run aground on a lee shore in any kind of wind and seas, you stand an excellent chance of becoming a shipwreck. Deep draft boats are more vulnerable in this sense than are shallow draft vessels with retractable centerboards (see following explanation)—but full-keel deep draft vessels are also generally more capable of "clawing their way off a lee shore." The Bahamas' windward shores are littered with shipwrecks of all kinds. [When you are on land, the windward shore faces the prevailing wind—when you are on a boat, a lee shore is one the wind can blow you against. Hence they are the same.]

This is the reason deep draft boats become shipwrecks if they encounter a lee shore: When a sailboat with a deep fixed keel runs aground it heels over—leans to one side. On a lee shore, the wind and seas drive the hull further aground, causing her to heel over further until her bilge (the curved lower side of the hull) encounters the ground. If there are rocks or coral, the hull is frequently punctured, allowing water to enter, and the vessel is wrecked. In the vulnerable attitude of lying on her side in wind and surf, the vessel is often pounded to pieces. Even in fair weather, a deep draft hull that runs aground is in trouble, particularly if the tide is ebbing, as she will still lie over on her side and be subject to damage. If the bottom is smooth sand, if there is no exposure to wind and seas, and if the next flood tide re-floats the vessel, there is no problem other than several hours of inconvenience (as in the groundings of *Fishers Hornpipe* in the Bahamas—see photos). However, one unfortunately placed rock or other hard, pointed object can still spell disaster, if it punctures the hull, and if the hull consequently floods. Today's manufactured fiberglass hulls are very vulnerable because they have very poor resistance to "point load impact." A fiberglass hull is strong only when all forces against it are equalized and distributed over a large area. Hence your average manufactured cruising or racing sailboat is the most likely of all vessels to become a shipwreck if she encounters a lee shore. Steel, aluminum, cold-molded wood and ferrocement hulls are less vulnerable to damage than fiberglass ones, but are by no means invulnerable. Often they are driven ashore and cannot be re-floated. Traditional plank-on-frame wood hulls are nearly as vulnerable as fiberglass ones.

Shoal draft vessels with retractable centerboards tend to remain upright when running aground. Even with centerboard down, as they encounter shallow water, the board simply is pushed up inside its slot or trunk. Often, when this happens, it functions as a warning that the vessel is in shallow water, and the board can be retracted, the boat turned, and further grounding avoided. If, however, the grounding is on a lee shore, in strong wind and moderate or large waves, and the vessel is driven aground, she will still remain upright, presenting her keel (the strongest part of the boat) to the bottom. Eventually the turn of the bilge may come in contact with the ground also, but the weight of the boat will still be primarily on the keel, and the hull will still remain more upright than a deep draft one. The chance of puncture is considerably less than with a deep draft hull. This will facilitate rescue or salvage when conditions permit—in many cases, the vessel may even rescue herself by placing a kedge (anchor) offshore and pulling herself afloat on the next high tide.

While *Fishers Hornpipe* was a pretty ideal sailboat in the open ocean, she was a very limited "gunk-holer." Gunk-holing is exploring coastal waters: sounds, bays, rivers, estuaries, lagoons, etc. Her draft of seven feet made her a poor choice for cruising in the Bahamas—however, we made the best of it, ran aground a lot, and had a blast anyway.

We sailed straight from Miami to Great Exuma—a five day trip—because we wanted to get there in time for the Regatta. Normally you would stop and formally clear into the country within 24 hours, but since George Town was a port of entry, we went straight there. One morning when Susan and I had the "graveyard" watch (midnight to dawn), Eliot popped his head out of the companionway to discover me lying down steering the *Horny Fishpipe* with my feet, with Susan sliding up and down on my rope-end (as we sailors call it). He promptly disappeared, like a jack-in-the-box—figuring we weren't ready to go off watch yet....

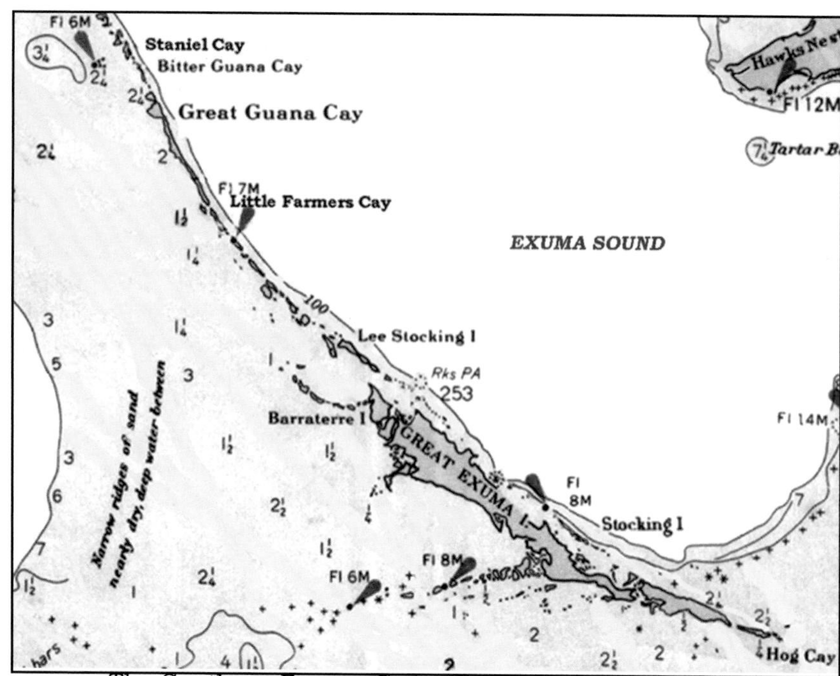

The Southern Exuma Cays. George Town, home of the Family Island Regatta, *is south of Stocking Island, which encloses Elizabeth Harbor.*

On April 23rd we anchored off the *Peace and Plenty Club* in Elizabeth Harbor, George Town, Great Exuma. We loved George Town, drank a lot of rum, and greatly enjoyed the *Family Island Regatta*. I got to race on *Diamond Cutter* out of Nassau as crew, but we came in last—too many white guys! The Bahamas were great to us. We ran low on money and went Native. Then it was the best—that's always when it is the best.

I started doing a lot more free diving (snorkeling) in the Bahamas—more than I had in Central America—and developed a taste for spiny crayfish and conch (which I gathered) and grouper and snapper (which I speared or caught on a hand line). Paul got very good at this also. Eliot didn't like to kill things, or deal with blood and guts, but he helped in other ways. We learned to use *Hawaiian slings* (long hand spears) because mechanized spear guns are illegal in the Bahamas—to give the poor fish a better chance of survival.

We moved over to Stocking Island, across Elizabeth Harbor, for quiet beaches and swimming. There is a beach on the windward (east) side of Stocking Island that is exquisite—three miles of pink sand, fine as sugar, littered with beautiful shells. On the lee side (Elizabeth Harbor), there are four interlocking lagoons, three of which qualify as "hurricane holes." There is a beach where the cruisers play volleyball, collect sand dollars and drink rum at sunset. There are sand dunes and cliffs and trails and caves, and the view from the cement beacon on the highest hill is wonderful. [All this has changed 25 years later—there are many more people—but the character of the place has survived. Visitors have cleared and maintained nature paths, and you can still find hour-long stretches when there may be no more than a handful of people on that perfect beach....]

On April 30th we crossed Exuma Sound, over night, to Cat Island, which we found beautiful and quiet. In the early morning, in a flat calm, we looked over the side to see huge, strange-looking baskets on the sea floor. We had the eerie sensation of floating in space. I sounded the depth with the lead line and was shocked to realize that the bottom was a hundred feet away, through crystal-clear water.

We spent several days cruising the "bight," or lee side of this 55-mile long island, and took a short hike up to the eerie, beautiful Hermitage (see photo). This architectural work of art was built by Father Jerome, an Anglican-cum-Catholic priest who designed and built numerous churches throughout the Bahamas during the first half of the 20th century. His remains were interred in the small crypt there upon his death in 1956, at age 80.

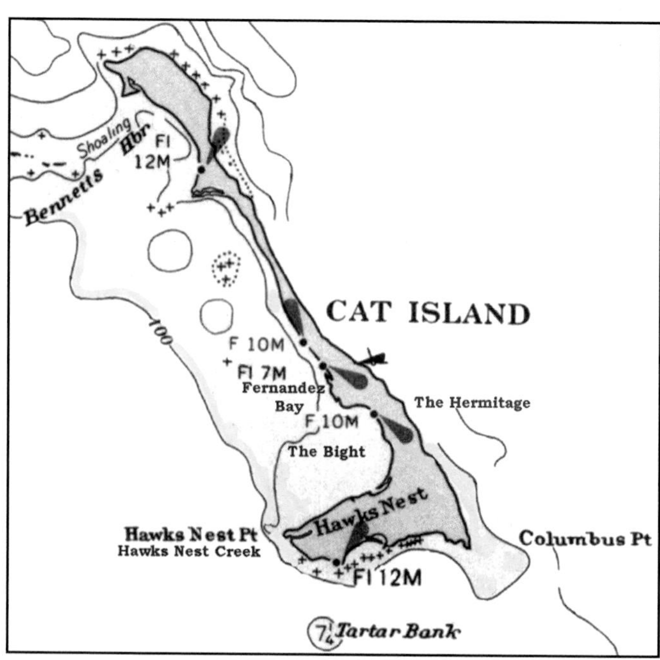

Cat Island. The beaches are among the most beautiful in the world.

On May 5th we entered Hawk's Nest Creek, on the southwest corner of the island, and moored between the small dock and some rocks. This almost brought disastrous consequences when the tide reversed and the strong current caught the *Hornpipe's* big keel. Coming back from the resort bar, we found her heeled over, twisted sideways to the current and straining her mooring lines nearly to the breaking point...good thing it was a strong dock! We also visited Fernandez Bay, where the Armbrister's beautiful resort is located, and anchored behind tiny Fernandez Cay seeking shelter during westerly winds (which was futile). Cat Island is no place for deep-draft vessels—the only shelter to be found is in the creeks, which are all very shallow, with the sole exception of Hawk's Nest.

I learned a lot about tides and currents in the Bahamas. Navigating in shallow water, among banks, islands and shoals, is very different from navigating across large, deep bodies of water away from all land. I learned to spend a few minutes thinking about the possible consequences of every situation—be it navigating a narrow cut between reefs or islands, or anchoring where there is a reversing tide. In particular, I learned that anchoring in strong tides that oppose the wind direction during either flood or ebb, would cause most boats to enter into the most bizarre "dance" imaginable. "Wandering" or "searching" at anchor is one thing—many boats, especially those with fin keels, do this. But when current and wind oppose eachother in an anchorage, boats can charge around in circles, race back and forth and jerk their anchors out, or spin around in place. We learned the technique of setting two anchors, one for each direction of the tide, or at 90 degrees to the tide flow, depending on the situation.

I also learned that both coral marl and sandstone can present such a hard surface that many anchors simply will not set in it, or have to be "started" by hand. This involves diving on the anchor while the vessel is pulling back on it gently, turning the flukes down (or the point of a plow), and guiding them under the surface. In our case, we almost exclusively anchored with the faithful 75-pound CQR plow, which never failed except when I failed to set it properly, or to pay out sufficient scope. We almost always anchored with all chain (except in very deep water), to provide extra weight and "catenary" to the rode, and so that the rode could never chafe on rock or coral. One excellent property of the plow anchor is that the vessel can reverse direction of pull, and not dislodge the anchor. In hard, rocky bottoms, however, I have found that nothing can match the old-fashioned fisherman (aka yachtsman) anchor for setting and holding, including during changes of direction of pull. The only failure I have ever seen of a fisherman anchor involved the chain rode wrapping around the upper fluke, dislodging the anchor and subsequently fouling and dragging it. I have seen that happen only twice.

We took on water at New Bight, Cat Island. This involved anchoring the *Hornpipe* as close to the beach as we could get her (actually running her aground on a flooding half-tide), and connecting many garden hoses together to reach a spigot up the beach by the road. The water was from an open well, and had a number of interesting things in it...including tadpoles! These we filtered out, and Bob adopted one as our pet. We named it *Sprout*, of course, for the little nubs that would become feet. Bob meticulously made a pool for it in a salad bowl, with a place for it to crawl out (or try to). Unfortunately, *Sprout* did not take to the diet of carrot peels and lettuce we provided, and croaked after a couple of weeks. I added chlorine to the water in the tanks....

There were several very elderly black men by the tiny bar/restaurant where we got the water, and one of them taught me to watch the stars at night: if they twinkled, it meant there was wind up high, and the next day would bring wind down low.

On May 6th we made another night crossing of Exuma Sound, back to the Exuma Cays. We anchored off Little Darby Island at 0715, which took several attempts, and when the tide ran out we found ourselves laid over on a 30 degree angle! (See photo.) An elderly local sailor came by in an outboard-powered skiff to ask us if we were all right (he turned out to be a famous *Regatta* captain).

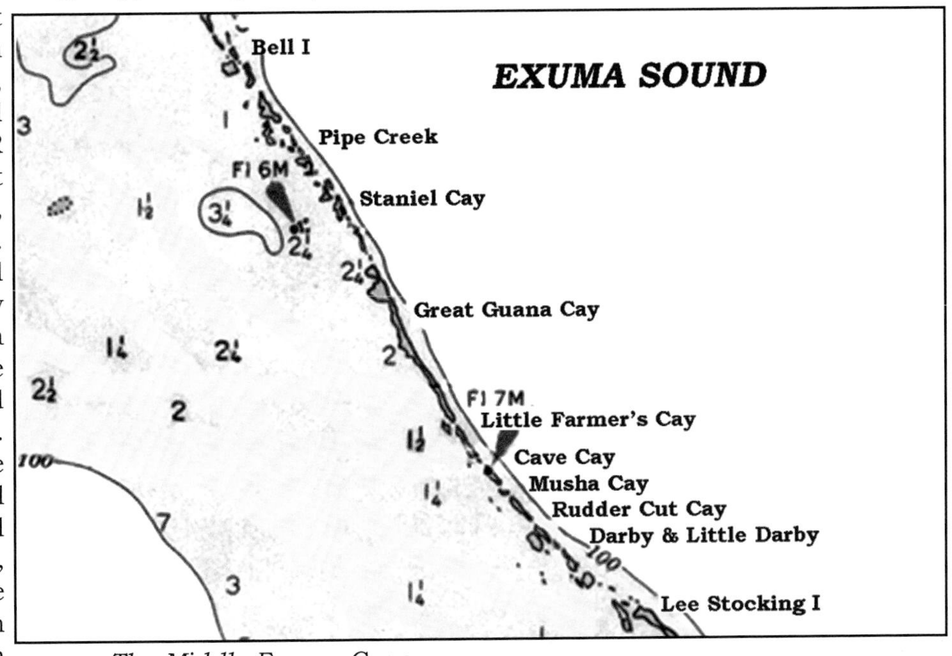

The Middle Exuma Cays.

Every place we visited, we encountered that kind of thoughtful consideration.

Two days later we visited Musha Cay, which was deserted and pristine. We wandered there for hours, and collected shells on the beach. We met the Lansing family, who had tried to buy Musha unsuccessfully. They bought instead the small cay just to the west (now called Lansing Cay), and were building a simple house there. [Early in the new millennium, Musha Cay would be completely raped by white developers.] And on 5/11 we anchored at Little Farmers Cay, which gave us a wonderful taste of an out-island native settlement. I must say that the black people of the Bahamas are as wonderful as the people of Isla Providencia in the southern Caribbean.

Next we visited Staniel Cay, which was a little touristy, but very nice. There is a small yacht club, with a clubhouse/bar/restaurant open to the public (sometimes), and the Happy People Marina, which is a legend unto itself. [Owners Kenneth Rolle and his wife have now passed on.] Thunderball Grotto (so named for the James Bond movie filmed there) is a small hollow island with a hole in the roof, and a large open cave inside full of tropical fish. Visitors dive through one of several short underwater tunnels to find themselves in a wonderland wilder than your wildest dreams. Take a zip-lock bag full of breadcrumbs in with you, and when you open it you will find yourself inside a big cloud of bright yellow and black sergeant major fish! This beautiful place is part of the Exuma Park system, all of which is a "must-visit" attraction in the Exuma chain.

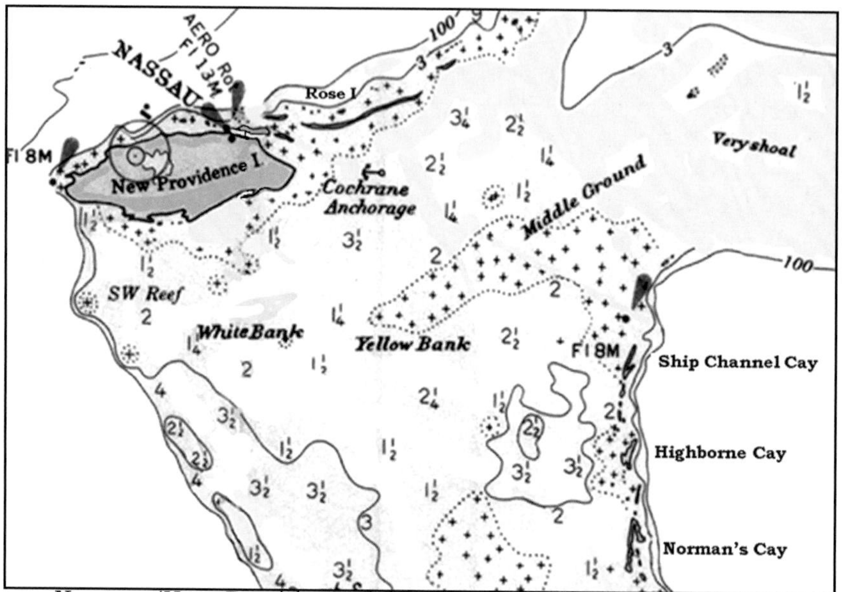

Nassau (New Providence Island) and the Northern Exumas.

On the 13th we sailed to Highbourne Cay, near the top of the Exumas, and thence on to Nassau, where we anchored off the Nassau Harbor Club. Things hadn't been going well for Susan—I know this was largely my fault—and we left her in Nassau to fly back to her dad in Texas. Susan and I had started the trip as new lovers, without knowing eachother very well, despite having become friends in Key West. After a few weeks in the Bahamas, it seemed to me we didn't really fit, and I tried to go back to being just friends. Well—no-one likes to feel rejected, me included, and that's how Susan felt. The final blow came when I was cleaning out a plugged-up fuel filter (my old nemesis), and put compressed air to it. The hose blew off, spraying dirty diesel fuel on some of Susan's beautiful clothing. She went ballistic, and was inconsolable. I felt like the lowest worm in the garboard [the hull plank just above the keel, traditionally infested with *teredo* shipworms]. I scrubbed her clothes for hours, but I couldn't get the stains out. That was the end.

After sending Susan home, we sailed to Rose Island to go diving on the beautiful coral reef there. It has coral canyons you can swim through, and was full of spectacular colors and fish. That night we departed for another night sail, this time across Northeast Providence Channel, for the Abacos (the northern Bahama Island Group). The Log states that we had an *excellent full-moon sail, in gentle seas and sweet easterly trade winds.*

At 1930 on 5/18, we anchored off Cherokee Point, Great Abaco Island—our deep draft did not allow us to enter the very shallow harbor there. The next morning, we sailed to Man of War Cay, where we had an excellent sail in *Gandy Dancer.* On 5/20 we sailed to Marsh Harbor, where I fell in love with singer David Crosby's Alden-designed centerboard schooner *Mayan.* I knew—and had known for a while—that someday there might be a schooner in my future, and perhaps a centerboard too. I was getting *very* tired of running aground, and I hadn't seen nothin' yet.... The more I saw of John Alden's designs, the more influenced I became by them—but *Mayan* completely blew me out of the water! (See photo.)

After playing in the bars and swimming pools (aquatic volleyball with bikini-clad tourist girls) of Marsh Harbor, we had yet another great trade wind sail to Great Guana Cay, where we hung out on the beaches for two days before sailing to Green Turtle Cay. We enjoyed New Plymouth immensely, with its narrow streets and prim, clean miniature houses, and provisioned at the small but well-stocked stores for the trip north. It was here that we first heard *The Gully Roosters* and fell in love with *soca* music. We also had a great party with David and Michelle on

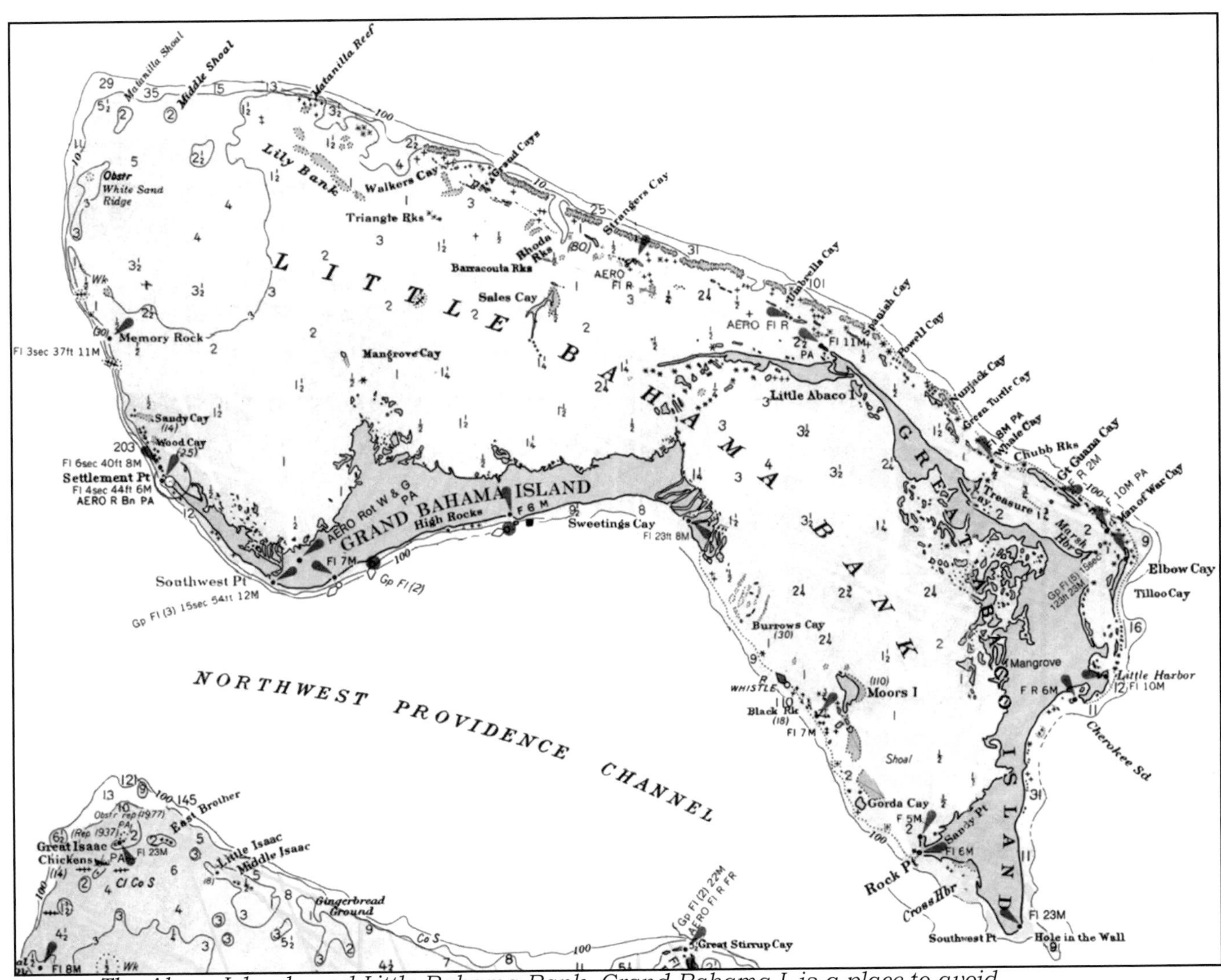

The Abaco Islands and Little Bahama Bank. Grand Bahama I. is a place to avoid.

Azulao, before they crossed the Atlantic. Someone baked incredible-edible hash brownies, after which (having eaten them all) we tried to wade out to a nearby island through the surf. The tide was flooding, and when the wave troughs got chest high, their tops would just sweep over our heads...we made it halfway before turning to body-surf back.

While we were in the Bahamas the Key West stowaway rat made herself known by chewing holes in things. Like the 5-gallon molasses drum—which drained into the bilges! Then she got the 5-gallon vinegar drum, the containers of grains, nuts, and rice—and finally even chewed through the hydraulic hoses to the transmission! Bob—having become used to coexisting with rats back at Starhill—tried various methods of catching her. But she outsmarted us all, and she wouldn't go near poison or traps, no matter how cleverly disguised. This "cat and mouse" (or should I say "Bob and rat") game went on for weeks.

* * *

We sailed offshore on 5/27 from Green Turtle Cay, in the Abacos, to Charleston, South Carolina. I remember several things about the trip—one was when my 24' long aluminum telescoping whisker pole folded in half. We were using it to hold the yankee jib out to windward while broad reaching in 20-knot winds and confused 6' to 8' seas. Next, near midnight on 5/28, we were hit by a violent squall, which broke the main boom bail and carried away my expensive snatch block. Then there was the toilet seat....

Around this time the *Hornpipe's* faithful old *Groco Skipper* (marine toilet) had taken a shit (no pun intended), and we were pooping in a five-gallon bucket. When around civilization, we would lower the bucket (half full of sea water) through the fore hatch, use it below, haul it back up on deck, surreptitiously look around for witnesses, and toss it overboard. This is a time-honored way of doing things. The only time it ever went wrong was when Paul hauled his used bucket up too rapidly, caught it on the drill press, and dumped it all over my work bench. [Years later, when I removed the drill press, I got a surprise.] When at sea, or if no one was around, we used the bucket on deck (or hung our asses over the side—equally time-honored). If anyone reading this has ever sat for long on the rim of a five-gallon bucket, you know how uncomfortable it is. You get this deep, round painful groove in your butt and thighs. I had a plastic camp-style toilet seat that fit neatly on the rim of the bucket—hence we usually used that. Well—around the time the whisker pole folded, I got up from using the bucket (on the lee side of the deck, of course), and the seat momentarily stuck to my ass. It was hot and sticky weather, you understand. The wind caught the seat before I could grab it, and I watched with great dismay as the damn thing took off like a frisby in that wind and sailed off on its own. I might have called a (wo)man overboard drill—as I had occasionally done when someone's favorite hat, or other item (the bucket itself on several occasions) had gone over the side—but the damn toilet seat sank like a rock. Besides—turning a cutter around with a jib poled out is a major ordeal.

The third thing I remember is that we overshot Charleston. I hadn't gotten a noon sight the last day of the passage (the last noon-sight fix was on 5/30), during which we gradually crossed the Gulf Stream, riding in it for several hours. Mariners must never underestimate the power of large currents—especially when sailing off the wind, as we had been. When we closed with the coast on 5/31, we found nothing but low vegetation and shallow water as far as the eye could see. No lighthouses, no city, no sea buoy, no breakwater. After searching around near dangerously shallow water (we had started taking soundings with the lead line), I found a small buoy labeled "2 BB." Which turned out to stand for "Bull Breakers." [Or "Bull Bay."] Anyone getting too close inshore would probably re-name it "Ball Breakers"; had a large sea been running, any deep-draft vessel running aground there would quickly be pounded to splinters. A shoal-draft vessel would simply run in and enter one of the dozens of creeks that riddle the marshes of a huge wildlife preserve.

I had hand-traced a chart for the Charleston-vicinity coast from friends on another boat in the Bahamas, and I had a small-scale (big picture) coastal chart. Neither showed "2 BB," and I couldn't find it in the *Coast Pilot*. I couldn't believe we had overshot Charleston by so far that we couldn't even see the powerful lighthouse (we should have seen it during the preceding night)—visible from about 50 miles away—but we had. The Gulf Stream had swept us 30 miles NNE of our dead-reckoning position! Hmmm, didn't this happen once already?

With tail between legs, we backtracked down the coast to the Charleston breakwater, and entered that beautiful historic harbor in the late afternoon. At 2100 we anchored just outside the Municipal Marina.

CHAPTER THIRTEEN—TO THE NORTH

"... In the destructive element immerse! ... To follow the dream, and again to follow the dream—and so always—usque ad finem...."

Stein in *Lord Jim*, Joseph Conrad

I fell in love with Charleston. This beautiful, historic city was in full bloom, and it was also full of beautiful, friendly people. Southern hospitality was alive and well in Charleston! We arrived in time for the wonderful annual Spoletto Festival, which we greatly enjoyed. There was art, music, theater, literature and great food everywhere—much of it outdoors.

We anchored between the City Marina and the Coast Guard station. [No longer practical since the marine expanded.] We went for long walks around the city, stunned by the architecture and living history in evidence everywhere. We loved the waterfront, and we hung out in the old slave market on the opposite side of the city, which was like a 'straw market' in Caribbean islands. There was music, art, food and beautiful women. There were discount clothing outlets, and I bought long pants and a jean jacket—things I hadn't needed for years.

While we were in Charleston, we finally got our rat—or rather, she got herself. We had moved everything she could damage out of her 'territory' (the enormous bilges of *Fishers Hornpipe*). She had done an unbelievable amount of damage, having chewed holes in dozens of storage containers as well as fuel lines, water hoses and hydraulic hoses. Finally, she found our unopened stash of rat poison, and chewed a hole in it—that was her demise. We found her body by the smell—under my bunk! I had been suspecting that socks had been disappearing out of my drawer—but as I didn't wear shoes, I didn't worry about it very much. The rat had used my socks to make a nest in a very hidden part of the bilge under my bunk—I had a hell of a time finding it and cleaning it out. And I felt bad about it—I would rather have caught her and released her alive. But she was too smart—or too stupid—to go into my *Hav-a-Hart* trap (I always carry one on board). We had an unceremonious burial at sea.

Bob left us in Charleston—slung his ancient Army-surplus pack on his back and walked to the freight yards to jump an empty box-car—his preferred mode of travel.

After the Spoletto Festival, we tried our first experience of navigating in the Intra Coastal Waterway (ICW). We crossed Charleston Harbor under full sail, and entered the waterway thus. As we approached the first bridge, I called the bridge tender on the VHF radio and requested that he open for us, informing him that we were under full sail. He said "Roger, Cap—bring 'er on up and I'll open for ya." As we rapidly approached the bridge—the flood tide current was with us, adding to our speed—the bridge didn't open. Having had no prior experience with this, I figured it must open really fast, and that the bridge tender would judge things pretty close. It still didn't open. At the last minute, I started the engine, spun the *Hornpipe* around into the wind, sails all aback (there was *just* enough room to turn) and flogging violently—then the bridge opened. After that, we rarely sailed in the vicinity of bridges...and I know now, of course, that in many places it is illegal to carry sail when navigating past bridges, even with the engine running.

While we found parts of the ICW very beautiful, we certainly couldn't compare it to coastal sailing or being in the open sea. In the ICW there was a lot of traffic. There were shallows and mud banks due to erosion (much of which is caused by the huge wakes from badly-designed power boats) and lack of dredging. We ran aground several times even in the middle of the channels. Constant vigilance was required navigating through narrow channels, among reversing buoy orientation (due to intersecting channels), through strong tidal currents, in heavy traffic in some places, and maneuvering around large ships and tugs with barges was often a nervous procedure. Navigating in the ICW is more like driving a car than sailing a boat—almost like a liquid I-95. Because the channels were often sinuous and surrounded by trees and buildings, sailing in the Waterway was all but impossible. Finally, I decided that the Waterway was useful when coastal conditions were undesirable—either due to storms or contrary winds, when tired or short-handed (in some parts you can stop almost at will), or when you want to visit someplace along it.

The trap I immediately fell into was that I didn't want to live in the north, on my boat, in winter—and I progressively found living in the south in summer to be undesirable. This is because of the intense heat and humidity (in the southeast US in particular), and because of hurricane season—roughly from July through November. So I became migratory—sailing north to New England in May/June—and south to Florida, the Bahamas and the

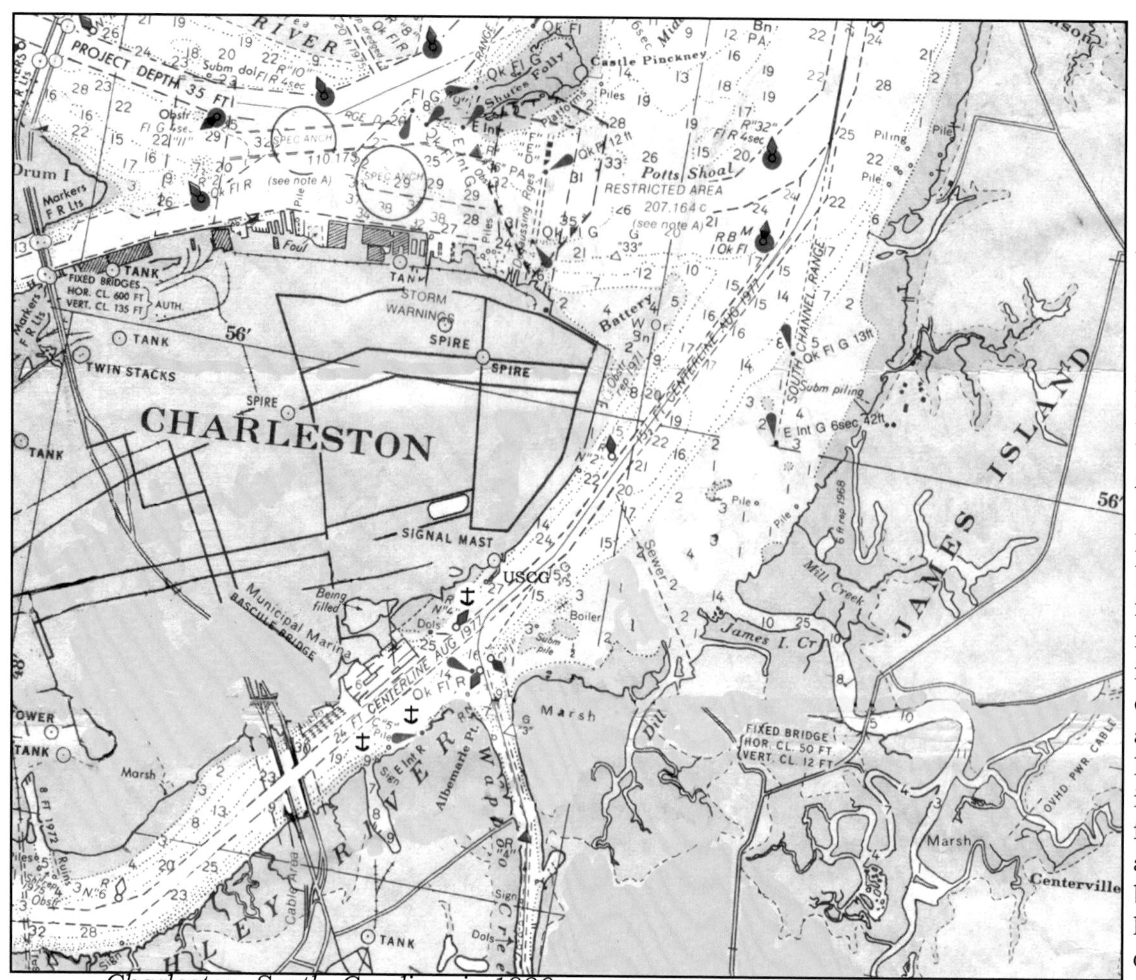

Charleston, South Carolina, in 1980.

West Indies in September/October. The problem with this migratory pattern is that in those months, sailing coastwise, the winds are not particularly favorable, and there are seasonal storms. Consequently, it is necessary to motor and motor-sail during most of the migratory trips, particularly if you don't want to spend literally months en-route. And, due to strong seasonal contrary winds, it becomes prudent to make a lot of the trip in the ICW.

Another approach is to travel the coast well offshore—riding the Gulf Stream current north, and sailing well outside the Gulf Stream coming south. *Sailing Directions for the World* indicates sailing nearly out to Bermuda, keeping East of the Bahamas, sailing through the Windward Passage, south of Cuba, and up through the Yucatan Passage through the Gulf of Mexico to sail from New York to New Orleans. Evidently a fast clipper ship could do that in ten days!

I found that I made friends along the coast, found favorite stops along the way, museums I liked to visit, races I liked to enter, and alternate routes to the "magenta Line" indicating the ICW on charts. Hence the migratory trip turned into a sort of cruise. I found that stopping at night became more the rule than the exception, and I found many beautiful, often isolated places to anchor (marinas were and are too expensive) all along the East Coast.

Somewhere in North Carolina we met Buck and Becky Smith [This book is dedicated to her memory] on their ferrocement Atkins 'Eric' *God's Bread.* Buck and Becky became life-long friends, and were instrumental in my eventual choice of Maine as my summer home. Buck is an internationally famous marine artist, perhaps best known for his beautiful drawings and paintings of gaff-rigged sloops sailing through the air. We would meet them many times in the years to come.

The Log Book for this first foray into the ICW is full of groundings. Between Charleston and Norfolk, we ran *hard* aground four times. Some of this was due to not staying near the center of the channel, some to not being in the channel, and some to poor choices of anchorages. *Some was because the channel simply was not seven feet deep anywhere.* Running aground in the ICW became a major source of anxiety and extreme frustration—especially when we couldn't get off and had to wait for the next high tide. Worst-case-scenario was running aground at high-water on a spring tide (the highest high tide in a bimonthly cycle). You could, theoretically, be stuck there for days, weeks, months, or even a year! In a storm surge, during the passing of a hurricane, it might take a major salvage operation (using cranes) to re-float your vessel.

We learned various techniques for getting off: placing weight (crew) near the bow to lift the (deeper-draft) stern free; swinging the main boom all the way out and hanging weight from it (people or a dinghy full of water); motoring forward while violently spinning the wheel (and rudder) side to side to "wriggle" a slot in the mud, through which we could then back out; setting a "kedge" (stern anchor) and attempting to winch ourselves back out the way we came in; and setting an anchor to one side (in deeper water), with which to pull our bow over. Often we tried several of these techniques together. Sometimes they worked—more often we had to wait for a higher tide. Sometimes we could take advantage of a large powerboat wake to "bounce" off in the lift of the artificial waves (perhaps the only positive use of powerboat wake). And on very rare occasion, another boat would take or give us a line and help pull us off.

The other item that appears too frequently in the Log is engine trouble. I had an Isuzu C-240—a sixty horsepower Japanese diesel, with a Borg-Warner 2::1 reduction/reverse gear. The engine really ran flawlessly—but the fuel filters and cooling system were inadequate. I had installed a single small filter/separator for diesel fuel, and it was not adequate for the task. Dirty fuel, poor quality fuel and fuel with water and algae purchased in third-world countries from unreliable sources (remember Mexico) took a tremendous toll. By the time we were relying almost exclusively on the motor to navigate the ICW, it was failing frequently due to fuel filtration problems and overheating. Live and learn! But the diesel engine itself was a jewel of design and manufacture—last I heard, it was still in *Fishers Hornpipe* after 25 years of service.

We traveled north in the ICW, greatly enjoying much of the beautiful scenery of the Carolinas (particularly the stretch north of Winyah Bay, which meanders so far inland that the water becomes nearly fresh), to Moorehead City and Beaufort, North Carolina, which we visited from 6/10 to 6/18. The people there were kind and friendly—the *North Carolina Maritime Museum* actually loaned us a beat up old truck to go shopping! This museum later became a rich resource for me for historical research for my books and designs. We discovered the *Dock House*, which had good ale on tap, reasonable food, and live music. I found myself sitting in with a bluegrass band, playing standup bass, which the band-leader went to get for me. I met a bright, interesting, beautiful woman who ran a dress shop in town, and we became lovers for the time I was there. It became clear to me that Beaufort was a magic place for me, and I knew I would always return, despite the overcrowded anchorage.

We continued in the ICW to the charming village of Oriental, on the Neuse River, from which we left the Waterway to sail out to Ocracoke on the Outer Banks. I had two charts for this area—Pamlico Sound—but there was a gap between them for which we had no information. It seemed like there was deep water up to the entrance channel to Silver Lake in Ocracoke—and I did something very stupid. I sailed *Fishers Hornpipe* at six knots right onto Royal Shoal—which I learned about the hard way. This was the only time in my sailing career I have ever had to cry *Uncle*—call the Coast Guard to come drag me off. Thank goodness they still helped people in my situation back then—nowadays they don't. At 1830 the Ocracoke Coasties' 41'er pulled the *Hornpipe's* bow around, and with all engines grunting we got her back afloat. The forces were so great that the *Hornpipe's* port bow chock was damaged. We followed the cutter into Silver Lake and anchored. Next morning, on 6/20, we moved to the Park Marina dock—which was free! [Alas—it isn't anymore.] We stayed there for four days, and I fell completely in love with this remote, windy,

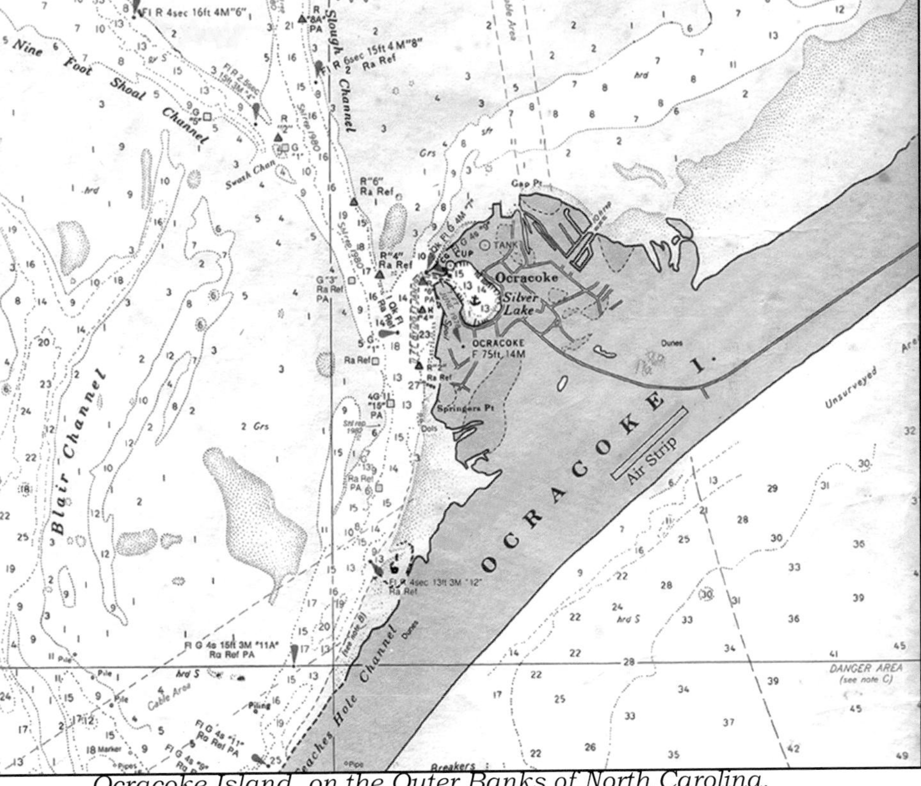

Ocracoke Island, on the Outer Banks of North Carolina.

beautiful barrier island of the Hatteras Seashore. To this day—twenty-five years later—I still go to Ocracoke every chance I get. I have many close friends there, I can often find crew there, and the quiet, tawny beaches and sand dunes go on forever.

While you cannot exactly drive to Ocracoke, there are three different ferries and a dirt airstrip.

When we left Silver Lake on 6/24, we had Gay and Karina on board—a high school teacher and a Swedish basketball player—whom we brought to Swanquarter on the mainland after a sweet day sail. We later anchored in Rose Bay—which *should* be called Horse Fly Bay! They bit the hell out of us while we were there.

After a stop in Bellhaven for propane (we were out) and lunch, we traveled again in the ICW to Norfolk. The three things of note involved the local wildlife: One morning, while hoisting the furled genoa, we found a large black and yellow snake coiled inside. Paul—Snakeboy—gently retrieved and freed it (I said *no* to keeping it as a pet). Another day we almost ran over a large black bear, who was swimming across the channel. We anchored one night at Pungo Ferry—where we had dinner ashore, and a note in the Log in Eliot's writing says *mungo pungo cheescake fruitcake waitress.* I guess he liked her.

On the afternoon of 6/30 we motored slowly up the Elizabeth River. None of us had been in Norfolk, Virginia before, and we were impressed by the US Navy's huge "mothball" fleet as well as by the dozens of active ships—especially the aircraft carriers and submarines.

We eventually arrived at Willoughby Spit—and were invited by Captain Lane Briggs [also in my Dedication], of the brand-new "tugantine" *Norfolk Rebel* (a schooner-rigged commercial tugboat), to come into Rebel Marine Service's marina. We had arrived home! The feeling was undeniable. Southern hospitality strikes again—and thus started a life-long friendship—for which I will always be grateful.

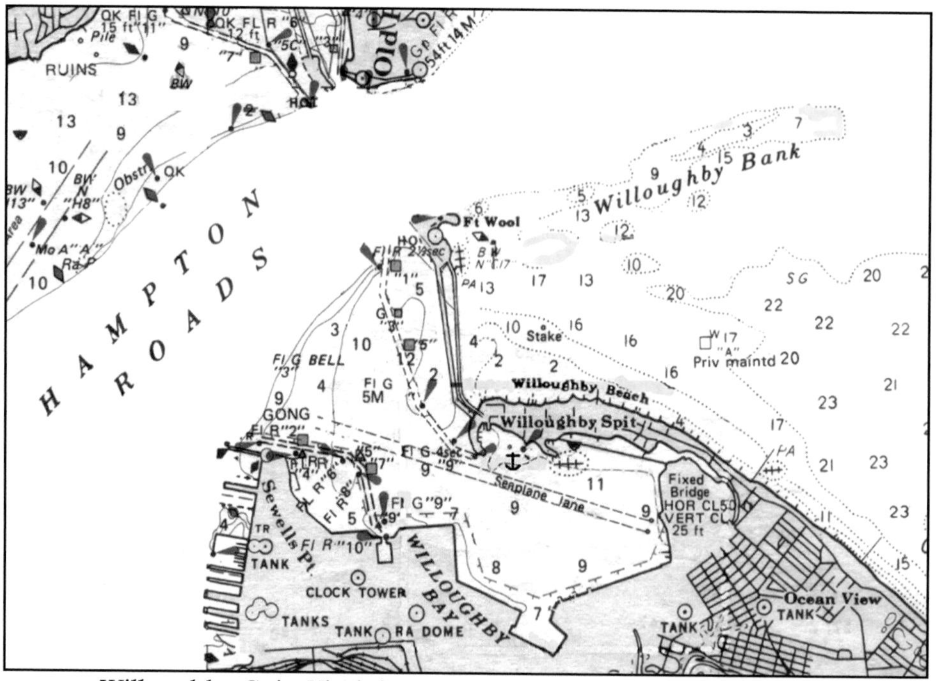

Willoughby Spit, Virginia. Captain Lane Briggs' Rebel Marine Services *is to the upper left of my anchor.*

Willoughby Spit is at the bottom of the Chesapeake Bay—where the tunnel goes from Norfolk across to Newport News (by Hampton Roads).

Captain Briggs always knows where the great parties are—'cuz they are usually his fault—and as he was in charge of the Forth of July Fireworks in Norfolk, we motorsailed to the Lafayette River in company with the *Norfolk Rebel* and the wooden ketch *Nike.* Once there, we rafted with Joe and Junior on *Nike* and partied for three days.

After one knock-down drag-out party on *Fishers Hornpipe* back at Rebel Marine, I woke up in bed with a voluptuous, intelligent, highly-spiritual woman...with whom I should not have been in bed! Thanks to her kind understanding, a life-long friendship ensued.

When we left Rebel Marine just after noon on July 6, with severe hangovers, we had kidnapped Captain Lane's secretary and her daughter for the trip to New York City. Kathy and Pagan Hill needed a sea voyage, and so did we, to clear our heads. This turned out to be the slowest sail ever—the wind decided to go to sleep for a week. We drifted in light puffs and calms all the way up the coast. Miles and miles offshore, with no wind at all, *the flies attacked!*

Millions upon millions of hungry, awful biting insects descended upon *Fishers Hornpipe* at sea—the only solid thing floating anywhere for miles around. [It turned out that this plague was caused by huge barges dumping millions of tons of garbage at sea from New York....] As it was horribly hot and humid, most of us were sleeping outside, naked. They nearly ate us alive. One bit Paul on the penis, which swelled up unnaturally, and after that we donned shorts! We sweated, slapped and scratched all the way to New York. Poor Kathy was unaware that I had brought no beer on the trip (I was trying to dry out) and went on an unscheduled withdrawal.... I had neglected to tell her that I don't drink when under way, and prefer that my crew not drink under way either. She was a very good sport about this, however, and wrote a wonderful poem, which she later mailed to us (see next page).

When we arrived in The Big Apple on July 9th, we had a great sail into N.Y. Harbor, and anchored in Great Kills Harbor, Staten Island. On the way there, we did have a minor mishap: While beating up the

Kathy's Hill's Poem (7/14/81)

TO THE CAPTAIN (and his hearty crew)
Of the vessel FISHERS HORNPIPE, Greeting:
Accept these lines as feelings true
And let our gratitude shine through
From both of us to all of you
For our stay aboard, though fleeting.

Despite the pestilence of flies
That caused the captain loss of temper,
And the dearth of beer (which lies
At my door—O, provisioning unwise!)
We saw the world with offshore eyes:
We've ocean sailing to remember.

Too bad you didn't find your bale;
Your eagle-eyes must spot it soon!
Meanwhile, may you sight a whale,
Keep dolphin company as you sail,
Leave ravished maidens on your trail,
And hear the oceans sing your tune.

With deep regret, we take our leave
Of such stout-hearted, naked men.
Shore life causes us to grieve;
But as soon as we believe
You're rounding Willoughby, REPRIEVE!
We pack sea bags to sail again.

channel, I was carefully watching a sailboat which was on a collision course with us, and I didn't see one of the channel buoys hidden by our big genoa jib. At the last minute, the other boat turned, and Paul yelled out *"port, PORT!"* I spun the helm, but it was too late, and we bumped hard into a huge green monster—which rolled kabump kabump down the *Hornpipe's* side. It did no damage to us—nor we to it—but I imagine a similar encounter in one of those flimsy tupperware yachts would have sunk it.

On the 11th we motor-sailed toward New York City, and tied up at the South Street Seaport Museum. Here Kathy and Pagan left us to return to Norfolk. [Because of our slow trip, and because Kathy had neglected to call Captain Lane to tell him we arrived safely, we later learned he had filed an over-due report on us with the Coast Guard.] The next day we departed to cruise up the Hudson River to Nyack. Paul's mother, Janet, joined us for the day sail to Edgewater, New Jersey, where Eliot and Janet left us.

It took me a long time to figure it out, but I finally realized I had met Janet years before, when I did some carpentry work on her house. While I was up a ladder installing a roof vent, I dropped my pry bar. A little boy retrieved it for me...it was Paul!

While anchored off Edgewater I had a meeting with David Beggs, who was in charge of work on the ships at the Seaport. Based on what he saw of my work on the *Hornpipe*, he hired me.

We sailed on up to Nyack, where Paul left to visit friends and family, and I had a reunion with Karren, my beloved partner who had helped me build *Fishers Hornpipe* back in California. Karren is from Rockland County, New York, and was home visiting relatives. She spent the night with me, and I felt awkward and lost and guilty with her. I was flooded with a thousand painful memories. Looking back, I realize Karren was essentially my second wife, or partner. She is a woman I loved very

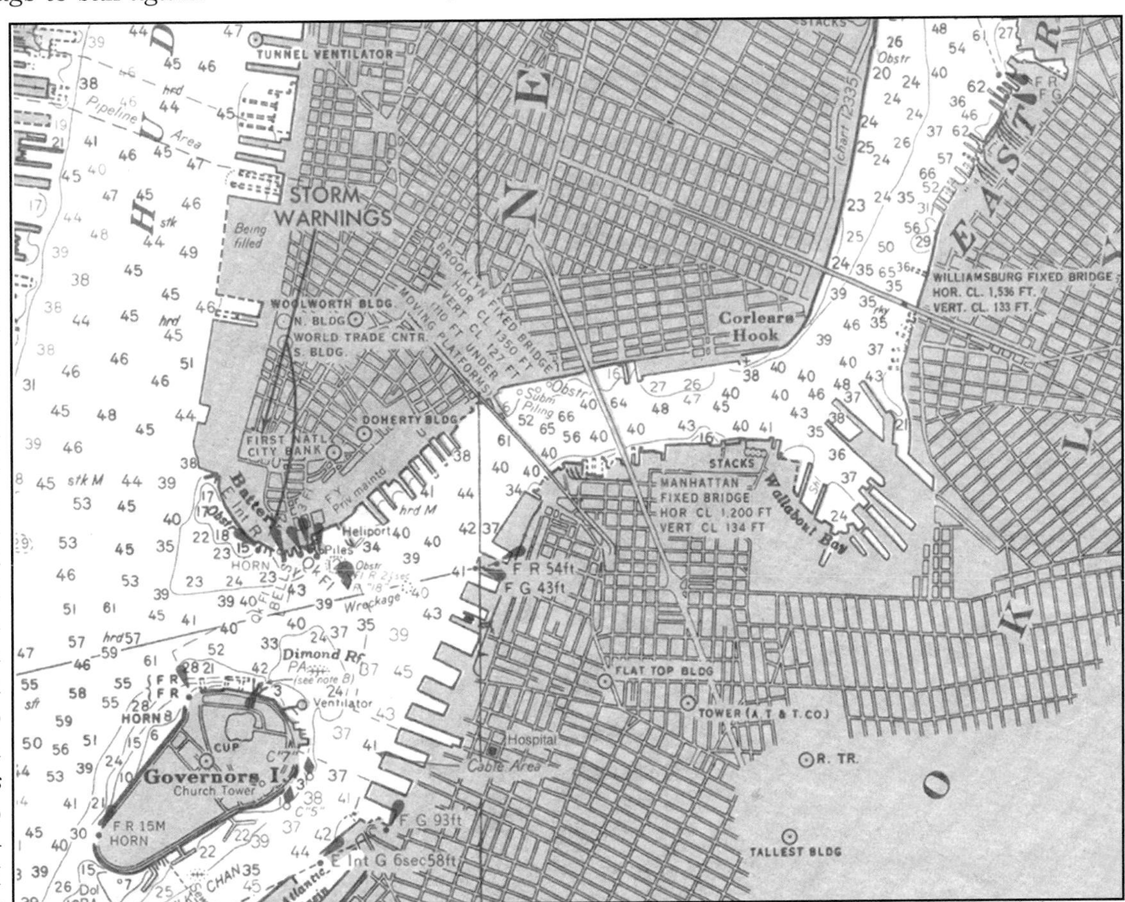

Lower Manhattan. The South Street Seaport is among all the piers to the right of the Battery. Of course the World Trade Center was not built yet.

much, but was unable to stay with when I became a sailor. I also realize that I was not worthy of her love.

Back in Manhattan, I started my job as shipwright at the Seaport Museum. The pay was lousy, but the benefits were great—a slip in the Museum, right in the historic Seaport. We woke up on the water with a view of Wall Street skyscrapers, the Brooklyn Bridge, and the East River. This was certainly different than the remote tropical anchorages we had become used to, but we made the most of it. We went shopping in Chinatown, walked along the Bowery, took the subway to movies, theater and music, hung out in the Village and Soho, cruised the art galleries, and stayed out of trouble, more or less....

Paul had an altercation with some "suits" in Chinatown: He was shopping with my bicycle *Air Force One* when a Mercedes cut a corner closely and side-swiped him. Paul dumped the bicycle on impact, but was not injured. The "suits" jumped out of their car and confronted him, one yelling at him that he would have to pay for the scratch on the side of his car, while the other one circled around behind him. Paul said "wait a minute...*you* hit *me*!" At the moment Paul realized these clowns were going to beat him up, *Wonder Boy* emerged, and clocked the yelling "suit" with a fast right, hard on the chin. The guy went down like a sack of potatoes! Out cold! Paul spun to defend himself from the other clone, who was backing away, holding his open hands out in front of himself while muttering ingratiating pittances...the two women in the car were frantically rolling up their windows and locking their doors. Paul grabbed the bike, the groceries, and booked it out of there! He was still shaking uncontrollably when he got home.

The working community of the Seaport was diverse, and I made some life-long friends there. The work was often frustrating, and I learned a lot about the problems that plague maritime museums. I would be replacing rail caps and coachroof trim on vessels that hadn't had a haulout in twenty years and were sinking out from under me. The priorities often seemed all wrong to me—the precedence of cosmetics to impress the tourists over structural emergencies to preserve the exhibits. But I gave it my best shot, I did what I could, I avoided museum politics, I didn't get a brown nose, and I knew it was only a summer job.

In New York, my love life continued to be good. One of the women who worked for the museum was attracted to the *Hornpipe* and her crazy hippy sailors, and was kind and helpful to us. I know in my heart that I owe her a big apology for what happened next, and I make that apology now (I know—it's a little late). While we were lovers briefly, I soon met someone else who swept my heart away: The museum hired college students in the summer to collect money and give tours. One of these "interns"—Lisan Martin—became very dear to me. She was a classics major at Brown University—very bright, very pretty, and full of vitality. Our 'courtship' started awkwardly—she thought I was a funny old man in overalls, bent under loads of lumber, always covered with sawdust.

I invited Lisan to dinner on board the *Hornpipe*, which I cooked. We found little to discuss that first night, to such a pathetic degree that Paul walked her to the subway to return home to Brooklyn. I figured, oh well, I tried. A few days later, she stopped me on the dock to say that she had a good time, and was willing to try harder to make friends if I was. Of course I was. I took her to dinner at a local restaurant—one of those esoteric, bohemian eastern-food hole-in-the-wall jewels that used to be in the Seaport neighborhood—and we really hit it off. Over a bottle of good white wine and a delicate meal, we discussed art, music, literature, philosophy—the classics—and mythology. We found that we *did* have a lot in common, intellectually if not experientially. She came home with me that night, and we found that we were a very good match in ways neither of us could have anticipated (I confess I had a feeling...).

Later I learned what had happened: When Lisan mentioned our dinner to the other interns she worked with, they became excited and wanted to know all about her evening on board the mysterious California Pirate Ship...and she figured she might have missed something. Perhaps it might be worthwhile to explore a little deeper....

And perhaps I should explain here that I believe lovemaking should include a lot of gentle touching and kissing—of *all* body parts (even toes!)—before, during and after sexual intercourse. I believe, especially in the beginning of a relationship, that sex should be slow, gentle and very thoughtful—that both partners should be attentive of the other's needs. Later, when partners really know eachother, passion may be urgent and intense and unusual (I can remember fucking someone up in a tree more than once), as long as that satisfies *everyone's* needs. I have no use for coercion, violence, pain, weird games, or restraints...if that's what someone wants—I'm out. On the other hand, I am not a "vanilla-sex" kind of guy either.... Despite the fifteen years between us, Lisan felt the same as me, and making love to her was fantastic.

* * *

The New York summer passed all too quickly. My job involved some strange responsibilities: The museum gave huge concerts out on Pier Six—and I remember when the *Taylor Family* (James, Alex, Hugh and Kate) performed. Years earlier, when I lived on Martha's Vineyard, I got to know several of the Taylors (even their mother). I doubt they remembered me, but I greatly enjoyed my job of watching over them, taking care of their needs (more about that), guarding their equipment and keeping fans off the Light Ship *Ambrose*, (which served as their dressing rooms). Well...a naked woman *did* get into JT's room, and I'll be damned if I know how.... And employing Paul and Eliot to run errands—mostly hand-carrying cases of Heineken beer to the band! Because the piers were packed rail to rail with solid humanity, the beer runs had to be made *outside* the rails—along the narrow edge of the dock. Negotiating this 12"-wide plank with a case of beer on your shoulder was a challenge my young crewmembers answered bravely to. After all, one slip and you went swimming in the East River!

By the time the Taylor Family concert ended, the band had given us a bottle of very good whiskey, in thanks for our help. We drank it. We had also, I'm afraid, been drinking Heinies with the band, and nature took its course. The only problem was that at three or so in the morning, the responsibility fell to me to use the museum's ancient forklift to take apart the speaker towers. This I somehow accomplished, without injuries or dropping anything, and the band—in conjunction with the sound crew—further plied us with gifts of alcoholic beverages. And someone gave us a large, gooey layer cake. That was a big mistake. When Paul and Eliot and I finally staggered down the narrow plank that connected the *Hornpipe* to Pier Fifteen, I grabbed a big piece of cake and plastered Paul with it. In retaliation, Paul plastered Eliot! What followed is lost to memory—but in the morning, heads throbbing with brutal hangovers (again), we had to face the most amazing mess I think I have ever seen.

* * *

While working for the museum I used to have lunch in a Fulton Street hole-in-the-wall called *Chapter Eleven*. There I met Tony Bianco, who was to become one of my best friends. Tony had been struggling with a 1927 Alden Malabar Jr. he had rescued from death in a Connecticut boatyard. He had been working on her restoration for seven years, and felt he was losing ground. He asked me to look at her, but told me if I laughed he would kill me! One rainy day he drove me out to City Island for my opinion, and the poor old girl looked so sad I broke down and started to laugh...I clapped my hand over my mouth but it was too late. However, Tony didn't kill me, and I recovered in time to give him a detailed recipe for saving the sloop. After my work period ended at the Seaport, Paul, Eliot and I moved the *Hornpipe* to a tiny anchorage behind City Island and went to work restoring the sloop, which Tony eventually named *Imagine*.

The story of *Imagine* is told elsewhere—In a 1985 article in *WoodenBoat Magazine* called *A Story of Priorities*—so I won't go into detail here. Except to say that Tony also was involved in another Fulton Street restaurant called *Ruben's Empanadas*—and that these became one of our all-time favorite foods. [To this day, in 2005, Tony still sends an occasional 'care-package' of empanadas to me.]

City Island is like a time-capsule of what New York was like one hundred years ago—with a few notable exceptions. The island is small—1/2 mile by 1 ½ miles—and is densely populated. Many of the old homes and buildings are beautiful. The island is a 'playground' for the less-moneyed New Yorkers—it is full of (mostly) inexpensive restaurants, bars, gift shops, 'antique' (junk)

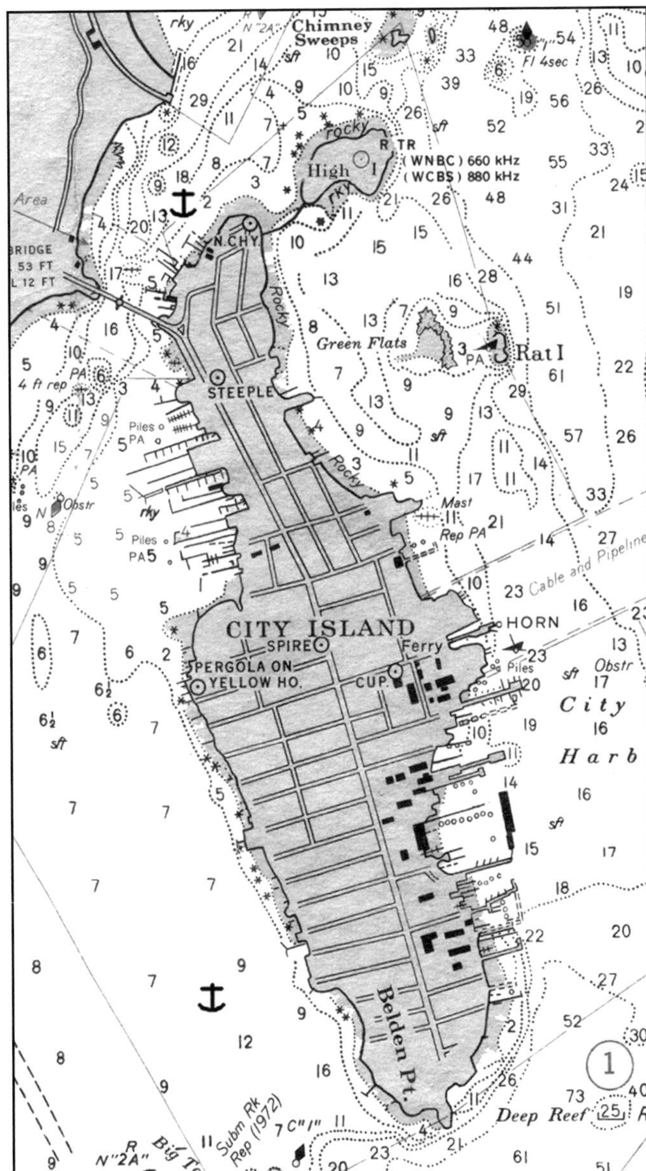

City Island, New York City. We restored Tony's Alden sloop Imagine *at* Sonny's Boat Club, *on the north end of the island.*

shops and the like. There are numerous marinas and boatyards—in years gone by Minneford's and Nevins were there, among others.

While we were on City Island, Lisan came to visit me. I remember her walking from the bus to the little boat club where we were restoring *Imagine*, and being on the opposite side of a very long fence from me—I wanted to hold her in my arms and kiss her, and the only parts of us that could touch were our fingertips! And I thought: This is so typical—this is my life—there is always a barrier between me and what I most want.... We had to walk what seemed a long way before we could finally embrace.

Next door to the boat club there lived an elderly artist (Teddy) and his wife. He taught me something I have always remembered: "Man has two heads, and the one above doesn't work until the one below finishes." Words to remember.

There was also a woman writer, who encouraged me to become a writer. She gave me my first copy of *Writer's Market*, and lots of tips about how to get started. She was interested in the restoration of *Imagine* and would stop by often to see how we were doing. One day she came in a beautiful pink cashmere sweater, when we were using tar (roof cement) as bedding compound—and of course her sweater got tar on it. We went next door to Teddy's to try to clean it—he was one of those people who had vast practical knowledge. He gave me some lanolin and I worked for a half-hour trying, in vain, to get the stains out. Why is it I always seem to be ruining women's clothes?

After planking, framing and decking *Imagine*, Paul, Eliot and I sailed out of New York on 9/26, late in the afternoon, and headed east into the Long Island Sound eating the last of a big box of going-away empanadas. We only got as far as Mamaroneck, from which we really started our journey the next morning, in search of a haulout and the colored leaves of New England's Fall weather.

We anchored at 0145 that following morning off Gardener's Island, inside the fishtail of eastern Long Island. The Log says we had a *hairy trip in.* We had been sailing east down Long Island Sound, towing *Gandy Dancer* in a light following breeze. Near midnight the wind rapidly increased until it was near gale force, and it became apparent that we had to find shelter or we were going to lose our faithful dory. The only nearby shelter I could find on the chart was in the lee of Gardiner's Island, inside the 'fish-tail' of Long Island's east end.

In the inky dark, with scattered squalls pelting us with rain, we ran through Plum Gut against a strong current, having trouble even finding the channel. We found very few lighted buoys, and had to leave them and venture into unmarked waters to find our anchorage. What we did was to take a course-heading from the last lighted buoy, run on it for a carefully measured time (having to accurately determine our speed), make a turn onto a second course for a second measured period of time, then take a final turn that would put us safely behind Gardener's Island, and sneak up on it slowly until the lead line showed the right depth for dropping anchor. This took some nerve, and perhaps some faith too. We couldn't see a thing in the storm. When the sun rose the next morning, we were right snug in the bight of Gardener's. We had slept well, so it was a good thing.

[For those who don't know—a lead line is a long length of small-diameter rope with a knot every six feet (one fathom) and a lead cylinder tied to the end. You swing the lead back and forth over the side of the hull, and toss it out as far forward as you can. As the lead sinks, you count the knots that disappear under water (in the dark, you can hear them go "blip...blip..."). As you pass over the line you pull it up and repeat the procedure. In this manner you can monitor the depth of water through which you are moving.]

The next day we had a very windy sail to Buzzard's Bay, Massachusetts. The wind started out around 20 knots, but reached over 30 by the time we anchored in Aucoot Harbor late that night. We left there in the early afternoon to have lunch, and tied up at the City Dock on the south end of the Cape Cod Canal. I ate a huge portion of fried seafood, for which I paid in more ways than one. At 1715 we left to transit the Canal with the tide, and when we entered Cape Cod Bay on the north end, we were hit hard by strong winds that we hadn't expected (winds in the Canal had been light). And I was hit by exploding fried food guts, which found me hanging over the lee side with my pants down while Paul and Eliot tried for all they were worth to keep *Fishers Hornpipe* from capsizing! We eventually got sorted out and headed for Provincetown (on the north end of Cape Cod), whence the wind again fell light. At about 2300 we entered P-Town Harbor—beautiful even at night—and shortly thereafter anchored behind the breakwater.

While on the Cape, I visited my dear friend Marcia Peaslee, whom I had gotten to know back in Key West, and whom I tried very hard to kidnap. She had just built a new house, and we made love on the third floor (literally *on* the floor!). She took me swimming in a nearby lake, and literally swam circles around me. We stayed on the Cape for a week, and I was feeling pretty depressed that Marcia wouldn't come with me. We had stayed in touch all year, and had been discussing this possibility in letters and phone calls, and I really thought she might come. Alas she did not, and never has since, though to this day I go visit her as often as I can, and we have remained friends.

Looking back on my youth, I know I seemed

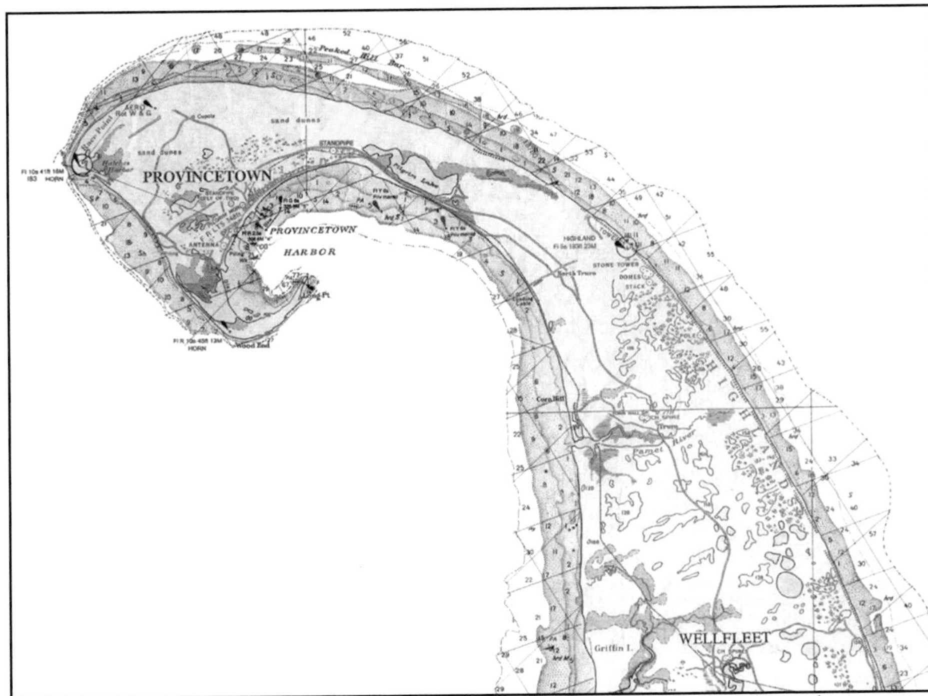

Provincetown, Mass, on the tip of Cape Cod. We anchored just inside the breakwater in P-Town Harbor.

"a bit of a rake" (as Becky Smith once put it) in those distant years—but I also know that I really loved Marcia Peaslee and wanted her to come with me as much as I have ever wanted anything.

We left P-Town on Oct 5th—very late in the year to head north—but that's what we did. My heart felt like it was in winter. I was cheered up a little by a group of migrating Humpback whales we sighted in the early afternoon. We had Jenny, a friend of Paul's and Eliot's with us for the trip to Maine (she joined us in P-Town). The next morning Paul wrote in the Log: *Saphire sea and rose colored dawn—dolphins playing with us, following and leaping.* And the following morning I wrote: *Have a flock of small land birds—I think American Gold Finches—make that a dozen!* (We were all working on our Haiku poetry....)

After two days at sea, we anchored off Burgess Marina in the Kennebec River at 1800. Finding out that they wouldn't haul us out, we left late the next morning for Booth Bay. We were unable to anchor there—the hook kept sliding across a rock ledge—and we finally picked up a mooring at Sample's Boatyard. They wouldn't haul us either. On the 9th we motored to Brewer's Yard in Ebencook Harbor, and they sent us to Robin Hood, who also said 'no way.' I don't know what the deal was—but I think all these Downeast wooden boat folks just wouldn't have a goddamn thing to do with one o' them ferryseement floating abortions. *Boat bigots!!*

I had had this fantasy that we would find jobs in a boatyard for the winter, anchor in a river, and ice skate to work. One chilly afternoon on Oct 10th, we were walking along the Kennebec River (wearing flip-flops as usual), when Eliot turned to me and said "you know we are going to have to start wearing shoes soon." "Oh no! Not that!" (I hadn't worn shoes since winter in Half Moon Bay—I didn't even *own* a pair of shoes!)

Realizing the truth of Eliot's words, we ran back to the dory, rowed out to the *Hornpipe*, raised our sails, pointed our bow south and headed for the Caribbean!

CHAPTER FOURTEEN—TO THE SOUTH

I don't care how fucking cold it is,
I see palm trees!
...a drop of pee on my leg.

Eliot Greenspan

But first we stopped in Gloucester, Mass, to see if maybe boat prejudices ran a little milder there than in Maine (we *really* needed a haulout).

At 1130 on Oct 11th, we came to anchor in Gloucester's inner harbor, and fell in love all over again. The port was a delightful mixture of working fishermen, beautiful old wooden yachts, and the Rocky Neck Artist's Community that we felt at home in.

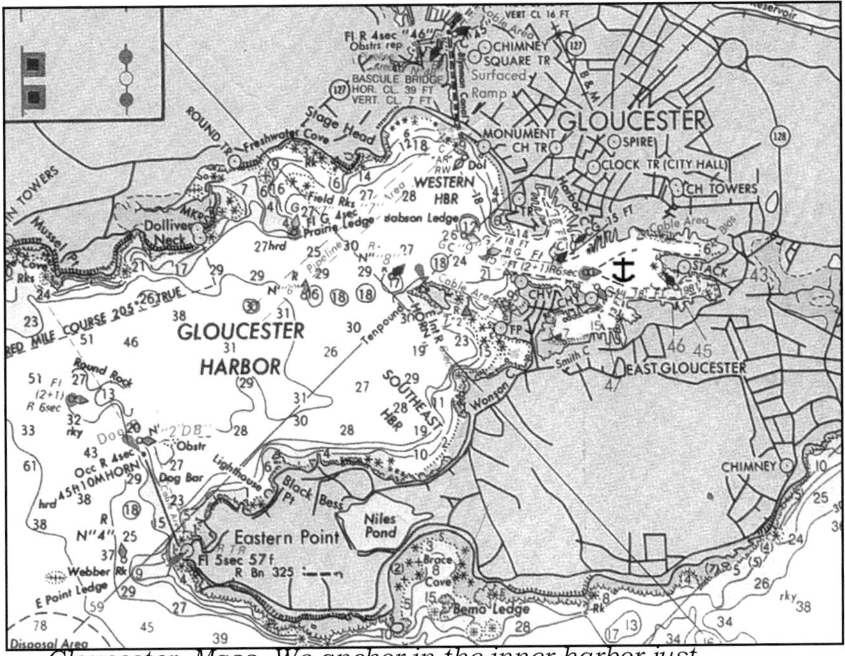

Gloucester, Mass. We anchor in the inner harbor just outside the mooring field (in the 1980's there were several free moorings available to visiting yachts). To the left of the anchorage is the Rocky Neck Artist's Community.

It was here that we endured the *Raid of the Polyester Pirates:* The local theater-group, all dressed up in weird-awful polyester stage clothes, jumped in anything that would float and attacked *Fishers Hornpipe* at dinner time! Fortunately, they bought a huge pot of lentil soup with them (which is when I learned to love lentils) and plenty of booze too! When they left, after a great spontaneous party, they left behind all their polyester clothes—which took me *years* to get rid of.

I found a new favorite breakfast joint—*Sailor Stan's*—in the Rocky Neck Community, and I still go there when I am in Gloucester twenty-five years later.

We got our haul-out, finally, at Brown's Boatyard, although it was much too late in the season, and the work didn't go as well as I had hoped. It was just too wet and cold. Trying to sand-blast and paint in drizzling rain really sucks.

We also found a new crewmember—Cynthia—who was a sweet person and a good cook. She was also a talented contortionist, and I remember watching her, dressed in black tights that conformed perfectly to her smooth skin, demonstrating a position in which her delicate and very pretty genitalia was (please forgive me, Cynthia) prominently displayed at waist height...and thinking, hmmm, I wonder what having sex would be like in that position? I never found out.

On the 28th we headed for Martha's Vineyard, my old stompin' ground, and we had some great sailing on the way. The tidal current through Wood's Hole was so strong against us that with the engine running full throttle and all plain sail up and drawing, we barely got through.

We spent Halloween night at Carly Simon's new nightclub, dressed up in homemade costumes (I wore Army fatigues, combat boots and my Army surplus gas mask—at least I was warm). We found my old artist friend Robbie MacGregor, who took us out to forage for oysters in the salty pond near where I used to live in West Tisbury.

We left the Vineyard on Nov 2nd and had a cold, blustery sail toward Newport, R.I.—but the westerly wind on our nose built up over 25 knots and drove us into beautiful little Tarpaulin Cove. The next day we sailed in a powerful norwester—between 20 and 30 knots all day—to tie up at Bannister's Wharf in Newport at 1350. *Fishers Hornpipe* was very close-hauled all day, and made an average devilish speed of 6.66 knots—not bad for a boat no *Downeast* boatyard would touch!

While we were in Newport, I took a bus ride to Brown University and spent a night with Lisan, hidden in her dorm room! This did wonders for my state of mind (and other parts), and it was with real regret that I got back on the bus next morning. Newport was fun (I particularly loved *Sala's* upstairs

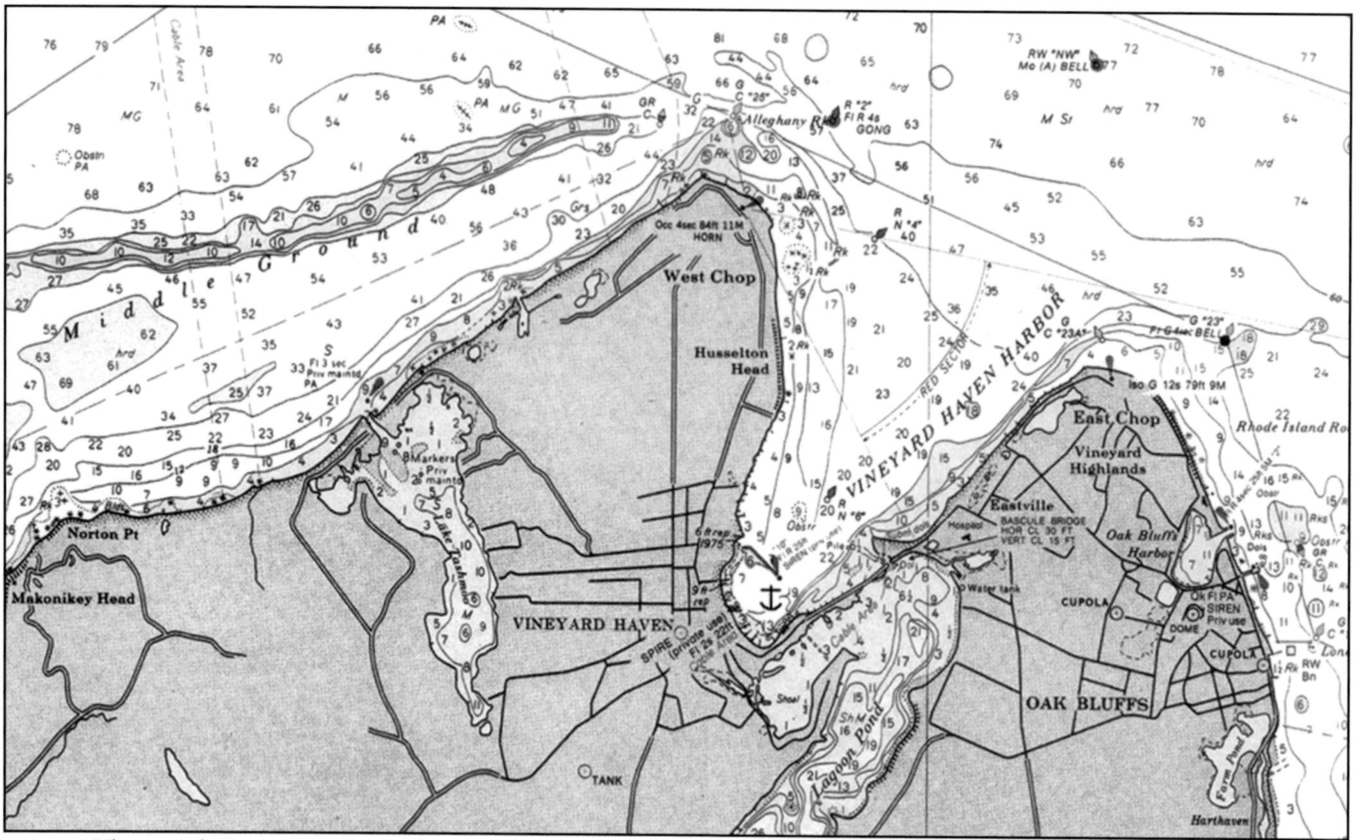

Vineyard Haven Harbor, Martha's Vineyard.

seafood restaurant), but winter was really on our heels, and we left on 11/5.

We stopped that night at Montauk Point, Eastern Long Island, tied to a small wharf in Montauk Lake. I had wanted to visit my folks in Bay Shore, but all conditions conspired against me and I had to blow it off.

On Nov 8th we went to sea and headed south. We sailed watch on watch, in winds 15 to 30 knots from WNW to SW. We were accompanied by schools of dolphins, and saw a large basking sunfish around noon the second day. That afternoon the wind died, and the school of dolphins that had been leading us all turned around and came back to see why we had stopped. When a little wind came back and we got under way again, the dolphins stayed with us. When we hove to later to cook supper, the whole school of dolphins stopped with us and patiently waited until we got under way again. Near midnight, when the wind died again, the dolphins finally gave up on us and left.

By 0230 that next morning the wind was back as a 25-knot nor'easter, and the *Hornpipe* was running like a scalded cat. We had a rough night in 12-foot seas, close together, but made good time of it until early on the afternoon of our third day out, when the wind fell light and died again. In the wee hours of our forth day, the wind came back as a light norther, and at 0930 we sailed

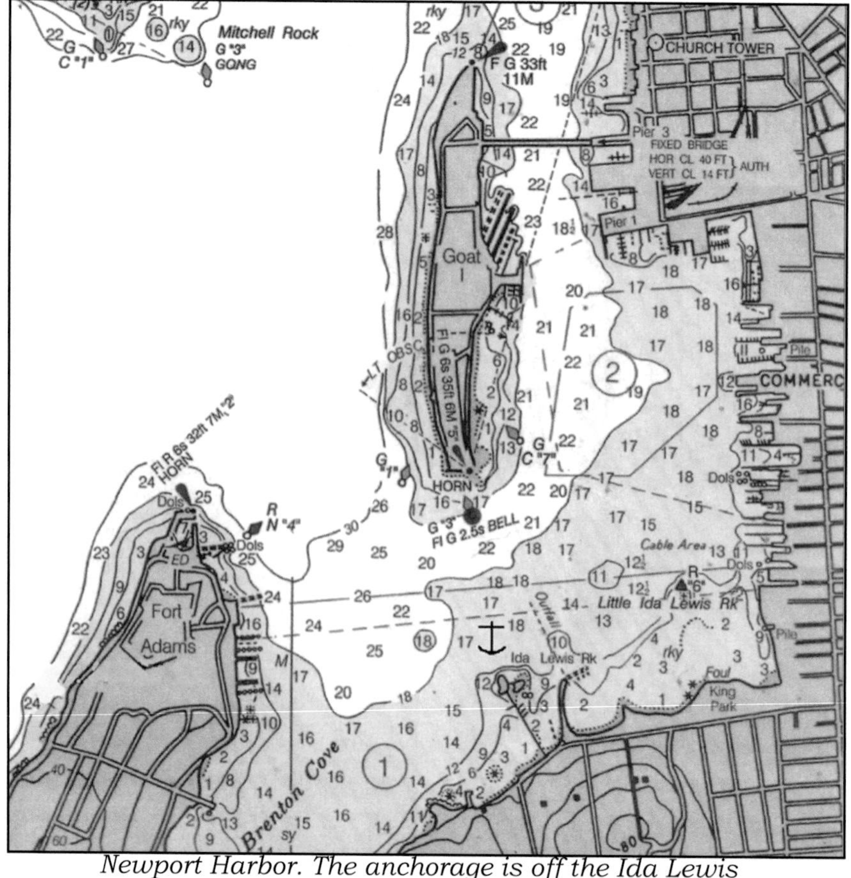

Newport Harbor. The anchorage is off the Ida Lewis Yacht Club.

right through a large pod of killer whales! I had not seen any since California, and was completely in awe of these beautiful black and white mammals. I was also pretty worried, having read that they are known to attack and sink small yachts at sea. An hour later, we had an uncomfortably close encounter with a freighter, which altered course to miss us at what felt like the last minute. The wind continued to increase, and once again became a nor'easter, blowing 25-knots all day.

That night—our forth one out—we entered the Chesapeake Bay in a full gale, which built in force as we raced to enter Hampton Roads. The breaking seas in the Bay were much rougher than outside in the ocean (due to the long fetch of the Bay and the shallow water), and we couldn't round up into them—nor did we have sea room to fall off—*we could not shorten sail.* The *Hornpipe* was so overpowered that I couldn't control her. I would ease the sheets to spill wind and fight the helm to get her to fall off a little, whereupon she would take off like a racehorse—then she would uncontrollably round up, allowing me to get a spoke down on the helm—whence she would fall off and race away again....

This went on for what seemed like hours, carving these big scallop-shaped-tracks across the Bay. *Fishers Hornpipe* was driven so hard that her pin rails, up above the turnbuckles on her shrouds, were in the water half of the time. Her bow-waves were blowing from her sides like a big powerboat going full-bore! I have no idea what her speed was, but I'm certain it was around ten knots—the fastest she has ever gone. Coming into Willoughby Bay—which is very shallow—we bounced across the bottom, the seas were so large. We were carrying a single-reefed mains'l and yankee jib, and we couldn't do anything but hang on for the wildest ride ever. Poor Cynthia, ever the good sport, asked Paul: "Is this normal?" "Why shoooore—we do this all the time" Paul drawled.

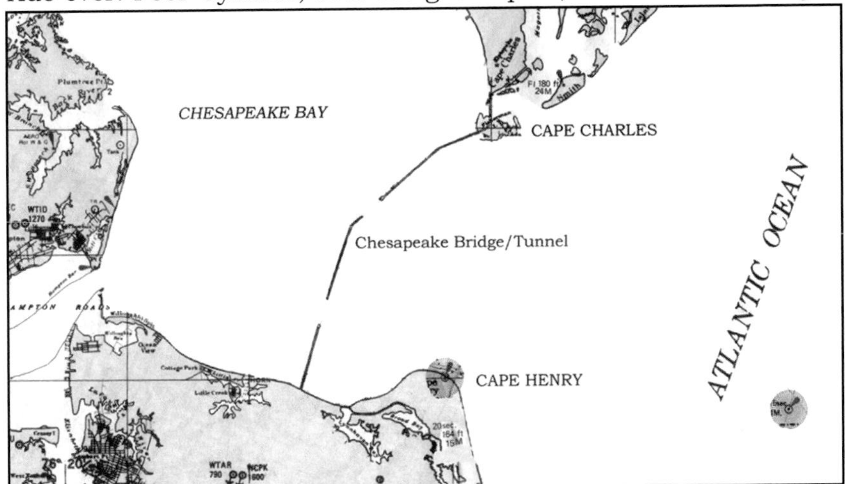

The Chesapeake Bay entrance. We crossed over the south tunnel of the Bridge Complex and sailed to Hampton Roads in gale-force winds and breaking seas.

Just after midnight, we got our sails down finally and motored into the fuel dock next to Rebel Marine Services—home again. That gale had become the winter's first major storm. We later learned we had been sailing in winds blowing 50 knots.

Newsletter, Nov 17,1981:

We stayed at Rebel Marine for five days—got cleaned up and dried out. I met Marine Architect Merritt Walter, and talked with him about a career in designing boats. He told me the pay is rotten and people sue you. As always, we threw a great party before we left. We never seem to leave anyplace without a wicked hangover. And once again, we kidnapped Captain Lane's secretary Kathy Hill for a week, to come with us to Beaufort. Lane handed her a quarter and told her "Now you have no excuse for not calling me." Paul took off to visit some friends and rejoined us in Beaufort, a week or so later.

Next door to Rebel Marine was a big motel called *Neptune's*, with a huge statue of Neptune himself on the roof eternally rotating on a turntable. We met a waitress there who was friendly and came to visit us on the *Hornpipe* after work. She was clearly lonely, and spent the night in Eliot's bunk... but he showed no interest in her—hence the next night she slept with me, and I was very interested. She was thin, and pretty, and very horny. So was I (is it a permanent affliction, or what?) I made love to her very slowly, letting the natural tensions swell, touching her and kissing her everywhere, as is my way. She was extremely responsive. When we came to the intercourse part, she was unique in a way I had never before (or since) experienced...maybe it was just because we were both so into it. She massaged me, in rhythmic, quivering waves, with her vaginal muscles. It was absolutely wonderful! Once again, we parted in the morning, when she went back to work and I sailed away. Story of my life.... [Years later, Kathy Hill told me she got married and raised a family—I hope her husband knows how fortunate he is!]

Since the Atlantic was still kicking ass, we took the ICW down to Beaufort, N.C., which was becoming one of my favorite stops. On the way, in the Alligator River, the sun came out bright and hot, and the Log states: *First naked day in months—though only for an hour....* In Beaufort we found our friends Buck and Becky Smith on *God's Bread* with their brand new baby boy

Bowen.

I hung out in the Maritime Museum library doing research, and looked up from my stack of books to see a tall, thin, attractive woman with long curly hair—*volcano goddess hair*—sitting across from me, also doing research. It turned out she was a commercial artist specializing in architectural renderings, and we soon became friends. As Thanksgiving was upon us—and since I do celebrate that holiday (the only holidays I celebrate are Thanksgiving and Halloween)—I invited Jean and her 10-year-old son to have a turkey dinner with us on board *Fishers Hornpipe*, which I cooked, with all the trimmings! She reciprocated by looking me in the eyes and making another, most intimate invitation. I got to use the line—for perhaps the only time in my life—"my place or yours...?" We chose hers—more room, more privacy. Sex with Jean was intense, athletic, enthusiastic—I remember we fucked our way off the bed, across the floor, and up against a wall...isn't it wonderful how different sex can be with different people? She asked me "are you always like this?" And I had to say "I dunno...it takes two to Tango—that's what my mother always says." Our brief time together was more Beaufort magic, and I was really sad to leave. Jean and I stayed in touch for a few years, and I think she might have come sailing with me, but there were some problems in the way of that (like school), and it did not come to be.

On Nov 28th we departed Beaufort for a night sail to Cape Fear. At dawn we were lost! The coast looked all the same, and for the life of me I couldn't find Masonboro Inlet. I finally called the Coast Guard on the VHF for descriptive information, and figured out we were too far south. We beat back up the coast for an hour.... *WRONG!* So we turned around again and ran back south, close to the beach, straining our eyes for anything that might tell us where the hell we were. The Log notes that it was *Primal Scream Time....* And I did, too. We eventually found the inlet, which had been recently dredged, re-marked, with a new breakwater, and didn't fit the description on the chart or in the Coast Pilot. Pay attention to those *Notice to Mariner* bulletins!

Just past noon we tied up to the floating dock at Masonboro Boatyard. I recognized this as the place where Paul had run us aground at high tide last spring—leaving us beached for 12 hours. Needless to say, we entered very slowly and carefully (Lucky for us, the channel had recently been dredged). Buck and Becky Smith had told us about Masonboro Boatyard—great people, good prices, winter community. Ed Lowe, who was the manager, loaned us a car to go shopping and catch a flick...more southern hospitality (I mean honestly—what Yankee would tell you to take his car for the evening?). *God's Bread* joined us shortly after we arrived, and we had a good visit.

Three days later, in the early afternoon we left Masonboro to continue south. We motored through Snow's Cut to the Cape Fear River, thence out the inlet and to sea. The inlet was surprisingly rough, because the powerful river ebb-tide opposed the wind, and because there was a large ground swell running. Cynthia had just fed us a delicious onion soup, and both Eliot and I tossed it up. Nothing like onion broth in your sinuses! Poor Eliot—I would call to him and say "Hey Eliot, watch this—*Eaauuuuaaagh!*"—as I barfed in the sink, and Eliot would stagger over to the sink and go "*Oh! Oooh! Oh no—aauuuoooghhhh!*" [Seeing me throw up always made him throw up too, and vice-versa. Oh, we were cruel.] Those of you who have gone sailing and encountered mal-de-mer have probably witnessed a shipmate down on his knees, talking to God on the Big White Telephone...perhaps even calling him by his first name, "*RALPH... RAAAALPH...oh God...oh God...RAAAALPH!*"

We motorsailed for a while, until the wind came up. The big swell should have clued me in—all that night we were in a light SW gale, which drove us further and further offshore. The wind blew up to about 40 knots, then gradually decreased to 10 knots by the next afternoon, and clocked to the NW. The Log notes: *lots of barfing.* By 2100 we were nearly becalmed, and ate a dinner of macaroni and cheese—our first food in 30 hours. Everyone was exhausted. But that night was beautiful—the sea was full of phosphorescence—until the wind backed and started to build again.

By morning it was blowing WSW at 30 knots, with a clear sky and building seas. We were close-hauled on the starboard tack, under storm jib and single-reefed mains'l. During the day, the wind increased to 40 to 45 knots with stronger sustained gusts, and the seas built to 15 to 20 feet. I was the sickest I have ever been in my life, and Eliot was no better. Cynthia and Paul blessedly did not get sea sick, and most of the physical work of handling the boat fell to Paul. I remember, at one point, seeing him up in the maelstrom in the cockpit hanging onto the "roll bar"—a massive steel pipe that ran across the front of the cockpit at chest height—screaming "*I LOVE IT...I LOVE IT...I LOVE IT...*" at the top of his lungs, just barely audible over the ear-shattering howling of the storm.

This went on for what seemed like years, but was only one day. I became a quivering lump of protoplasm, curled in a corner of the aft cabin under the table, wedged in place, with a towel under my face and a little cup of water. I had thrown up until nothing came out but green paste—the bile from my liver. Then I had the dry heaves.

For 10 hours there are no log entries—the

only such omission ever. During the afternoon, the mains'l flogged so violently that the leach line wore through the leach tape and wrapped itself around the port intermediate shroud (shrouds and stays are the wire ropes that support the mast) and tore the mains'l to ribbons. Paul came down and asked me what to do—I told him to get it down, if possible—and put up the stays'l, if possible. Paul—alias *Wonder Boy*—did just that, but it took him a couple of hours, working with solid green water breaking completely over the *Hornpipe's* foredeck.

I wasn't sure it would work, but the ever-amazing *Fishers Hornpipe* continued to beat into towering twenty-foot gray-beard Atlantic seas, making very good time (6.5 knots), under storm jib and stays'l alone—a feat that should not have been possible. And not only that—she continued to steer herself. The seas had become so large and violent that they began to break across *Fishers Hornpipe's* raised quarter deck and burst like a fire hose through the tiny opening that was our only source of fresh air in the great aft cabin.

At 1840, with conditions easing up gradually, I was able to crawl to the VHF radio and place a general call ('radio check') to see if anyone else was out there and could hear us. I made radio contact with the USS *Makanerie*, who gave me her position as 32 degrees N by 78 degrees 59 minutes W. This did not constitute a 'fix' for us, as we could not see this ship—but we at least knew approximately where we were as she could 'see' us on her radar screens (which put us within 5 miles of her location). The wind dropped to variable at 5 to 15 knots, and Eliot was able to come on watch and steer back towards shore. At 2300 I contacted another ship, southbound, and got a good position. I was up and about by now, but weak as a kitten. At midnight I was able to come on watch, and at 0343 I found the sea buoy for St. Mary's Inlet—the northern-most inlet in Florida.

By 0915 on 12/5 we were tied up to the "Florida Welcome Dock" in Fernandina Beach, and we were close to that condition where you fall down on your face and kiss the sweet, beloved Earth! We really felt welcome, too. But never before had we been so badly beaten up by any ocean—not even the *Gulf Stream* off Cuba. Everything in *Fishers Hornpipe* was wet. In places her woodwork had been stripped bare! Water found it's way through every pinhole, every loose fastener, every chainplate, every wire through the deck, every portlight, skylight and companionway. All the mattresses and our bedding were soaking wet, as were all our clothes. *The books on one shelf amidships had jumped their fiddle rails, all together, and landed in perfect order under another bookshelf six feet away to port, neatly turned 180 degrees so you could still read their titles—albeit upside down!* It was a year and a day since our arrival in Key West—and we were back in Florida.

After several days of cleaning up, drying out and patching up, we dug out my old spare mains'l and bent it on. We had to bring all our mattresses out on the dock, wash them in our 55 gallon drum in fresh water, squeeze them out and dry them—which took days.

We departed before noon on Dec 10th, in the ICW (no more oceans for a while, thank you very much), for St. Augustine, and promptly ran aground (the Log entry says *Dumshit on helm* in Eliot's handwriting. We anchored that night in the St. John's River, and continued south next morning. At 1415 we ran hard aground again, this time near high tide. The Log entry says *Don't even ask who was on the helm*—in Eliot's writing again. It took us until 2000 before we (Log entry) *Got the fuck off.* We anchored south of Pine Island for the night, and came into St. Augustine a little after noon the next day. We anchored north of the Lions Bridge so we could get to sea without having to deal with a bridge opening (I really don't like the feeling of being trapped with no access to the open sea)—and celebrated Cynthia's birthday.

We stayed in St. Augustine for three days and had a good time. I ran into one of my old Key West lovers—she was driving a horse and buggy to haul tourists around. We discovered the *Mill*, an upstairs bar which has really great music.

On the 15th, at noon, we weighed anchor and headed out the inlet, ready for the ocean again. The Log says: *St. Augustine Inlet rough and hairy.* (It's

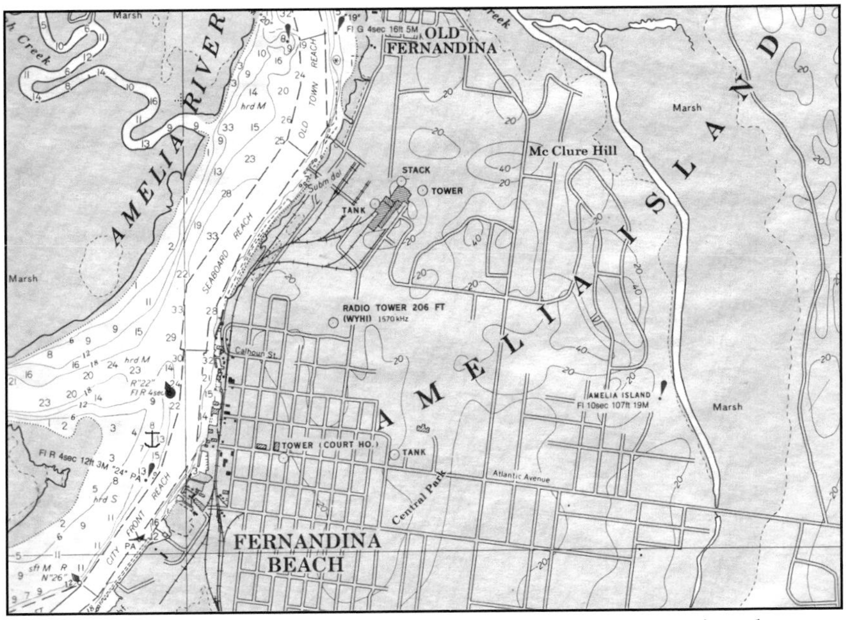

Fernandina Beach, Florida—just inside St. Mary's Inlet.

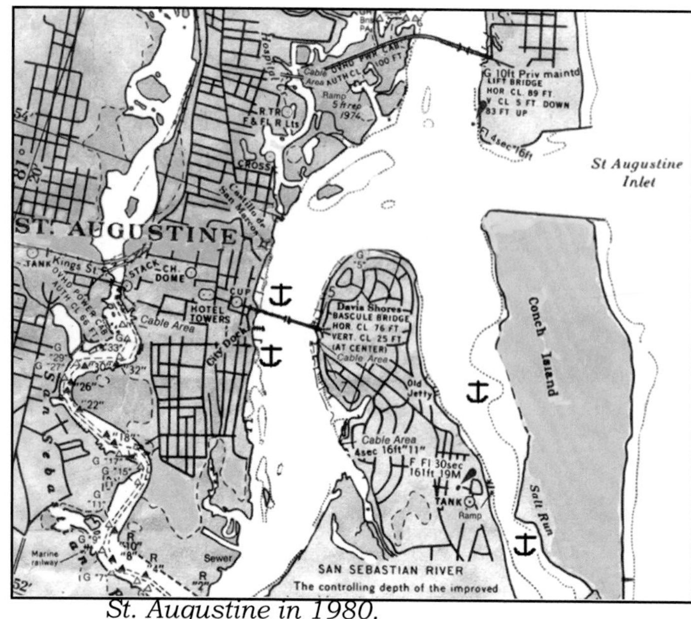

St. Augustine in 1980.

famous for that...you work diligently to stay in the center of the channel, with huge white breakers roaring over bars on both sides of you.) At sea the wind was WSW at over 25 knots (too familiar). We had to hand (take down) the worn old mains'l, and close reach under jib and stays'l, now that we had learned that that unlikely combination of sail worked. In the night, the wind moderated, and we put the main back up and had good sailing on a beam reach with 10 to 15 knots wind. The wonderful old *Hornpipe* reeled off the miles at a steady 6 knots. We sailed like this for three days, staying well offshore to round Cape Canaveral, but otherwise staying "inside" (west) of the Gulf Stream to take advantage of a slight counter-current. The wind gradually clocked through to the north, but never blew over 15 knots—very sweet.

Just before midnight on 12/17 we anchored in Lake Worth, just inside the inlet. The next afternoon we moved to the anchorage between Singer's Island and Peanut Island, where President John F. Kennedy's fallout shelter was located—and where he reputedly had love trysts with Marilyn Monroe.

Newsletter, Dec 18, 1981:

Palm Beach, Florida: Well here it is coming on Christmas again and I've been down so many roads I confess I'm lost. I haven't sat behind this old typewriter in a long time, and the keys stick. Salt air. There are many of you—my people—whom I love and care about, and I've blown it trying to write individual letters to everyone. There are over a hundred of you I want to write to and hear from—so please forgive this mimeographed newsletter. Call it a Christmas card from someone who doesn't observe Christmas. And I will keep it brief—I haven't money for many copies and postage. (I am a living study in living beyond one's means.) But I want you all to know I'm still out here doing it—moving sailing living loving flowing—remembering to stop and smell the flowers!

Fishers Hornpipe *is alive and well after over fifteen thousand miles of much of three of the Earth's seven seas caressing her keel. But we are both showing signs of age and we both seem to need some work. My boats are rough and tired, but sound. My head I am less sure about.*

I must admit that something in me is tired, and that I long to be out from under the burdens and responsibilities that come with this lifestyle; but I'm damned if I know what else I would do. Despite the hassles, living and traveling on the water is terminally addictive—as rich and full and rewarding as life on Earth probably gets. The problem of finding good female crewmembers is always a major hassle, and I don't mean girlfriends or lovers—that, happily, hasn't been a problem. But there are precious few free, adventurous women in the world who can and will take off traveling by small sailboat, and have their trips together and their heads in a healthy place.

So life goes on and life is good. And the world around us is desperate, as usual. I try to pay attention and be aware, to put my energy in positive places—and still I wonder, still I search.

* * *

Cynthia left us in West Palm, where she found work—and to be with an airline-pilot

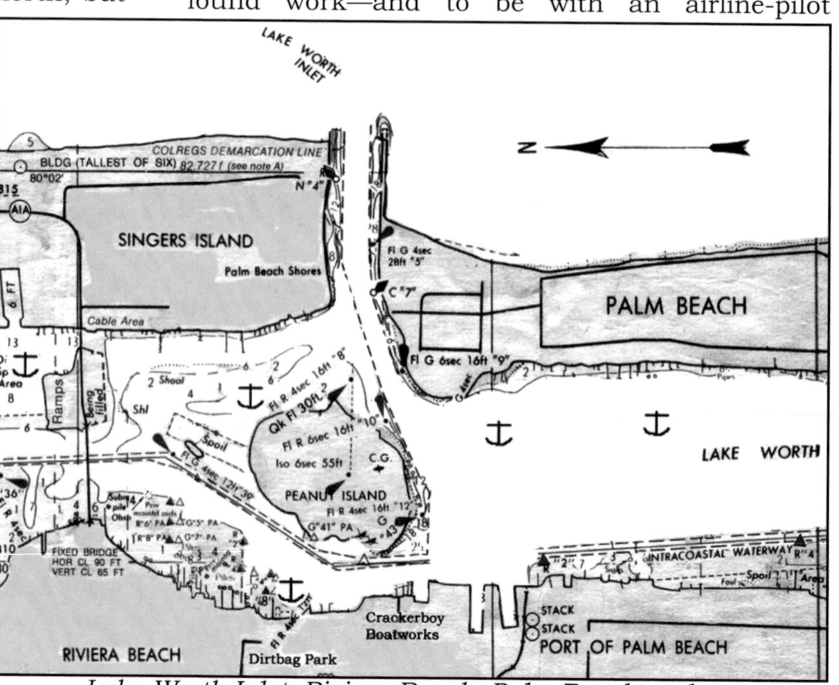

Lake Worth Inlet, Riviera Beach, Palm Beach and Crackerboy Boatworks.

boyfriend. We stayed in touch for a while, then lost it. She was a real good trooper—went through sheer hell with us—and I hope wherever she is, she's having a great life. Paul went to New York to spend Christmas with his family.

On Dec 21st, Eliot and I went to sea and sailed back up the coast to Cape Canaveral, to spend Christmas with my family. We took my mother, stepfather, aunt and uncle out for a day sail. I showed them what their condo looked like from the ocean. This was the only time my parents ever went for a sail with me—they never approved of my lifestyle and salty wanderings. I think they enjoyed the day, but they clearly didn't understand Eliot, and the whole visit was awkward. At my aunt and uncle's condo later, my aunt saw Eliot touch his bare foot while eating from a plate of cheese and crackers. She took the plate into the kitchen and dumped it in the garbage. We had removed our thongs at the door, as always, as any civilized person would, and we sat on the floor cross-legged on the pure-white shag rug. They must have thought we were from another planet. The Logbook makes no mention of the visit or the day-sail, and it took me a while to even remember why we went to Canaveral. It was a strange, awkward, unhappy Christmas.

Around noon on the 29th we left to travel in the ICW down to Ft. Pierce, where Paul joined us, to look for work. We were all stone-cold-broke. We spent nearly a month tied to the dock at Cracker Boy Boat Works, and worked for Pete (the manager) on his vintage Huckins powerboat, *Target II* (from Bay Shore, where I grew up). While there, we also worked on the *Hornpipe* some, and finally planked the inside of her transom with exotic woods I had carried halfway around the world for that purpose. One afternoon Pete came aboard looking for me, and found Paul and Eliot in the aft cabin stark naked, having a sawdust fight! Sometimes *even I* have to wonder what people thought about us....

The Florida weather she was warm. We spent January kicking around the coast. We blew out our tired genoa jib beating in the ICW, blew out one of my hand-made halyard blocks, and ran aground some more. We went down to the other Cracker Boy yard, in Riviera Beach, and did a major haulout. Paul found a girlfriend named Stacy, who would join us later. Eliot found a girlfriend too—a tiny, incredibly sexy creature who was stunningly beautiful—and I mean it! Eliot disappeared into connubial bliss for a few days, and it was fantastic to see Mister Abstinent Buddhist expend all that chi! (When they surfaced, they could barely walk....)

We met Tish and Mira from Miami, and worked on repairing sails and making canvas awnings and sail covers on Tish's floor. I liked Tish—she was a strong, pragmatic woman—and we became lovers briefly. Then I met her sister...and I remember Tish saying "Yes Reuel—she's your kind of woman—complicated...." As happens so often in my life, Tish and I became friends, and I never saw her sister again.

In a way, my luck ran out. I had sex with a woman who worked in *The Crack*, as everyone called the boatyard (crack in the wall of doom...crack in the ass of reality...). And I got Herpes Simplex II. This episode changed my life forever. Herpes found, in me, the ideal host—and the ideal victim. For the first year I had constant, painful attacks—five days on, five days off. I had to pretty much abstain from sex—by now you can imagine what that did to me. I felt like my life was over—I had lost my sexual freedom, which was as dear to me as breathing air! I was in a prison of my own making, and I knew deserved it (which only made me feel worse). But my own ethics deemed that I must not give this nasty disease to anyone else. I know perhaps I don't seem to be a moralist, but I live rigorously by my own ethics and values, and chief among them is to *do no harm to others*—for me this includes all life on Earth (OK—not mosquitoes!). Such was the inevitable price for all that delicious fucking around. But perhaps, in a way, I got off easy: Within a few short years we had diseases like Hepatitis C and AIDS—maybe by slowing down when I did, my life was saved....

By mid-march of 1982 we had earned some money, packed in stores, found crew, and spruced up our *ARK*—we were ready for the islands!

VOYAGE THREE PHOTOS

Photo 1

Key West, Florida
Reuel & Susan
Scottish tender

Photo 2

Key West
Marcia Peaslee

Photo 3

Key West, April Fools cruise
Note Mariel Boats on seawall

Photos 4 through 8

Fort Jefferson, Dry Tortugas, Florida

Photo 9 Bahamas Crew: Susan, Paul & Eliot

Photo 10 Aground, Darby I.

Photo 11 The pristine Beach at Musha Cay, Exumas, Bahamas

Photo 12

The Hermitage
Cat Island, Bahamas

Photo 13 David Crosby's Alden centerboard schooner *Mayan* in Marsh Harbor, Great Abaco

Photo 14

Naked Photographer
Abacos, Bahamas

Photo 15 Eliot

Photo 16 *Azulao* in the Abacos

Photo 17

Michelle & David on *Azulao*
Fishers Hornpipe wing & wing

Photo 18

God's Bread and *Fishers Hornpipe* in Masonboro, NC

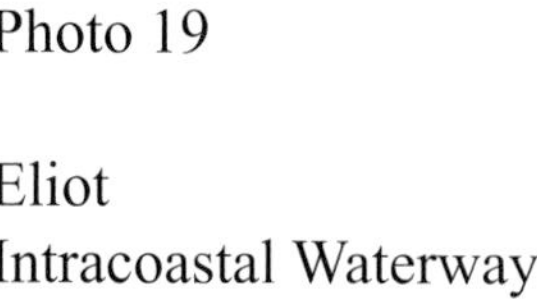

Photo 19

Eliot
Intracoastal Waterway

Photo 20 South Street Seaport, Manhattan

Photo 21 South Street Seaport, making roof trim for the Light Ship *Ambrose*

Photo 22

Imagine, City Island, N.Y.

Photo 23

Tony Bianco, City Island

Photo 24

Eliot sanding deck beams
City Island

Photo 25

Eliot, Paul & Jenny
In the Gulf of Maine

Photo 26

Coming into Maine
Kennebec River

Photo 27 Cynthia & Reuel

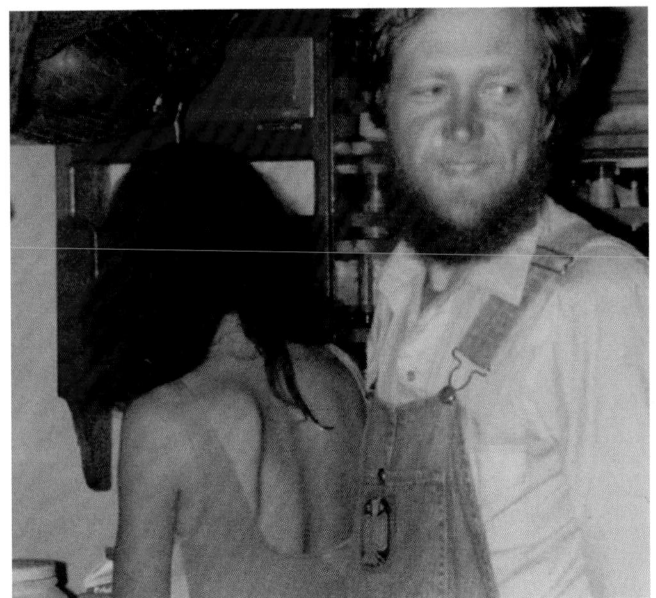

Photo 28 Eliot (Cynthiaphoto)

Photo 29

Martha's Vineyard, Mass.
Robbie's cabin in the woods

Photo 30

Martha's Vineyard
Paul with a new friend

Photo 31

Drying clothes in the aft cabin
Sears & Roebuck coal stove

VOYAGE FOUR: THE CARIBBEAN

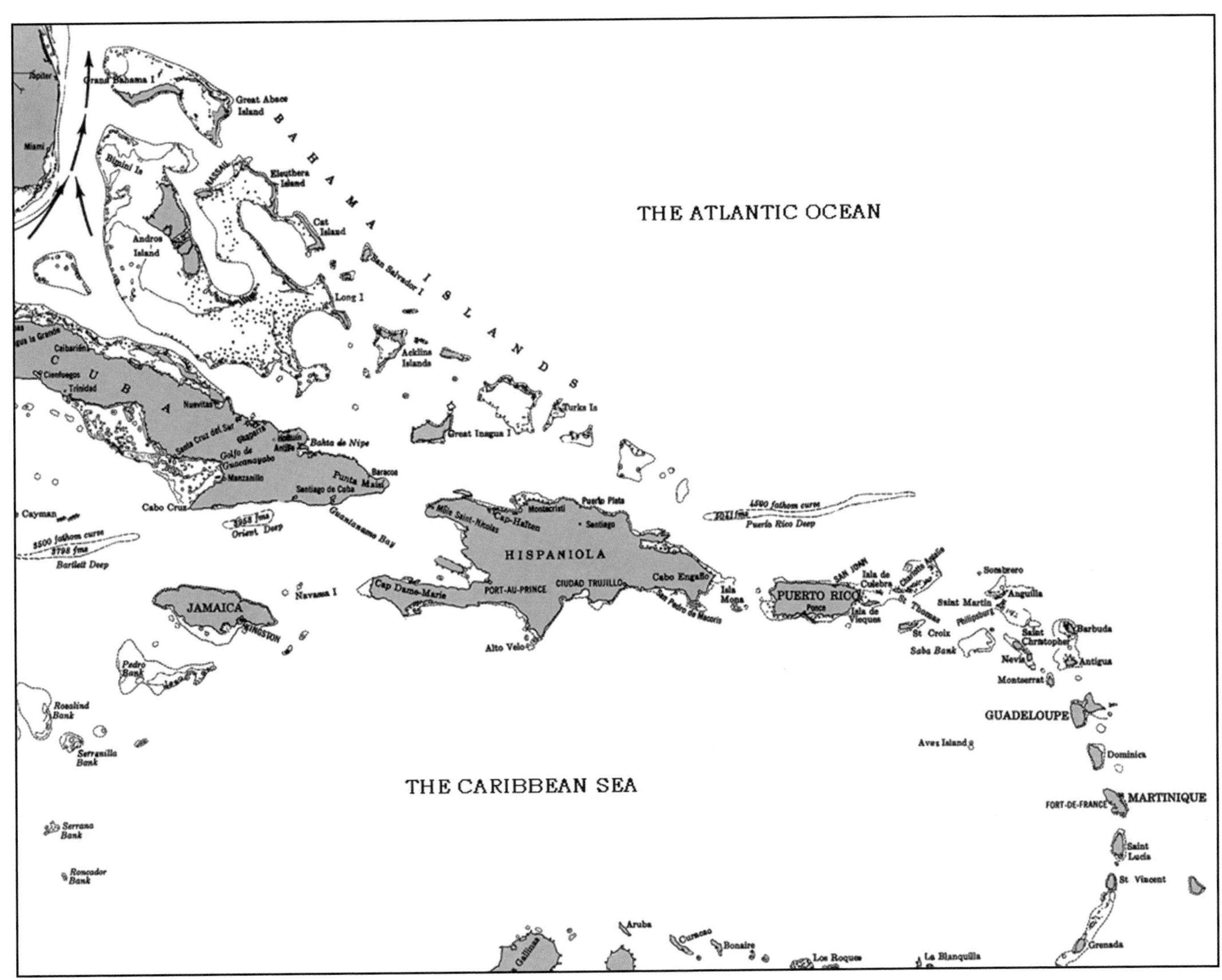

Voyage Four—from Florida through the Bahamas, Turks and Caicos Islands, Haiti, Dominican Republic, Isla del Mona, Puerto Rico, The Virgin Islands and the Lesser Antilles to Grenada and back (the Caribbean Sea).

CHAPTER FIFTEEN—TO THE ANTILLES

Destiny belongs to those of us who find the power, freedom and fortune to mold it in the shapes of our dreams.

Reuel Parker, 1983

On March 16th of 1982 we went to sea just after midnight to cross the Gulf Stream and head for the islands. Paul was back from spending Christmas with his folks, Eliot had been working with me, and we had a new crewmember with lots of spunk—a 21-year-old woman named Loretta—out on her first "walkabout." We also brought our friends Tish and Mira for a two-week sailing adventure down to Great Exuma.

We had an excellent cruise through the Bahamas, and played lots of music with Tish and Mira. I don't know if I have mentioned it previously—Paul and Eliot are both avid musicians, and many of our parties include making music. During this time I also spent more time painting with watercolors, which I found very relaxing and rewarding, even though they definitely had 'no commercial value.'

After a slow, lazy four-day sail, we tied up at the Nassau Harbor Club dock at 1030 to await Customs and Immigration officials. When they didn't come, we moved to the Customs Dock by the straw market, cleared in, and moved back to anchor off the Harbor Club. I mention this to illustrate that it is often more expedient to go to the officials instead of waiting for them to come to you...and it saves "taxi fees."

On the 20th we sailed across the White and Yellow Banks down into the Exumas. We visited Allan's Cay, Highborne Cay, Hawksbill Cay (where we anchored and weighed anchor the next morning under sail alone), Warderick Wells, Staniel Cay (we arrived in time for Happy Hour!), Musha Cay (where we visited our friends living on Lansing Cay), and finally George Town, Great Exuma. Hawksbill Cay is part of the Exuma National Park system—it is uninhabited, and is a beautiful naturalist's paradise. High up on a sand dune near the south end of the island is an old mailbox where cruisers leave messages to eachother.

We had beautiful sailing, swimming, diving, music, food, and more. Coming through Wax Cay Cut, we caught a 12-pound grouper on the hand line—our first one! We also caught a number of barracuda, which we still ate in those days, despite the danger of ciguatera poisoning. Our rule of thumb was to not eat any 'cuda over two feet long—and never eat one if flies didn't land on it! As the Bahamians say: "Barracuda is a *sweet* fish." I took my crew into Thunderball Grotto off Staniel Cay, and I'm sure they will never forget that wonderland of coral and tropical fish—like a giant swim-through aquarium.

I had developed a crush on Mira (despite herpes—after all, there are condoms), but she wasn't having any of it. She surprised everyone (including him, I suspect), by sleeping with Eliot. Smart girl!

On April 9th we tried to move into George Town's inner harbor (Kidd Cove) as a front (norther) was approaching, and the Log says: *hard fucking aground—wind pinning us.* We got off in the late afternoon and didn't go in there any more. We put Tish and Mira on a plane back to the states, and rowed out to the *Hornpipe* just as the norther struck. She was pitching so hard in the steep, short seas of Elizabeth Harbor that her 6"x12" Douglas fir bowsprit was flexing where the anchor rollers are through-bolted. We moved over into the lee of Stocking Island.

But George Town was taking its toll on us—the Log says, under Notes: *Lost our momentum in GT—bogged down, work, suburbia, beer, stout, rum, etc. Like psychic quicksand—low biorhythms and windy squalls—tangled anchors.*

One night, while the *Hornpipe* was anchored across the harbor by Stocking Island, we took *Gandy Dancer* and *Tuphlm Grdlphmp* (Penguin for 'tuba player'—see early *Bloom County*), our new little plywood tender, and went to the Peace and Plenty Club for a goodbye party (for us). We took some friends from another boat with us. While there, yet another norther came through, and when we staggered back out to the dock, the dinghies were leaping up and down in the storm, half full of water. It was too rough to row *Tuphlm Grdlphmp*, and we had too many people for *Gandy Dancer*. So we decided to tow one dingy with a few people, and put the rest in *Gandy* and motor home.

We had come over using the British Seagull Silver Century—the only outboard motor I have ever used on a tender—and it wouldn't start. I yanked and yanked (having to wind the cord on each time) until I thought my arm would fall off, all the time in the dory, which was jumping up and down in violent seas. Paul tried—yanked and yanked. The fucking limey bastard wouldn't even go "poot." It had done this before—stranded us somewhere—and then, after we got home, started the next morning

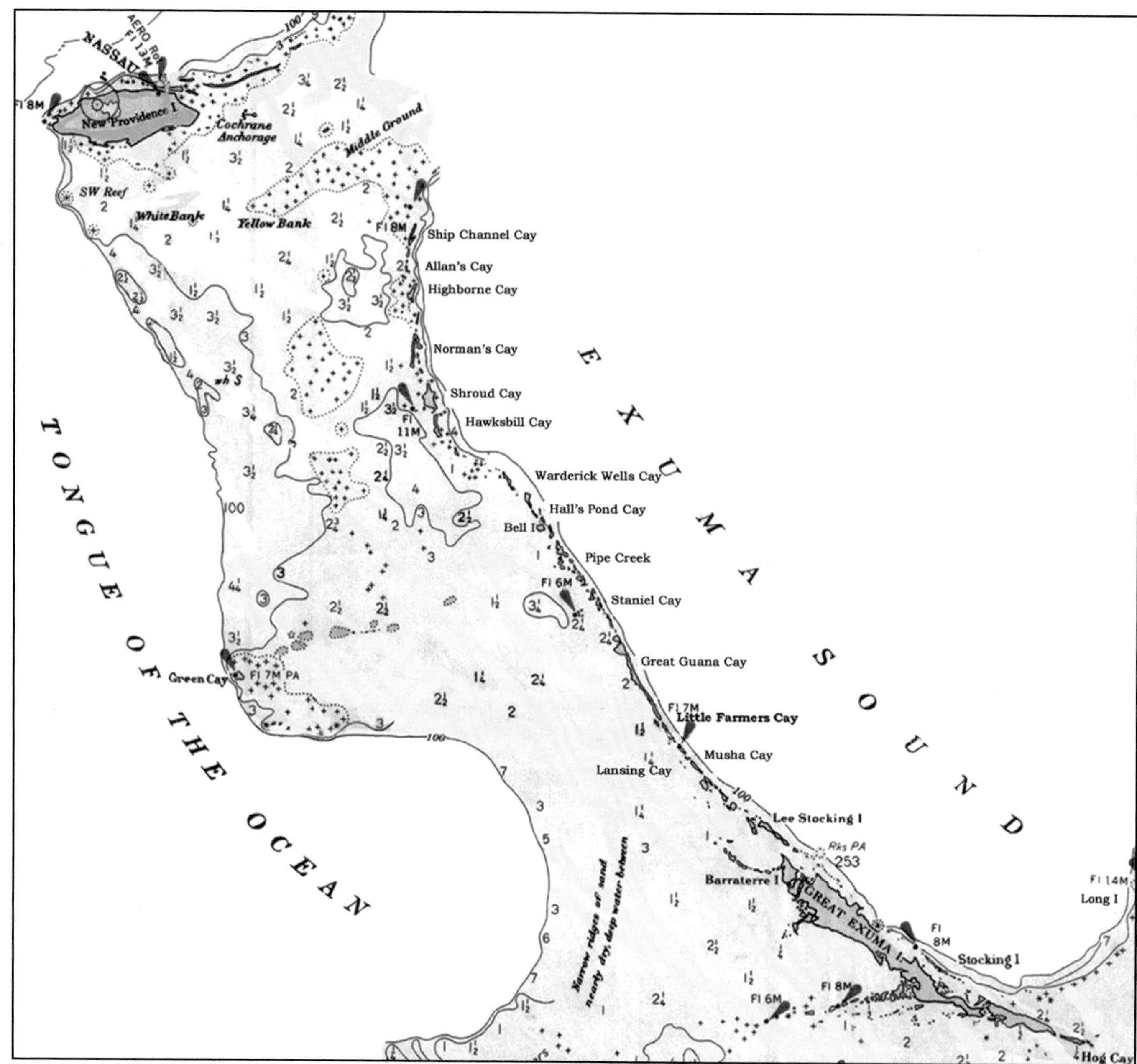

Nassau and the Exuma Cays; the tip of Long Island is on the right.

with a single pull. I don't know what it is with these engines—I think maybe they are inhabited by malevolent spirits...or perhaps only Englishmen can understand them. So I rigged and sailed *Gandy Dancer* (thank the Dear Goddess I had her rig in the boat!), tacking to windward with four people, towing a second boat with three people, across two miles of storm-tossed water, in gale-force winds, in the dark. I was so pissed off at the Seagull that when we finally got back to the *Hornpipe*, soaking wet and exhausted (no longer very drunk), I hung the motor on a fender board and forgot to tighten the clamps.

Two days later, on the morning of the 14th, we left for Long Island, bounced over a coral head on the way out, and began tacking into the brisk trade wind. On one tack, the whipping "lazy" jib sheet grabbed a-hold of that goddamn outboard motor, whipped it up into the air, spun it around in three big circles and threw it into Davy Jone's Locker! I gasped, moaned, swore bitterly—and then thanked my lucky stars...I was free of the bitch at last!

We sailed to Clarence Town on Long Island, and met up with a man who insisted on taking us to the best bar on the island...and this was a *long* island! He took us on a wild, high-speed station wagon ride, slamming over potholes in the dirt road with long-dead shock absorbers, children and livestock scattering before us, out to a remote straw shack that did indeed turn out to be a great bar. When we got there, he blew the horn until someone came rolling out of the house in a wheel chair, started up a noisy generator, and opened the bar for us. We had a great time there, and the bartender taught me how to make Bahamian fish chowder, for which I am eternally grateful! It is the quintessential Bahamian breakfast—served with grits. Here is the recipe:

Bahamian Fish Chowder

> Dice some potatoes and start them boiling.
> Melt a slab of pork fat (or butter) in a heavy-bottom pan.
> Dice a big yellow onion fine and sauté it in the fat.
> Throw a big piece of fish in the pan—grouper, snapper, hogfish or sheepshead.
> Add the potatoes and water—season to taste with salt and pepper.
> Serve with hominy grits and butter.
> Die and go to heaven!

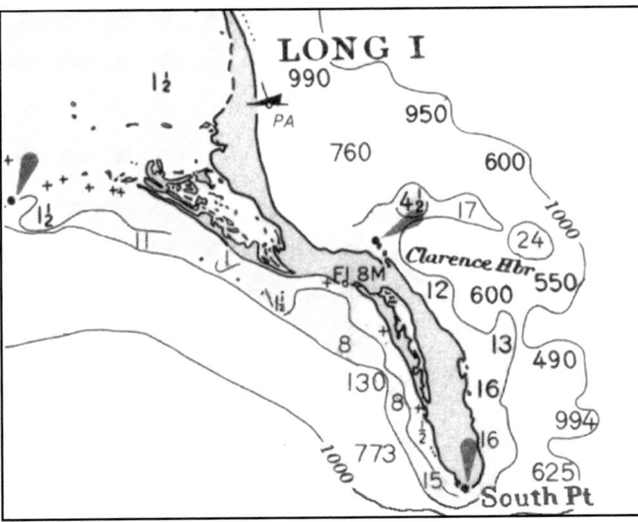

Long Island, southern half. Clarence Town is in Clarence Harbor.

On April 17th, in the late afternoon, we got under way for Landrail Point on Crooked Island—a long beat to windward. We arrived the next morning and had a nice visit in the immaculate settlement of Seventh Day Adventists who live there.

I know a woman who runs the small resort at Landrail Point, who is one of very few people to have been attacked by a barracuda. When diving on the reefs in the Bahamas, you pretty much always encounter these large, spooky predators. There are like "a bad dog that you don't know if he's going to bite you" as Larry back in Half Moon Bay put it. In general, the 'cudas just hang in the water a few feet away—and watch you. You are, after all, in their territory, and they're curious as to what you are doing there. The real danger is wearing anything flashy—anything that reflects light—like a watch, or jewelry, or a stainless steel diving knife. They will hit that thinking it is a fish. Their large, numerous teeth are razor sharp—capable of slicing right through bone. Which is what happened to the woman from Landrail Point: She was walking in very shallow water —less than a foot deep, literally, wearing sneakers to protect her feet, which made a sucking sound as she walked. A huge barracuda—three-feet long—shot into the shallows, rolled sideways, and bit her ankle. Evidently the 'cuda thought she was a ray caught in the shallows and thrashing in distress. Rays are a common food source for 'cudas. The woman had to be airlifted first to a hospital in Nassau—and when doctors there saw the severity of the bite—to a special surgical unit in Miami. The 'cuda had bitten almost entirely through her ankle—even the bone! It took several operations and several years' healing before she was able to walk with any semblance of normality. She figured hers was an isolated, freak incident, until she met a man in the Miami hospital having an operation for the identical problem. Interestingly, there is no record of any such attack on anyone walking *barefoot* in the shallows, as do Bahamians...evidently the sneakers are the problem.

By this time we were well into what are referred to as "The Bahamian Out Islands." The farther out you go in the Bahamas, the quieter things get. Only a small fraction of cruisers ever sail beyond George Town. Thank goodness! There are fewer services, but the people are even friendlier. The trade winds blow stronger and steadier, the temperature gets warmer, and the feeling of being in a very different part of the world intensifies. People are more independent, very poor, and yet they seem to be more content. Amazingly, they give more of themselves...though perhaps not at first.

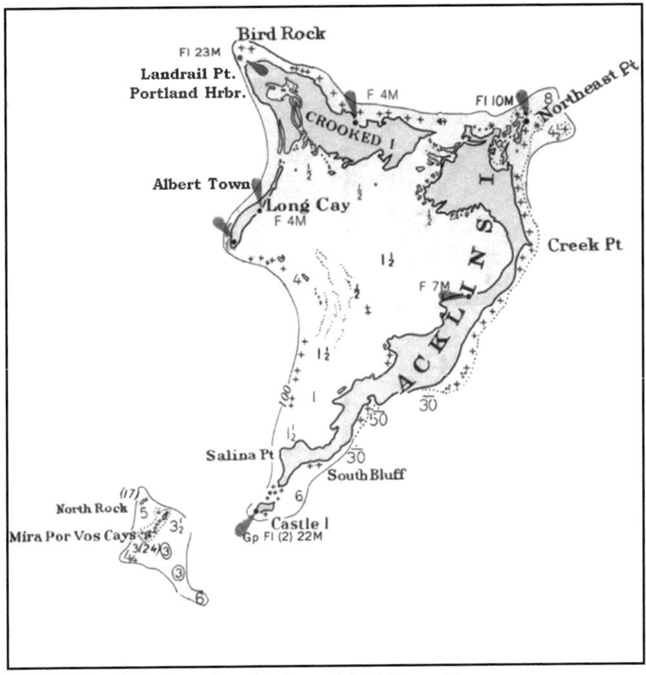

The Crooked Island/Aklins Group. We anchored in Portland Harbor.

On the 20th we left for the continuing long beat eastward. A day later we came to anchor in Abraham's Bay in Mayaguana. This is the most easterly of the Bahamian Islands, rarely visited by yachts, and here we would have to wait for Loretta's passport to catch up to us. We had been told that a driver's license was inadequate for entry to the Turks and Caicos Islands (our next destination), and for the countries of Hispaniola. Although we waited a week, the passport never came, and we chanced going without it.

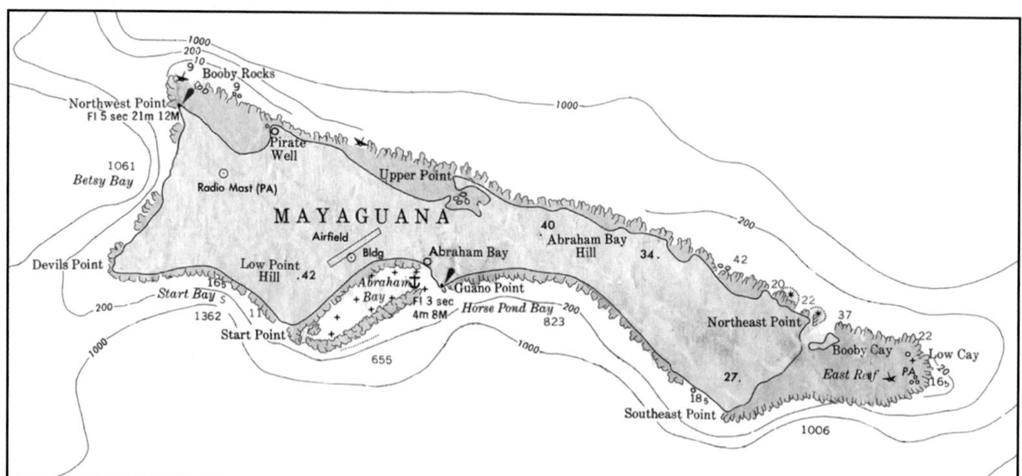

Mayaguana.

We had a good time in Abraham's Bay. This was a place that had never seen a tourist, and rarely saw even a cruising sailboat. At first people were suspicious of us long-haired American hippy sailors, but they were always polite. The young fishermen, in particular, were slow to open up. We kept asking them where to dive for conch, and when they finally agreed to show us, it was because I said I would make conch fritters for them. That worked almost too well—for every day after that, one or another of us got picked up early in the morning, and every afternoon found me slaving over a hot stove cooking up the catch! I kept apologizing for my conch fritters: "these are *Florida* conch fritters, mon—not as good as *Bahamian* conch fritters—but it's all I know how to do...." They ate 'em all.

Before we left, they threw a party for us in one of their tiny pink houses, and we barely made it back to the dory after all the rum we drank and pot we smoked!

[After twenty-five years of cruising extensively in the Bahamas, I have to say this: although Bahamians may well be the kindest, friendliest people on earth, they *very* rarely invite foreigners into their homes. Perhaps they are shy. Perhaps they are embarrassed of their poverty. But when and if you are invited into a Bahamian home, know that you are a very blessed person, and thank your lucky stars for your good fortune. It means you are truly accepted by some of the finest people on earth.]

We also went to church on Sunday. Now I am no Christian—never have been, never will be—but Bahamian churches are the exceptions to all my rules. If you ever experience one, you will understand, especially in the Out Islands. In Abraham's Bay there were two churches—both Baptist, and rivals. We had to choose one, and this happened when a young man asked me if I could repair his Fender amplifier. He actually played electric guitar in the church service. It turned out just to be a bad RX-7 tube, and we got a couple flown in from Nassau. So we had to go to that church. I think we went to the other one once too—so as not to hurt anyone's feelings (this was a very small community). The churches had men they called "beggars"—whose job it was to harangue the churchgoers for money during evening services. He got me good! Eight bucks—which I really couldn't afford—but how could you ever tell a Bahamian that?

On the 28th, at 1550, we left for Providenciales (Provo) in the Turks and Caicos Islands. Late in the afternoon we sighted a pod of large, black whales, apparently sunbathing. The wind fell light, then calm—very unusual for that latitude in April—and we had to motor-sail on and off for much of that night and the next day. At 1426 on 4/29, we anchored under sail off Gussy Point—where we stayed for over a week. Here Paul's flame Stacy joined us to sail to the Virgin Islands. And I found a job doing some cabinet-work for a Canadian who wanted louvered doors made of cypress for his new house.

As our anchorage was on the quiet side of the island, it was a long walk to the town. Still, we went there often, for provisions, to visit friends in the marina there, and to enjoy the night-life. I remember there was a wild bar, belonging to an expatriated Texan, where there was 'dwarf-tossing' at night (as well as rum-tossing). And I remember falling in lust with a beautiful Brazilian girl, the first one I ever met. My attempts at kidnapping failed—I can't speak Portugese!

I guess I should explain what dwarf-tossing is: this is when a couple of big guys get up on the bar and throw the smallest person (preferably female) as far across the room as possible, where a bunch of other drunks (hopefully) catch him or her with a minimum of broken bones. It was a popular

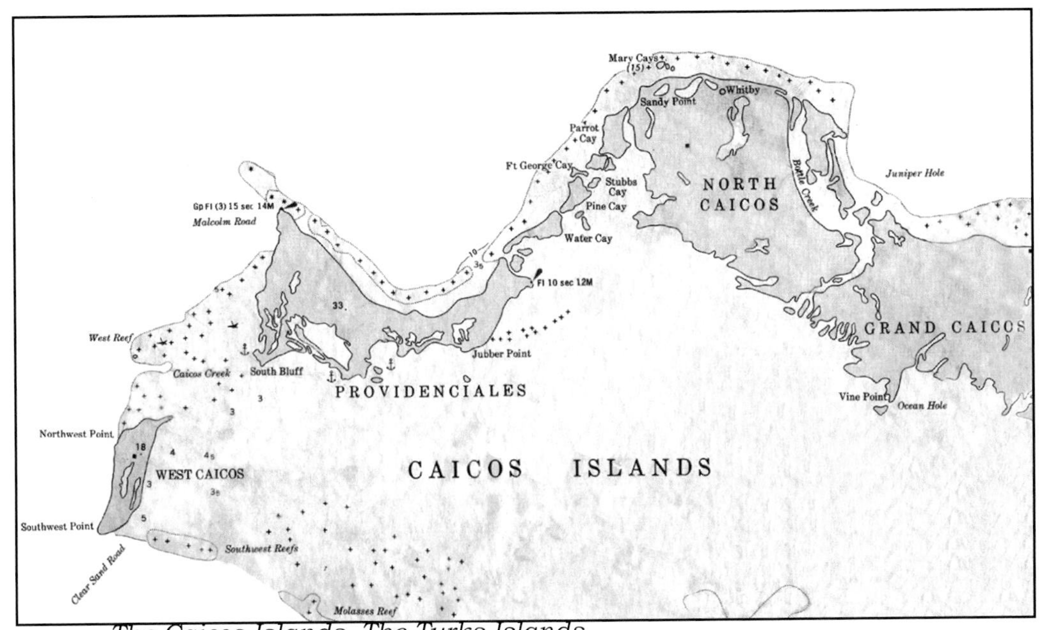

The Caicos Islands. The Turks Islands are just to the East (right).

pastime there.

One afternoon when I was walking across the island to go to my boat, a truck picked me up, and the driver (a white guy) invited me to his house. He asked if I wanted some coke, and though I was unsure of what he meant, I said sure. (I just hoped it wasn't that disgusting soft-drink, which I can only choke down if it has a lot of rum and lime in it....) He brought out a jar with aluminum foil over it, and proceeded to fire up a healthy rock of cocaine. This was my first and only experience with 'free-basing'—the predecessor to smoking crack—and I have to say it was an effective way of doing coke. I went home with a good buzz!

On May 10th we sailed over to West Caicos and caught a 'cuda for supper. I only remember that I was unimpressed with this island—indeed I did not particularly like the Turks and Caicos Islands, and cannot recommend them as a place to visit—except as a way point on the way from and to better places. They were low, desert-like and ugly, they felt very exploited, too full of weird white people, and too focused on drug traffic.

The next morning at 0930 we set sail for Cap Haitien, Haiti. On the trip, we caught a huge kingfish (see photo), around 75 pounds, whose fillets made gifts for the many port officials and other cruisers in Cap Haitien.

We had been very excited about going to Haiti—mysterious, smoky, mountain Voodoo island. We all know we will return there someday. Haiti is unique in this part of the world—much more like Africa than a Caribbean island. The people were engaging—sometimes too much so. They were mostly friendly, and seemingly non-violent by nature. Poverty was everywhere we looked, in dramatic, shocking evidence—much worse than anything I

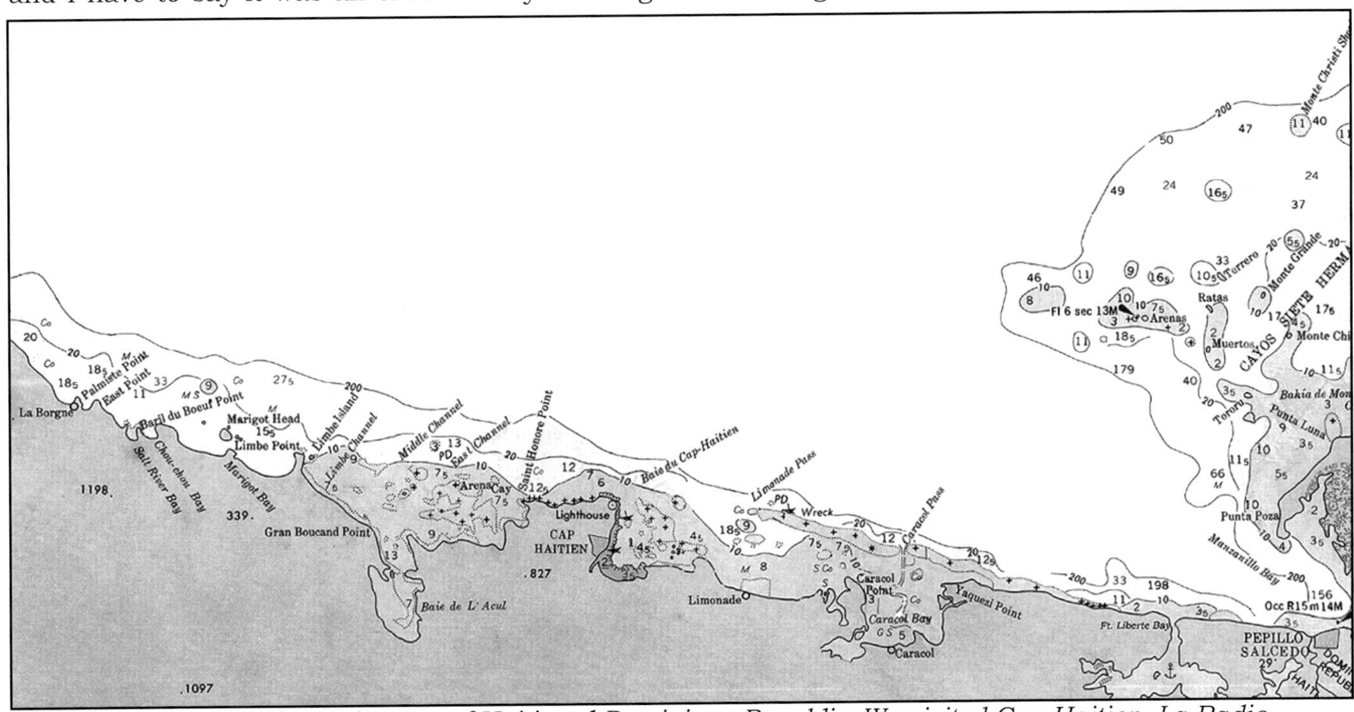

A section of the north coast of Haiti and Dominican Republic. We visited Cap Haitien, La Badie (to the west) and Ft. Liberte Bay, before entering the D. R. at Pepillo Salcedo.

had seen in Mexico or Panama or Columbia. Haiti has had a rough history—having become the New World's first black nation in 1804, and being bled nearly to death by its rulers ever since. The island is environmentally a disaster—the soil is gone, the trees have all been burned for fuel, the gold has been torn from the earth—yet still it is beautiful. We found new friends in Haiti—among the young blacks who "work" the tourists and the docks, among the white "aristocracy" engaged in exporting art, weaving fabrics (friends of Paul's father), photographing and painting scenes of the land and people, and among historians documenting the restoration of King Christophe's magnificent and terrifying Citadel.

Paul's father's friend was a fascinating man, and we visited him several times. He was weaving native sheep's wool into beautiful, natural fabrics, which were exported all over the world. I looked at his carding machine, to try to repair it—but I was unsuccessful. [I learned, years later, that this man had died of AIDS—one of the early victims. AIDS was believed to have entered the western hemisphere in Haiti—having come from Africa.]

We got to know some of the white sailors who returned time and again to Haiti—some for their own dark reasons. One of these—a white man in his 30's with a taste for dark, young female flesh—introduced us to a local black man in his early twenties, the equivalent to a Mafioso in other places (I don't believe he was Ton Ton Macout—but I don't know that he wasn't, either). They both took Paul, Eliot, Loretta and myself on a nighttime tour of bars and whorehouses that I will never forget. This went on through most of the night, and we had to cross and re-cross police checkpoints as we went further into places unlike anything I have ever seen before or since. We finally ended up in a concrete blockhouse bar full of young black women who descended on us like locusts. Sexual intercourse cost $5 US. Being tired, a little drunk and over-stimulated, we were all drawn off, protesting weakly, to tiny rooms on the second floor above a miniature courtyard. This left Loretta and our handsome young host alone, looking into each other's different, mysterious eyes....

This is the second time in this book that I have had sex with a prostitute (these are the only times), and I feel I should say something about that. While I vehemently do not like the exploitation of *any* people, prostitution is an enigma. I have been around it all my adult life—starting with my first trip to Mexico in 1965. I knew several prostitutes in the Houseboat Community in Sausalito—and they were clearly exploiting themselves—they liked both the money and the perverted excitement of having sex with total strangers. They had no men controlling them—no pimps! In countries like Mexico, Costa Rica and Haiti, this is clearly not the case. The motivation for prostitution in places like these is economical, social, even religious—and hence is very ugly. Why did I do it? I was curious, I was horny, I was a selfish pig. To gain a glimpse about how utterly horrible prostitution can be in Mexico, read Cormack McCarthy's novels.

Eliot left us in Haiti to attend Naropa Institute in Boulder, Colorado. His parents were unhappy that he was "wasting" his life bumming around on a sailboat, and all concerned had reached a compromise in which Eliot would go to the school of his choice, to study what he wanted to study. He chose poetry and literature at Naropa, in the company of such great men as Alan Ginsberg and William Boroughs.

Before he left, we all went to visit the Citadel—Roi Christophe's mountain fortress, built on the blood of his own people (of the slaves carrying stones up the mountain, every tenth one was supposedly murdered, his blood and bones mixed with the mortar to strengthen it). Here we were accosted by boys with donkeys for hauling our white asses up the mountain—a hike considered much too long and steep for tourists. We politely refused—we wanted to walk, we were used to walking everywhere—but they followed us, waiting for us to give in. We didn't. On the long walk I tried to make friends with a young German tourist who also refused to ride. Although he spoke English, he clearly didn't like Americans (who can blame him?) and it took a long time for him to respond to me. I was not insistent. Eventually he became friendly, as we all explored the Citadel, and we invited him to the boat. After we got to know Heinz (57 Varieties, he told us) Schlegel, we asked him to join us on the sail to the Dominican Republic. He graciously accepted, and moved into Eliot's bunk before it cooled off. Loretta didn't waste any time with Heinz—she saw a good thing and she grabbed it! We were standing in the aft cabin, naked, when Loretta seized Heinz by his hawser and towed him off to a snug harbor.... Heinz was a handsome, intelligent, educated young man. I wish he had stayed with us longer, but he was on his way to Central America, and had a limited amount of travel time. He was new to sailing, and perhaps he was curious about the lifestyle of what seemed like an American floating commune.

I took Heinz well offshore in *Gandy Dance*r one afternoon to go fishing in deep water. While out there, a nasty squall line came up very suddenly out of the north, and we turned tail to scoot for safety. The first squall overtook us long before we fetched the harbor, and we had to reef the sail by removing the sprit and folding the sail in half. Heinz was quite alarmed—the wind built to 30 or 40 knots in seconds, and the seas to 6 or 8 feet within minutes.

I was too busy to be terrified. Down in the troughs we could see nothing but angry water! While I ran before it, Heinz frantically bailed water that came in as fast as he tossed it out. Other than a few bad snap rolls before I got the daggerboard out, *Gandy* surfed in like a duck. We both sat in the bottom of the boat for ballast, wet and cold, but the trip was quite exhilarating. We didn't catch any fish.

Friends on other boats told us to try to visit a primitive village nearby called La Badie, which was forbidden to cruisers, and on 5/18 we told the harbor officials we were "going fishing." They were alarmed, and tried to prevent us leaving, but we insisted and left. Perhaps because of the big kingfish and all those steaks we had given away, they believed us. We anchored off La Badie and went ashore, where we were greeted by the village Chief, who showed us around and invited us to stay for a Voodoo ceremony that night. Much as we wanted to, we knew we would get into who knows what kind of trouble if we stayed. After all, we had only gone fishing. We were all interested in learning more about the religion Voudon—but this wasn't a time when we could stay.

The Chief showed us some drums that he had made, and Paul's eyes lit up. We haggled a surprisingly expensive deal for a "baby" drum, which sounded and looked like no other drum any of us had ever heard or seen. [A year later, Paul studied with a Haitian drum-master in New York City, and shortly thereafter joined the Haitian dance troupe *Macondal*—the only white face among the many black. Another close friend of ours, Elizabeth MacAllister, was so intrigued by our stories of Haiti that she began visiting there regularly, became friends with Paul's drum master, and was eventually initiated into the religion Voudon.] I traded a keg of nails for a "mama" drum, which twenty-two years later is in the next room. We returned to Cap Haitien before nightfall—without a fish—and rafted up to our friends on *Sin Duda*.

The next day we sailed to Ft. Liberte, further along the north coast of Haiti. All I remember is that it was a quiet place, where we explored the ruins of ancient forts, all overgrown with jungle.

On May 21st we moved across the invisible border to the Dominican Republic—a couple of hours away—entered the country and anchored off the city dock. My Newsletter for this time says the *Dominican Republic occupies the east half of the very large island of Hispaniola, while Haiti occupies the west—but they are as different as Africa is from Spain.* Pepillo Salcedo was a small industrial town, and while walking around we were 'adopted' by two young men whom I didn't trust. We bought them beers at the bars we went to, but they clearly wanted more from us. When Heinz and Loretta went ashore that night—against my advice—they had a harrowing experience with these two, who tried to rob them and rape Loretta. They had to run for it, and barely made it to the beach and into the dory on time. They rowed for their lives under a pelting of rocks from the beach.

We left the next day and had a good windward sail among the Seven Brothers Cays to Monte Christi—a beach resort. On the way we caught two small black-fin tuna, which made us a good supper. I got very sick in Montecristi—something I ate on the beach again, I think (will I ever learn?)—and we stayed at anchor for a couple of days until I recovered. We left on 5/25 to continue working our way east. This time it was Paul who got sick—that scared me because he *never* got sick—and we put in to the tiny harbor of Pt. Blanco. The wind

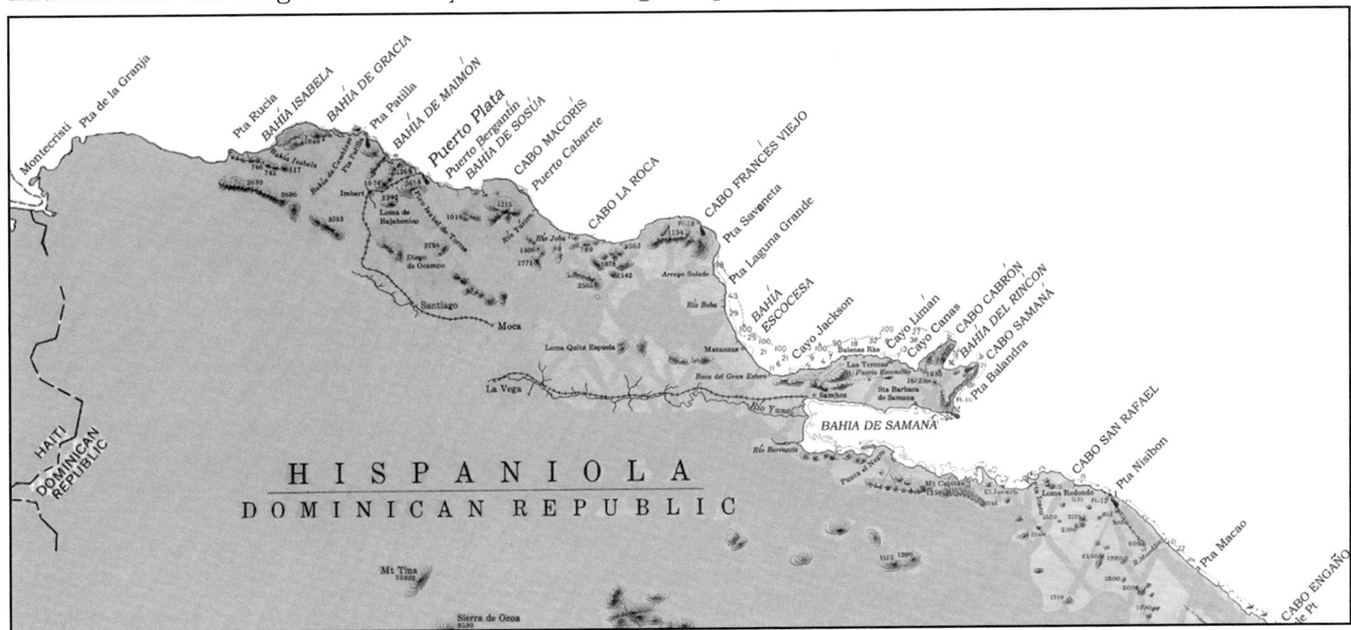

The Dominican Republic's north coast. We visited Montecristi, Puerto Plata and Sosua.

outside was 15 knots out of the ESE (on the nose), and was increasing. There was a military vessel in Pt. Blanco, and the captain politely kicked us right out, saying the harbor was restricted—no yachts allowed. So out we went, while the wind increased to 20 and then 25 knots, and we beat up to Puerto Plata, where we anchored late that night.

We enjoyed Puerto Plata very much, and found new friends and great hospitality. Here Heinz left us to continue in his travels to Central America, and we were all sorry to see him go. We met an excellent musician who spoke almost no English, but played great drums, and Loretta worked like hell to soften the stony visage of the Capitania del Puerto to let him visit us on board. She sure had guts, because this guy scared the shit out of me. When the port officials all came on board to clear us into the country, I went through the boat with them. They never touched the belongings of men—but thoroughly searched those of the women. We found out later what they did if they found anything: There is a vacant, private warehouse where the women are interrogated and searched...and bargains are made. It turns out that the previous year, the Port Captain had made a little mistake in protocol, which resulted in a couple of DR citizens leaving the country on an American yacht. The Capitania spent several months in one of his own prisons. After that, he made no compromises. Loretta was treading on thin ice—but she *almost* persuaded him!

The Brugal Refinery is located in Puerto Plata, and they make some of the finest sippin' rum in the world—especially the dark estate-bottled stuff in the net bag. Once a week, when a new batch was finished, they set up a stand on the sidewalk outside the refinery and served little paper cups of rum. Needless to say, I found myself back in line a few times...jeeze that stuff was good! We also met a European man—from one of those tiny countries I can never remember the name of—who told me that the DR was *Heaven on Earth*. He had moved there a few years ago with a modest amount of money, and was living like royalty. He found a beautiful young wife he loved, hired servants, bought a big house in town, started a family, and opened a European restaurant in his dining room. He had us over to dinner—for free—and the food and company were excellent.

At some point, by bus, we visited the beach community of Sosua, on the Bay of the same name. This is a beautiful, quiet place, where German refugees settled during the Holocaust of World War Two. There we found delicious yogurt and ice cream. We regrettably did not visit Bahia de Samana, which we were later told is probably the highlight of any cruise to the D.R.

In Puerto Plata I met multihull designer Chris White and his wife Kate, on their new cruising trimaran *Juniper*. We were side by side—moored Med-style, stern to the public docks—and we became friends and traded boat tours. *Juniper* was the first multihull to really capture my imagination—a big, practical, simple and beautiful cruiser. We watched *Juniper* sail out of the harbor (she had no engine), and she moved like a huge graceful animal in harmony with the wind. Heaven knows what they thought of the *Hornpipe*—she is *Juniper's* diametric opposite. Both boats were very pragmatic and not highly finished—*Juniper* as a weight consideration, and the *Hornpipe*—er—just had never been finished. I still had unpainted plywood bulkheads with construction notes, bad poetry and graffiti scrawled all over with magic marker! Back in California, years before, I had had to make the decision whether I was going to screw around forever building this boat—or go sailing. Sailing won.

CHAPTER SIXTEEN—PUERTO RICO AND THE VIRGINS

The friends who met here
And embraced are gone,
Each to his own mistake.

W.H. Auden

On June 7th at 1830, we left Puerto Plata to continue our long beat eastward. Our destination was Mayaguez, Puerto Rico. That first night—perhaps you have noticed that we almost always began voyages at night—was a very rough beat in 20 knots of ESE wind. An hour out we blew the tack pennant on the genoa jib, and had to wrestle it down in the moonlight, then put up the yankee and the stays'l. We were carrying a lot of sail, driving the boat very hard, trying to make good time and close tacks. Early the next morning the wind eased off a little, and the sailing was gentler. We beat to windward for three days, having all kinds of wind from calms to squalls, and finally tied up to the Commercial Wharf at Mayaguez. The Mona Passage had lived up to its notorious reputation—rougher than shit and full of freak waves, unpredictable winds and dangerous currents.

The reasons for night departures are several: Often a passage is likely to be longer than twelve hours, making it impossible to enter a new, unknown harbor in daylight. Entering in darkness is manifestly risky—even if a harbor has well-marked channels with lighted buoys, the mariner simply cannot see all possible dangers. Also, port officials do not generally work at night, and in some countries it is frowned upon, if not illegal, to enter a port without clearing in almost immediately. Finally, night winds, in much of the world, are gentler than day winds—hence seas may be smaller and gentler too.

We were all immediately intrigued with Puerto Rico. The people are proud of their reputation for hospitality, and they certainly proved it by us. Virtually everyone we met was kind, warm and generous. People seemed to always go out of their way to be helpful, and this was true of everyplace we went on the island. Quite a contrast to some of your New York City 'Ricans! (I say this having had a knife to my throat, having been robbed, and having been beaten up because I couldn't speak Spanish—all in New York.) What was also intriguing was knowing

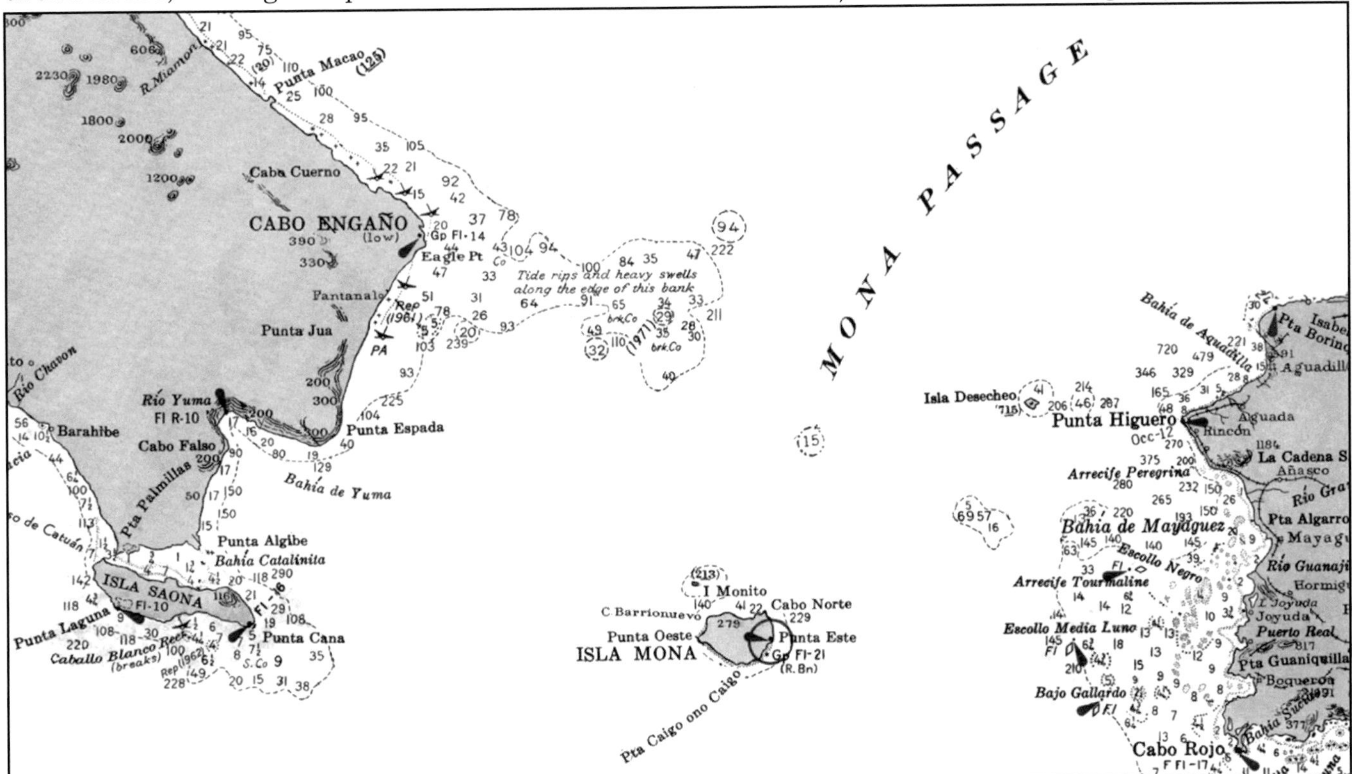

The Mona Passage, between Hispaniola and Puerto Rico—a place of strong winds, powerful and often unpredictable currents, and rough seas. Boquerón, which we visited longest, is in the SW corner of Puerto Rico, just above Cabo Rojo.

that we were Americans in America—sort of—and that Spanish was definitely the national language. I fell in love with Puerto Rico, and will always return there.

On the 12th we sailed down the coast to Bahia de Boqueron, and anchored off the village. We had wanted to visit quaint Puerto Real—but the harbor looked too narrow and shallow to me from sea, and I chickened out. Some of our cruising pals were at Boqueron—*Satisfaction* and *Allonz-Y*—and we soon made friends with the people on boats that were new to us.

Everyone was talking about Isla del Mona, in the middle of the Mona Passage between Hispaniola and Puerto Rico, and I wanted to go visit it. None of the other boats had dared attempt a visit—in addition to the rough, potentially dangerous passage, Mona has no real anchorage. The island, roughly seven miles in diameter and more or less round, consists primarily of steep, rocky cliffs. Only on the west side—usually the lee side in the easterly Trade Winds—is there a beach, protected by a small reef which forms a tiny basin. There is a single, narrow break in the reef, through which it is just possible to run a small vessel. Once inside, you must round up and anchor immediately, and there is only room for two or three small boats. If for some reason the wind shifts to the west—which it can do during storms—any vessels in this anchorage find themselves right on a lee shore, with virtually no protection from storm seas which sweep over the narrow reef and break across the basin. You can see why no-one goes there. So we had to!

As we talked about our proposed adventure in the anchorage and in the village, we soon found many others who wanted to go also, but had been afraid to. So we put together an expedition crew, which consisted of the following:

The Isla del Mona Expedition Crew

Fishers Hornpipe	Paul, Loretta, Stacy, Reuel
Satisfaction	Shawn, Cheryl (12-year-old twins)
Allonz-Y	Irene
Nail Cakes	Jim
Blue Boat	Ross
Boqueron Village	Minerva

Ten people was quite a large crew for the *Hornpipe*—but the tropical weather was such that most of them would sleep on deck. If it rained, we had the settee in the great aft cabin, which could sleep three, and we could sleep six in our cabins, assuming people didn't mind sharing berths. I admit that I wanted Minerva to share mine, but she wasn't interested. I later learned why, possibly, when I met and became friends with her ex-boyfriend and father of her son. She was still working things out with him, it seemed. Or perhaps she just knew better than to get involved with a transient hippy sailor who would soon sail away. Finally, there is the distinct possibility that she was only interested in becoming friends with me, and nothing more. I asked her if she had any interest in cruising, and she replied that it just wasn't something she wanted to do then, particularly with a six-year-old.

I first saw Minerva sailing across the Bay (Boqueron is quite large) on her *Sunfish* in a 20-knot trade wind breeze. She was wearing a bikini, and was hiked way out to windward to hold the hull of her little boat flat to the water so it would plane. She was leaning way back over the water—so far that she could dip her head and long black hair into the sea. She was so alive and so beautiful and so totally a sailor that my heart jumped into my throat and thumped like hell. I was out sailing in *Gandy Dancer*, and though I tried, I couldn't catch her.

On the 16th at 1915, we departed Boqueron with our crew of ten and sailed to Isla del Mona. The passage was rough in confused seas, and we rolled heavily running downwind wing and wing, although the winds were pretty light—around 10 knots. At 0340 we came right up on Mona—having never seen the tiny light on the cliffs—and had to jibe quickly to run north around the island. As we ran along the vertical gray cliffs that encircle most of the island, we could see, even in the dark, that they were riddled with caves. Above, there was verdant tropical vegetation pouring over the cliff tops. At 0640 we carefully entered the tiny basin and anchored. The view we saw with the rising sun was one of the most beautiful imaginable.

Since I had been up all night, I went below to my cabin to get some sleep. We had caught a fish on the way in, and someone was cleaning it on deck above my cabin, after which they dumped a bucket of salt water on the deck to rinse off. *Fishers Hornpipe* has portlights set into her hull just below her rubrails, and the one in my cabin was open to get some fresh air. I woke up with a shock, screaming bloody murder as several gallons of salt water, fish guts, blood, and scales came cascading all over my naked butt—to say nothing of my bed!

It took two trips in *Gandy Dancer* to ferry everyone ashore—though a couple of people swam in to the crescent white-sand beach. On shore we met the island's Puerto Rican park-caretaker, who was fluent in English. Paul—a lifelong fan of iguanas—immediately wandered off in search of some. He quickly came back, holding his hands as far apart as they would go, looking a little dazed and muttering strange imprecations.... The park ranger started laughing—he knew Paul had seen a

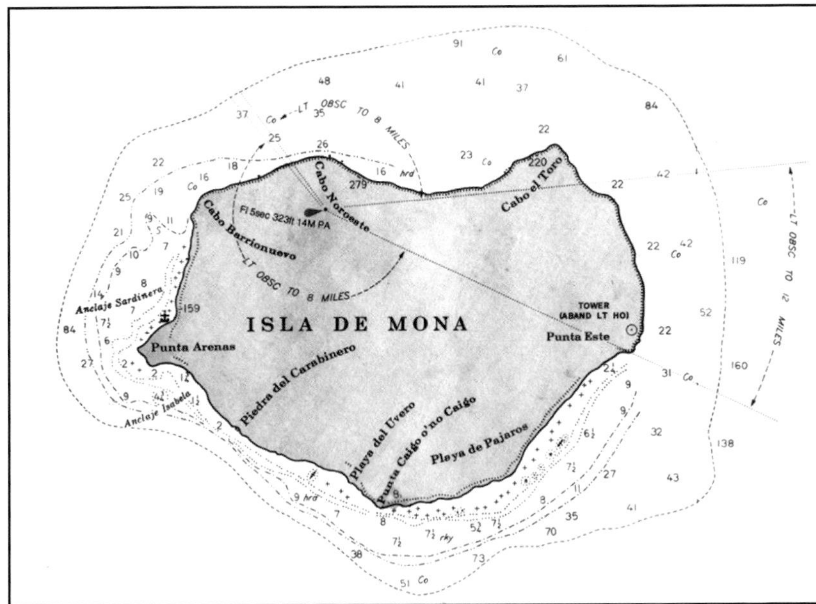

Isla del Mona (Puerto Rico). We anchored in Anclaje Sardinera, off the ranger station. The island is riddled with caves, giant Iguanas, and is a National Park.

legendary giant iguana!

The ranger (only inhabitant of Isla del Mona) took us to see several of the famous caves. This time we remembered to bring flashlights! The caves were huge, amazing, and plentiful. Indeed, the whole island was riddled with caves, and we later heard of a legendary secret expedition in which some geology students from Puerto Rico had traversed the whole island underground through caves, having to accomplish large parts of the journey with scuba gear.

We took long walks in the jungle rainforest, and the plant and animal life were astounding. I felt as though I had stepped back in time a million years. I remember looking into a huge bromeliad, full of rain water, and seeing a tiny multi-colored frog the size of my little fingernail. I realized that each bromeliad contained its own miniature eco-system.

During all my travels to remote places in *Fishers Hornpipe*, I became more and more convinced that the most important challenge facing humanity is the preservation of the Natural Earth, of biodiversity, and of wilderness areas *for their own sake*. These feelings were not new—they were fundamental to everyone at Starhill—but they were growing ever more important, ever more urgent, in my mind and spirit. [They continue to do so.]

At 1805 we regretfully left Isla del Mona, and began the long night sail to windward back to Boqueron. Just as I started the *Hornpipe's* diesel, the raw water pump died, spraying salt water all over everything in the engine compartment, and I had to shut it down. I explained to everyone that we had just become a "true" sailing vessel. We would have to leave this very tight spot under sail alone, and beat back 'home.' We raised the main, paid out the main sheet so we would be able to turn downwind to get out, and had crew ready to raise jib and stays'l the moment our anchor broke the surface. Which turned out to be a problem, as the anchor wouldn't let go of the bottom! This time Paul was spared, as Shawn immediately jumped overboard. Not only did he free the anchor, but he also came up with a large "bug" (spiny crayfish), proclaiming excitedly "they're all over the place down there!" We slipped the "bug" surreptitiously into a bucket and I told Shawn to leave the others in peace—we were, after all, in a park, and all wildlife was protected.

Once again in the Mona Passage, we had a rough ride in the intersecting cross-seas and swirling currents. But Jim took that bug below and made lobster crepes! He was a real trooper to cook under those conditions, and I wasn't surprised when he hurried on deck and tossed his cookies. Jim was a commercial fisherman—you *know* it's rough out when a commercial fisherman barfs! We tacked into 15 to 20 knot trade winds all night, and at dawn, as we approached Puerto Rico, the wind died. We were 20 miles from Boqueron, and we couldn't get there! We would catch a puff and start sailing only to have the powerful currents carry us away. We tried different approaches—went back out in the Mona Passage and tried to find lasting wind. We tried to find less current. Nothing worked. *It took us 15 hours to cover the last 20 miles!* Finally, at 1820, we anchored off the village, and a very tired—but not unhappy—crew went home for a long sleep.

Loretta had a troublesome love affair in Puerto Rico (with Minerva's ex-partner), and ran out of money at about the same time. She left us to go work in San Juan, the capitol city on the north coast. She was gone, but not forgotten, and we got back together later, thousands of miles away, as you will see.

Paul and I had been eyeing a very beautiful 30' sloop beached by one of the previous year's hurricanes—and we were so reminded of Tony's Malabar Jr. *Imagine* that we started planning how we might save her. The boat was rough, but structurally sound, as the storm surge had simply put her up on the beach unharmed. It turns out she had been the last boat built by an elderly master shipwright in Puerto Real, who had since died. The little sloop had been used as a commercial fisherman, and had a large diesel engine in her—and nothing else. After asking around town, we located her owner, who offered to give her to Paul

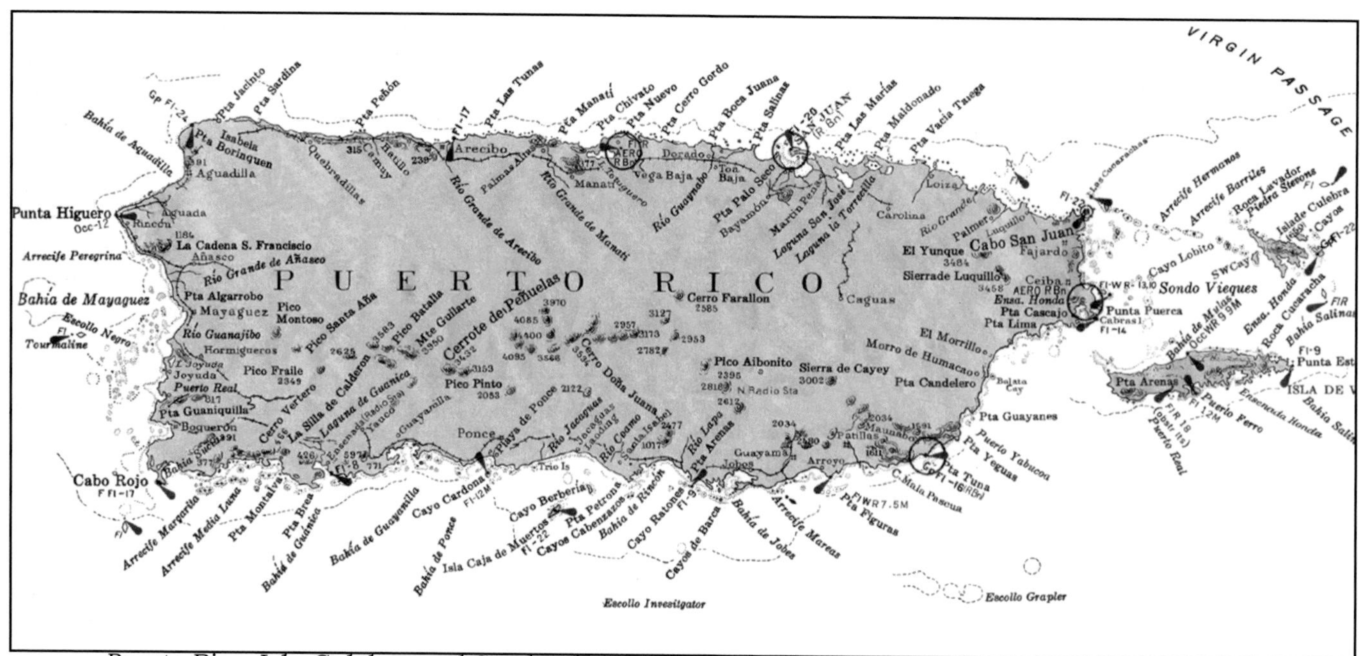

Puerto Rico, Isla Culebra and Sondo Vieques. Isla Caja de Muertos, which Paul and I explored, is in the middle south coast. We cruised all but the north coast.

if we would remove her diesel and return it to him. Someone else had taken her sails, and told us we could have them back. Another man who had a restaurant nearby told us we could restore her in his yard—for free—and that he would help us buy materials for the work. I made some drawings for converting and restoring the sloop as a pocket-cruiser, and Paul became very excited about having his own boat. Unfortunately, when he called his folks back in the states to ask for money to finance the project, they said absolutely not. We sadly had to thank everyone for their kindness, and leave this rare jewel to rot on the beach.

The new raw water pump for my diesel cost $130 to replace—and I was lucky to find one. We stayed a month in Boqueron, and became so comfortable there that it was difficult to leave. We even left one time, spent the night in La Parguera, and came back, as Paul became sick.

While in Parguera, we met up with a woman introduced to us earlier by Minerva, who was attending the oceanographic institute there. She gave me a guided tour of all the marine biology projects, and that night she took us to Bahia de Phosphoro—the most phosphorescent place on Earth—in her outboard-powered skiff. It was a dark night, with no moon, and I stayed on the bow watching the lightning flashes of fish darting out of our way. Then she anchored, and we all took our clothes off to swim. *I will never forget the beautiful glowing image of her naked body as she dove into the crystal clear water.*

We finally escaped the magic spell of Boqueron on 7/8, and started cruising the beautiful south coast of Puerto Rico. After another brief visit to La Parguera, We anchored off the Ponce Yacht Club at 1815 on 7/9. We had *robust sailing*, according to the Log, beating into 15 to 25 knot ESE trade winds. We enjoyed the city of Ponce de Leon—especially the Art Museum and the Dunkin' Donuts! The people were very kind, as usual—while riding *Air Force One* with a big block of ice in the basket, a man in a pickup truck stopped and gave me a ride.

We left for the uninhabited island of Isla Caja de Muertos (Coffin Island) on the 13th. Paul and I explored (bush-whacked) this beautiful natural island, and unknowingly were very intimate with some kind of horrible poisonous plant, which left

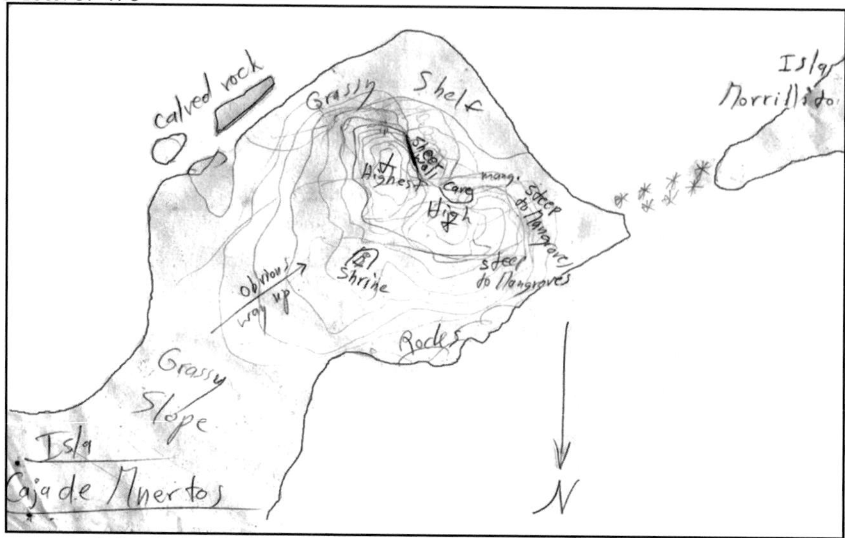

Isla Caja de Muertos (Coffin Island)—one of my many crude Sketch charts, made when Paul and I climbed the island.

us with poison ivy-type rashes that took weeks to clear up.

On the next morning we continued east, anchoring for the night in the lee of Punta Viento—Windy Point—and it was. We left early the next morning and sailed to beautiful Culebra, anchoring at 0150 on 7/16 above Punta Soldado. Culebra was one of those well-kept secrets that eventually got discovered. The island is small, with several pretty bays, hills and tropical trees—a very special place. [I shudder to think what it looks like now....]

We left for St. Thomas early the following morning, but had to re-anchor 20 minutes later when I realized I had to re-seize several track cars to the mains'l luff—the constant beating had simply worn them out. Beating does cause a lot of wear and tear—but running does also. The dream of the sailor is to have nothing but endless beam reaches.

We sailed into Long Bay, St. Thomas, at 1930 that same evening, and anchored in our first real Lesser Antilles island. The next afternoon we moved across the Bay to Hassel Island to anchor in what the locals call "Commie Cove"—which was to become our hangout in Charlotte Amalie. Hassel Island was very pretty, quiet, had beautiful cliffs, canyons, ruins, tiny beaches and wildlife, and the people who lived there—expatriates of several nations—adopted us. We found a "pet" octopus on a beach that could only be reached by dingy or a long, slightly arduous climb, and went nude sunbathing on the huge flat rocks on the south side of the island—facing away from the troubled 'civilization' of Charlotte Amalie.

Stacy had to leave us to return to Florida, and we hoped Eliot would rejoin us, depending on when his classes started at Naropa. I obtained a post office box, and actually had business cards printed. I was finally hanging out my shingle proclaiming that I was a marine architect...but I didn't give up my "day job" as shipwright.

Newsletter, Aug 1, 1982:

St. Thomas, USVI: Fishers Hornpipe *lies at anchor off Charlotte Amalie—the tropical city sprinkled upon lush green hills and looking so deceptively peaceful from this anchorage a half-mile away. The Lesser Antilles have been a cruising goal for me since California, and finally, three years later, here we are.*

Here, among the Virgin Islands, I will now set up a new "home base" from which to work and cruise for an indefinite time. We arrived nearly broke, as

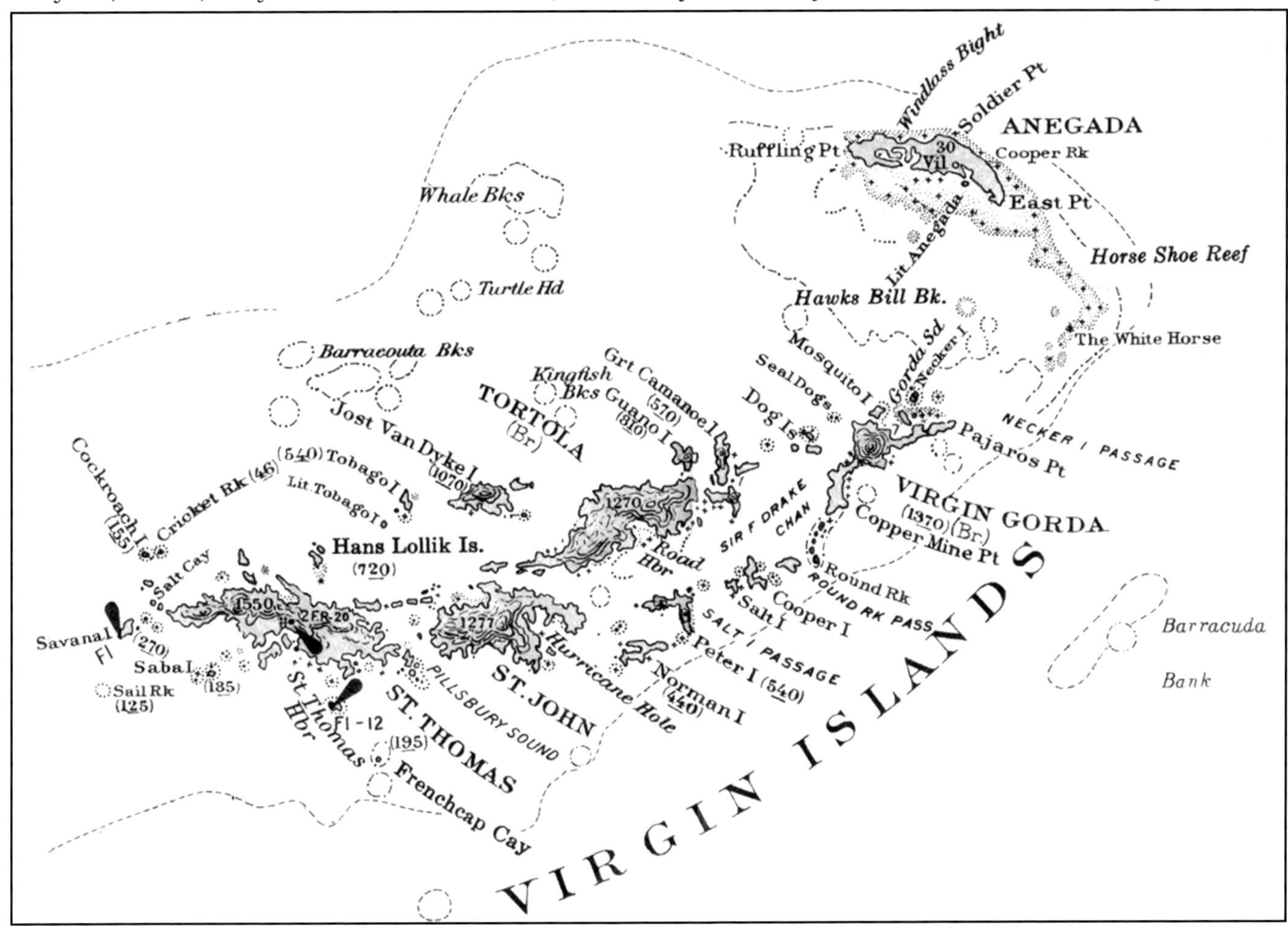

The Virgin Islands (minus St. Croix), at the top of the Lesser Antilles.

usual, but have already found work and new friends. Our first job is a major interior reconstruction of the Ring Andersen schooner Orianda, *which belongs to Neil Pern of the Canadian rock band* Rush. *Neil has the money and taste to do things right, and we are excited about the project. The work will take place in Tortola, BWI, where* Orianda *does high-class charters, and we may have to pay income tax there.*

Six months of sailing adventure lie between this newsletter and the last one. We worked in boatyards in Florida to earn enough money to make this trip. While we were there, I designed three cruising sailboats: a 57' steel ketch for my friend Allan, a 46' steel sloop for Pete and Ursula at Cracker Boy, and a 50' plywood/epoxy cruising sharpie for my new friends Michael and Joan Polvere. So—I have really launched my new career as a marine architect, despite Merritt Walter's admonitions back in Virginia.

The Virgin Island summer was hot and wet, but blessedly without hurricanes. Paul was my only remaining crew. Being stuck in one place, things soon became strained for us, and we needed a break. We were both experiencing some health problems—I used to joke that we were walking compendiums of tropical diseases—but really it wasn't that serious. After Paul eventually left, I was overcome with a terrific feeling of sadness and loss. I somehow felt he was leaving for the last time. Paul and Eliot are bright lights in my life—I will always miss them both.

Paul returned to his mother's home in Rockland County, New York, and wrote a long essay about his adventures and learning experiences on *Fishers Hornpipe*. He had been part of an experimental high school program called *SWAS—School Within a School*, which encouraged alternative approaches to education. Based on his years of travelling in foreign countries, his learning experiences on a true cruising sailboat, and on his extensive reading and self-education (by the time Paul and Eliot lived and traveled with me, there were over one thousand books on board), Paul was graduated from high school. I also trained both Paul and Eliot to be shipwrights and carpenters, and they both used these new skills to earn their livings at times.

Now, I ask, could there possibly be a better way for young people to grow than to be allowed to follow their own natural learning paths? To be allowed to apprentice themselves to the adults they choose, and to be accepted and taught by those adults? If the doors of all the work places in the world were left open to adolescents—as well as the doors of more formal educational "institutions," young people would come and go and would learn unhindered, and un-imprisoned. Youth should all, of course, receive guidance and direction from their elders—*all* elders in their community, including all lines of work and occupation.

* * *

I lived in the Virgin Islands for five months, during which I made numerous trips between Tortola and St. Thomas, as well as to neighboring islands like St. John (which became my favorite of the US Virgins), Jost Van Dyke and even Puerto Rico. I got to know the neighborhood, and I found some great people there. I met professional yacht captain Brad Miller, who became my life-long friend. I met Morgan Sanger, who ran the West End Shipyard, Jim and Trish who lived ashore and had the beautiful ketch *Laissez Faire* (see photos), some of the well-heeled folks from Steel Point (see photo), and the wonderful brother and sister team who ran the bar/restaurant *Bananas*. I also met Michael and Kieth—captain and mate of *Orianda* (more about which presently). But I never felt at home—as much because I was troubled as well as because the Virgins were not the right place for me to bury my anchor for long.

My home base was Soper's Hole, West End, Tortola. I took over the old Fleet Indigo Charters building next to Bananas bar/restaurant (which old-timers know as Poor Richard's). I moved my tools ashore and set up shop—and went to work remodeling the schooner *Orianda*. The work was fulfilling and lucrative, and led to more work and more still. Much later, I was even asked to return to Tortola to remodel *Orianda's* remaining cabins, by air if necessary, tools and all, all expenses paid. I never did.

I was able to spend some time with the members of the Canadian rock band *Rush* (whose drummer, Neil, owns *Orianda*). When our work was finished, we all went sailing on *Orianda*, and had a blast. I was very flattered when Neil visited with me on *Fishers Hornpipe* and we played some of my hand drums together! The members of *Rush* are very mellow people, considering they are a very hot rock band. In saying this, I am comparing them mentally to other rockers I have known—like the wild, wonderful folks associated with Neil Young, the Taylor Family, or even my beloved Red Legs.

I had two intense love affairs, which didn't work out, and left me feeling empty, lonely and inadequate. During my time in St. Thomas, I met and started spending time with a Canadian woman sailor named Tracy Ireland. She was very bright, and very beautiful, and she came out to visit with me when I was anchored in Commie Cove. We went swimming and sunbathing together, naked in the hot island sun, and we went for long walks on Hassel Island. She was seeing someone else at the same time—a local doctor—and she chose to be with him rather than sail off into the sunset with me. [Twenty years later we caught up to eachother—she married a different doctor, taught him to sail, moved to New Zealand, got divorced—but we were three thousand miles apart and were unable to arrange a visit.]

In Tortola I met a woman sailor named Susan, who had just bought a beautiful Swedish mahogany sloop named *Gracil.* We raced *Gracil* in Foxy's Wooden Boat Regatta (on Jost Van Dyke)—and won! I felt my life was changing for the better, especially after a romantic dinner and night aboard *Fishers Hornpipe.* But Susan also ended up with another man—a mechanic friend from St. Thomas—and I was crushed. Once again, I stupidly thought I had found my life's cruising partner, only to be blown out of the water.

I started drinking heavily—those dangerous rum-and-cranberry/squeeze-of-lime drinks at *Bananas.* One night I really overdid it (we were playing drums too loudly) and I was politely thrown out of the bar. Paul took me back to the *Hornpipe* where I stood at the lifelines and screamed out my frustration and heartbreak over Susan. The next morning, he told me what I had done—I had no memory of it—and I was horribly embarrassed and depressed. I wanted to die. Time to change my life. Within days, Paul left.

I lived alone for a month—sorely needed solitude. I was becoming concerned about finding crew to continue down island, and *Fishers Hornpipe* was overdue for a haulout. I needed help. A South African sailor named Peter helped me scrub the *Hornpipe's* large and very foul bottom. We then sailed her from Tortola to St. Thomas on 10/5. Back in Commie Cove, the US Coast Guard boarded the *Hornpipe* and searched her for drugs, under the usual pretense of 'safety inspection.' She passed—no drugs, no violations—but I felt violated.

I met a chubby young California hippie girl named Darlene, and she sailed with me to Las Croabas, Puerto Rico, where we gave the *Hornpipe* her desperately needed haulout. We spent some time in the village of Fajardo, which I liked very much. There were indigenous daysailing sloops in the harbor, which took tourists sailing among the islands in Sondada Vieques. They were small, light, all wood, with tall, very-raked masts, and they fairly flew over the water. [One of these days I will return to Fajardo and find one hauled out, copy her lines, and perhaps adapt the design for cold-molded wood construction....]

On 11/20, we sailed back to St. Thomas, and after another visit to St. John, I returned alone to West End, Tortola. Was I fated to become a single-handed sailor?

CHAPTER SEVENTEEN—THE LESSER ANTILLES

It is a delight of souls to become moist.

Heraclitus

On Thanksgiving of 1982, there was a great communal feast in West End, during which I met Holly, Karen, Tom and Roy. They had arrived on boat delivery jobs, had a few dollars in their pockets, and wanted to look around a little before returning to the States. They all expressed an interest in sailing south with me—my prospects were improving! On 12/1, I sailed back to St. Thomas to start provisioning the boat. It turned out that Karen had to return to the states suddenly, but I met a young (male) Dutch hippie named René who wanted to come with us in her place.

My plan was to sail to Trinidad, with only a few stops along the way, thence on to Venezuela, and up the huge, jungle-girthed Rio Orinoco. We all got the necessary inoculations and malaria pills in St. Thomas, before leaving.

On the morning of Dec 17th we weighed anchor for Martinique. We popped the cork on a bottle of *Möet* and toasted our voyage. We had a long, lazy four-day sail down to Martinique, during which we watched the Antilles islands drift slowly by 30 miles to windward. Tom in particular was very displeased with our slow progress, and couldn't understand why I didn't start the diesel and charge along—too many deliveries. The weather was hot, the wind very light, and we all wore little or no clothing. Half my crew slept on deck.

One morning, while Tom was half asleep on the raised quarter deck, Holly (who was completely naked) came and squatted near him, and seeing he was waking up, said good morning. Tom thought things were looking up, and started a conversation. A few minutes later Tom came bolting below with a look of shock and outrage and told me "She...she... she was taking a *shit*!" "Well, I guess that's why we call it the poop deck," I told him. My dad once told me the most effective way for a woman to repel a man's unwanted attention was to take a big shit in front of him. It worked a little too well.

We arrived in Martinique during the early hours of 12/21, and cleared in at Fort de France. Tom announced he was jumping ship, and to our dismay, Roy announced that he was leaving also. It turned out that Tom had only come because he was romantically interested in Holly—and when she made it perfectly clear that he was wasting his time, he just wanted off. The reason he gave us was that he was terrified of contracting herpes from me.

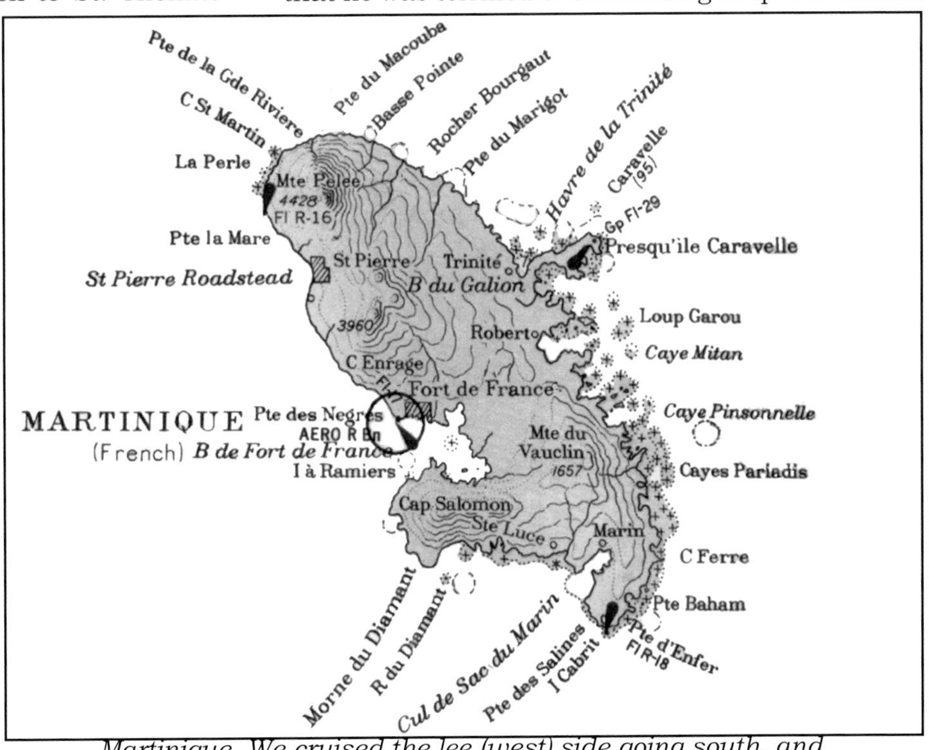

Martinique. We cruised the lee (west) side going south, and the windward (east) side going north.

He flat out refused to believe me when I explained that that could only happen with intimate sexual contact. Roy said that was also his reason—and we lost a third of our crew. Perhaps Roy had only come for the same reason as Tom. [Ten years later I ran into him in Camden, Maine—but I never did ask him.] Looking back, I think they were just the wrong people for us, and vice-versa.

We nevertheless enjoyed our stay in Martinique immensely. French wine could be had for seven francs a bottle—a little over a dollar. We visited Anse de Cocotiers and Grand Anse d'Arlet, where Holly and I had Christmas dinner at a tiny beach restaurant named Tamarin. We each ate a whole fish, prepared with a blend of French and Caribbean culinary wizardry that altered my whole concept of how to cook fish. The French wine was equally exquisite. But Holly's company was becoming the most flavorful spice in my life.

We advertised on a bulletin board for crew, and found a Belgian woman who had just crossed the Atlantic, and wanted to do some island cruising. Jacqueline joined us in Fort de France, and at 1045 on 12/29 we departed for Bequia.

The 23-hour trip was one of contrasts—calms and squalls—and during the night a turnbuckle pin worked its way out, causing our jib to sail off to leeward with the forestay. Because the *Hornpipe* has twin forestays I was able to put up the other jib—there are almost always two jibs hanked on—while I repaired the disconnected stay. Depending on wind conditions, I carry a genoa and a yankee, or a yankee and a storm jib, one on each stay. Running downwind, both sails can be carried simultaneously, using a whisker pole attached to the sheet of the jib on the more windward side.

The Northern Grenadines.

We anchored in Admiralty Bay, on 12/30, and I promptly fell in love with Bequia—adding it to my list of favorites.

An unforgettable experience was celebrating the 1983 New Year's Eve at the beachside Frangipani Hotel. To further celebrate, the next day we sailed around the island to Friendship Bay to go exploring, but the anchorage there was so rough that we came back to Admiralty Bay on 1/3. The sailing was surprisingly rough also—35-knot winds and 15-foot seas, and we took several waves on deck. Locals told us that the weather was the worst in 15 years.

I found Bequia to be unique among all my favorite islands, though it reminded me a little of Providencia in the southwestern Caribbean. The people ranged in color from very white to very black, but there was no sign of racial prejudice—indeed, everyone was either a friend or relative. Bequia is a small island, but it has atypical weather for a small island.

In the Lesser Antilles, the large, high islands make their own weather—clouds form above the mountains and volcanoes, which trap moisture and make rain, and dense, verdant forests grow under the rain, which in turn create more moisture. Hence the existence of rain forests. The smaller and lower islands do not have rain forests or clouds, and are swept over by the relatively dry trade winds. They tend to be arid, have sparse vegetation, and are frequently barely hospitable to animal life, including humans. But the steep, high, verdant islands have less coral reef around them, as they are like mountains whose tips pierce the ocean surface, whereas the low, dry islands are often surrounded by extensive reef systems because they are flat both above and below the surface of the sea. It is interesting that many of the Caribbean island nations include one island of each kind—the high islands have farms, orchards, plantations and herds, and the low islands have abundant fish. Another feature of the low, dry islands is that they frequently include boatbuilding operations, while the high islands provide the wood, although these days most of the plank-stock comes from South America.

Bequia is unique because it is a small island paired with St. Vincent, which is high, mountainous, volcanic and extremely verdant. One would expect Bequia to be dry—it has only low hills—but Bequia lies only nine miles from St. Vincent, in a southwesterly direction, and manages to draw and hold some of St. Vincent's cloud cover and tropical rain. Hence Bequia is a tropical paradise, bursting with life of many kinds, including the eclectic life of the reef. Until shortly before our visit, Bequia had also been perhaps the last place in the tropics whose inhabitants hunt whales under sail and oar.

Many aspects of Bequia captured our love and admiration—and one of the most meaningful for me was the local skill for designing and building boats. The Bequia "two-bow-boat" is famous the world over for quality construction, longevity, seaworthiness and beauty. I fell in love with the boats I saw there. The sheer physical beauty of the island—and its diversity—found a way into my heart such that I considered swallowing the anchor and never leaving. Holly and I went for long walks—a thing we found ourselves more and more devoted

The Southern Grenadines.

to. I think we were happiest wandering around the countryside of the many islands we visited together. In the marvelous book *Clean Sweet Wind* by Douglas Pyle, we are informed that the grackles of Bequia sing "Bequia, Bequia, t'sweet, t'sweet," while on nearby St. Vincent, they sing a different tune.

All four of us sailed over to St. Vincent on the island schooner *Friendship Rose*, to see the big island, and to procure visas for Venezuela at the embassy there. The decks of the big schooner were covered with chickens, pigs, produce, children, bicycles, trunks and clothing—even appliances and televisions, and lots of happy, colorfully dressed people. It was a priceless experience.

On Jan 6th we continued our journey south, stopping next at Clifton, Union Island, and Palm Island (the Tobago Cays), for hiking and diving. Jaqueline and I climbed the Pinnacle—a steep, rocky hill on Union Island—and got pretty torn up in the thorns and cactus. The view—many miles in every direction—was worth it! We had a hell of a time getting back down—we never found anything resembling a trail. I got the feeling that we were the only people to climb up there in years.

We sailed to Granada on the 9th, and anchored in the Lagoon by St. George's. Here we discharged René and Jaqueline, and Holly and I decided to

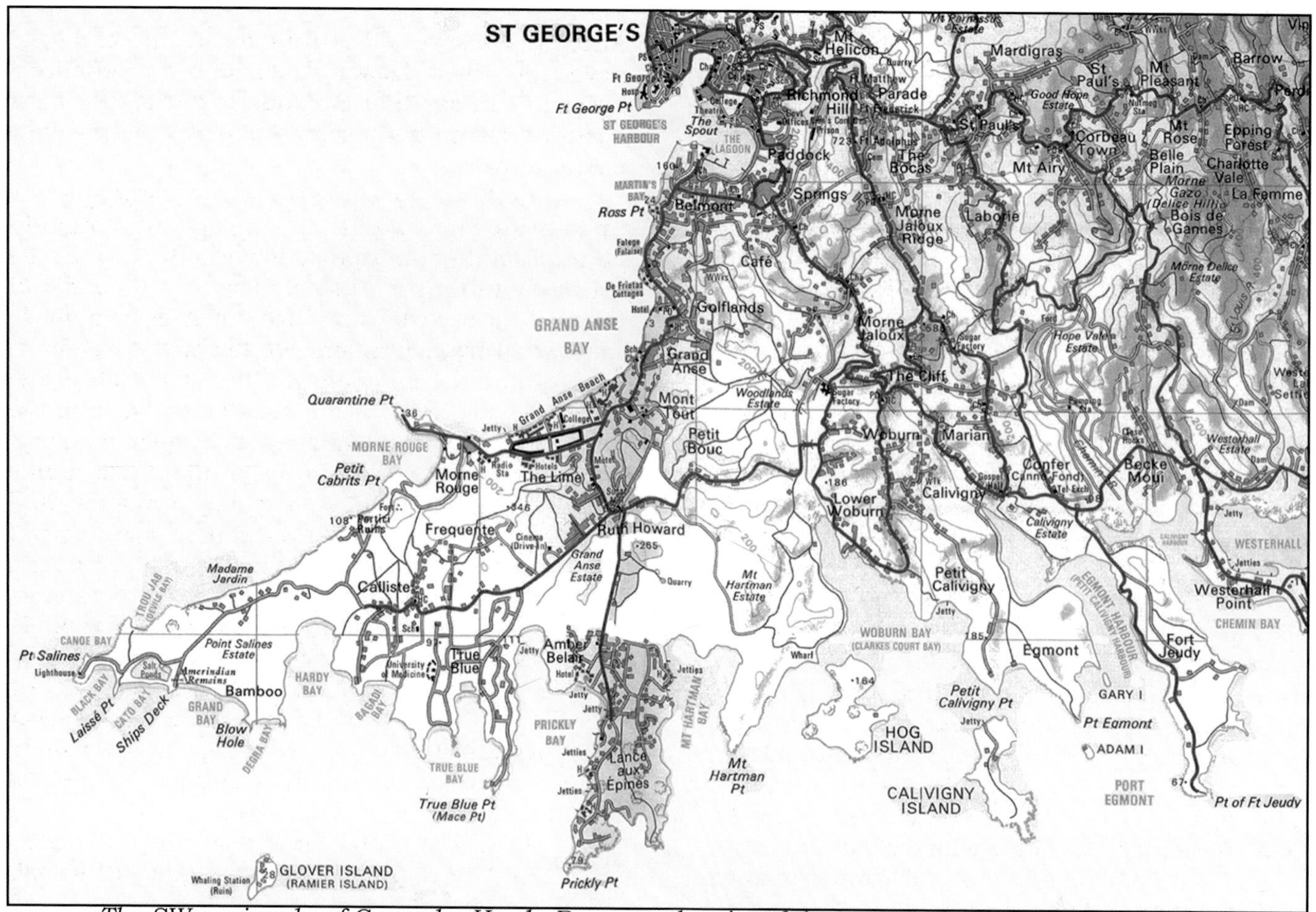

The SW peninsula of Grenada. Hardy Bay was the site of the controversial airport under construction. Hog Island was "off-limits"—but we obtained permission to visit it. St. George's Harbor and the Lagoon are top center.

spend some time alone, just the two of us. After discussing it, we had realized that we didn't have enough confidence in our crew for the ambitious trip to the Orinoco. Besides the language barriers, Holly, René and Jaqueline were in no way seasoned sailors, despite Holly's delivery and Jaqueline's Atlantic crossing. René had never sailed before. The winter trade winds were blowing strong—often over 30 knots between the islands, and the seas were often large, short and steep. The crew also did not get along famously, nor did everyone seem to be doing their part.

Holly and I spent an idyllic month in Grenada. We relaxed and took life easy and slow for a change—took some time to get to know the island. We went swimming—Holly's exercise passion (after running), diving (I finally started getting good with a spear gun), walking on the exquisite beaches, and going for long walks, hikes and bicycle rides. We explored the countryside, the settlements and jungle rain forest. We sailed out to visit some of the nearby small islands. We met friends, fellow travelers and local folks, from whom we learned a lot. We felt we could stay forever.

Among the folks we met were Chuck and Anne Cole on *Sun Spirit*—a 23-foot Block Island Cowhorn (see photo). They had sailed from Wellfleet, Massachusetts, with a cat, dog, infant son and no engine. They even sank once, recovered their boat and kept going! We were to see them again, even on Cape Cod much later, and they have become life-long friends.

When we arrived in Grenada it was still under home-grown socialist rule. Grenada's previous ruler, Geary, had been a despot, filling his own pockets with the island's resources while clamoring about space aliens. The way the Grenadians tell about the coupe is this: "Well mon, we is all sittin' on de fence, and she break—and we is all fallin' on de same side." A man named Elvin Bishop became the new leader—with solid backing from the people. He formed a new government, which he called *The New Jewel Movement.* He saw that a modern socialist government would most benefit the people of the island, but knew he would need help from outside. He turned to various countries in the Caribbean and Central America, with limited success. He turned to the United States—going so far as to request audience with the president—and was refused.

Every country in modern history that has had what the people themselves considered an "American-style revolution" has been condemned—often violently—by the U.S. Government. These include Fidel Castro in Cuba, Ho Chi Mihn in North Vietnam, the Sandanistas in Nicaragua, and Elvin Bishop in Grenada, to name a few. The U.S. Government is infamous, on the other hand, for backing right-wing dictatorships all over the world. Do I need to enumerate them? [As I make my final edit of this book in late 2005, the US is deeply involved in yet another heinous war in Iraq. It does appear to me that we learned *nothing* from Vietnam, and that American youth and the soldiers and civilians of any country that either crosses us or has what we want, are destined to die by the tens of thousands. I am deeply ashamed of, and afraid for, America, my country.]

Bishop, in desperation, finally turned to Cuba, and was accepted with open arms. Bishop had an uneasy relationship with the Grenadian military. The military was pushing for militant communism; Bishop was against this. Cuba sent in advisors for all branches of government. Holly and I saw several agricultural projects and made friends with the Minister of Agriculture. As Grenada's airport was small and could not accommodate commercial jets, a plan was initiated to build a new airport. This is what probably triggered American military concern—the airport was not seen as a boost to tourism, but as a military base.

Parts of Grenada were "off-limits" to foreign cruising yachts. One of these was the beautiful anchorage at Hog Island, which was located near the military base. Upon entering the country, I had made friends with the Immigration Officer, because we found we were both dedicated to reading 19th-century English literature—especially Thomas Hardy. We began to trade books. I eventually talked him into giving us permission to spend a week anchored off Hog Island. We had a rough sail around the south end of Grenada on the morning of 1/16/83, and spent three memorable days alone in this virtual Garden of Eden. From the top of the hill on Hog Island, we could see the military base, and watch the soldiers in training. It was a very small base, and it did not strike me as "a major buildup of military personnel," as later accusations indicated.

While we were there, we dove for conch (pronounced "konk") and collected several. We took them to the beach to clean them (a messy process), and were joined by a local man who was doing the same. During the cleaning, you remove a long, clear "noodle," which West Indian men always swallow whole. This caught Holly's attention, and she asked what the noodle was...the man blushed (black people do blush), and said "oh, dat's not for you, missy, dat's only for de mon." Cleaning the next conch, Holly took out the noodle and swallowed it. This cracked up our new friend, who laughed and laughed. She had just eaten a raw conch penis!

We also spent time in Prickly Bay and Grand Anse, which were as beautiful as any anchorages I have ever visited. Looking back on my experiences, I think I can say that Grenada might be the most beautiful place I have ever seen, in all my travels to beautiful places.

Early one morning Holly and I caught a bus up to the top of Gran Etang—the highest mountain on the island—and walked down to the lake in the volcanic crater (see photos). The whole middle of Grenada is a park—and most of it is completely untouched by civilization. We followed a primitive trail around the perimeter of the lake, and on the far side, hiked off into the rain forest. Deep in the jungle we came upon a barefoot old man, who was very shocked to see white faces there. His name was Rufus, and he was trapping armadillo and opossum, prized for the flavor of their meat, to put his daughter through college in Trinidad. Although we were all speaking English, it was almost impossible to understand eachother. He proudly showed us his catch, and I was grateful that Holly had a strong stomach. When she asked him why he was barefoot, he explained that shoes were never worn by West Indians except to go to town or to church—shoes were strictly a status symbol and had no practical value whatsoever.

The hike took us along a sketchy trail on the park boundary, and down the mountainside through old plantations and citrus groves. We encountered several very remote camps, and caused great surprise. Everyone we met was polite and friendly. Grapefruit were rolling around everywhere on the lower slopes, and we packed our day packs with those we couldn't eat. The trees were strange (see photo) and the bamboo groves were enormous, but we never found the remote waterfalls we had hoped to see. Finally, late in the day, we emerged in a tiny village above the road, and as we walked through, gathered a large entourage of giggling children. By the time we hit the coastal road, we were very footsore and tired—and hitched a ride back to St. George. The hike turned out to be more ambitious than either of us anticipated—and we were avid, buff hikers—but it was a unique life experience of incomparable value.

I went to high school with a friend who founded the medical school on Grenada. We went to find him, but were unsuccessful—I can't remember why. When American forces later invaded Grenada, protecting American students was given as one of the main justifications. But a horrible tragedy had already occurred.

Weeks before the invasion, Elvin Bishop and his prime ministers were placed under house arrest by the overzealous military commander, supposedly prodded by his Cuban advisors, who claimed that things were moving too slowly. Within days, Bishop and his government, backed by a large group of supporters, walked into the military compound to talk. The soldiers opened fire, killing Bishop and several of his supporters. While the U.S. invasion has been described as an incredible farce (talk to the soldiers who were there), it was also inevitable and necessary.

Early on the morning of Feb 5th, Holly and I left Grenada (after one last farewell blowout dinner at *Mama's* in the Lagoon), and sailed to nearby Carriacou. Holly and I had become a good sailing team, and found that we could handle *Fishers Hornpipe* quite well with just the two of us—even entering and leaving crowded anchorages under sail. The way I expressed it in one of my Newsletters: *I can close my eyes and see Holly's golden perfect body cranking the windlass, long blond hair blowing in the breeze while I haul up the mains'l,* Fishers Hornpipe *slowly falling off and gathering way over rippled turquoise water under a brilliant blue sky with big puffs of trade wind cloud sailing above. I could die right now and never feel cheated by life.*

Holly's long golden hair was due to be trimmed, and since I know how to cut hair, I was elected. Naked, in the tropical heat, I gently snipped away with the shears, inevitably touching Holly's neck, shoulders and back. Holly wept—getting her hair cut makes her cry...I, on the other hand, suffered a throbbing erection—cutting her hair was terrifically, painfully erotic.

While in Grenada, we had received a letter from Bob Tillotson [how did we all communicate before email?], and made arrangements to meet him in St. Lucia. We also made arrangements to meet Holly's friend Carleton in Martinique.

We spent a couple of sun-drenched days in Carriacou exploring the island and looking for boat-building projects—for which the island is known, along with its professional sailors. Of note is the beautiful anchorage at Saline Island, where we found interesting rock formations.

We worked our way slowly north, stopping again in Union Island and the Tobago Keys. We sailed to Cannouan on 2/9, where we met two sweet little girls who made us promise to be their pen pals. Months later, I got a touching letter from them saying to send money! On the 10th we had a good sail back to Bequia, and felt like we were coming home. We stayed for a few days, and sadly bid farewell to "Bequia t'sweet" on Feb 13th.

We left in the evening and sailed overnight—our first such sail with just the two of us—arriving in Marigot, St. Lucia next morning. We picked up Bob, sold Paul's old bicycle to a happy boy for very little money, and sailed to Martinique on the 15th. The sail took only 5½ hours, but Bob was horribly seasick in the rough seas between islands. I held him in my arms while he moaned and puked his guts out, and felt terrible for him.

We anchored off Marin Club Nautique to clear customs and Immigration, then moved in the afternoon to Plage St. Anne, which is a wonderland—a tiny French Caribbean waterfront village. Here we climbed the zig-zag steps up to a mountain shrine, with beautiful stone carvings of the stages of the Crucifixion at every turn. At the top were millions of devotional candles swept into a small canyon, and as we were living at night by candlelight, we stuffed Bob's backpack full to bursting, all the while furtively looking over our shoulders for a priest to come out of the rocks yelling "Sacrilege! Sacrilege!" at us in French. Bob—ever the scavenger—was in candle heaven.

Looking in the Log during these idyllic times, I see that I was being more informal. Instead of logging exact arrivals and departures, I was now writing *morning* or *afternoon*.

We decided to cruise the windward east coast of Martinique, after talking to some French cruisers. Again, I hand-copied some of their charts, with directions to the best places to go. We found that there were no American boats—they were all afraid of the lee shore—not realizing that eastern Martinique has protective reefs, islands, and several beautiful, quiet harbors.

Carleton joined us at Club Nautique in Baie Francois. On the 19th we moved to Petit Granade I. by Pte. Vauclin, where we celebrated my birthday by having dinner in a quaint restaurant—we even had truffles!

On Feb 21st we moved to Havre du Robert, where we ran hard aground and were stuck for two tides (18 hours). We had a very hard time getting off—but meanwhile we had a good shopping spree in town—Carleton was wealthy, and contributed to our cruise by providing excellent food and wine. On the 22nd we moved to Baie du Tresor (we didn't find any), and on 2/24 at 1940 we set sail for Dominica.

Dominica is a lush, verdant island, with volcano and rain forest. The people are poor, and before we even entered Prince Rupert Bay we were accosted by children vying very competitively for our business in anything they could con us into, from buying fruit to guided tours. Some of them were delightful characters—one enterprising lad actually sailed a funky homemade raft offshore to be the first to harangue us—a very risky proposition—as the nearest land downwind was Central America.

We took *Gandy Dancer* up the beautiful jungle Indian River that flows into the Bay—but were unable to go without hiring a guide—totally unnecessary as the route was obvious and there was no danger of getting lost! The boys on the waterfront figure that this is *their* river, in *their* country, and if we wanted to see it, we had to pay. We tried to take a long walk on the slopes of the volcano—but the

Dominica. The beautiful Indian River flows into Prince Rupert Bay, where we anchored.

boys insisted we needed a guide for that also. I can understand, but it rankled me anyway. Somewhat disgusted with the constant harassment, we left on the morning of 2/27 for Guadaloupe.

On this trip Bob invented a solution for seasickness—he danced with the waves. First he set his mind to his task, and as we entered the rough seas and strong trade winds between the islands, he stood on the *Hornpipe's* heaving foredeck in a Tai Chi stance, and rode the boat like a huge surfboard. It worked, and on the eight-hour passage, he did not become sick. He was, however, completely exhausted!

At 1710 we anchored in Petit Cul de Sac Marin, Pointe a' Pitre—perhaps not as as beautiful as it sounds—as there is a large international airport there. The following morning Carleton left us, after treating us to one more French feast. Carleton was a kind, understanding man, but his presence on board had been very painful for me, and I'm sure he knew it. Seeing the woman you love being intimate with someone else is a hard thing to endure—but I tried my level best to be a good host, and to hide my frustration.

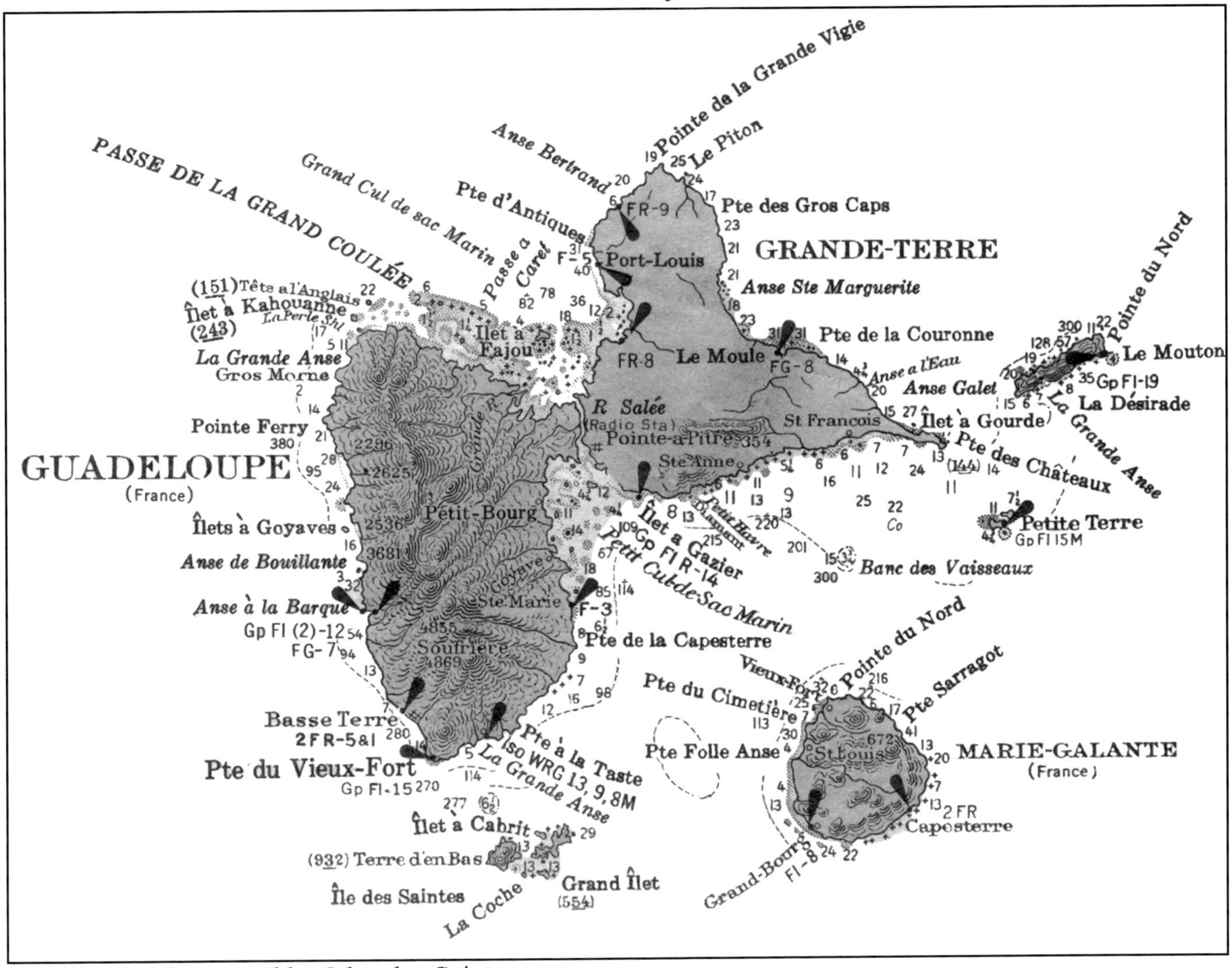

Guadeloupe and les Isles des Saintes.

Was Holly the woman of my dreams? The sailing partner I so desperately wanted? Perhaps, had I not contracted herpes, she might have been...but Holly absolutely drew the line at sexual intercourse and any possibility of catching my nemesis. (We were both opposed to condoms, which really do ruin the joys of intercourse.) She was my dear partner for months of idyllic cruising in some of the most beautiful islands on earth. We were very close, and we loved eachother very much—but we were not to be partners. I lived with the pain of that day and night, like a bleeding wound that could never heal. I had fallen completely in love with Holly Hunter and I knew I could never have her.

That afternoon we moved to Le Gosier Island, and on the afternoon of 3/1 we sailed to Isles de Saintes. This small group of islands was very pretty, but the anchorage I chose was very deep and had a tidal surge. I used a ground tackle device called a 'lizard' when anchoring, which consists of a nylon line leading from the mooring bitts over an anchor roller and through a very heavy-duty steel block shackled to the cutwater bobstay chainplate. From there, the line was hooked onto the anchor chain with a cast-steel chain-hook. The 'lizard' changes the angle of scope (pitch) of the anchor rode by transferring load from the anchor rollers down to the chainplate right at the waterline—a height of over six feet. This makes it possible to anchor with less rode, but still achieve the desired scope (five lengths to one height is normal). But the lizard also acts like a giant rubber band, because nylon is very stretchy, and because the chainplate is at the lower end of the bobstay, the anchor rode does not lie against the bobstay—which causes chafe and helatious noise.

In the deep, surging anchorage at Isles de Saintes, the shackle pin holding the lizard block at the cutwater loosened and worked its way out. I did not have a spare—this was a 5/8" stainless steel shackle, which had cost a small fortune to buy, even wholesale. [Price one next time you go into West Marine and be prepared to swallow your tongue.] So I dove for the pin. Fortunately the water was crystal clear—unfortunately it was deep. I fought my way down toward the bottom, popping my ears over and over while straining to see the pin. I was amazed how far away the bottom was (Holly had dropped anchor, which was fairly common, so I didn't know how much rode went out.) After each dive, I rested on the surface, face down, breathing deeply through my snorkel. Each dive took me deeper, until I finally spotted the shiny pin. I made a huge effort to reach it, and stopped only a few feet away, my lungs fairly bursting for air. On the surface, I hyperventilated for a long time—perhaps five minutes—than dove and swam like hell for the bottom. I got the pin! As I turned to start up, I saw with dismay the tiny image of my large sailboat hull far, far above. I swam like hell for the surface, suppressing the increasing feeling of panic—and broke the surface like a breaching dolphin, gasping desperately for air. On deck, after replacing the pin and tightening it for all I was worth, I sounded the bottom with the lead line, and found I had free-dived to 44 feet.

On March 5th we sailed to Basse Terre, the mountainous half of Guadaloupe. After port formalities, we moved to Anse a la Barque, and spent the next day climbing Volcan Soufriere. The volcano was steep, high and green, its head in the clouds, with numerous craters and cracks leaking steam—a beautiful but somewhat spooky place (see photo). Bob loved it, and elected to spend the night in a cave in the cliffs. It turned out to be a cold, wet, uncomfortable night—and he spent many hours in the sun trying to warm back up.

Holly and I were picked up by a local man on our way down to the harbor. He took us to his home that evening for a delicious shark dinner. Our host was an avid hiker, and his other guests were a group of Germans visiting the island to hike the many beautiful trails there. Basse Terre has hidden waterfalls and hot springs near the volcano, and we wished we could stay longer to see them—but our money was running out. Time to head north.

Holly and I sailed alone the next morning up the coast, while Bob walked and hitch-hiked to enjoy the scenery and people from a closer vantage point. Near the north end of Guadaloupe, *Fishers Hornpipe* came out of the island's wind shadow very unexpectedly, into the full blast of the trade winds. We were about to anchor in the harbor of Deshaies, to meet Bob and spend the night, and were carrying full mains'l and our large genoa jib. A powerful gust laid us over while a rogue wave dashed into the close-hauled genoa, bursting the sail at two seams. I spent hours sewing it back together—the result looks (once again) like a patchwork quilt. Considering three years of constant abuse, the sail is a real credit to the Henderson Brothers Loft back in San Diego.

On March 9th we sailed to Antigua, anchoring in the famous yacht haven English Harbor. It was beautiful and reeked with history, but it was very crowded, so on the 11th we had a rough sail over to the Green Island anchorage. Here it was quiet and very pretty, and we swam ashore and walked on the beaches with no need of bathing suits. The Log says the diesel quit again, and I should mention, sadly, that we continued to have frequent fuel problems all through the Caribbean. Draining and cleaning the fuel filter, bleeding the injectors and swearing a lot over bloody knuckles always got her running again—but the whole thing was an ongoing pain in the ass. Looking back, I attribute the problem to bad fuel, lots of dirt and water in the tank, which got stirred up in rough water, and inadequate filters as previously mentioned.

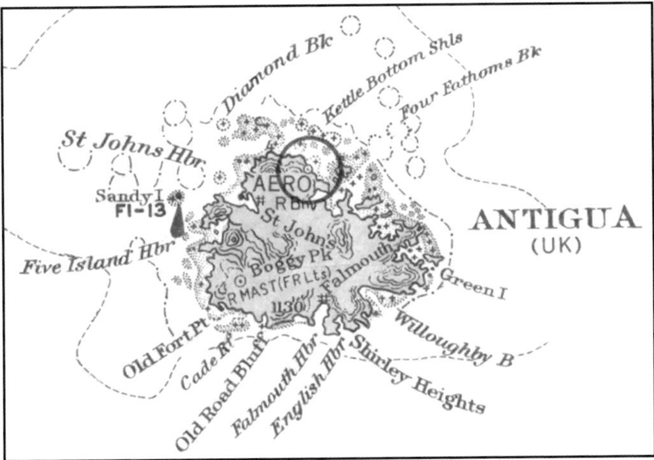

Antigua. Our favorite anchorage was behind Green Island, on the east side.

Next we sailed to Dickinson Bay, thence to St. John's Harbor to get provisions and clearance papers. At 0900 on the 16th we sailed to Barbuda.

Barbuda is another of the low, flat, dry islands—a desert park belonging to Antigua. The landscape was like something out of a scary science fiction movie—but the surrounding reefs are praised for some of the best diving in the world, with very abundant sea life, and over 350 known shipwrecks, some of which are reputed to contain treasure. The island was so loaded with fish that you could fall off the boat right in the anchorage with a spear-gun, and be surrounded by the most varied choices for seafood feasting the imagination can comprehend.

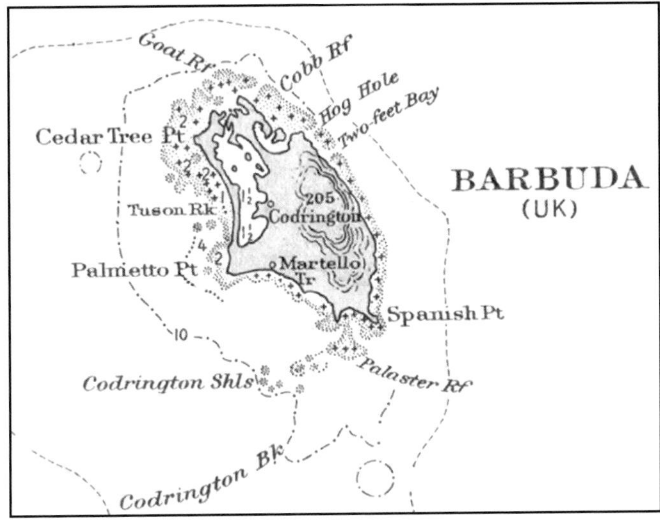

Barbuda, companion island to Antigua.

We went for long walks on deserted beaches and across surreal plains—bizarre patterns of cracked sandstone—carefully skirting cactus and sandspurs. At one point Holly was convinced her feet were as tough as those of Rufus back on Grenada, and she went ashore barefoot. The landscape was so abusive, and *hot*—that I had to carry her home on my back! After three days of solitude and fresh fish dinners, we sailed to Saint-Barthelemy (St. Barts).

We anchored outside Port Gustavia at midnight on 3/19—the inner harbor was so full of boats we didn't dare attempt it at night. We found some old friends, including Michael on *Starbuck* (whom we hadn't seen in years), and acquired new friends on the large Bermudian ferrocement cutters *Venus* and *Moon*. Michael organized a music party, which took place in the *Hornpipe's* great aft cabin. Among the guests were Marlene—a singer/guitar player from Washington state, and a talented and beautiful teenage fiddle player from the Bermudian cruisers [who is now known as Holly Neir]. The party was a great success, the music was wonderful, and Marlene stayed on board with me for over a week (which I *really* needed!). For many wonderful days, Marlene and I hung out and played music in bars together, like *Le Select* in Gustavia, and *Pinnochio's* on St. Martin, to which we sailed on the 27th.

At *Pinnochio's* there was a brilliant Scottish musician, with whom we played on his last set each evening we were there. The club owner took a liking to us, and after we finished the last set, he introduced us to his home-brewed fruit liqueur, whose tropical flavor (and kick!) I will never forget. At 0200, when Pinnochio's closed, we would wander down the beach to a fancy French casino/club to listen to an excellent jazz band, with whom Marlene would sing a song on their last set. Fine memories!

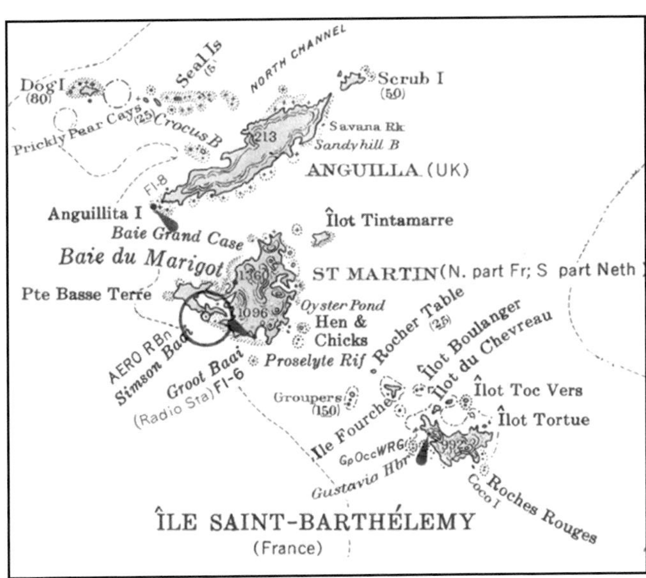

St. Bart's, St. Martin and Anguilla.

On March 31st we bid many sad adieus, and sailed overnight back to the Virgin Islands. All our plans were up in the air, we were all totally broke, and none of us knew what to do next. Bob received some money in the mail, and flew back to the States. I sold my trusty old *Airco* arc welder/generator to *Allonz-Y* for enough money to sail back to America.

Holly and I sailed back to Tortola on 4/7, to visit friends and watch the races that weekend from *Orianda*. On the 8th we sailed over to Roadtown, where I ran into Darlene, the hippy girl who had helped on the *Hornpipe's* haulout the previous year, and arranged for her to sail west with me. We raced against *Orianda* from Roadtown back to West End on 4/10, and tied them. Not to be outdone so easily, they soundly pelted us with water balloons! I then kidnapped Cindi, *Orianda's* cook, in retaliation, and forced her to sign on for the trip west.

On the morning of 4/11, the four of us sailed back to Hassle Island near Charlotte Amalie, and on the 13th, Holly Hunter disembarked to fly home. I felt flooded with sad, confused feelings, including one that I was losing the love of my life. My cruise of the Lesser Antilles was over.

VOYAGE FOUR PHOTOS

Photo 1 Loretta & Tish in the Bahamas

Photo 2 Loretta

Photo 3 Paul & Kingfish

Photo 4 *Fishers Hornpipe* at sea. Clockwise from lower left: Reuel, Stacy, Paul, Loretta... Not your typical *Cruising World* photo! Note the cockpit layout, folding dodger, forward-facing companionway, 2" pipe "roll bar," center-mounted halyard winch and stove pipe. *Air Force One* is to the upper right.. There is an awning rigged over the aft cabin hatch.

Photo 5

The Fortress at Cap Haitien

Photo 6

Cap Haitien Harbor
Native craft

Photo 7

Cap Haitien Harbor
Seawall & native boat

Photo 8 Cap Haitien street

Photo 9

Cap Haitien
Town Square

Photo 10 Cap Haitien street

Photo 11

La Badie
Village Chief
(seated)

Photo 12 Steel Point, Tortola, British Virgin Islands

Photo 13

The schooner *Orianda* in Tortola

Photo 14

Susan & *Gracil*
Tortola

Photos 15 & 16

Laissez Faire
Tortola

Photo 17 Fort de France, Martinique

Photo 18

Martinique house

Photo 19 Bequia Boats

Photo 20 A Bequia two-bow boat

Photo 21 Bequia, windward side

Photo 22 Holly & Kick 'Em Jenny

Photo 23 Reuel (Hollyphoto)

Photo 24 Holly Hunter

Photo 25

Holly

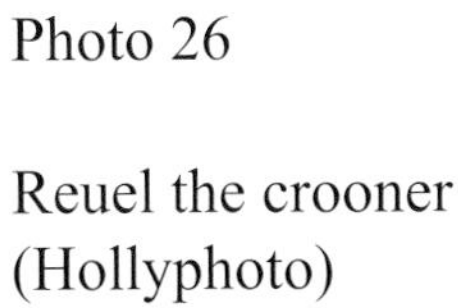

Photo 26

Reuel the crooner (Hollyphoto)

Photo 27

Holly in the *Hornpipe's* galley

Photo 28

Lake Grand Etang, Grenada

Photo 29

The view from
Mt. Qua Qua
Grenada

Photo 30

The view from the lower slopes
Mt. Qua Qua, Grenada

Photo 31 Jungle Reuel (Hollyphoto)

Photo 32 Jungle Holly, Grenada

Photo 33 Reuel (Hollyphoto)

Photo 34 Jungle tree, Grenada

Photo 35 St. Georges, Grenada

Photo 36

Hardy Bay, Grenada
Site of the controversial air field

Photo 37

Sun Spirit
Sailing in Grenada

Photo 38

Gandy Dancer sailing
in the Lagoon, Grenada

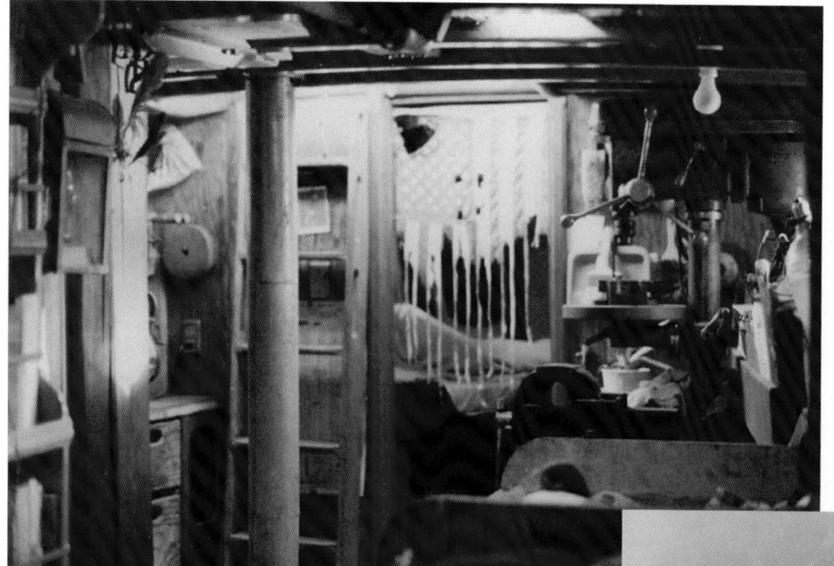

Photo 39

Fishers Hornpipe
Forward cabin (shop)
Looking toward foc's'le

Photo 40 Bob Tillotson (Hollyphoto)

Photo 41 Volcan de la Soufriere, Guadeloupe

Photo 42

Port Gustavia, St. Barthelemy

VOYAGE FIVE: ENDINGS

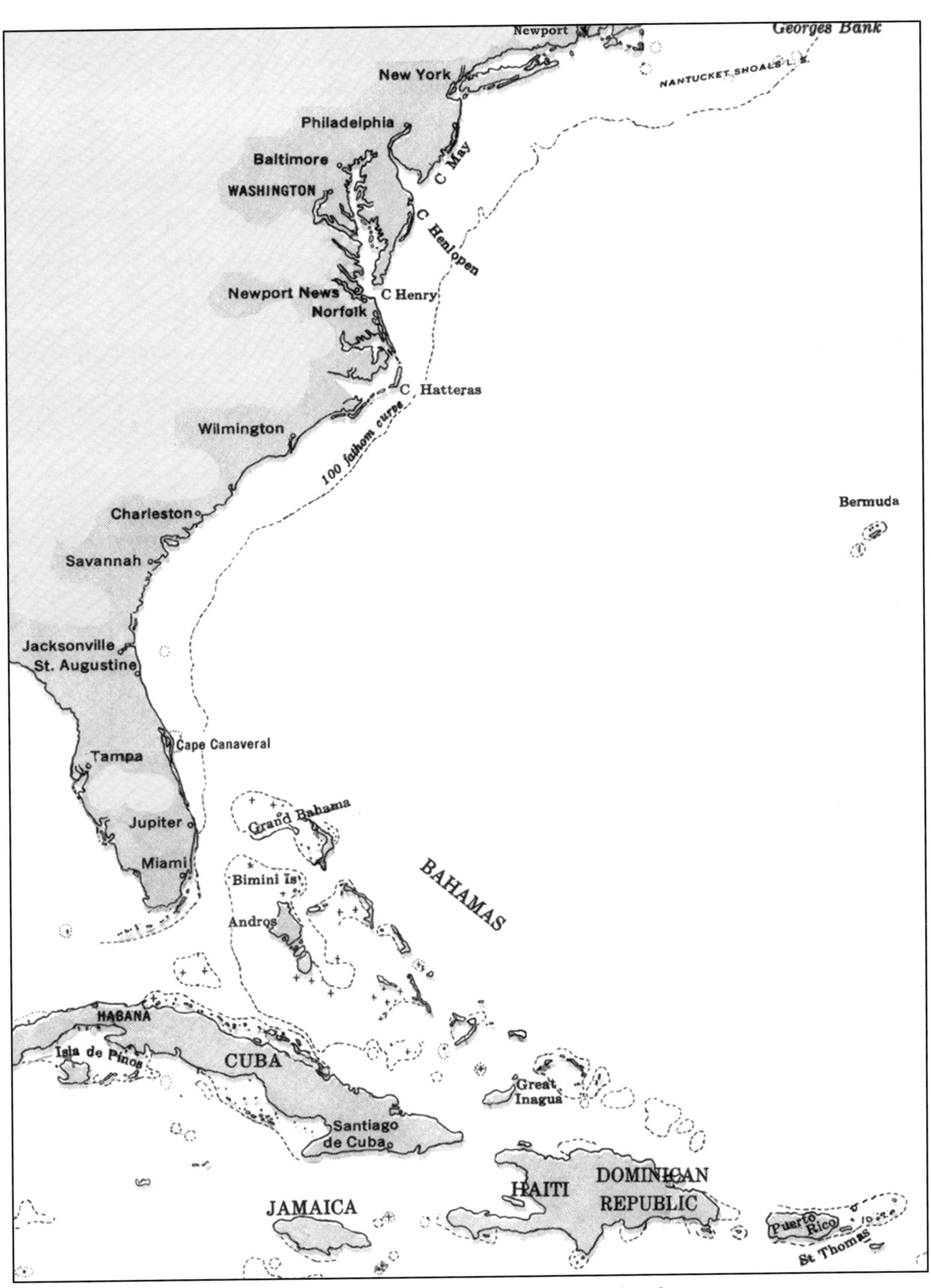

Voyage Five--The Virgin Islands to Newport, RI, back to Florida, to the Bahamas, and ending back in Newport.

CHAPTER EIGHTEEN—ONE MORE ROUND

There is no solace for us,
For such as we,
Who search for some hidden city
We shall never see...
Instead there is only the road,
The dawn and the wind and the rain
And the watchfire under the stars,
Then sleep...
And the road again

John Masefield

Early on the afternoon of April 14th, 1983, Cindy, Darlene and I weighed anchor for the Dominican Republic. Both women had limited sailing experience, and I felt concerned at first, but Cindy turned out to be an excellent shipmate, a fast learner and a great cook (she was, after all, a pro). Darlene was sick a lot, and on her worst days couldn't even stand watch. Because neither woman had gone cruising under sail, nor done much traveling of any kind, I tried to plan the voyage to take in some of the more interesting and beautiful places I had visited previously. I also wanted to make a fast trip, so I planned on fairly long jumps—some over 300 miles—with stays of a day or two at each stop to rest and enjoy the scenery.

From Charlotte Amalie we sailed west through Sondada Vieques, and headed out to sea near Culebra. We found moderate wind and fairly large seas once in the ocean, and made over six knots broad-reaching along the north coast of Puerto Rico. Darlene got seasick during her first watch and had to go lie down. (The Log shows that

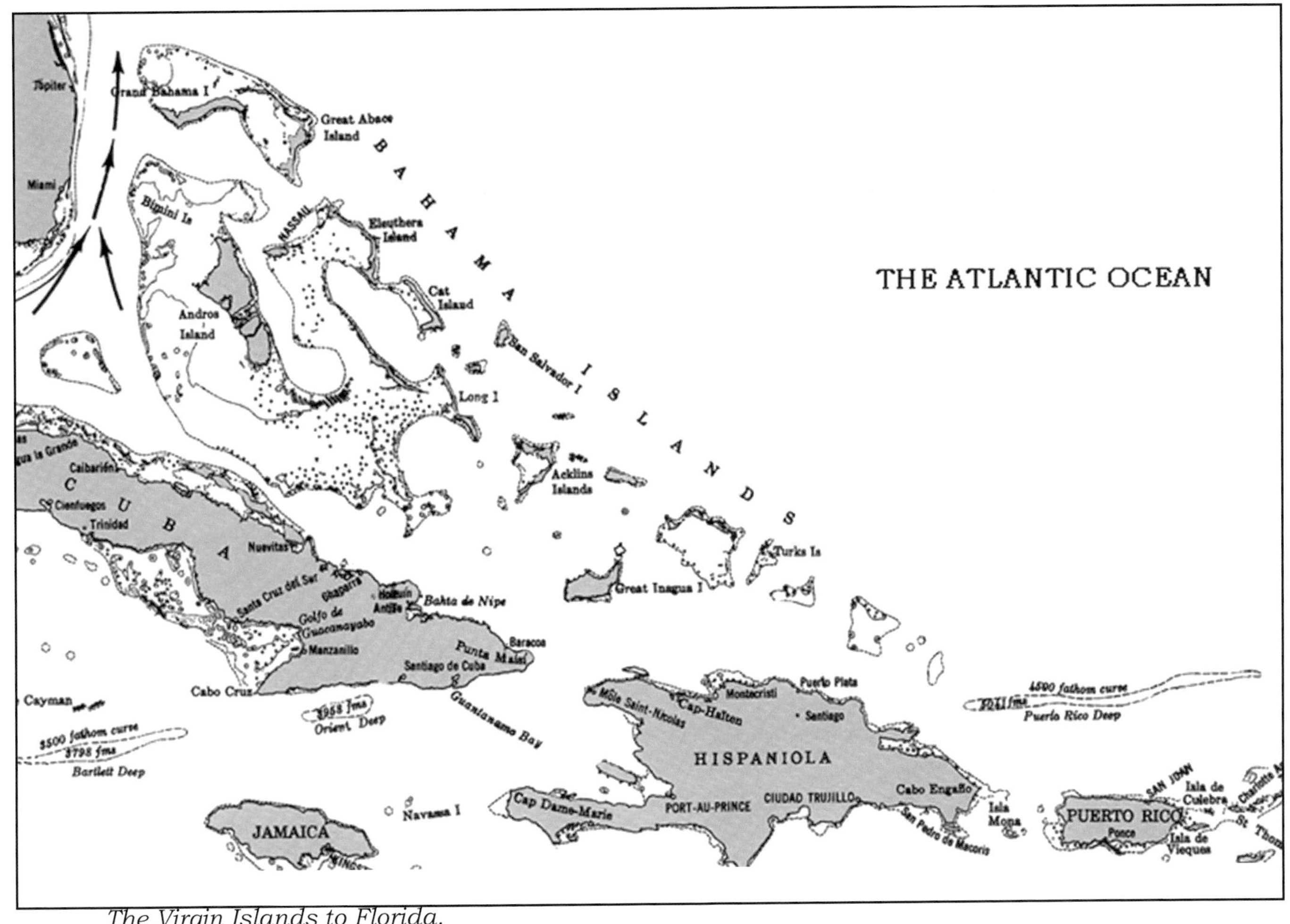

The Virgin Islands to Florida.

although she stood many of her watches later, she wasn't able to help with sail changes or cooking. We all know what it's like!) The next day we had good sailing in seas that were *a little rough* according to the Log, and that following night conditions eased a little.

On the morning of the 16th, I felt concerned that I couldn't see land. After checking my charts and courses—and no small amount of head scratching—I thought to use the hand-bearing compass to check the ship's compass, and found a ten-degree discrepancy. Running back below to plot the course we had actually been steering, I found that we were further offshore than expected, and heading for a dangerous offshore reef (the Silver Bank). I plotted a new course, corrected for the new deviation, to bring us into Puerto Plata. And I realized that my big *Airco* arc-welder was the cause of the problem—or rather its absence was! For five years—all of my sailing—it had been bolted to the deck under the cockpit roof, a couple of feet from the compass. Removing all that steel rendered my compass deviation correction rose useless. I would have to make a new one—and meanwhile I would have to confirm every course with the hand-bearing compass. The lesson here is obvious, but I must stress the old seaman's rule: *Never rely solely on one source of information for navigating or determining your position.*

We continued to have good sailing on the 16th, with the genoa jib out to windward on the 24' whisker pole, but I was unable to get a noon sight. At 1725 we spoke with a tanker on VHF radio and obtained a fix, after which I altered our course slightly. A half-hour later we caught a 35 lb. Kingfish using a cuttlefish lure. By noon on the 17th we were tied stern-to-the-pier in Puerto Plata awaiting customs and immigration officials. That big Kingfish once again greased the wheels of bureaucracy, fed most of the other boats on the dock, and provided us with three large dinners.

I must say this, because I haven't yet: Catching, cooking and eating your own fresh fish is one of the greatest delights of living on a cruising sailboat, and one of the natural joys of living on planet Earth. *We must protect our oceans!* Whenever I am sailing, unless in storm conditions, I am also trolling for fish.

We spent five days in Puerto Plata and visited nearby villages and beaches. Cindi and Darlene ate lots of local ice cream (arguably the tastiest in the world) and bought gifts for friends and family in the States. Prices were cheap, and the American dollar went a very long way in those times.

While we were in Puerto Plata, a friend of mine and his girlfriend arrived on a sailboat they were delivering to Florida. Port officials—and I know how unbelievable this sounds—found marijuana seeds varnished into the cabin sole, and arrested him (not her, fortunately). He would have rotted in a DR prison were it not for the fact that he had worked briefly in Charlotte Amalie as a policeman, and had his police ID card in his wallet. The moral here is clear: Never, ever enter *any* country with drugs, drug paraphernalia, or even prescription medications without the doctor's prescriptions. My friend persuaded the officials that he was an undercover cop posing as a delivery skipper, working to bust a big drug ring. They let him go.

Some other friends of mine weren't so lucky. They were chartering their schooner to tourists for whale-watching expeditions from the Dominican Republic, when a jealous competitor told officials that they were secretly running drugs. Their schooner was confiscated, they were imprisoned without a trial, and they nearly had their first baby in prison. It cost a lot of money and time to reveal that the charges were a hoax, and they were lucky to get their schooner back and leave the country. Forever.

At 1430 on April 21st we left the Dominican Republic. The offshore view of her green mountains in the late afternoon sunlight was one of grandeur and beauty. The human mind's ability to remember images amazes me—I can close my eyes and still see this picture. The sea was dark blue, a 12 knot NNE wind had us reaching under full sail, making six knots at a gentle heeling angle of six degrees. *The Hornpipe* was in her element, strutting her stuff. The Log says: *Beautiful Sailing!* Darlene was feeling better, standing her watch, and the Log also says: *Darlene singing loudly out of tune with Cindi's Walkman—where's that rotten fish head?* The wind held direction and force for three days, only growing lighter at night.

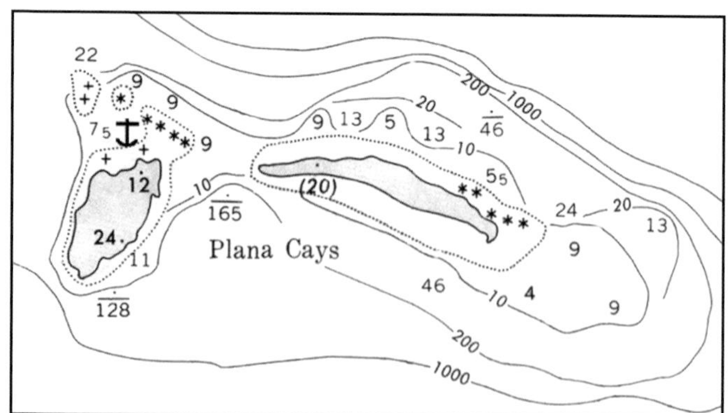

The remote Plana Cays, rarely visited.

We anchored in the lee of the Plana Keys in the Bahamas—a small group of remote, uninhabited islands. We caught up on sleep, did some beach-combing, explored the Spanish ruins there, and left the next morning for George Town, Great Exuma. The trade winds returned to a SSE direction, but

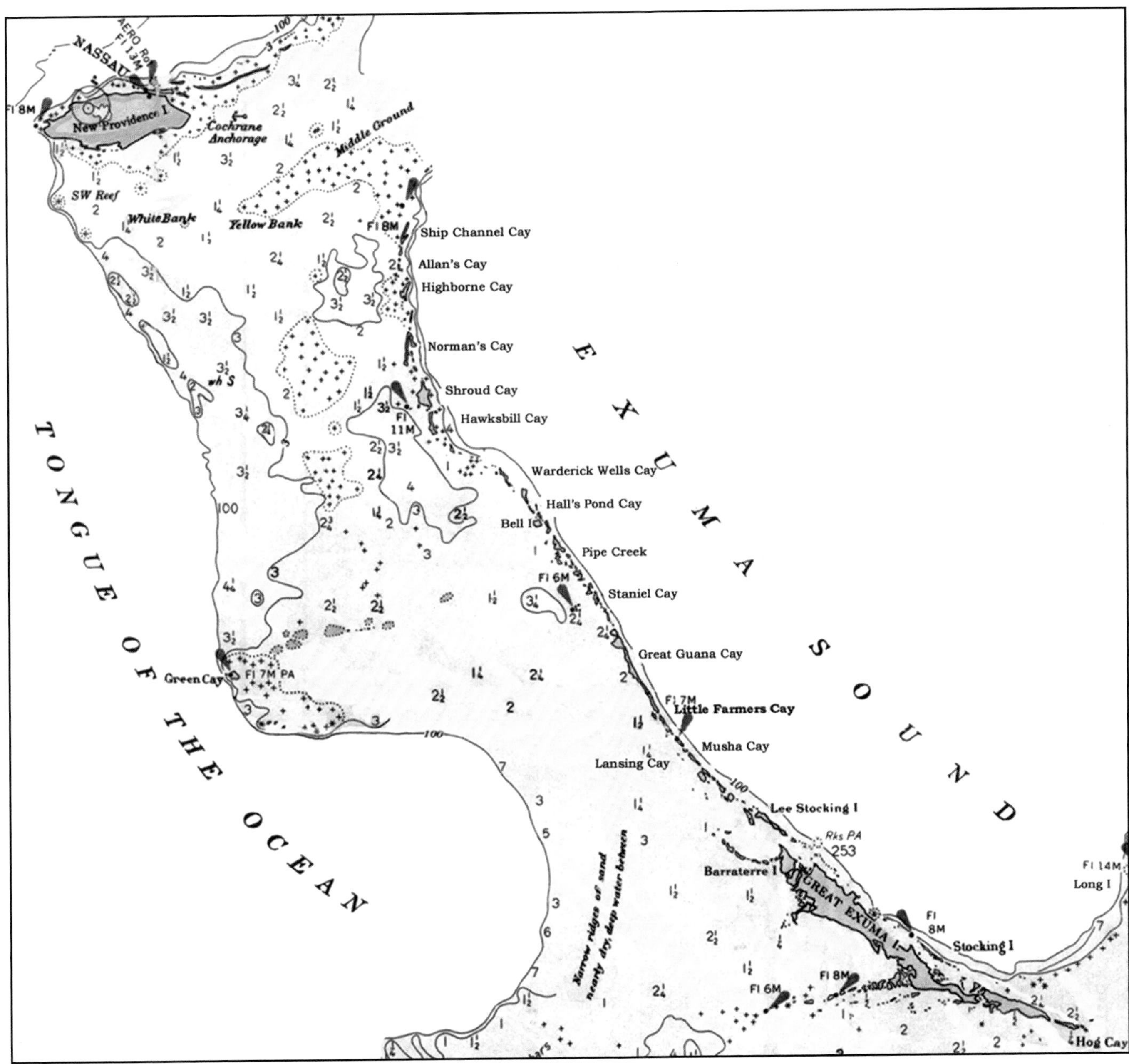

Great Exuma to Nassau.

gradually clocked around to SW and fell light. By the dawn of the 25th we were running along the coast of Long Island, and the wind continued to clock into the NW, heading us. By 1030 the wind was blowing 20 knots, and we were pounding to windward in short, steep chop, trying to get around the north end of Long Island, when we caught a large barracuda on the hand line. As he was too large to safely eat, due to the danger of ciguatera poisoning, I released him alive—a dicey procedure unhooking my lure from that big mouth full of razor-sharp teeth. I stuck my fish club—the cut off end of an oar—in his mouth while reaching down his throat with a pair of pliers. His gullet was so big I realized I could slide my whole arm down his throat! A sobering thought....

The barracuda's teeth are markedly different from the shark's—while shark's teeth are for ripping and shredding (the shark attacks, then waits for its prey to bleed to death), the barracuda's teeth are for slicing—and can even sever large bones, as I described earlier (the woman from Landrail Point).

At 1645 that afternoon, we anchored off the Peace and Plenty Club in George Town. This was my third visit there in as many years. We had missed the Family Island Regatta by one day. But we had a good visit anyway, and found some old friends.

On the morning of the 27th we sailed up to Musha Cay, and again visited my friends on nearby Lansing Cay—they fed us a lunch of Spam sandwiches! We sailed Gandy Dancer to Moon Cay (just north of Musha), so named for its lunar landscape and unearthly natural beauty, and collected some beautiful shells. This tiny island is a bird-rookery, and we were very careful not to step on or disturb the eggs. I dove for conch, which I cooked into Bahamian-style chowder and fritters.

We sailed to Staniel Cay on the 29th, where I took Cindi and Darlene diving in Thunderball Grotto. While we were ashore in the yacht club, *Fishers Hornpipe* dragged anchor and attempted to destroy a J-24. We rowed out to her frantically and got everything untangled without damage, but Don on *Not Easy* has never let me forget it! At that time Don was a sailing instructor in Key West, and later our paths were to cross often—he now owns and operates a big Chris White-designed charter cat named *Fish Head*.

The *Hornpipe* very rarely dragged her anchor, and the handful of times she did (having anchored literally thousands of times), was always my fault. I guess it's always the captain's fault—after all a boat doesn't consciously decide to drag anchor, even though it seems at times that they must. What had happened is that I anchored on a sloping bottom in a crowded tidal anchorage, using minimal scope. When we anchored, the tide was pulling the anchor uphill on the flood. Then the tide reversed (at maximum height—minimum scope), pulled the anchor downhill, and consequently popped it loose. The 75-lb. CQR plow almost never tripped—but it did that evening, much to my great embarrassment.

On the 30th we sailed to Shroud Cay and anchored in its lee—a very pretty spot according to the Log. On 5/1 we sailed to Nassau across the White and Yellow Banks, keeping a lookout for isolated coral heads, and anchored as usual off the Nassau Harbor Club. My crew was now getting the hang of things, and the Log notes happily that we never even started the diesel that day, weighing and dropping anchor under sail alone, even in Nassau's crowded Harbor. This is really not noteworthy for most small sailing yachts with competent crews, but the *Hornpipe* was a large, heavy boat—54' over all and with 46,000-lbs. displacement. She carried a powerful rig, only one center-mounted sheet winch (for both outer jib sheets), and large, heavy ground tackle—weighed with a manual windlass. So my new crew and I felt good about our small accomplishment. We went ashore for fresh-water showers, pizza and rum.

The next afternoon we weighed anchor for Florida, and after a pleasant downwind sail, tied up to the night Customs Dock at 0130 on 5/4 in Riviera Beach. There was a "hot-line" customs phone there in Sailfish Marina, and this time the 1-800 number worked. We were cleared by telephone into the US without problems.

Here I want to explain the differences—and the sailing strategies—between the outbound trip to the Virgin Islands, and the return trip: [Readers not interested in this may skip the next five paragraphs.]

The outbound trip to the Lesser Antilles the previous year involved sailing into the powerful trade winds, and against their attendant ocean currents, a distance of about one thousand miles. I chose to "island-hop" on that voyage, both to enjoy the sights and to stop and rest along the way. The alternative sailing route from Florida to the Virgin Islands is to go directly to sea and sail at least 900 miles to windward on the starboard tack (the wind coming over the starboard bow). Sailing to windward is analogous to climbing a steep hill on land—sailors even call it "upwind" and think of it as going "up."

In sailing to windward, the boat's sails are sheeted in flat, close to the centerline (fore and aft axis), the boat is "heeled over" (leaning sharply to the side), and the hull is punching into the waves. Hence the ride can be rough, wet, and exhausting. On the plus side, most well-designed sailboats will not require steering going to windward—the helm (tiller or wheel) can be lashed in the optimum position.

After sailing these 900 or so miles (the idea is to reach the longitude—or location due north of—San Juan, Puerto Rico), the boat is tacked onto the port tack. Eventually she reaches the Virgin Islands, having "beat to windward" in the open ocean the whole distance—sometimes more than 2,000 sailed miles.

The way I made the trip—sailing among the islands—was seemingly a more direct route—but was not. We still had to tack—beat to windward—most of the way. The differences are two: First, we could wait for favorable wind—such as when an approaching cold front might supply westerlies (usually available no further east than Hispaniola); Second, we had beautiful islands to visit along the way, and hundreds of places in which to stop and rest. On the down side, our trip through the islands took several times longer, and our actual distance sailed was probably *at least* 2,000 miles.

The return trip involved sailing with the wind and current—"down wind," or "down hill," by analogy. Much easier, much faster, and with much more comfort, as a boat sailing downwind does not heel over much or "pitch" (jump up and down in the bow) as she does when beating (it's called beating for good reasons!). The return trip is much shorter—closer to the straight-line distance (about 900 nautical miles), except for weaving among the islands. Although sailing downwind involves the possibility of "rolling" (rocking side to side), this is usually more comfortable than pitching—and it can be eliminated by steering to keep the wind off the quarter—not directly from behind.

Hence our outbound trip involved a sailed

distance of over 2,000 miles, mostly to windward, which took *four months* (from 3/16/82 to 7/17/82). And our return trip involved a sailed distance of a little over 1,000 miles, and took *less than three weeks* (from 4/14/83 to 5/4/83). It's true that we were in no hurry on the outbound leg, and that we were in a hurry (I was broke!) coming home...but the difference, as you can see, is profound.

* * *

On the 6th I moved the *Hornpipe* over to Cracker Boy Boat Works, where I stayed for most of May and June, working on boats in the yard as a contractor. I also did a lot of work on the *Hornpipe*, finishing neglected parts of her and giving her a major haulout.
Newsletter, May 22, 1983:

Riviera Beach, Florida: It seems I have put off writing this newsletter, because my head has been up in the air about many things, which I thought might clarify themselves with time. But since everything continues to be in a state of change, I finally just sat down behind this old typewriter.

This past year has had some ups and downs, and I have been struggling to change some aspects of my life. Sound too familiar? When I last wrote, I was looking for a home base in the Virgin Islands. I didn't find it there. Paradise is in your head—in your perception—the Virgins were a peculiar blend of Heaven and Hell. Or perhaps they were my Purgatory.

It is now the 25th of May. I have been working at the "Crack" on a big, ugly Tupperware sailmonster to earn enough money to do a haul-out on Ms. Hornpipe, *get the hell out of this Godforsaken oven called Florida and up to New England where the weather and folks suit me better. It looks like mid-June for an escape.*

My plans are somewhat vaporous, though I have as many dreams as ever. I truly need to escape this very demanding lifestyle for a while, and I want to change some things in my life. I want very much to visit friends in Massachusetts, New York, California and Colorado. I am involved in a new career in marine architecture, for which I am even considering returning to school. And I am admittedly weary of the shoestring vagabond life I have been living. On the other hand, cruising includes so many of the best things in life that I can't conceive of giving it up for very long.

Fishers Hornpipe *and I have sailed over 25,000 miles now. I have had over forty crew members, most of whom I have taught to sail and live this lifestyle. I have learned (sort of) two new languages* [Spanish and French], *and greatly broadened my skills, attitudes and appreciation of life. This could have come in no other way. It has been very good. It has also been hard, and frightening at times. It has been a hell of an education!*

Now I wonder if I am ready to do something else, something different with my life and energy. Change is seductive, and also intimidating. There is so much to see and learn in traveling, that I don't ever want to give it up—but I do want to change some of my methods. I have always lived awfully close to the edge.... Despite all the wonderful lovers and friends, I have been lonely at times, and I think about having another partner. Life is damned short. I stand in the crossroads again, as I did a decade earlier in the redwood forest in California, when I conceived this long, strange, beautiful trip. Destiny belongs to those of us who find the power, freedom and fortune to mold it in the shapes of our dreams.

Fishers Hornpipe *is tentatively for sale. I would need to find the right person in the right circumstance. This has been a painful and confusing decision to make, but I feel it is unfair to her to leave her neglected while I do other things. Eventually I imagine I will build another boat. I cannot predict my own future—nor do I have any desire to—but I hope I can sense the directions in which I might best go, and sense the changes I might best make. To choose the best paths to walk in the future, I must also review and understand the paths I have taken in the past.*

* * *

I am approaching the end of my story. I have not been able to find a Newsletter that follows that one. But in my life, there was another year of living and traveling on *Fishers Hornpipe*, another eleven pages in the Log Book, and many more adventures. Even more important: I was to meet more remarkable people, who would change my life as I changed theirs....

On June 20th *Fishers Hornpipe* went to sea, with a crew of three besides her captain. Among them was a Cuban woman, Teresa Rodriguez, who was to become one of my very closest life-long friends. John, her ex-boyfriend, and Liz were the other crewmembers. Liz also became a dear friend. She is the New York woman introduced to me by Paul, and she is the one I told about earlier who became so interested in Haitian culture and religion that she became initiated into Voodon. We had good sailing up the Florida coast in the northern extremity of the trade winds, and caught a 12-lb dolphin (dorado) on the second day out.

We were at sea for four days, loping along at four and five knots, but picking up extra speed by hovering near the western edge of the Gulf Stream. This made for slightly rough sailing at times, but we chose stay with the current. The Log says: *Beating in the Gulf Stream sucks.* During the morning of the 23rd we rounded Cape Fear and decided to take a break.

We entered Masonboro Inlet, having no trouble finding it this time, and arrived at Masonboro Boatyard in the evening. We stayed there for a day, and then went back to sea for an overnight sail to Beaufort, North Carolina. There, at the Dock House, I found *Hot Shandy*—not a boat but a folk-duo I knew from Key West.

We had arrived in Beaufort on the day of the annual re-enactment of the Pirate Invasion (a true historic event), and we all dressed up as pirates to help Sinbad with the invasion. We hoisted the 'Jolly Roger' on *Gandy Dancer* and went marauding in the harbor. We got so pelted with water balloons that we nearly sank. My two lovely female pirates got a lot of attention (especially once they were soaking wet)!

On the 25th, in the late morning (some of us needed extra sleep to recover from hangovers) we entered the ICW, to head for Norfolk. On the 30th we arrived at Rebel Marine Service in Willoughby Bay—home again...but not for long.

After a pleasant three-day visit with Captain Lane and the folks at Rebel Marine, we departed near midnight of 7/2 for Fire Island (Great South Bay, Long Island, New York). We sailed and motor-sailed for four days at sea, with very-light following winds. We were completely becalmed at sea for one twenty-four hour period, and the Log notes: *Fucking bugs at sea again!*

Entering the Fire Island Inlet was a nerve-wracking experience with seven feet of draft (see chart below). The Inlet is very shallow, with uncharted shifting sand bars. I had a bow lookout, and proceeded very slowly. It went well.

By 1115 on July 6th, we were anchored off Saltaire in the Great South Bay, and I was home—this time the home of my New York childhood. After resting and cleaning up, we sailed over to Bay Shore and tied up at the Maple Avenue Dock. I called my parents, and my brother who was visiting from Colorado, to come and visit.

I was nervous about how this would go—but it was better than the Christmas visit in Florida. It was a benchmark experience for me, sailing my own long-distance cruiser, that I built with my own hands and sailed halfway around the world, into the Bay of my childhood. I was a completely different person than the young man who went west in 1964, and I felt something akin to vertigo at visiting the world of my past.

My mother and stepfather still figured I was a complete fool to be frivolously wasting my life bumming around third world countries on a

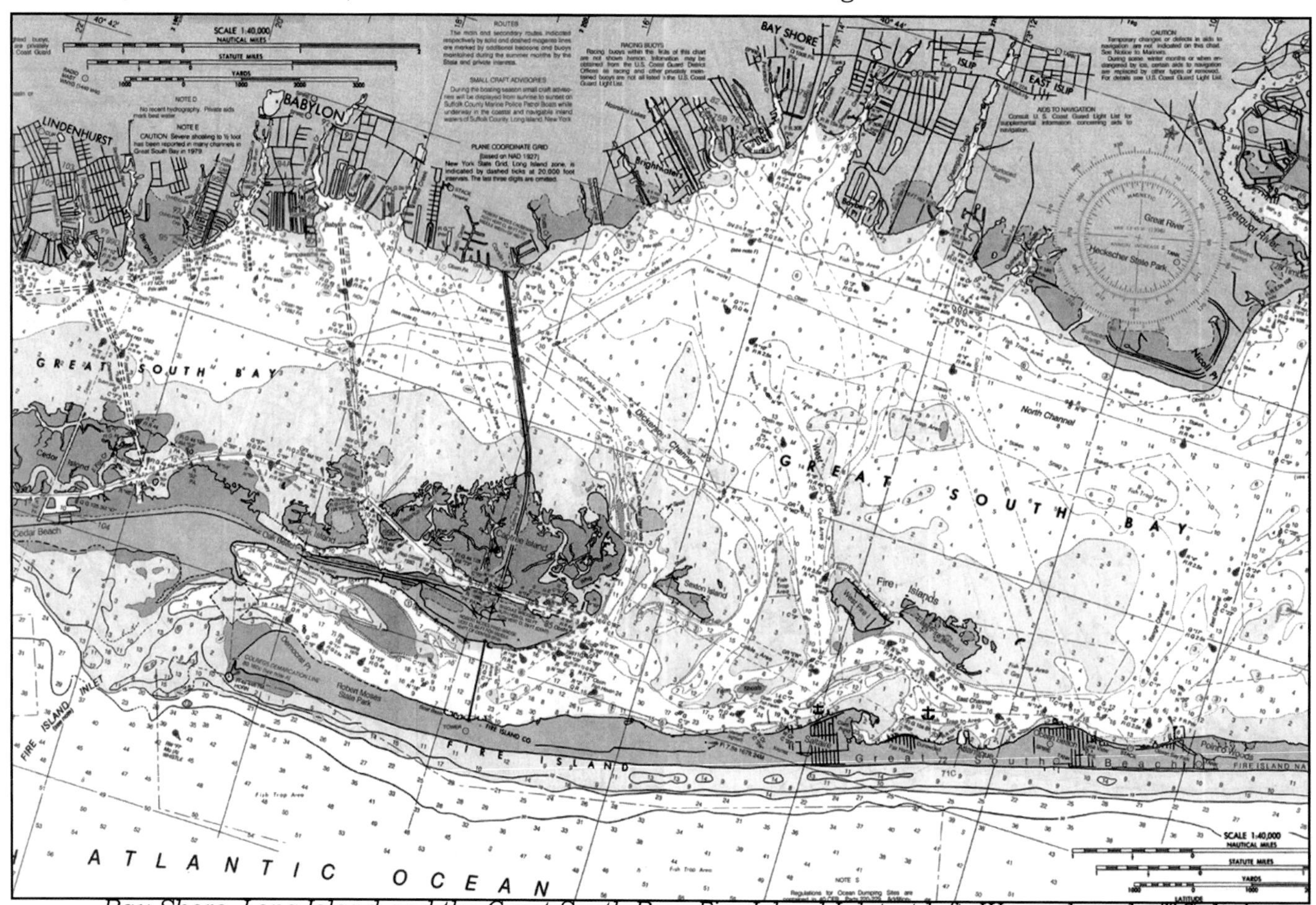

Bay Shore, Long Island and the Great South Bay. Fire Island Inlet at left. We anchored off Saltaire, Ocean Beach and Atlantique on Fire Island—a magical place—or at least it was.

sailboat. They never respected any of the myriad challenges and experiences which were, to me, so conducive to personal growth. They just didn't get it. And of course I came across as arrogant, false-worldly and conceited—utterly self-centered and selfish—looking down my nose at their ugly bourgeois suburban house full of plastic televisions and appliances and hideous furniture and tasteless art. And what the hell did I think I was I doing sleeping with this Cuban girl who dressed like a dyke and never brushed her hair?

Liz left us in Bay Shore to return to Manhattan, and my brother David came on board for a visit and some sailing (see photos). On the 8th we sailed across the Bay to Ocean Beach, where we anchored for the night, but found ourselves aground by morning. We got off using a stern kedge, and re-anchored off Atlantique. On the 10th we sailed to the wonderful little Suffolk County Maritime Museum for an afternoon visit, then back to Bay Shore. After visiting with my family for another five days, we left for New York City on the morning of the 16th.

The Log notes my exasperation with a drastically wrong National Weather Service forecast. I have noticed, over many years, that forecasting wind speed and direction frequently eludes all the organizations that attempt it. Some people even say that humankind was better at predicting the weather in the mid-nineteenth century—before they had any sophisticated electronic equipment to confuse them! I was also burning out on the day-to-day frustrations of my lifestyle...I was going to need a break soon.

After a long, frustrating day, we anchored in Gravesend Bay, Brooklyn, shortly after midnight on 7/17. Later that morning, we left to motor-sail through New York Harbor and the East River to City Island, where we spent nearly two months completing the restoration of Tony's Malabar Jr. sloop, *Imagine.*

An interesting footnote here is that Tere's Cuban family in Coral Gables (Miami) could not know what she was doing, or where she was. I think I am safe telling this story all these years later—Tere's mom and dad still don't speak English. Tere, who was 20 years old, invented this wonderful elaborate yarn about being in school someplace. Her folks would have disowned her—or worse—had they known she was living in sin with a degenerate Yanqui hippie sailor, seventeen years her senior, on a boat, in New York City—the ultimate den of iniquity. But Tere and I had a grand time messing about in Manhattan when we weren't busting ass working on *Imagine.* We became very close, we lived and worked together very well, and continued to do so on and off for many years. I learned a lot from Tere, though perhaps she doesn't know this (sometimes it's hard to say the most important things). I should clarify that we were lovers only briefly—part of that total exploration process that happens between some people—and what came out of it was a solid, lifelong friendship. I deeply love this wonderful crazy intense *Cubana*—there is no one else in the world even remotely like her. Tere was an excellent first mate, co-worker, fellow traveler and best friend! [She still is.]

In early September we launched *Imagine* from Sonny's Boat Club on City Island with a crane, and sailed her for her first time in many decades. She was a *very* sweet sailboat, and sailed like a dream. Years later, I wrote the following recollection:

The experience was like living poetry. Heeled sharply, close-hauled to weather under full sail in

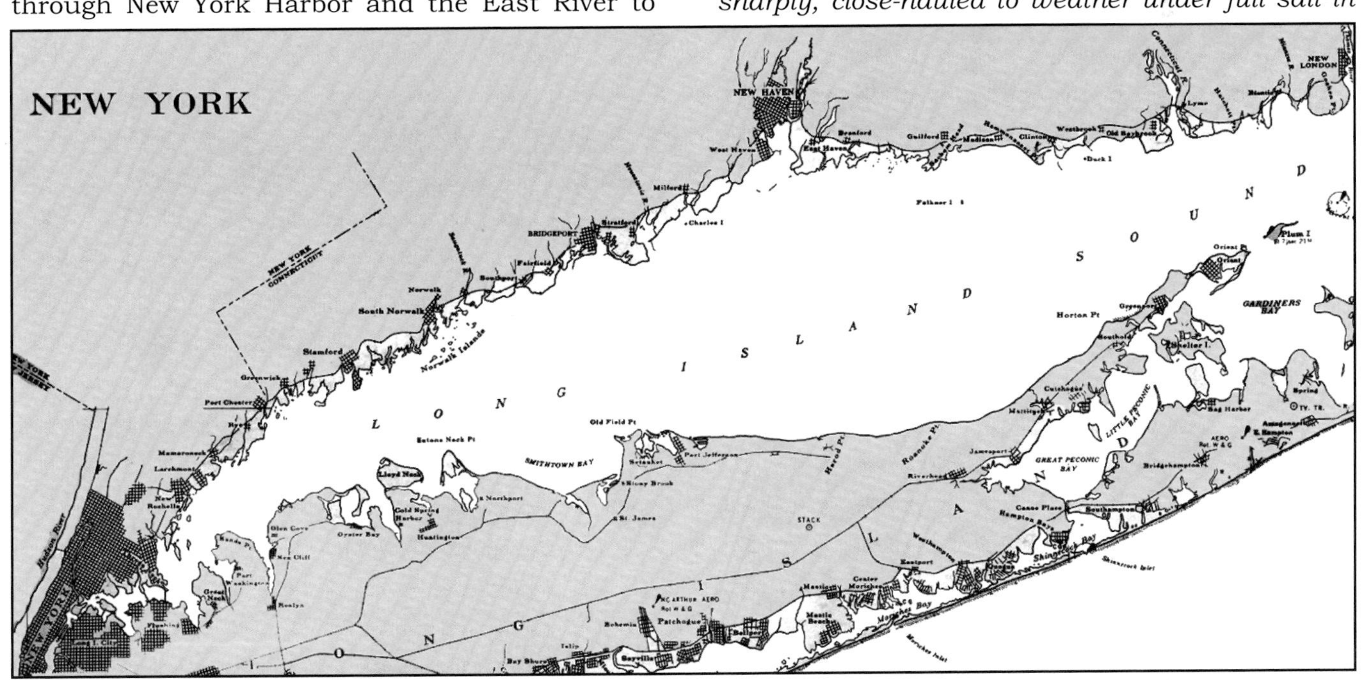

Long Island Sound.

twenty knots of wind, Imagine *laid her lee rail right to the edge of the water in such a perfect curve that the sea slid along her side exactly parallel to the rail cap and released cleanly from her transom. She sailed like a fish swims, like a bird flies. She out-pointed and out-paced a 30' go-fast fiberglass racing sloop one memorable day on Long Island Sound. The sailors on that plastic and aluminum caricature of a boat were bundled in layers of foul weather gear, and looked soaked to the skin. Those of us on* Imagine *were dressed in street clothes, and were as dry as if taking a stroll on Seventh Avenue. I will never forget the looks on their faces as we passed them!*

Tony was as ecstatic and flustered as a new father, and Tere and I had some cruising money in our pockets.

On the morning of Sept 12th we weighed anchor for points east, feeling very glad to escape New York City. As much as I love it, I have to take it in small doses, like any other powerful, dangerous narcotic. For crew I had Tere, Janet (Paul's mother) and Denise (a friend of Tere's). We worked our way along the north shore of Long Island, anchoring in Mamaroneck, Eaton's Neck Basin (where we gathered mussels, with which I cooked mussels marinara that evening), and Mt. Sinai Harbor, where my crew departed.

Just before noon on the 19th I set sail alone to single-hand *Fishers Hornpipe* for the first time. At 1920 I anchored in Mattituck Creek, where Loretta (who had sailed with us from Florida to Puerto Rico) joined me. On the 20th, we sailed to Block Island, R.I., which has become one of my favorite islands ever, anywhere, and we anchored in Great Salt Pond. I have always noted the friendly hospitality of Block Island dogs, and the Log includes the following entry:

Had local tour-guide dogs all day—black lab accompanied us to the dock tonight, where we met a small orange cat, whom the dog attacked. She held her own, and they both followed us down the dock. Perhaps I shouldn't have petted the cat.... The dog attacked her again. She fell in the water and drowned almost immediately! Fucking bummer! I looked for a long time in case she was clinging to a piling under the dock—then I looked for her body—no luck. Will look again tomorrow morning. The black lab was very curious about all this, and jumped in the water to follow us in the dory. We had to bring him back ashore. What upsets me is the feeling of futile incompetence because I didn't react quickly enough to save this precious flame of life. Why are cats so dear to me? (Why am I horribly allergic to them?) Next morning: The cat is alive! We saw her!

Block Island is a great place to visit. It is full of nature trails, cliffs, beautiful beaches, and is perfect for long walks and bike rides. The restaurants are excellent and reasonable and the bars are fun (especially *The Oar House*). The two harbors are full of cruising boats (especially Salt Pond), and Race Week (in mid-June) draws serious sailors from all over the world. The *Java Lounge* is the place for great coffee and beautiful women (and men).

We sailed to Newport the next day, which was a total zoo-scene, as the 1983 America's Cup races were in progress. The Log notes another completely erroneous weather forecast—looks like this was becoming an issue for me. We went sailing with our new friend James on a boat he borrowed the next day to watch the final race, and saw the Aussie's whip America's butt and take our cup away

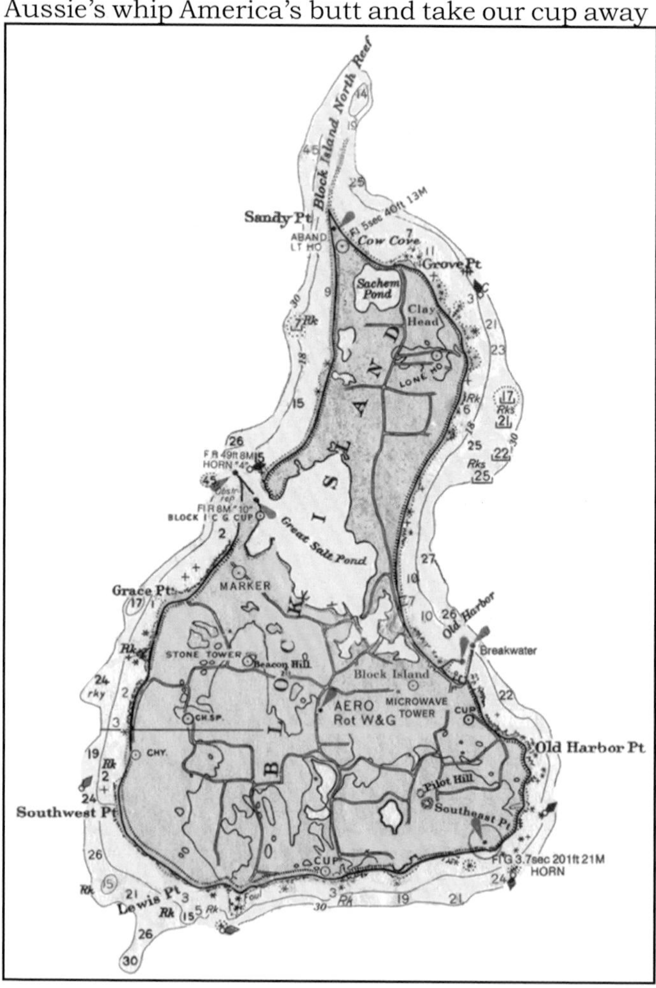

Block Island, Rhode Island.

for the first time in history! Alan Bond's *Australia II*—with her radical new wing keel—terminated the New York Yacht Club's 132-year vice grip on the cup, beating Dennis Conner's *Liberty*. Thus ended, also, the dominance of 12-meter yachts in ocean racing—and I for one welcome the new innovative open-classes which have followed, encouraging new design ideas.

Within a few days, one of the Thames Street

art galleries featured a poster in the window, of *Australia II's* designer, Ben Lexcen, sitting naked in a chair, with an enormous penis dangling out onto the floor! I guess that's what all this racing is *really* about!

Loretta left—we weren't getting along very

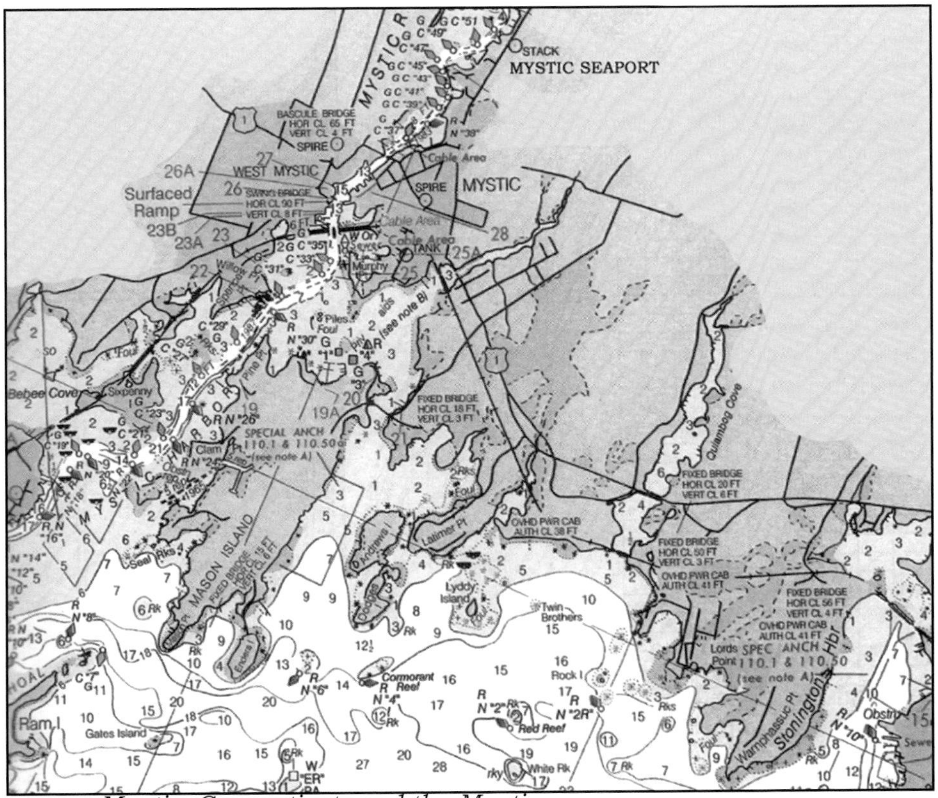

Mystic, Connecticut, and the Mystic Seaport Museum.

well—and Tere re-joined me. I think Loretta was going through some difficult times with her family, and just couldn't cope with the authority figure of a captain. I hasten to add that I am about as low-key as captains can get before total anarchy ensues—I even ask my crews' opinions about destinations and schedules. This conflict made me very sad, but Loretta and I have seen eachother since, years later, and found that our friendship survived.

On Nov 3rd Tere and I sailed west to Noank, and thence to Mystic Seaport for a visit. I love Mystic Seaport, and never tire of stopping there. Their hospitality and open friendship have been a real boon over many years. I especially am thankful for use of their library for my various researches, and access to the archives of vessels that are not on display.

We continued west, anchoring at Niantic, and Port Jefferson, where we tied up at Bayles Dock. The manager there very kindly gave me an antique one-handed adze, when I admired it. After I explained that I was a shipwright, he wanted me to take it and use it. [Which I still do.] We sailed to City Island, and thence motored through the East River again, to tie up at South Street Seaport, where we stayed for a week.

I left New York and went to sea with Paul, Liz and Tere for crew—a wonderful combination of crazy people. The weather forecasts were continuously, completely, unbelievably wrong, but we made it to Atlantic City on the afternoon of the 17th, where we anchored in Clam Creek...and went gambling! It felt strange to walk through Atlantic City's poor neighborhood to the absurd opulence of the boardwalk and casinos. We all concluded that Atlantic City is a sick, unbalanced place—one we would probably not visit again. [Read John McPhee's story: *The Search for Marvin Gardens.*]

We sailed to the Chesapeake Bay on the 18th in light winds (lucky for November), and anchored in Willoughby Bay early on the morning of the 20th. Paul and Liz had to leave to fly back to New York, and Pagan (Kathy's daughter) and James, with whom we had sailed to watch the America's Cup Race, joined Tere and me. We motored for several days down the "ditch" (ICW) to Beaufort, where Pagan left us to return home to Norfolk.

On Oct 30th we went to sea in a strong nor'easter, which gave us a fast run down the coast to Charleston, N.C. Steering downwind was a chore at times, and the Log notes that I greased the steering box. I had salvaged it in a junkyard near Half Moon Bay (for $10) from a 1948 White bus, and it still works great. We had an exceptional run of 84 miles in 11 hours and 10 minutes—averaging over 7 knots—really ripping along for the fat old *Hornpipe.* We spent a couple of days enjoying the sights and tastes of Charleston, including a Halloween dinner on board of broiled *bonita* and steamed vegetables with butter sauce (we had caught two *bonita* at sea).

We went back to sea on Nov 2nd, with all flying, in a sweet NE wind of 15 knots. My speed check was so extraordinary that I concluded we had a 1-knot current (counter-current due to the Gulf Stream) with us. The following evening we anchored off Fernandina Beach, Florida, and next morning moved to the Welcome Station Dock and celebrated Tere's birthday. The Log notes, in Tere's handwriting, that we had a wonderful party, and that I cooked a *far-out pizza, with sardines even!* Amazing, as the only fish I *don't* like are little bony, smelly, oily ones. I bet I left them off of my half....

On Nov 5th we sailed to Port Canaveral, where we spent the night at a fuel dock (we were running on fumes), before sailing on to Cracker Boy in Riviera Beach. We tied up in a slip there on the 9th, and I took over the wood shop in the boatyard as resident shipwright, where I lived and worked for the winter.

Thus ended our second cruise of the U.S. East Coast.

CHAPTER NINETEEN—THE LAST VOYAGE

No single thing abides, but all things flow
Fragment to fragment clings; thus all things grow
Until we know and name them. By degrees
They melt, and are no more the things we know.

Globed from the atoms, falling slow or swift
I see the suns, I see the systems lift
Their forms; and even the systems and the suns
Shall go back slowly to the eternal drift.

Thou too, O Earth—thine empires, lands and seas—
Least, with thy stars, of all the galaxies,
Globed from the drift like these, like these thou too
Shalt go. Thou art going, hour by hour, like these.

Nothing abides. Thy seas in delicate haze
Go off; those mooned sands forsake their place;
And where they are shall other seas in turn
Mow with their scythes of whiteness other bays.

Lucretius (*Titus Lucretius Carus*) 96?-55 BC

Working for the winter at Cracker Boy Boat Works was not much fun. Riviera Beach is really a pretty awful place—a very depressed neighborhood with a high, violent crime rate, prostitution, alcoholism and rampant drug use, especially "crack" cocaine. The area has an extremely high incidence of AIDS, Hepatitis C, and other diseases transmitted by unprotected sex and the sharing of needles used for intravenous-drug injection. But I completed many unfinished projects in *Fishers Hornpipe*, gave her a haul-out, and earned some money.

By mid-March I was getting anxious to be sailing, and I put together a crew consisting of Tere and Liz, my beautiful pirates. On 3/21/84 we set sail in the late afternoon for *Fishers Hornpipe's* last cruise to the Bahamas. We had waited for the easterly trade wind to clock around, heralding an approaching cold front, and crossed the Gulf Stream with light westerly winds. The Log states we had a slow trip, rough and lumpy, with little or no usable wind. Late the next afternoon we approached West End, Grand Bahama Island, and started working our way very slowly along the south coast. The cold front never really materialized—not unusual for so late in the winter season—and by evening the trade wind returned, easterly at about 10 knots, causing us to make tacks on and off shore.

On the morning of the 23rd we gave up trying to sail east, and went into the port of Lucaya to clear Customs and Immigration. I had never set foot on Grand Bahama before, and immediately decided I never would again. The island is being tastelessly overdeveloped for tourism, and Lucaya was like a huge shopping mall. There was no anchorage, and we had to pay $25 for a slip for the night. Entering the country also cost several times more than it does in Nassau at the Customs Dock.

Liz had run out of time and had to catch a flight back to the States. We were sad to see her go—we never even got to anyplace we wanted to show her. This is the most frequent problem with crewmembers who are too tangled up in the "straight" world—they never have enough time.

Sailing does not happen on a New York schedule—it happens when the weather, the wind, the current and the sea allow it happen. When you go sailing, you must throw away your calendar, your watch, your busy schedule—and go with the flow! Most people cannot do this, unless they are very young or very old—or have learned to arrange their lives around Nature and not the inanities of "civilization."

Much of our following abbreviated Bahamian cruise will be repetition of places I have already taken you to in previous chapters—so I will only describe new places and a few highlights. By this time I had purchased my first Olympus OM-1 35mm camera, and it will be apparent from the photos at the end of this last Voyage that my interest in photography (which has always been keen) increased more than ever.

Tere and I sailed along the Berry Islands, down to Nassau, where her friend Jean joined us.

We caught a lot of fish everywhere we went—more than ever before. Then we headed for Eleuthera, a 90-mile long, narrow island first settled (by Europeans) in 1649. We sailed down the Bight of Eleuthera to Hatchet Bay, a rock-enclosed harbor I had never visited. We found it to be funky and low-key—no tourists.

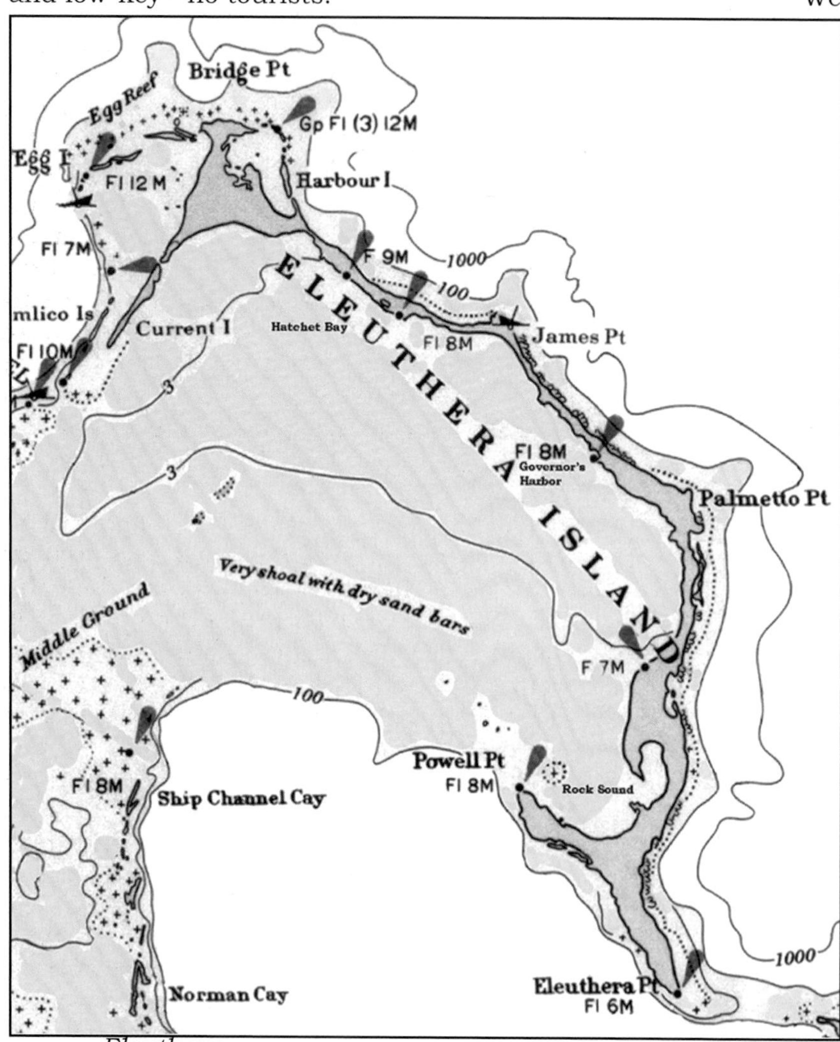

Eleuthera.

The Bahamas are riddled with caves, and the caves north of Hatchet Bay are well worth a visit. If you like to surf, Surfer's Beach is a place you may never be able to leave—the break is perfect. A word of caution—since the nearby chicken farm closed, the local sharks have had to change their diet!

On April 6th we sailed to Governor's Harbor, anchoring in the lee of Cupid Cay, another pretty place (see photos), but with a surge that made the *Hornpipe* roll a little. Governor's Harbor is a fascinating village with houses that show centuries of patina and character. There is a large basketball court, and even if you don't care for sports, like me, you *have* to see Bahamians play basketball. There is simply nothing quite like it anywhere else. The tiny bars and clubs have pool tables, if you go for that. I have to admit that I only play pool in the Bahamas—nowhere else would I even think of it (except that one time in Sausalito I told you about...). A walk over the hill to the windward side of Eleuthera takes you to a different reality. The beaches are the best in the world. I won't talk about the Club Med. [Thank goodness it's gone now.]

We sailed down to Rock Sound, near the south end of Eleuthera, which has an airport handy for swapping crew. Although the Log neglects to say it, Jean left us there.

Sailing across the bights (lee sides) of all the large Bahamian islands, and on the Banks behind the chains of cays, provides the best sailing on Earth. Beam-reaching in strong, steady trade winds (the islanders call this "clean, sweet wind"), across flat, turquoise water, while gazing on sandy beaches studded with palm trees—is sailor's heaven. Sailing on the Bahama Banks, in the lee of Andros, Great Abaco, the Exumas, the Jumentos, or inside the barrier islands of the Abacos is perfect. Shallow draft is a big help, and my growing addiction to sailing in the Bahamas eventually led me to design, build and own large, centerboard schooners built using cold-molded wood construction.

Teri and I departed Rock Sound on the 10th —bouncing across the bottom—and came to anchor off spooky Poison Point, then later in the evening, with the flood tide, Sound Point. We went diving and caught a grouper and three crayfish—a feast for dinner. The next day we crossed Exuma Sound to anchor in Paradise Bay at Little Bell Island. I know I abuse the hell out of superlatives, but this was yet another incredibly beautiful place. We explored the island, visited the caves on Dundee (see photos), and sailed down to Staniel Cay.

Sailing with Teri was a real pleasure—her company is excellent, and she is a strong, competent sailor (after all, I taught her). The two of us could sail the *Hornpipe* to the ends of the Earth, if only we had the time and money. This last mini-cruise in the Bahamas might seem like an anti-climax to my Voyages, but it was, for us, a mellow and very sweet time.

If you ever have the good fortune to visit Staniel Cay, take a walk across the airfield and over the dunes to the windward beaches. Do this on a day when the trade winds die, before a norther comes, and bring your mask and fins. The reef-strewn waters and tiny pink sand beaches are awesome. After a couple of days of anchoring off the Yacht Club, we anchored once again behind Thunderball Grotto so Teri could see it. I guess you can tell I like the place.

On April 15th we sadly turned our bow north. We came to anchor off Norman's Cay in the afternoon, and we caught the largest grouper ever—maybe it was even a mythological Jew-fish—it fed us for days.

The next morning, trying to leave, fate snagged us again, leaving us hard aground for seven hours. We went to explore a small, pretty cay east of Norman's, with which I fell in love (see photos). I ever I find myself a wealthy old man (very unlikely), I might do everything in my power to lease or buy this island (a strange thing for someone to say who does not believe in ownership of land). It is a place I wouldn't mind living—in the winter, anyway.

We dove for some conch, and motorsailed off the bar around 1600. The genoa jib jammed in the raised position, running us out of control onto *another* sand bar at high tide! I had to go aloft in the bosun's chair to free the jib, and found that the uppermost jib hank had worn through and broken, causing the down-haul to twist around and jamb the next jib hank down. Negligence on my part—the entry in the Log is so vulgar even *I* can't repeat it here. Two small dingys from neighboring cruisers came over to help, and we set a stern kedge and winched ourselves off in a hurry, before the tide could ebb.

That night, after anchoring in the deepest water we could find, we had our Yugoslavian neighbors from *Princess Mistral* over for dinner, most of which they brought—but I cooked up a quick Bahamian spicy conch chowder...I never get tired of it!

Reuel's Conch Chowder

> Dice some new red potatoes into small chunks and boil in lightly salted water.
> Sauté diced onion, garlic, celery and lots of conch in olive oil.
> Dice half (or less) of a small habanera pepper very finely, having removed seeds. (Note: you can use any hot chili pepper—even canned jalapeno.)
> Drain most of the water from the potatoes and add sautéed items.
> Add a can (or two) of diced tomatoes.
> Season with salt, basil, thyme, fresh lime juice, sherry and love.

* * *

A little about Norman's Cay: This is the island that was taken over by Medellin Cartel drug-lord Carlos Lehder in the seventies. It was used as a trans-shipping waypoint for cocaine, until an American cruising couple were reputedly murdered, and their boat set adrift on the Banks. In a huge DEA bust, Lehder and his gang were captured and locked up to rot in a US dungeon for eternity. When I first visited the island in the early 80's, there were still armed military guards posted at the old Cartel residence. [Things there are different now—the old resort buildings are in ruins—but there is a great little bar just beyond the airstrip near the north end of the island.] Norman's Cay is known also for the wreck of a DC-3 drug plane—right in the middle of the shallow bay (see photo). This bay is a breeding ground for conch—you can see them in every stage from tiny seedlings to young adults, at which stage they migrate to deeper waters. North of the small neighboring islet I fell in love with are some beautiful small beaches and meandering tidal creeks—crystal-clear turquoise water flowing through pink sand channels—where you can lie down and take a whirlpool bath. To the east of "my" islet is another small bay full of fish and lobster (spiny crayfish).

On the morning of the 18th we started for Nassau in light winds. We didn't make it very far, and had to creep into Highbourne Cay late that afternoon—where we ran aground, of course. The next morning we tried again—the Log says *no engine today, please.* Though our progress was slow, at 1400 we came to anchor off the Nassau Harbor Club.

As a tip to other cruisers who might read this: The main anchorage for visiting yachts is in the west end of the harbor—my chosen anchorage is the east end. Although less convenient to downtown Nassau, there is a huge shopping center across the street, and there is less crime. The busy downtown waterfront includes many water rats (the two-legged variety), who will paddle (or swim) out to the anchored boats and rob them. The east end has no convenient place from which to do this—the waterfront consists of wealthy homes (many of which are actually tasteful) and the Nassau Harbor Club, which is gated and guarded. It is sad that Nassau is now a place of extremes—that it has a dangerous criminal element—but that is the nature of waterfront cities all over the world. Nassau has always been a haven for pirates, smugglers and numbered bank accounts.

From Nassau we sailed for Florida, and the only thing of note was that we tried to cross the Bahama Bank on Easter Sunday instead of taking the deep-water route in Northwest Providence Channel. I was nervous about isolated coral heads, because of the *Hornpipe's* seven-foot draft, and when darkness fell, we anchored. During the night, the wind and seas became too intense, and near midnight we weighed anchor, which was a bitch

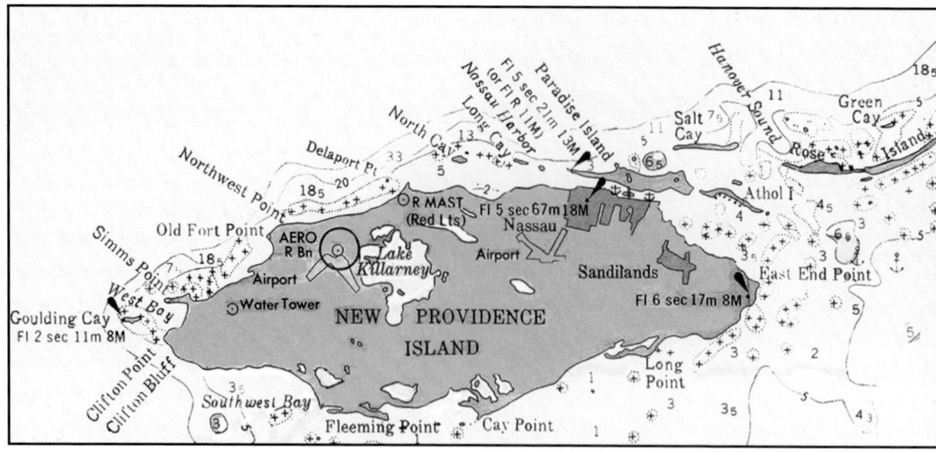

Nassau, on New Providence Island. The Harbor is between the city and Paradise Island off the NE coast. I prefer the right-hand anchorage. There is good diving north of Rose Island.

with the bow plunging up and down, and sailed on—damn the coral heads! Within twenty minutes I sighted, with great relief, the South Bimini radio tower, and set a new course by it. At 0200 we anchored in the lee of Bimini, and settled down for a short, uncomfortable night.

At 1000 that morning of 4/23, we departed to cross the Gulf Stream. As we closed with the Florida coast that afternoon, we approached a long line of rain showers. I studied them carefully, and seeing no sign of strong wind, continued to carry full sail. *Wrong!* The wind hit with no warning, laying *Fishers Hornpipe* over nearly on her beam-ends. As I jumped out of the cockpit to get the jib down, I heard that sickening riiiiiiiiip sound as the mains'l blew to ribbons. We were six or eight miles off the coast, and the wind gusted to 60 knots.

We somehow collected our wits and shredded sails, and limped into Sailfish Marina to clear Customs near midnight. I no longer trust my judgement of squall lines. The next morning we moved over to a slip at Cracker Boy.

At the *Crack* I tied up some loose ends, repaired some sails, and headed north on May 16th. Tere left me to go to school *for real.* I found a college student named Peter as crew, who had never been cruising or to sea, but had raced on J-24's a few times.

I had finally decided to put my beloved *Fishers Hornpipe* up for sale in the meat-market of Newport, Rhode Island, in the annual *Used Boat Show.* Getting there on time was a real challenge—the show was in two weeks!

We motorsailed in the ICW for a couple of days as another norther was blowing down the coast (some years they just don't quit), anchoring the first night in Vero Beach, and (the next night) tying to the fuel dock at Cape Marina in Canaveral. There I got into an altercation with the owner, who insisted I pay a night's dockage, while I insisted that I had come in late at night and was waiting for the fuel dock to open. I figured filling my tank was costing me more than enough money—but he refused to sell me fuel unless I paid dockage. He prevailed in the end, and I felt like I got fucked. I will certainly never go there again.

There are many marinas which dislike sailboats and make it clearly felt. Sailors are almost always on a tight budget; power boaters are used to spending money. I can live like a king for a year on what some powerboats consume in fuel in a week. I could hear the marina owner mutter under his breath as we cast off: "fucking stick-boaters...."

We went out Canaveral Inlet to sea and tacked offshore to get into the Gulf Stream current. We traveled at sea, in the vicinity of the Gulf Stream, for three days, watch on watch. I did not get any noon sights, and the taff log kept clogging with sargassum—so I radioed ships occasionally to get their positions. The wind made several changes in direction and force, causing us to make frequent sail changes. All this was exhausting work for only two people, in the shipping lanes, with no autopilot.

On the evening of May 20th we came into Charleston, took on water at the Municipal Marina, and anchored for the night. Late the next morning, after catching up on badly needed sleep, we went back to sea. The first day out we had good wind, and enjoyed a fast beam reach, but it didn't last.

We rounded Cape Fear motor-sailing in light winds, and came in Masonboro Inlet. We tried to come into Masonboro Boatyard, and ran hard aground in the channel. Ed (the manager) came out and helped us kedge off. *I was extremely exasperated with deep draft and running aground.* We ended up having to anchor at Wrightsville Beach, which I came to like—it has a Laundromat [now a T-shirt shop], grocery store (*Robert's*), several good bars and restaurants, and a huge beach—all within a five-minute walk from the Public Landing near the causeway.

On the 23rd we had a long day-sail to Beaufort, N.C. I took Peter to the *Dock House* for food and drink, and we left next morning for the ICW. We made as fast a trip as we could, arriving in downtown Norfolk late on the evening of the 26th—right in the middle of *Harborfest.* We got stuck in a huge maritime traffic jamb, watching the fireworks. Very late that night we sneaked into Rebel Marine in Willoughby Bay.

Peter was completely worn out, and jumped

ship. Like so many young folk, his first taste of the real world sent him packing back to school—the womb with a view. I found new crew—Ginny, who wanted to learn about the sailing life, and Tom, a naval architect who worked designing structural ship interiors. We had a pleasant, if abbreviated visit at Rebel Marine, and left on the 28th. The channel out of Willoughby Bay was badly silted in, and we ran aground *three times* getting out, and had to be towed by Captain Jesse Briggs (one of Capt. Lane's four sons) in the tugboat *Steel Rebel*.

As we headed out to sea, the forecast called for a moderate southerly gale, and Ginny asked me if I didn't think we should turn around. "Hell no," I said—"once we get clear of the land, and hang a left, we will have one hell of a sleigh ride!" The seas kept getting bigger and rougher, and when we passed the bridge/tunnel complex near the mouth of the Bay, Tom and I went out on the bowsprit to change jibs. We were in seawater up to our armpits, one hand for the ship and one hand for dear life, but we changed jibs, reefed the main, and headed into the gale. Poor Ginny was about shitting bricks, and I think Tom just didn't know what to think. Thank goodness neither of them got seasick.

Once well clear of the land, we came to a northeasterly course, set a whisker pole on the yankee jib, a preventer on the reefed mains'l, and took off like a scalded cat. Steering was a bitch in 25- to 30-knot winds and 12- to 15-foot seas, with large rogue waves and the occasional breaker. The helms-person had to stand—literally—the two-hour watch, legs far apart, both hands on the wheel, struggling to control the *Hornpipe* while she tried for all the world to surf her bulbous ass down those big, steep waves. We built some biceps and pectorals! It was wonderful! Ginny and Tom were very good sports about it—they soon realized they had been shanghaied into a trip of whose nature they had no clue.

There was enough traffic at sea that we contacted ships to get our fixes, saving me from trying to get noon sights in heavy overcast and rough water. We made a beeline for Block Island, and watched a 97% solar eclipse at sea on the afternoon of the 30th. Trailing my hand lines as always, we caught a 6 lb. Bluefish and had broiled fish, rice and salad for dinner—our only real cooked meal on the trip. That same night, at midnight, we anchored in Old Harbor, Block Island, and slept like the dead. *Fishers Hornpipe* had sailed 355 miles in 56 hours and 40 minutes, at an average speed of 6.27 knots. What a sweet sea-boat she is!

Very early next morning, I awoke with that sailor's sixth sense that all was not well, and discovered that my plow anchor was gently dragging through a massive bed of kelp. After re-anchoring, we went ashore for breakfast. At 1000 we left for Newport in a calm, and after days of the southerly gale, the wind turned around and became a strong norther—dead on the nose. We reefed the main and started beating into it, adding the motor to point higher. Perhaps my dear girl knew I was taking her to the auction block, because entering Narragansett Bay, her engine quit! I dove below with a 5-gallon jug of fuel, disconnected the fuel hose from the filter and plunged it straight into the jug. Bled the injectors, fired her up—and got her into our slip in the Treadway Inn just as the Used Boat Show opened.

Tom left to go back to work in Norfolk, but Ginny stayed on for a little while. She had been considering getting a boat of her own, but wasn't sure if she would like the life. As we had been beating out of Chesapeake Bay into a gale on the ocean, she was absolutely terrified. Waves were crashing over the bow and streaming along the decks, and she was sure I was taking her to an early death. She vowed that if she ever got back to land alive, she would never set foot on another boat! But by the time we arrived in Newport, her life had changed before her eyes. She thanked me, very sincerely, for showing her what the sailing life is *really* all about, and what sailing on a real cruising boat in the ocean is like. She was no longer afraid, and she did eventually buy her own sailboat and move aboard—another convert.

* * *

Now, as I write this, I find myself fighting to hold back the tears. During the Used Boat Show, one man kept coming back to look at *Fishers Hornpipe*, and on 6/14 I sold her to Captain Paul Dunn. But first, there was a haulout and survey at Point Judith Marina on 6/4, a day sail, and some negotiating.

I have to explain here that ferrocement boats are not, and have never been, well-respected, and that they usually don't sell well. Almost all are amateur-built, and most of them look it. *Fishers Hornpipe* was unique, and she was almost never identified as ferrocement. Mostly, folks thought she was European steel. She was fair, beautiful, well appointed, and she had 35,000 miles of blue-water sailing under her powerful keel. She was painted with dark blue polyurethane, always sprayed, never brushed, and her rail-caps were varnished ash. She was flush-decked, with massive skylights and hatches, all near her centerline for safety, and her spars and rigging looked commercial. Her 7x7 wire-rope stays and shrouds were hand-spliced—not swaged or clamped, and her rigging screws were plainly over-sized. She looked like a boat you could go do surveys in Antarctica with, and I had even installed large wood internal frames in her forward underbody to back up external stainless steel bow plates (never installed) for just that kind of work.

Paul Dunn had been skippering crew boats out to offshore oil rigs, and knew a seaworthy boat when he saw one. When my crew told him about our trip up, riding the waves of a gale at sea for three days, he knew that she *was* what she *looked* like. I sold her well, but it still broke my heart.

I found myself standing in yet another crossroads. I had never felt so lost in my life. I rented a tiny cottage on the beach next to Point Judith Marina, and Ginny stayed on to help with one last bottom job. Then we put the *Hornpipe* out on a mooring, and day after day I sat on the tiny porch of my cottage and watched her. Tere came to visit, and tried to make me feel better. I guess I came out of it when I opened a bank account with more money than I had ever dreamed of in my life—and it helped when I realized that Paul Dunn really loved his new boat.

I also realized that it was time to embark on a new dream, and that I had the money to invest in my career as a marine architect. I started thinking about the schooner that had been growing in my mind—and what it would cost to build her. I thought seriously about buying an old house in Newport to remodel, but quickly learned I didn't have that much money. I bought some recording equipment, and sat in that cottage for weeks playing music and taping it. I set up a drafting table on the tiny porch, and designed the schooner (for the Polvere family in Ft. Pierce) that would become *Sarah*, my first Exuma-52. I bought a planer/jointer, a big table saw, an industrial air compressor, and a number of hand tools. I became close friends with Michael (one of the owners of the boatyard) and Ruth Waldman, and fell in lust with their beautiful daughter Karen (Ruth wouldn't let me near her!). I spent a bittersweet summer in Rhode Island, which I came to love, and took stock of my life and dreams.

In September of 1984 I returned to Florida, by truck this time, towing a hand-made trailer (soon dubbed *The Taco Stand*) full of tools. I had my beloved *Gandy Dancer* on the roof of my old Scout—I bought her back from Paul for a thousand dollars—worth every penny! *Air Force One* had rusted away to oblivion and sadly went onto the boatyard scrap heap. I joined Michael and Joan Polvere in Ft. Pierce, where Eliot also joined us, and we started construction on *Sarah.* Wood was always my medium, and I had been thinking long and hard on a new construction method. All my cruising experiences on *Fishers Hornpipe* had been brewing in my mind, and I had many ideas I wanted to see take shape. I was off and running.

The last entry in the *Hornpipe's* dog-eared old Log Book says:

Goodbye Baby—Good luck!
Good Sailing!

VOYAGE FIVE PHOTOS

Photo 1

Reuel, Liz (behind) & Tere
(Davidphoto)
Fire Island, N.Y.

Photo 2

David Parker

Photo 3

David & Reuel--bad hair day
(Terephoto)

Photo 4

Paul, Reuel & Tere
Sonny's Boat Club
City Island, N.Y.

Photo 5 *Imagine* in the slings

Photo 6 *Imagine* at anchor

Photo 7 Tony Bianco, *Imagine's* owner

Photo 8 Tere in *Fishers Hornpipe*

Photo 9 Cave entrance

Photo 10 The cave, Eleuthera

Photo 11 Governor's Harbor, Eleuthera

Photo 12 Governor's Harbor--kites

Photo 13 Jean & Tere, Cupid Cay

Photos 14, 15 & 16

Cupid Cay, Governor's Harbor
Eleuthera

Photos 17, 18 & 19

Governor's Harbor

Photo 20

Parrot's nest in
Coconut palm
Eleuthera

Photo 21

Basketball
Governor's Harbor

Photo 22

Tere & the old well
Eleuthera

Photo 23 The windward beach, Governor's Harbor

Photo 24 Tere climbing up the anchor chain

Photo 25

Bugs in the pot
Eleuthera

Photo 26

Grouper
Eleuthera

Photo 27

Yellowtail Snapper

Photo 28 (above) Tere in the cave at Dundee

Photo 29 (below) The cave at Dundee

Photos 30 & 31 Giant starfish, Normon's Cay

Photo 32 Trilobite

Photo 33 Sponges

Photo 34 Rock snails

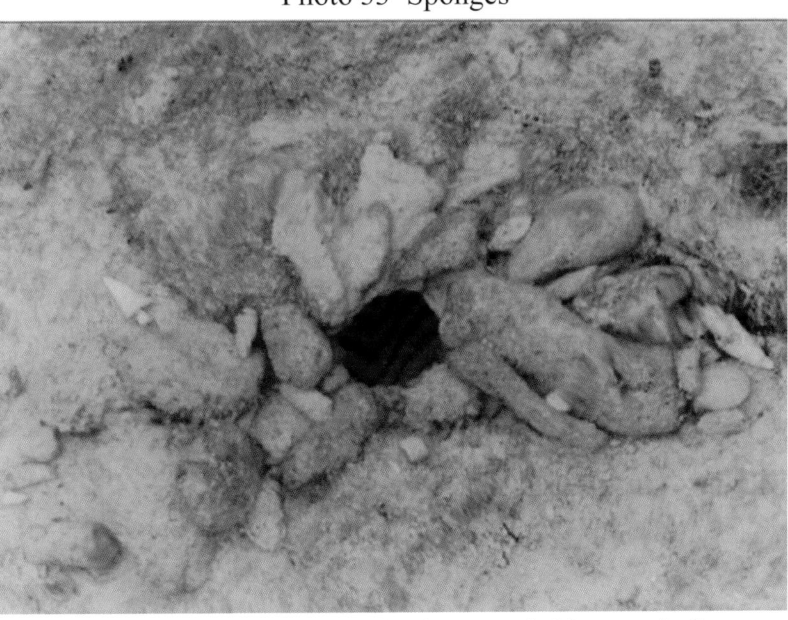

Photo 35 Rock fish nest (under water), Normon's Cay

Photo 36 The beach at my favorite island, near Norman's Cay

Photos 37 & 38 The *Hornpipe* and Tere, aground at Norman's Cay

Photo 39 The crashed DC-3 drug plane at Norman's Cay

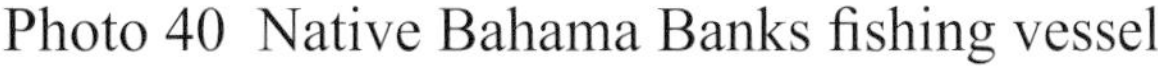

Photo 40 Native Bahama Banks fishing vessel

Photo 41

Paul Dunn kissing his new baby
Point Judith Marina, R.I. June, 1984

Photo 42

Paul Dunn

Photo 43

Ginny

Photo 44 *Fishers Hornpipe* hauled out at Point Judith Marina

Photo 45 Tere in Point Judith

Photo 46 Reuel in Pt. Judith (Terephoto)

Photo 47 *Fishers Hornpipe* on her mooring in Snug Harbor, Point Judith, R.I.

APPENDICES

APPENDIX ONE—NOTES

NOTES ON NAVIGATION

We always trailed a Walker Mark IV taff-log while passage-making. This consisted of a brass spinner connected by a stiff braided line to mechanical odometer mounted below the *Hornpipe's* starboard taff rail. The log recorded our progress through the water—from which we could deduce our speed—but it could not measure our progress over the bottom of the sea. Hence it was always necessary to know what currents we were sailing in, and to compute their vector (direction and strength) in our course.

We used a Danforth Constellation 5" compass, with a home-made "deviation rose" so we could correct our compass directions for magnetic disturbances caused by ferrous metals in and on the boat. It is also necessary to adjust compass directions for variation—the difference between the Earth's magnetic poles, and humankind's mathematically established "true" poles.

I also carried a hand-held magnetic bearing compass—which you sight across at a distant object whose magnetic bearing (compass direction) you desire relative to the position of your boat. Three accurate magnetic-bearing sights give you a "fix"—your vessel's exact location. Of course, it is necessary to positively identify the objects you are taking sights of!

Finally, there were the two plastic sextants—one cheap, and the other cheaper. I had never learned as much celestial navigation as I should have, back in California, and all I knew was how to take a noon sight with my sextant and reduce it mathematically to get a "fix." Noon fixes are subject to several factors which affect their accuracy. If the sun is almost directly overhead—as when you are near the equator—accuracy is poor. If the sky is overcast or hazy, accurate sights are difficult or impossible. If the vessel from which you are taking sights is in rough seas, sights will be inaccurate. If the horizon is indistinct, sights will be thrown off. What I did was to take a series of sights, several minutes apart, before, during and after local apparent noon, recording the exact time of each sight with a chronometer (I used a battery-powered quartz-crystal watch, set to *coordinated universal time* from short-wave radio). I then went below and plotted the sights on graph paper, where sextant angle was the vertical axis and time was the horizontal axis. I then drew, by freehand, a careful, symmetrical curve that intersected, insofar as possible, all of my "points" (sights). I folded the graph paper in half, with the crease at the highest point of the curve, and the halves of the curve overlapping. The top of the curve represented our latitude, and the crease represented our longitude. I next used the current *Nautical Almanac* to "reduce" the esoteric mathematical angles and times into our actual position on the face of the Earth. Then, I frequently ran up on deck and threw up.

Dead Reckoning refers to using everything available to you to plot your speed and direction, and extrapolate your position, from your last fix. Christopher Columbus was one of the world's great "DR" navigators, and could frequently maintain an accurate position for his vessel for days at a time without a fix. I think I got pretty good at DR navigation too, though sometimes I wonder. I usually have a sense for my vessel's direction and speed, as well as the sea and wind conditions, even below asleep in my bunk. This sounds like a tall tale—but most long-time professional mariners will tell you the same thing. Nevertheless, there were times, especially during long storms at sea, when I simply had no idea where the hell we were—and that is one of the most uncomfortable feelings I have ever had.

In shallow water—or approaching the shore from the sea, we took soundings with a lead line. This consisted of a five-pound lead cylinder with a concave bottom. When it is desirable to see what the sea bottom consists of, the concavity is "armed" with butter or tallow (creamy peanut butter works also), to which bottom material will stick. Many charts and pilot books describe the bottom in great detail, which in older times was a vital tool in determining a vessel's position. Old-time New England captains relied heavily on this method, particularly in foggy weather. Although many tall-tales are told 'down east' about their abilities, these seasoned professionals could often find their way into port in pea-soup fog, and anchor by judicious use of the lead line, the currents, wave forms, wind direction, and a keen sense of smell ("Ayup—Aunt Martha's chicken coop is five miles to larboard....").

Fishers Hornpipe had an electronic depth sounder, but it never did work right. She also had a radio direction finder (RDF) which I bought in a marine flea market—but it never worked either. I had better luck with a battery-powered am/fm radio—I took it on deck, found a station that identified its transmitter location, and slowly rotated the radio (antenna down) to find the strongest and weakest reception. When the antenna pointed toward the strongest signal, I found the magnetic bearing via the compass, and thus deduced approximately what direction from the broadcast tower we were in. Needless to say, this was not very reliable or satisfying.

I am eternally glad that I learned to navigate "the old way"—and hence when all the modern electronic gadgets die (and they always do)—I still have a chance of figuring out where I am. But I must say that when GPS (Global Positioning System) became available, I was greatly relieved to know that I wouldn't have to go below anymore to reduce sights—no more barfing! (From that cause, at least.)

NOTES ON FISHING

About fishing: On all the boats I have owned, I fish almost constantly with hand lines, using Cuban reels or "yo-yos." These are open, asymmetrical spools held in one hand and worked with the other hand. By turning the spool perpendicular to the trailing line, the line pays off rapidly. To wind the line in, you rotate your hands around eachother almost like pedaling a bicycle. I use mostly 80-lb test polyester braid, with a wire leader and clip.

For lures I use everything—feather jigs, spoons, Magnum Rapallas ("swimming" fish lures), cuttlefish or squid jigs, small whole bait fish, etc. I often troll with two lines, port and starboard, when I am not trailing a taff-log spinner—although there is a risk of horrible tangles if the lines get crossed. Sometimes I try to keep the lure in the shadow of the boat, but usually I just trail the lure far astern, one or two waves aft, or around 75-feet away. When possible, I fish the drop-off of the continental (or island chain) shelf—frequently at a depth of a little under 100 feet. I also troll inlets and inter-island passages, sometimes using a "diving minnow" lure just above the bottom, especially in coral. In the tropics, I use pieces of conch or fish for bait, and "jig" the bottom for grouper, snapper, hog fish, sheepshead, and even squirrel fish. When all else fails, I free dive either with a spear gun or a Hawaiian sling. I also gather spiny crayfish (langosta), conch, crab, mussels, clams, oysters, scallops, whelk—almost any edible sea life. I catch a lot of fish...I eat a lot of fish.

NOTES—ENGINES, COOLING SYSTEMS AND FUEL FILTRATION

A valuable lesson I learned from the *Hornpipe* is that big boats should have big engines—especially if they are heavy, deep draft, and have tall rigs. The *Hornpipe* had an Isuzu C-240 four-cylinder diesel rated at 60 HP—which I think may have been exaggerated—coupled to a Borg-Warner 2::1 reverse gear.

In a 54-foot, 23-ton sailboat, with 7' draft and a 54' tall mast (plus the windage of rigging), this would be considered a "cruising auxiliary." The engine could not quite drive us to hull speed (8 knots) on flat water with no wind—a sustained speed under power alone was likely to be around 7 knots maximum.

The *Hornpipe* motorsailed beautifully, where the motor would boost our speed and pointing ability, but the motor was inadequate for extended motoring, especially against wind and tide, and was hopeless for getting us off when we ran aground (most motors are). In addition to being under-powered, the cooling system and fuel-filtration systems—as mentioned earlier—were sadly inadequate. When I chose my diesel, I thought it would be just right—and when I designed my systems, I believed I was matching them correctly to the diesel.

The lesson here is that you should think very carefully about the kinds of traveling you are most likely to do with your boat, install the largest engine you think will do the job (including adequacy for emergency situations), and install large, redundant cooling and fuel-filtration systems. I now install large fuel filters (with plastic bowls that can be drained of contaminants and water) in parallel—that is side by side with plumbing and valves that allow one filter to be isolated and the other to replace it in a couple of seconds. This allows draining, cleaning and cartridge replacement without even shutting down the diesel.

We had similar problems with our small raw water filter. It would frequently get plugged up with debris in the ICW. I now install two clear polycarbonate plastic water strainers in parallel to allow switchover and cleaning, using removable basket strainers. In the Pacific, my small, single filters were adequate—on the east coast they were pathetic.

I also had problems with my raw water (sea-water) pump and my heat exchanger. These items were added to the manufactured diesel by the company that converted it for marine use—and they skimped on size in both cases. The ½" pump should have been ¾", and the heat exchanger should have been larger. All water hoses could have been larger. Unfortunately, economy is often the over-riding factor—it certainly was in my case—and compromises must be made. At the time I thought 60 HP was fully adequate—now I know 75 or 80 HP would have been much better, although it would have driven up my installation, fuel and maintenance costs.

NOTES—SAILS, WINCHES AND RIGGING

The jibs are the real power sails on a cruising cutter or sloop, and they can be a lot of work to handle. The *Hornpipe* has one big Barient two-speed winch, mounted on a very stout through-bolted base outside the after cockpit coaming. The winch is centered, and both jib sheets lead to it via fairlead and turning blocks inside the bulwarks on the raised quarter deck. During a tack, one sheet is cast off, and the other wrapped on and cranked in. As the helm is directly forward of the winch, about four feet away, one person alone can come about. This is done on your knees on the seat cushion, on the forward edge of the quarter deck. This position is very secure and protected, and the jib can be tacked very quickly and efficiently with the two-handed handle on the two-speed winch (it helps to have a second person tailing).

At something like $2,000 apiece for big winches, I have never understood why no other cruising boats use this arrangement. I find it much more convenient, especially when sailing short-handed (endemic on cruisers), than casting a sheet off on one winch, climbing over the helmsman and/or cockpit table, to take in the other sheet on a winch on the other side of the cockpit.

The work of changing jibs is the hardest, and most dangerous, of all the common jobs under sail (unless you have a square-rigger!). The old saying is that *the right time to shorten sail is when you first think of it.* Taking a reef in the mains'l is often the first step—as the wind increases and the boat heels over more, weather helm increases, making steering harder. (Weather helm is a boat's tendency to turn toward the wind, requiring that the rudder be turned to hold the boat on her course.) Shortening sail at the mains'l decreases sail area aft (in a sloop, cutter or schooner), shifting the sail plan's center-of-effort forward, thereby easing weather helm.

But the time comes when the jib must be changed. On an old-fashioned cutter like the *Hornpipe*, this involves going out on the bowsprit to collect and furl the jib coming down, and to cast loose the gaskets on the jib going up. With a single outer forestay, you also have to hank on the new sail and change the halyard. In a storm at sea, all this is exhausting, if not life-threatening, and a good tactic is to run downwind (on a very broad reach) while crew are on the bowsprit.

Good lifelines, safety nets and a bow-pulpit are helpful, but a safety-harness is very strongly advised. In most cases, the jib sheets have to be untied from one jib and tied to the clew of the jib going up, but at least this can be done on deck.

The *Hornpipe* has two outer jib stays, rigged port and starboard, and separated at the tops of the rigging screws (turnbuckles) by an eight-inch hardwood strut, to keep the stays from fouling each-other. (In strong wind, one stay could cross under the other, and the jib hanks could catch on the unused stay, unhooking themselves.) The twin-stay arrangement also creates redundancy, such that if one stay broke, the mast is still supported; but it also allows two jibs to be hanked on. In addition to simplifying the process of changing jibs, this also allows twin jibs to be carried downwind—one held out to windward on a whisker pole attached by car and track to the front of the mast, the other sheeted conventionally. The twin jibs act like a large spinnaker, but are much easier and safer to control. When turning up to windward, the windward jib can be lowered, thereby skipping the two crew-intensive steps of lowering and gathering a spinnaker (often quite a project) and raising a jib.

Another safety feature of twin jibs is that in gusty weather, the slot between the stays opens to spill a little wind. But the real advantage of twin stays is that one jib can be lowered and another one raised, with much less time, effort and danger. It is necessary to have the correct two jibs hanked on—but even if you don't, it's easier to change jib hanks while a jib is up on the other stay, with a jib that is already down on the stay you are working with. Or you can add a new jib above the one that is down—though this is not a good idea in rough weather (having too many sails furled out on the bowsprit invites damage).

I always tried to anticipate which jibs I would be most likely to need *before* starting a passage. The *Hornpipe* even has twin inner forestays (staysail-stays) allowing twin storm jibs to be carried downwind in heavy weather, and also providing redundancy of rig.

My stays'l even had reef points, so that it could be shortened way down in severe heavy-weather conditions (I never used them).

I have found that sailing under bare poles is dangerous and very uncomfortable, increasing the chance of capsize under the force of a breaking rogue wave. Even the tiniest sails will provide steerage, dampen rolling, limit the period of roll, and keep the vessel moving with wind and seas. Plus I puke less....

APPENDIX TWO—EXERPTS FROM PAUL NEWMAN'S *JOURNAL OF TRAVEL*

All my life I've had pipe-dreams of sorts, but everything was just that—a pipe dream. Seemingly untouchable. My thoughts are still filled with dreams, but now everything seems a little more possible. I can tell now of how I'd love to tour South America, or how, when I go to Europe, I'd love to travel the North Sea—follow the routes of the Vikings; to spend half a year sailing the fjords of Norway. All these are still dreams, but I've made the step that bridges the dreams with reality. The reality is that the world is now accessible to me. Not any smaller, but closer. With the proper resources, I can go anywhere in the world on little more than a whim. The only problem seems to be survival when I get there.

How lucky I feel, when I think of what is within my grasp. Most people in our world have no means to travel. Survival is a day to day struggle. In most places the majority of the people have never seen the boundaries of their own countries: many seldom leave their villages. It is true that a few people born into the third world have means or spirit to get up and go, but the world of cruising yachts is a very elite group. Very few, other than Europeans or Americans, cruise the sea just for pleasure.

The year I spent before my travels, I studied in a class the idea of what is "pleasure" and why the people of the world not only lack pleasure (by our definition) but are going day to day without even the bare minimum of food. I studied economic theories involving the hunger of the world. The facts shown to me were hard and made me think, but I had only my own experience to relate to. Now those numbers have become people. My experience doesn't just relate to the world of Rockland County [New York] *and a classroom of S.W.A.S.* [School Within A School], *but to the world of Colon, Panama, where the suffering walked with me through the streets. The experience is now first-hand.*

[Paul, when I visited him in Rockland County in the early 1990's, was growing food for poor people in the area, in a churchyard being gardened for that purpose. His tiny studio in the woods where he lived had no electricity at the time because rather than work to earn money for his own pleasure, or even comfort, he was devoting his time and energy to see that people in his community would have enough food to eat.]

We spent a day or two working before venturing out into the city of Colon. We strolled out of the front gate [past the armed guards], *separating our secure world of the Canal Zone from the city, and began exploring. We searched for a central market and a few other shops. Starting through the streets, we asked directions, and got lost with every turn. The streets were like nothing I've ever experienced. The most* [depressed] *parts of our American cities did not compare with the slum in which we walked. The smells of poverty overwhelmed me. The stares of the people made me feel totally out of place, not just that we didn't belong, but that we were hated. The stares were intensified as we ventured further into the city. Replies to our questions were frequently instructions to go back, as if the people were saying "Why do you want to come here? Why do you want to add to our pain?"*

We finally found a supermarket and settled for vegetables wrapped in plastic and Ronzonni spaghetti. We left the city, returning through the gate and into the Yacht Club, but the feelings that we had experienced were not left behind. I carry the memory like a scar across the face. I had never before felt that I wanted to be anything else but myself, but there, if I only could be black! I didn't feel I had directly done anything to these people and yet they hate me. They are hurt by what I stand for, and their outlet of aggression is toward me as a symbol.

More importantly, these people are hungry. They live in a city that smells of death. One finds magic only in an occasional smile or friendly word, but this loses all power when overshadowed by the ugly, violent surrounding world. Most people here have little security to their survival and many times they steal to live. The crime in a city like Colon is unbelievable. You can be assaulted and mugged anywhere. A friend had been met in a local pharmacy by three men wielding knives. While two men held him, the third cut all his pockets, stripping him of everything. And they take everything.... These things happen with extreme regularity. They are a way of life in Colon.

Death is also a way of life in Colon. Although in these instances of robbery it is common to be left unharmed, this is not due to the sympathy of the assailant, but due to the fact that it is easier to rob a man of his clothes while he is alive than when dead. Your death would make no difference in the penalty suffered by your assailant. On these streets, it's shoot to kill. [Our friend Rob had seen thieves shot down in the street.]

* * *

As the history books will [demonstrate], *Portobelo was the hot spot in the early days of the South American continent. All the wealth and riches in precious metals plundered from the Incan empire was stored in the fortifications of Portobelo. Many a battle was fought there over greed for Inca gold. Many galleons carrying the riches of the king were lost in the dangerous reefs surrounding this small, well-protected harbor. When we arrived, Portobelo was again the hot spot. The gold is gone, but this is replaced once a year by the richness of the people in celebration. It was the time for the* Festival of the Black Christ.

In the early days of Spanish imperialism in South America, there was a large push to convert the natives to Christianity. One of the [promoters for converts] *was a governor of a large region on the continent. He, being a good Catholic and wanting to show his people the faith, asked the King of Spain to send him a statue of the Savior. He asked also if the statue could be portrayed as being dark-skinned (this may very well be true, for Christ was an Arab Jew)....*

For two days we watched the people roll into this town for the ongoing six-day [Festival]. *By the sixth and final day the festivities peaked. Over 20,000 people, all black, filled their hearts with peace and their stomachs with the local liquor. The people crammed into the plaza and narrow streets. Men carried the Black Christ, surrounded by hundreds of glittering candles, for hours around the town. There was dancing in the streets and the party didn't stop until dawn.*

[I don't know why neither Paul nor I took photographs of the *Black Christ Festival*. They would be priceless to me now. Perhaps it was because a camera might have seemed intrusive or even sacrilegious.]

* * *

The area [of the San Blas Islands] *is on the eastern coast of the land that separates Central America from the lower continent of South America. It is mostly uninhabited. There are no roads, so boat is the common means of travel.... The few tribes of indians that inhabited the inner Amazon jungle have either been almost wiped out or relocated in a program very much like the one used a century ago in our mid-west. The land on which they lived has been harvested for rubber and cleared for agricultural use, or for the transcontinental highway. Clearing the land has destroyed the delicate balance of the rain forest.*

On the Caribbean side, running down the coastline of Panama and upper Columbia, are the three hundred and fifty islands of the San Blas. Here there exists an Indian culture which survived, but not without change. Modern man and his dollar have opened these Indians' small world to our large world around them.

These are the Kuna Indians. The Kuna have tried very hard to preserve their culture while also opening themselves up to the outside world. They have a very tight community structure and a vastly matriarchal society. The villages are composed of grass huts arranged by family and clan. The women dress in traditional clothes. With brightly-colored panels of fabric, they create tropical designs and these are made into blouses. These panels of fabric have brought the Kunas their fame. They are called molas.... Some molas are very beautiful and are considered a unique art form.

Out of the 350 islands, only a very few have villages. All the islands are used, though.... Islands are divided by family clan, and are used to produce coconuts. The only large growth on the islands besides mangroves are coconut palms. Coconuts are the islands' agricultural export. Each of the thousands of trees are owned, and each palm has its own proper name.

All of the islands are very low and sparse, no higher than three feet above sea level. A heavy storm would completely wash the islands away. It is a wonder the Kuna have lived there for centuries. It becomes apparent that the hurricanes do not drop this far south in the Caribbean. There is, lately, concern that the weather patterns are changing. The last two season's [hurricanes] have dipped farther south than ever before in known history, with some of the most violent storms recorded. There is evidence showing that the changes in the upper Amazon regions may have contributed to these changes in weather patterns. This adds to the argument against the destruction of rain forests in the equatorial region.

The Kuna have survived very well culturally, but there is speculation as to how much longer this will last. The corruption of the dollar has taken its toll, but the weather could very well be the deciding factor in the fate of this beautiful lifestyle....

The islands [on the coast of Panama] *form small clusters and keys. Each are surrounded by coral heads, making access by large boat difficult. Most of these keys have channels which can be followed through the reefs to a protected anchorage inside.... Navigation tends to be tricky. It is only safe when the sun is high. At mid-day, when the sun pierces down through the water and reflects off the sand, it is possible to see the bottom at sixty feet. So, with chart in hand, and mate on the bowsprit, the captain can find his way through the weaving channels. Problems arise occasionally because coral is a living, growing creature and some of the charts were recorded in the early 1900's....*

We tended to stay out of sight of the Kuna population because they didn't appreciate our constant nudity. There is very little reason to wear clothes when it's 90 in the shade and 80% humidity.

...I have to admit I didn't miss them at all.

Almost every day I dove the reefs in search of dinner. I had purchased from a friend a speargun, and Tage had bought one new in Panama. Together we speared lobster [spiney crayfish, called "longosta"] *and crabs 'til I was actually sick of my favorite seafood!*

Between the lobster and crab, and Reuel, Anne, Jean-Paul, Silda and myself (Tage cooked all of one meal in eight months) something was always cooking. Feasting never stopped. No sooner was breakfast finished when somebody would be cooking fried bananas or plantain for a snack. This pattern continued through the day 'til finally after dinner we would have dessert.

The feeling of enchantment was ever-present in the San Blas. The fact that the islands and inland regions are only accessible by boat...adds to the magic. The appearance of the magic in physical aspects was most predominant: the crystal blues of the water, the delicate balance of land and sea. The islands sometimes dropped off at the shore line to dark blue depths. Others spread out, submerged in the shallows of green sea grass and the iridescence of reflecting sunlight, for a quarter mile before falling back into the sea. The small islands dot the rugged coastline, and the mountains of the mainland rise quickly to the sky. Clouds and mists run down through troughs and valleys toward the sunlit islands to be dispersed by the sea breeze and evaporated by the afternoon sun. The outer bars and reefs feel the weight of the pounding ocean surf as they protect the tranquil waters that lie inside their walls.

Under the smooth surface that lies between island and ocean reef, you can enter into a new realm—the world of the coral. The life there is as abundant as in the air-breathing jungle. The layers of this undersea world are as densely populated as the layers of the forest canopy. The magic of the world under the waves is found as easily as putting on a mask and stepping off the beach.

I have traveled much in my short life—more than many people three times my age. I've seen American Indian dances and celebrations in the different cultures of the native people of the southwestern United States, but nothing thrilled me more than when I walked through a Kuna village. We were shown through the winding paths between grass huts to the home of a new friend who introduced us to his family. While the others talked, I communicated with the children through their games. The young people were amazed by Reuel's beard, and shrieked with joy at touching it. It was such a culture shock.

* * *

My real sailing education started on the passage to San Andreas. I had gotten to know Fishers Hornpipe *very well by then, but she had only really shown me what she's made of, which is solid concrete, 'til this trip. For three days we rode the wind full speed at almost all times, slapping into the oncoming seas that reached 15 feet in height.*

When sailing with four people you have six hours off and two hours on watch, steering the boat. Most of the time I would sleep for four hours and hang out for two, in any order, in between watches. [During] *these hours, you're always on call or ready in case you're needed.... Sometimes a sail had to* [be] *dropped and another be raised. If things get really rough, somebody would sit up with the person on watch. More and more, Reuel came to depend on me. I would find myself waking out of a deep sleep and onto the deck in the rain with 15-foot waves smashing over the bow, changing the jib. It was not a matter of Reuel picking on me, but a matter of necessity. The captain has a terrible strain on him when at sea. Whereas I knew the working parts of the boat, Tage might have to have Reuel explain or show him, and that is just one more unneeded hassle. So if there is such a title as first mate on* Fishers Hornpipe, *I took that responsibility. Even so, the worst work in the worst conditions is somehow tolerable if not enjoyable. It must be a spirit of adventure.*

There is a lot of time on a boat to hang out. I spent a lot of time reading and writing. We have a very extensive library on board which contains over 1,000 books and many magazines. Reuel's interests in literature coincide with my own, so I had an overabundant source of reading material. I also spent time making jewelry, using local materials—shells, coral, amber—and have made a number of necklaces and bracelets. This is something I will continue doing because I enjoy it and it can be done anywhere. Although there isn't a large amount of money to be made, there is a market.

[On *Fishers Hornpipe* I carried a large inventory of threads and beads, as well as tools for many kinds of crafts—hence we all passed many pleasant hours making jewelry.]

Out at sea, times can be difficult because of the constant motion, which can be very violent. Although I've never gotten seasick, reading or doing tedious work can be quite nauseating. At times during a passage, especially in rough weather or seas, the sailing itself can be so tiring that when there's nothing to do, I want to do just that—nothing.

* * *

We stayed only a few days at Providencia, but under different circumstances the stay would have lasted much longer. The season of the northers, which can blow for days at a time at gale force, was just beginning, so we didn't have too much time to get to Key West.

The night before we left, we were invited to a rum-dum, a sort of get-together dinner. When we arrived there were twenty or thirty people around the fire, some helping to cook the fish chowder, but most were just sitting around smoking joints and listening to reggae music. We sat there until very late, eating fish soup and socializing.

I talked with one man for a number of hours. We were both equally interested in the different worlds in which we live. At the end of the night, he told me that if I wanted to stay there in Providencia, he could have it arranged. His cousin was in charge of immigration, and I could [have] *very easily* [obtained] *the necessary papers to stay. He said I could help him tend his small plantation, and we would have food enough to live. If we wanted fish, we would go out to* the reef and *catch them. It all seemed so simple. I could pass the days on this beautiful island, without all the cares of the outside world. But there is too much to see in the world for me to stop* [now]. *Maybe someday I'll return to Providencia, and if I do, I think I'll stay much longer.*

* * *

Before we left [Isla Mujeres] *it seemed to us the weather had died down, but in fact it was only taking a short breather. The seas were reaching twenty feet, and we were running smack into them. Even though the wind was blowing a steady 30-knots at times, we averaged only two or three knots through the water. Just as we'd begin to build the momentum needed to move, we'd slam into a series of large waves. The first two would slow us down, and the third would stop us dead in the water. If I didn't know the currents to be helpful, I would have thought at times we were moving backwards. It became very frustrating having enough wind to move us very fast, but getting nowhere.*

On that four and one-half day passage, we ate only two meals. Otherwise I lived on peanut butter by the spoonful, complimented by an occasional slab of cheese. I slept nearly all my free hours, just as an escape from the violence of the sea. The storm lasted the whole trip. The seas didn't die down until we were practically inside the shipping channels of Key West. The trip was mostly miserable, but there were times, such as sunrise, that were so beautiful it made the misery bearable.

Key West was a shock to the senses. Traffic lights, loud hotrods and neon signs bombarded my head. The smell of the pizzeria began to tell me that I was home, but I still felt as if in a foreign land... or in a dream. I could understand all that was said around me and I found myself staring at one table, trying to get things into focus, or normal perspective. Through my auditory perceptions, I seemed to be not one out of three people sitting at a table, but rather a microphone in the middle of a crowd, condensing the separate vocal sounds into a constant [drone]. *I took a few days to get used to the United States once more.*

This portion of the trip is over, but I didn't feel as if it had reached an end. I had learned much aboard Fishers Hornpipe, *knowledge that will enable me to crew on a variety of sailboats. But, whereas I plan to gain experiences taking short cruises on other boats,* Fishers Hornpipe *has become my home. Reuel and I have become good friends and plan to cruise together for a while. Now the whole world is mine to see. What the future holds, I don't know. I do know, though, that the traveling has just begun.*

* * *

[I have included most of Paul's *Journal*, both here and throughout my story, because I wanted you to see through the eyes of a unique seventeen-year-old young man, the wonders that I saw. Paul's *Journal of Travel* stood as a high-school thesis, and SWAS (*School Within a School*) graduated him with a diploma based, to a large degree, on this paper.]

APPENDIX THREE--ALBUM

Photo 1 *Fishers Hornpipe* at Cracker Boy boat Works, Riviera Beach, FL, 1984

Photo 2 Aft cabin settee and table--note rolled charts between deck beams

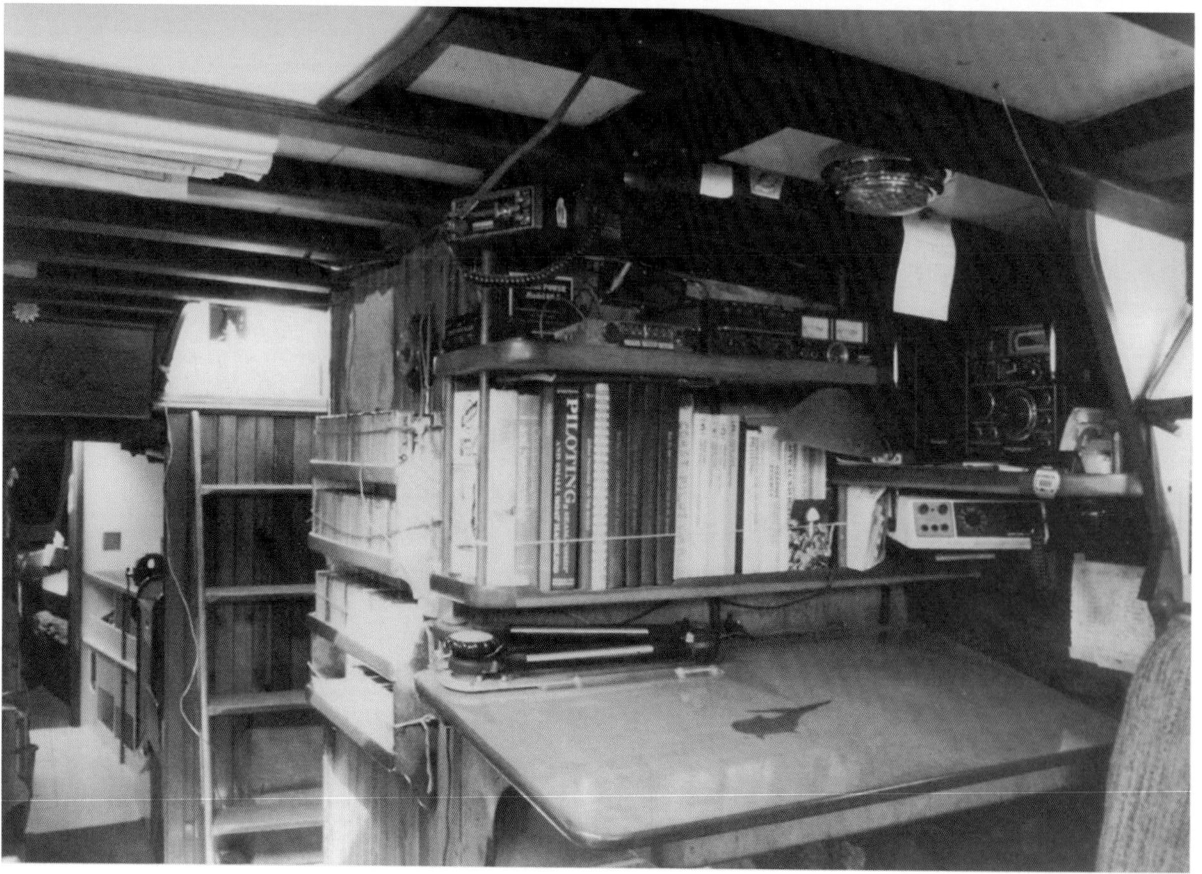

Photo 3 Aft cabin navigation desk and main companionway, looking forward

Photo 4 Aft cabin galley, looking forward

Photo 5

Aft cabin head & Harvey, my philodendron

Photo 6 Master cabin, port side looking aft

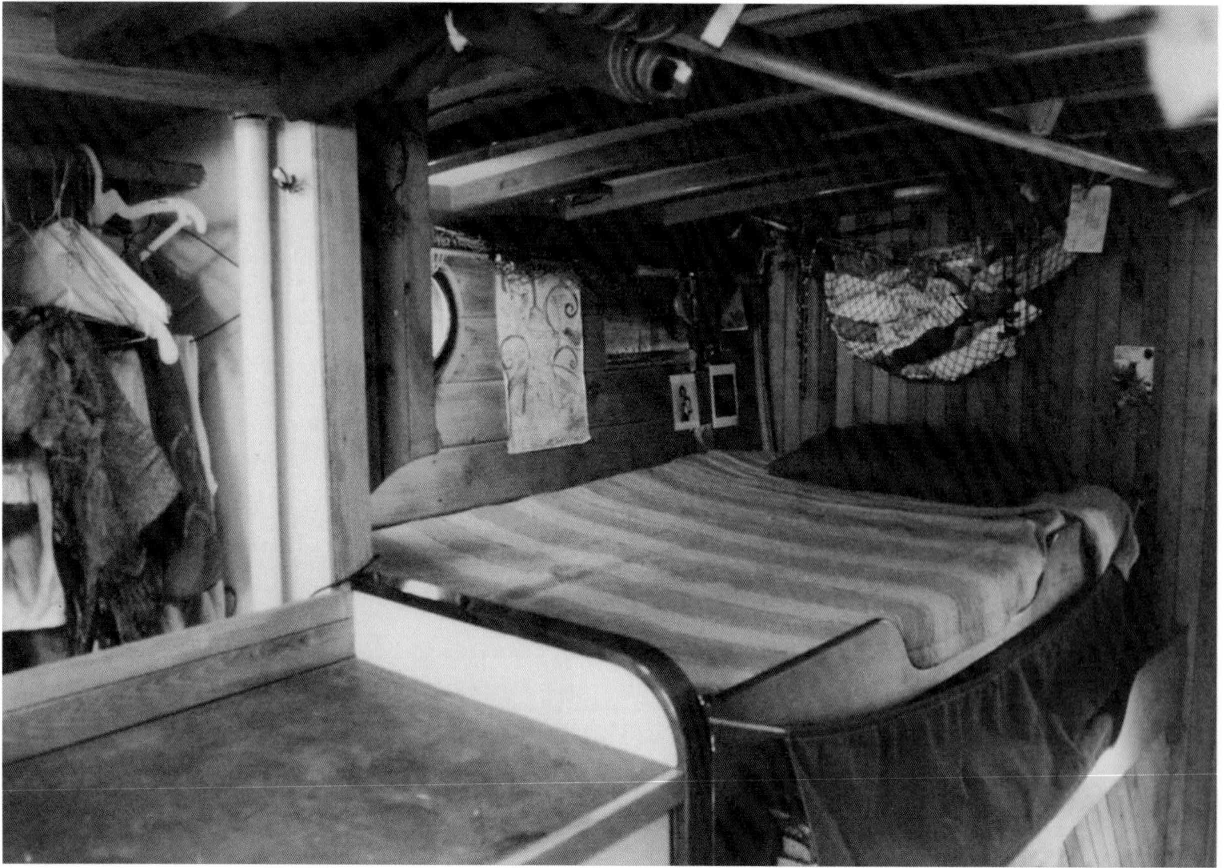

Photo 7 Starboard cabin set up as double berth (the top slides in to create two singles)

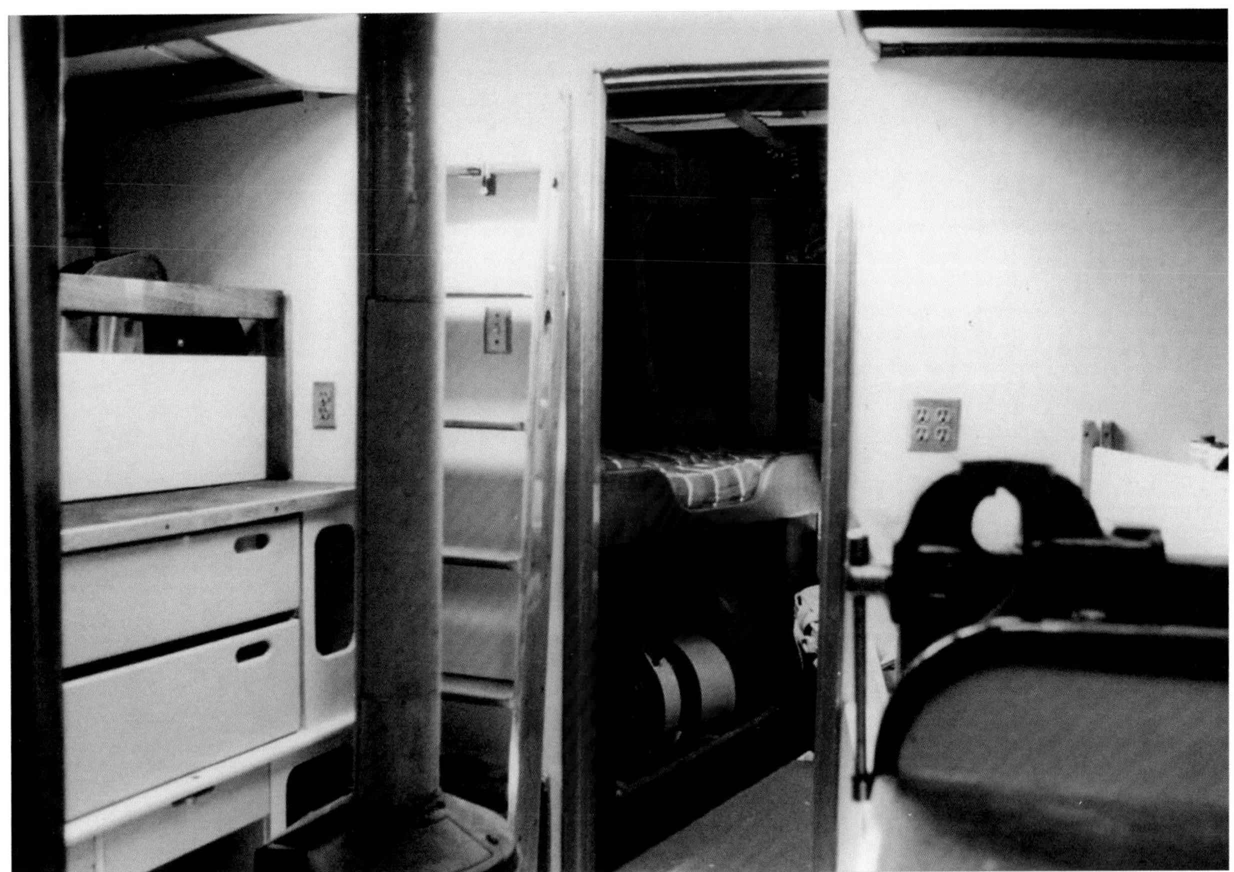

Photo 8 The shop, looking forward--drawers and bins P & S

Photo 9 The fo'c'sle, mooring bitts and chain locker forward

Photo 10 Mast detail--wire halyard winches for jibs; custom-made "traveling" halyard blocks for main and stays'l: These sails are raised using single-part halyards (wire above, 3-strand Dacron below) until nearly hoisted, at which point the rope halyard is passed around a mast-mounted cheek-block (at bottom of photo), thence around the "traveling block" (at top of photo) and down to a belaying pin on fife rail, thus making a 2 to 1 purchase for sweating the sail luff tight.